THE POKER -TOURNAMENT- FORMULA 2

THE POKER
-TOURNAMENT-
FORMULA 2

— ARNOLD SNYDER —

CARDOZA PUBLISHING

FREE GAMBLING NEWSLETTERS
Sign Up Now!

Sign up for Avery Cardoza's email newsletters and you receive three for free: *Avery Cardoza's Poker Newsletter*, *Avery Cardoza's Gambling Newsletter*, and *Avery Cardoza's Online Gaming Newsletter*. Our newsletters are packed with tips, expert strategies, special discounts, free money sign-up bonuses for online sites, prepublication discounts, poker and gaming tournament schedules, news, and words of wisdom from the world's top experts and authorities. And what's best—they're FREE! Sign up now!

www.cardozabooks.com

Cardoza Publishing is the foremost gaming publisher in the world, with a library of over 200 up-to-date and easy-to-read books and strategies. These authoritative works are written by the top experts in their fields and with more than 10,000,000 books in print, represent the best-selling and most popular gaming books anywhere.

FIRST EDITION
Copyright © 2008 by Arnold Snyder
- All Rights Reserved -

See page 496 for free book offer!!!

Library of Congress Catalog Card No: 2008927148
ISBN: 1-58042-226-8

Visit our web site—**www.cardozabooks.com**—or write for a full list of books and computer strategies.
CARDOZA PUBLISHING
P.O. Box 98115, Las Vegas, NV 89193
Phone (800) 577-WINS
email: cardozabooks@aol.com
www.cardozabooks.com

About the Author

Arnold Snyder is a gambling legend revered by millions of players who have made money from his advice. He makes his living as a professional gambler and consistently ranks in the top 5 percent of professional tournament poker players. In the 2007 WSOP, for players who entered at least ten events, he ranked among the top five players, percentage-wise, for cashes per tournaments played. He is the author of many titles, including the sensational companion book, *Poker Tournament Formula*.

Widely regarded as one of gambling's top analysts and strategists, he has often appeared as an expert witness in industry-related court cases and has lectured on the mathematics of gambling at major universities including Cornell University in Ithaca, the University of California at Berkeley, and the University of Nevada in Reno. He was inducted into the Blackjack Hall of Fame in 2003 as one of its seven charter members. He lives in the mountains west of Las Vegas with his wife and gambling partner, Radar, and their five cats.

for K,
for gambling
on me

TABLE OF CONTENTS

PART III: STRATEGIES............257

9. THE FIVE PHASES OF A POKER TOURNAMENT............259

10. PHASE ONE: STACK BUILDING—TAKE THEIR CHIPS WHILE THEY'RE NAPPING............265

PART IV: FOR HARD CORE PLAYERS ONLY 373

INTRODUCTION

Most Of What You Know Is Wrong

If you want to make money in pro-level no-limit hold'em tournaments, you must abandon a lot of what you already know about playing poker. If you've been playing cash games for years and you consider yourself a solid player, that's a handicap when you start entering tournaments. Likewise, while there are a lot of books on the market today on how to play tournaments, and some of the tips in these books are excellent, for the most part, the authors who have written these books are handicapped by being a bunch of poker players, or worse, mathematicians! Coming from backgrounds of years of poker play or too much higher education, they focus so much on poker and the mathematics of poker that they miss most of what's really important about optimal tournament strategy. A tournament is not a poker game, and the mathematics of tournaments is not the mathematics of poker.

In this book, I'm going to teach you how to play pro-level no-limit hold'em tournaments. You should understand from the start that unless I state otherwise, I am specifically discussing and analyzing multitable no-limit hold'em tournaments that begin with full tables (nine or ten players) and play down to a single winner. I am not writing about satellites, limit tournaments, pot-limit tournaments, or short-handed or heads-up tournaments. I'm also not writing about cash games. Much of what I disclose will likely be applicable to some of these other types of tournaments, but make no assumptions. Also, my personal experience in these pro-level events has been exclusively in live tournaments, though I

INTRODUCTION

have attempted to address online differences that would be caused by the increased speed of play.

Your poker skills and experience will serve you well in these events if you can incorporate them into the optimal tournament strategies, but poker skills without optimal tournament strategy are pretty much wasted in a tournament. A slow-structured no-limit hold'em tournament isn't about pot odds, effective odds, implied odds, or reverse implied odds. It isn't about how many outs you have for your nut flush draw. It isn't even about which starting hands you should play and how you should play them based on your chip stack, position and the action in front of you.

You need not be a mathematician to make money playing poker tournaments. I will explain the math as necessary, but it's a lot simpler than most authors would have you believe. Tournaments, and especially no-limit tournaments, are comparatively easy to make money in if you stop thinking like a poker player.

HOW THIS BOOK IS DIFFERENT
FROM MY FIRST POKER BOOK

If you have read *The Poker Tournament Formula* (let's call it "*PTF1*" to distinguish it from this book), then you already have a pretty good foundation for strategic thinking in pro-level tournaments. The bigger buy-in pro-level events, like the "fast" small buy-in tournaments I focused on in *PTF1*, are all about structure, though the structural differences make for some very different optimal strategies.

This book will focus on these slow tournament strategies, picking up where *PTF1* left off. Specifically, we'll be focusing on live tournaments with blind levels that last 40 minutes and longer (with 60-minute blind levels being most common). If these are the tournaments you are playing (or want to play), then this book is for you. Still, I would advise you to read *PTF1* if you haven't already, as that book provides a foundation for thinking about all tournaments, and every tournament becomes faster as the blind levels increase. I'm not going to rehash in this book everything I've already written in *PTF1*, though some of the concepts from that book will be expanded upon as necessary.

This book will also show you how to optimize your strategy for each specific tournament you enter. Pro-level tournaments are not all created equal. If you play in a lot of the events during a WPT or WSOP Circuit series, there are important structural differences between events with different buy-ins. Even if all of the events you play are no-limit hold'em tournaments with no rebuys, full tables (nine or ten-spot) and hour-long blind levels, the different amounts of starting chips in these events will have enough of an effect on each tournament's structure to significantly alter the optimal playing strategies. The optimal strategy for a $1,000 event will be very different from the optimal strategy for the $3,000 event, and this will differ significantly from the optimal strategy for the $10,000 main event.

To help you understand optimal playing strategies based on structure, I will also introduce the important concept of *chip utility*, and provide a simple method for ranking tournaments according to their respective utility factors. None of this requires difficult math and there isn't any difficult math to do at the tables. Once you understand a specific tournament's structure, and how that structure changes as you go through blind levels and players are eliminated, you'll be able to play much more by "feel" and much less by using the formulaic systems based on flawed mathematical logic that have dominated much of tournament thinking for decades.

Again, as I stated in *PTF1*, the cards you are dealt are the least important factor in your tournament success. If your idea of a great poker book is one that has lots of sample hands with instructions

INTRODUCTION

on how to play them, you will be happier with any of the dozens of other tournament books on the shelves at Barnes & Noble. Neil D. Myers wrote a book of hand examples as a companion guide for *PTF1*, and he seems to be good at this job. But fast tournaments lend themselves very well to formulaic strategies, provided you base your play more on your *position* than your cards. I'm not sure if Neil can do the same thing for the strategies in this book. And I'm not going to spoon-feed you a lot of hand analyses because I never read them myself.

I've rarely seen hand examples that answered the questions that have to be answered in real-world tournament situations in order to make a decision. This book will teach you to ask new questions, and give you the means to answer them.

In *PTF1*, I provided "basic strategies" to cover a wide range of situations because fast tournaments simply don't allow for much fancy play. The simple position basic strategies described in *PTF1* for fast tournaments can also be applied selectively in slow tournaments, and I use these strategies myself in slow tournaments and with great success. But slow tournaments also require a greater range of tournament skills and strategies to get you to the money. Slow tournament structures call for more creativity and unpredictability. There are many more options on how to play the same hand, even when you are in the same position and face the same opponents with the same size chip stacks at the same blind level. There are fewer automatic plays.

Some of the tactics covered in this book include small-ball theory, long-ball theory, approaches to playing a short stack, approaches to playing a big stack, early strategies, late strategies, bubble strategies, final table strategies, how to play when you're card dead, how to play a rush, and changing gears.

This book will also discuss specific techniques for bluffing, calling suspected bluffs, creating a table image, and reading your opponents. But the emphasis in all of these discussions on tactics and techniques will be on how they relate to the overall tournament structure and your chip utility.

I'm going to start this book by focusing on how you should be thinking when you sit down to play a tournament. When you look out at the sea of players surrounding you, each one with a stack of chips in front of him the same as yours, your goal is not just to see if you can win some money playing poker. Your aim is to bankrupt every player in this event. You must finish this tournament with a virtual mountain of chips, more chips than you have ever had in front of you, or that you have ever seen in front of any player in a regular poker game. You don't accomplish this goal by thinking about which hands you should enter the pot with. You can throw the mathematics of poker out the window. It's time to start thinking about the mathematics of fear.

I'm not going to include a lot of advice for rank beginners in this book. I'm going to assume you understand the common jargon of poker and that you do not need a primer on how to play the game. I assume you know which hold'em hands are generally considered strong and weak, and you have no trouble reading the board. If you need a primer on no-limit hold'em tournaments, I'll refer you to *PTF1* which covers all of that and a lot more.

> YOU CAN THROW THE MATHEMATICS OF POKER OUT THE WINDOW. IT'S TIME TO START THINKING ABOUT THE MATHEMATICS OF FEAR.

I felt conflicted writing this book because I'm actively playing pro-level tournaments myself, and I'm making money in these events. I've asked myself why I would want to give such valuable information to potential opponents. I seriously considered calling my publisher and telling him that, contract or no contract, I had decided against sending him the manuscript. I have no desire to put my name on a bad poker book that contains nothing but a lot of rehashed fluff, and the book I've written—in which I greatly enjoy tearing apart a lot of the accepted ideas on how to make money in pro-level events—is really too valuable to publish.

In the end, I wrote this book for the many tournament players who have written to thank me for *PTF1*. I basically view this book as a gift to them. And because this book contains a lot of information that is contrary to the material in other books on how to play poker tournaments, I'm sure many players who have read all the books will disagree with what is revealed within these pages. How can everybody else be wrong? Some noted "authorities" on the game will attempt to refute my findings, just as they tried with *PTF1*, and since people don't abandon their gurus very easily, I don't really think I have to worry too much about making the fields of tournament players I'm facing significantly stronger. Besides, my experience in three decades of professional gambling has been that even when players know exactly what they should do, most are unable to do it if it requires any guts.

In any case, if you number yourself among the few who aren't afraid to question authority, and you have the guts to do what you need to do to win, this book is for you. So hang on tight. As race car legend Mario Andretti put it: "If everything seems under control, you're just not going fast enough."

PART I: PRINCIPLES

THE BIG SECRET: CHIP UTILITY

I began my research for this book at the Rio Casino on July 1, 2006, at the $2,000 buy-in event of the WSOP. In the third blind level ($50/$100), with my chip stack still around the $2,000 in chips I'd started with, I was moved to a new table where I immediately recognized John Phan, a highly successful young tournament pro known for his hyper-aggressive style. In 2005, he had taken second place in *Card Player's* Player of the Year standings, barely edged out of first by Men the Master, and I recognized him from photos I had seen of him.

When I got to the table, Phan already had a huge chip lead. The average chip stack at the table at that time was around $3,000 in chips, while I estimated Phan's stack to be in the neighborhood of $15,000 in chips. Maybe more. There were few high-value chips on the table this early in the tournament, and the stacks in front of Phan, mostly black and green, looked like a mountain. He didn't sit, but stood behind his chips looking down at the mere mortals below him. He was smiling broadly and attempting to make small talk with a player to his right who seemed to know him, but that player looked just as somber as everyone else at the table.

In each of the first five hands I witnessed, as I sat there trying to get settled, Phan entered the pot with a preflop raise and never got a single caller. Each time, he made a big show of peeking at his hole cards, then acting as if he'd just looked at pocket rockets—not acting so much as overacting, hamming it up. Hand after hand, he added more blacks and greens to his towering chip stacks. Finally, he said, "Am I the only player at this table who wants to play poker? Didn't you guys come to play?"

I had never seen a player in any tournament so clearly in charge of a table while maintaining such an easy and humorous style. He was like a laughing Buddha.

After Phan had collected a lot more chips, one player finally tried a move on him. Phan had called his preflop raise from the blind, and then came out betting when the flop came down with an ace and two rags. The player pushed all in. Phan instacalled. The player who pushed in had missed the flop with his K-Q. Phan turned over his cards to show A-6, and another victim bit the dust. I understood the move the player had made. He was tired of not being able to play poker with Phan to his left, and I'm sure he had decided in advance to push in on Phan no matter what came down on the flop. Bad timing.

In another pot where Phan was involved out of position, he bet on the flop and his opponent started reaching for chips as if getting ready to reraise. Phan immediately started loading up both of his hands with chips and laughing, saying, "Uh-uh-uh! Be careful!" This was enough to discourage the bettor. He mucked his cards and Phan took down another pot.

On another hand where Phan used this same "Uh-uh-uh! Be careful!" to discourage a raiser behind him, the player raised anyway. With great comic styling, Phan started shaking his head and laughing, saying "I told you, don't bet. Why did you bet? You can't beat me!" Then he reraised enough to put his opponent all in. What was most sick about it was that all he had to do to make this reraise was slide out one tall stack of blacks from the stacks and stacks in front of him. To him, it wasn't much of a bet at all. His opponent agonized over his decision for a full minute while Phan jabbered away in his relaxed and animated style: "You can't beat me. I have the best hand. I told you not to bet." His opponent finally folded.

Phan's chip stack, combined with his aggressive style of play, literally had the rest of the table frozen, even though most of the players had very viable chip stacks in relation to the blinds. A small raise to Phan was a huge raise to any opponent. A minor risk to him could put any opponent to a life or death decision. Phan was simply able to play poker at a level no one else could afford.

If Phan was involved in a pot, or was positioned behind a player so that he could still become involved in the pot—and he involved himself in an awful lot of pots, maybe 50 percent or more—any player who bet had to be prepared to commit all of his chips. While he talked continually, laughing and always smiling, everyone else at the table was quiet, waiting with a grim expression for a trapping hand. For the hour or so I was at that table, I would estimate that Phan took down close to 90 percent of the pots he played. He only threw away two hands that I recall when players bet after the flop, and one was when an opponent pushed all in on him. By the time I busted out, Phan had increased his mountain of chips by about 50 percent. Though I always keep close track of my opponents' chip stacks, I never even made an effort to count Phan's chips at that table. The exact total would not have had any relevance to any decision I would have had to make.

I spent the entire following week trying to figure out what had happened at that table. I couldn't stop thinking about it. I'd never seen anything like it before. It was the first time I realized that all it takes is a single player with a monster stack—who really knows how to use it—to cripple the ability of an entire table of players to play poker. Again, most of these players had what would normally be considered viable chip stacks given the blind level. One of the players at that same table was Chris "Jesus" Ferguson. I don't believe he entered more than one pot in the hour I was there, and it was a pot in which John Phan had already folded. I talked to a few players about the experience and they told me that Phan was known for lording over his table like that. They said his relentless aggression was similar to Carlos Mortensen's and David "the Dragon" Pham's.

The next time I saw John Phan was about ten days later in the second WSOP event I'd entered on my research project—a $1,000 buy-in event. This was at a much later blind level, probably about eight or nine hours into the tournament, when we were getting close to the money. I was in pretty decent chip shape when Phan was moved onto the table where I was playing. He arrived with just one rack of chips in his hand. I remember feeling intense relief, thinking that he would not be able to ruthlessly punish this table as he had done the last time I played with him.

My relief was short-lived. Within a few seconds of Phan's arrival at the table, one of the tournament directors arrived with the rest of his chips—rack upon rack upon rack—probably five or six racks of chips in all. All I could think was, "Oh no, here we go again!"

Phan went on to take second place in that event, which paid $289,000, and I continued to obsess about what the hell he was doing. How did he acquire all of those chips? (Each time I'd seen him, he'd already built his monster stack.) What most intrigued me was his ability to literally freeze the play of every opponent at his table. I realized that Phan knew something about playing tournaments that few players understood. Later, in a number of California tournaments, I watched the play of David Pham, a former student of Men the Master, and though his style was less arrogant than John Phan's, I realized that Pham understood the same secret. By then, I had figured out the basic principles behind the effectiveness of their play and I set out to learn how to acquire such a stack without busting out too often to make it worth it, and how to actually use the chips to achieve results like theirs.

The first time I ever had a Phan-sized chip stack was in the later stages of a tournament several months later. I was playing very loose and experimenting with post-flop stealing moves. After a series of lucky catches on speculative hands, and winning four out of four races, I found myself with a very big chip lead on my table. I continued to play aggressively and continued to win, which culminated in my busting out two all-in players on the same hand when my pocket kings held up on a raggy flop against a player with pocket jacks and another with a nut flush draw.

When I finished stacking up my chips, I looked around and it appeared I had half the chips on my table. I counted my chips—$194,000. I looked up at the tournament clock and it showed 42 players remaining, with the average chip stack at $34,000 and change. I had almost six times the average. I continued to play loose, raising preflop with virtually any "playable" hands, including any ace, any two high cards, and most connectors suited or not, but I found that no one wanted to play with me. I just kept picking up the blinds and antes. During the break, I saw players coming around from other tables to point at my chip stack. I heard one of them remark, "Geez, that must be $200,000!"

On one hand shortly after the break, where I'd entered with a raise from late position with A-5 suited, I got a call from the big blind—the player who was second in chips at the table, with about $65,000. The flop came down with a king and two rags, one of which paired my 5. He bet the size of the pot. I sat there wondering for a moment if he'd actually hit the king or if he was just trying a resteal. I thought my bottom pair with the ace kicker might actually be the best hand. I decided to raise for information to see where I stood. I bet out the size of the pot to see if he had really made top pair. My information bet took very few of my chips.

My opponent looked at my bet, started counting the chips in his stack, and asked the dealer to spread out the chips in the pot. If he pushed all in, I would fold in a heartbeat, but as he agonized over his decision, I realized that he had probably hit top pair. He had a king. But he didn't like his kicker. If he had A-K, he probably would have reraised me preflop. Maybe he had K-J or K-9 suited?

I knew he had king-something. But as he was stacking out chips to call my raise, and adding up the chips in the pot, he seemed to realize that if he simply called my bet, there would be more chips in the pot than he had remaining in his stack. He wouldn't be able to play after the turn, so calling was out of the question. He had to decide right then and there if he should push all in with top pair and less than top kicker. He was second in chips at the table—or at least he had been before he'd gotten involved in this hand—but he couldn't afford to play poker with me beyond the flop. He mucked his cards and I took yet another pot with what I am sure was not the best hand. At that moment, I remembered John Phan laughing and the hopelessness of all the other players at the table where I'd first seen him in action.

The stories above illustrate a concept that is crucial to making money in pro-level events—the concept of *chip utility*. I cannot overstate the importance of this concept in tournaments and I will be returning to this concept over and over in my discussions of every facet of play in pro-level tournaments. Chip utility is the key factor in determining who makes money in poker tournaments and who doesn't. It's the "big secret" that separates the winners from the losers, the difference between the live money and the dead money.

This chapter on chip utility and the following two chapters that explain how to quantify utility so that you can use it strategically are the most important chapters in this book. If you want to know the secrets to building a monster chip lead so that you can push the players at your table around, you need to understand chip utility so that you can make it work for you.

You may be unfamiliar with the term "utility" as I will be using it, but I will take care to explain it as it's essential that you understand it. When you win chips in a tournament, you are really winning utility, and at the same time you are diminishing the utility of your opponents. When you lose chips, you are losing utility, while your opponent who took your chips is gaining utility. Understanding the concept of utility is the first step toward understanding optimal pro-level tournament strategies, because all of your most important decisions in a tournament come down to chip utility decisions.

If you've taken courses in economics in college, you probably have a pretty good feel for the concept of utility as it is defined by mathematicians, and especially as it relates to game theory. If not, that matters little. Suffice it to say that mathematicians recognize that when utility is a factor it is a mistake to ignore it if you are attempting to mathematically analyze a problem. I will be defining utility specifically as it relates to poker tournaments, and the concept is easy to put into laymen's terms. I'm not going to go into any advanced math in this book because it's unnecessary. The mathematics of utility as it relates to poker tournaments is very straightforward and logical, and if you ignore it, you're putting yourself at a significant disadvantage in today's tournaments.

A very basic definition of chip utility would be the *usefulness* or *serviceability* of your chips. Later, we will further explore the idea of chip usefulness or serviceability by looking at the real world applications of chip utility. But I want to start this chapter by disabusing readers of a common notion that many of you may have about your chips.

CHIPS ARE AMMUNITION— NOT MONEY

Never think of your tournament chips as money. In a cash game, your chips are money. In a tournament, chips are simply the ammunition you use to attack your opponents, take all of their chips, and earn yourself one of the prize payouts. Your chips themselves are not a payout. They're just ammunition. When a tournament begins, all players start with the same amount of ammo. As the tournament progresses, the skirmishes begin and the victors of these battles are awarded ammunition from their opponents' stockpiles. The more ammo you have, the more ways you can use it. The less ammo you have, the fewer ways you can use it. The skills you have—and I'm referring to both your poker skills and your tournament skills—are the *weapons* you bring to the battle. When you have a lot of ammo, your weapons make you a formidable opponent. With little ammo, your weapons themselves become useless.

When you capture any amount of an opponent's ammunition, two things occur. You increase the value of the ammo that's already in your stockpile because you have increased the ways that you can use that ammo. Your weapons (skills) have become more valuable because you can put them into action. And at the same time you decrease the value of the ammo remaining in your opponent's stockpile because you have curtailed some of the ways that he can use his skill. By taking any substantial amount of an opponent's ammo, you can make his remaining ammo nearly worthless because you will have curtailed the use of so many of his skills.

One of history's most brilliant war strategists, the Prussian General Carl von Clausewitz, in his 1832 classic, *On War*, said that one of the most important tactics in a successful campaign is to *take away your enemy's ability to make war*. It doesn't matter how brilliant your enemy's plans, how superior his position, how experienced his commanding officers, how massive his troops, or how formidable his weapons—if you cut your enemy's access to ammunition, he is a goner.

THE FUNCTIONS OF CHIPS IN A TOURNAMENT

We can loosely categorize the usefulness of our chips in three separate divisions: preflop utility, post-flop/turn utility, and river utility, all of which are important functions.

PREFLOP UTILITY FUNCTIONS

1. Chips can be used to steal blinds and antes

With a moderate to big chip stack, you can do this in any unraised pot from any late position seat. With a really big chip stack, you can frequently steal blinds and antes from early and middle position seats. Likewise, with a big chip stack, you can frequently steal pots from preflop limpers simply by raising. The bigger your chip stack, the more ruthless and aggressive you can be on these preflop steals.

With a small stack, you may be able to go after the blinds from the button or cutoff seat, but you must play more cautiously because any play back at you may cost you more chips than you can afford to lose. In other words, a player with a big stack can make these types of position plays with just about any two cards, because it's cheap to get away from the hand if the steal attempt fails.

Players are also much more hesitant to call preflop raises from players who vastly outchip them, unless they have premium starting cards. How many times have you watched as a chip leader stole the blinds and antes over and over with no callers? It just happens as a matter of course at every tournament table when the chip discrepancies get big. The rich keep getting richer because it's so easy for them to do so. The smaller your stack, the more likely an opponent will be to shoot back at you, so the more important your cards become. If you're a very short stack, it may take an all-in bet just to steal the blinds. A desperately short stack may have no stealing function at all. Any all-in bet by a player who is on the verge of death will likely be called by any player with a lot of chips and a marginally playable hand.

2. Chips can be used to see a greater number of flops

The more chips you have, the greater the number of speculative hands—such as small pairs, medium connected cards, and suited cards—you can play. These hands often must be thrown away after the flop, but if the flop hits a hand like this, the implied odds can be tremendous.

With a big stack, you can even make raises or call raises with these speculative hands. To do so effectively disguises your hand from your opponents who are likely raising or entering a raised pot with big cards, which not only enhances your implied odds if the flop hits you, but enhances your opportunities for stealing when it misses you. With a short stack, most of these types of speculative hands must be abandoned preflop. With a desperate stack, your only preflop move with a speculative hand, other than folding, would be to push all in. Seeing flops with speculative hands is simply another chip function of great value to a big stack that's unavailable to short stacks.

3. Chips can be used to sit and wait

A big stack gives a player the luxury of changing gears at will, and using patience during times when he is not getting decent cards and the pots seem too dangerous to get involved in. In other words, chips allow a player to be selective at those times when selectivity is the best strategy. Short-stacked players cannot be as selective, as the blind and ante costs will be eating away too big a percentage of their precious few chips.

THE POST-FLOP/TURN UTILITY FUNCTIONS

1. Chips can be used to drive opponents out of pots (eliminate draws)

Say that you have an overpair to the board, which shows potentially dangerous straight or flush draws. You can drive players on draws out of the pot by making a bet that makes it too expensive for them to try to draw out on you. This bet would also eliminate players who simply held an overcard to the board, say an ace, which would beat your hand if an ace appeared on the turn or river. The more chips you have compared to your opponents, the easier it is for you to make it too expensive for them to stay in a pot with you. With very few chips, you may have to pot-commit yourself just to make the odds wrong for opponents to call. That's dangerous. And a very short stack loses even this basic chip function. He often cannot make it too expensive for an opponent on a strong draw to call.

2. Chips can be used to make continuation bets (which are often bluffs) post-flop

If you raised before the flop, it usually makes good strategic sense to bet after the flop, even when the flop doesn't hit you, and even if an overcard comes down that could have hit your opponent's hand. This is because most of the time the flop will not have hit your opponent, and he must respect your preflop raise and post-flop bet as indicative of a strong made hand. It's easy to steal pots from players who may have a better hand or a better draw than you if you have more chips than them. They often cannot afford to call with marginal hands or on draws without jeopardizing either the viability of their chip stack or their tournament survival. A really big chip stack can often be used with ruthless aggression in stealing from opponents in this way. A player who flops top pair, but with less than top kicker, will often relinquish his hand to a bet from a player who outchips him. Short stacks get very few legitimate bluffing opportunities post-flop, and all of them—including simple continuation bets—are costly and potentially dangerous.

3. Chips can be used to semibluff when you have a strong draw

The semibluff not only builds the pot for a player when he does make his hand, it also often gets him a free card on the river. With a big chip stack backing up a semibluff on the flop, the check by an opponent on the turn is almost guaranteed. In fact, a big stack can often steal the pot with a bet on the turn, even without making his hand. Semibluffing is very dangerous in a tournament if you cannot afford to lose the chips you bet with. The bigger your chip stack, the more you can utilize this function.

4. Chips can be used to bet for information

If a preflop raiser bets after the flop and you believe the bet may be merely a continuation bet, a big stack allows you to raise to see if your opponent really has the hand he's representing. In these cases, your reraise will usually fold a bettor who was just trying to keep the lead, winning you the pot. This is especially true if you outchip your opponent by any significant amount. With a short stack yourself, however, that information bet may be too expensive to make. Without a strong read on your opponent, you may have to fold the best hand because you simply cannot afford to lose the chips you would lose if you call or reraise and find out you were wrong. Poker skills—such as the ability to read opponents—definitely play into this. But with no clear read, the information bet is a very valuable utility function.

THE RIVER UTILITY FUNCTIONS

1. Chips can be used to bet for value

When a player believes he has the best hand, a big stack permits him to bet an amount that an opponent with a good or marginal hand will call simply because of the size of the pot. Value bets add to a player's chip stack with little danger, though they are much more dangerous for short stacks because of the possibility of being put to a test with a reraise from an opponent that could put you all in, or cripple you if you call and your hand does not hold up. An aggressive player may even bluff you out of the pot if you attempt a value bet when you are short-stacked, but he would rarely try this kind of bold bluff on a deep-stacked opponent. In fact, value bets from deep-stacked players always look dangerous because it appears the player is trying to get more money out of you. If you value-bet when short-stacked, you must usually do so when you feel so strongly that you have the best hand that you are value-betting with the intention of calling any raise. If you do not feel your hand is strong enough to call a raise, then you must often dispense with the value bet.

2. Chips can be used to call down suspected bluffers

In fact, a big chip stack will often deter players from bluffing in the first place, because they can see that the big stack can well afford to call. Big chip stacks get much more of the true value of their cards when they hold competitive hands than small stacks do. Short stacks will often be putting their tournament life on the line when they call suspected bluffs. There is a value to keeping your opponents honest—to keeping them from taking shots at you when you have a legitimate hand but the board presents dangers. In the chapter on attitude, we will discuss how valuable this type of call can be to your table image when you are right. But like all of the above uses we have for our chips, this chip function diminishes with your chip stack.

3. Chips can be used to call for information, just to see what your opponent has.

Many times I have called another player's value bet on the river, knowing I was beat (as I did not hit my draw), but for the value of seeing what he was betting with if I couldn't put him on a hand based on how the betting had gone. This is valuable information that I may be able to use later when involved in a pot with this player. With a short stack, I cannot afford to waste the chips it would cost me to get this information. (And occasionally, a call when you "know" you are beat wins you the pot when your opponent's alleged value bet turns out to be a bluff, and your busted draw hand actually beats his trash!)

SHORT ON CHIPS EQUALS SHORT ON UTILITY

If you've played many tournaments, the value of chip utility may seem obvious to you—something that all tournament players would figure out pretty quickly on their own. Of the ten common chip utility functions described above, every single one of them is made possible by your chips, and every one of them can be severely restricted by having a short stack. The less ammo you have, the more dangerous it is to employ your weapons.

Also, note that these ten common functions are not by any means all of the utility functions that exist. For highly skilled players, there are other more sophisticated plays that also require a decent amount of chips to pull off—for example, calling on the flop in order to steal on the turn, or calling on the flop and turn in order to steal on the river, or check-raising to steal at any point in a hand. The more experienced a player you are, the more non-standard moves you might think of that would earn you chips, but all of these fancy moves require a sufficiently-sized stack to pull off and are less accessible to you the shorter your stack.

If you've ever been short-stacked, you've probably sat there looking at hands like 9-8 suited and 5-5 and other speculative hands you'd like to see a flop with, but mucked because you felt you had to conserve your chips for a better opportunity with a stronger starting hand. It's particularly exasperating when you muck your marginal cards, then the flop comes down and you see that you would have hit your set or flopped a straight. You can't help but think, "Geez, normally I would have played that hand and earned a huge pot!"

Every tournament player has also had the experience of being at a table with deep-stacked aggressive opponents who continually freeze the action with overbets. For example, you've got $4,000 in chips with the blinds at $50/$100 a little over an hour into the tournament. You started the tournament with $5,000 in chips, but a few hands you played didn't go your way so you're down a bit.

Normally, you'd figure it's no big deal. It's early. The blinds are cheap and there are no antes yet. The problem, however, is that two aggressive players at your table have already doubled up and are sitting there with $10,000+ in chips. It seems like every time you or some other player come in with a standard raise, say a bet of $300 to $400, one of the big stacks reraises to $1,200. Twice this has happened to you, once when you had A-Q off suit and once when you had K-Q suited. Both times you mucked your cards, feeling your hand wasn't strong enough to get involved in such a big pot preflop with a player who not only had you outchipped but had position on you. Your gut instinct told you you were being bullied out of these pots, not because of any read you had on the reraisers, but simply because you noticed they were playing too many hands too aggressively for it to be likely they had been dealt that many premium starting hands. But if you reraise, it would take all of your chips, or pot-commit you, and if he's got A-K, he'll never fold and your hand is dominated. And even if he has a medium pair he may feel he has sufficient chips to call your raise.

Do you really want to get involved in a pot this early in the tournament for most or all of your chips with a hand that's moderately strong at best? (I'll answer this question later...)

Most of the "experts" will tell you that if you have a chip stack totaling 40 times the size of the big blind, you are in great chip shape—especially if the antes have not kicked in yet—and you should be fully functional as a poker player. But the real value of your chips is based on their *utility*, and if one or more aggressive players at your table are restricting you from using your chips the way you'd like to use them, it doesn't make much difference how many big blinds (or rounds of play) your chip stack equals. Let's say you continually find yourself thinking things like:

1. "I wish I could see the flop with this hand, but not at that price," or...
2. "Man, I can't even take a shot at the blinds anymore with that maniac to my left," or...
3. "I have no control over the pot size at this table with those aggressive overbettors involved in so many hands," or...
4. "I'm sitting here getting pushed out of pots, slowly being chipped away, waiting for an opportunity to trap one of those deep stacks, but I'm just not getting the cards I need..."

If any of these situations are the case, you are simply experiencing what happens when your chip utility is constrained. It happens to virtually all tournament players in every tournament played. Because the chip utility functions are so important to your success, you must base your overall tournament strategy both on striving to maintain the full utility value of your chips, and on acquiring a bigger stack than your opponents so that you can freeze as many of their chip utility functions as possible.

> **YOU MUST BASE YOUR OVERALL TOURNAMENT STRATEGY BOTH ON STRIVING TO MAINTAIN THE FULL UTILITY VALUE OF YOUR CHIPS, AND ON ACQUIRING A BIGGER STACK THAN YOUR OPPONENTS SO THAT YOU CAN FREEZE AS MANY OF THEIR CHIP UTILITY FUNCTIONS AS POSSIBLE.**

In a cash game, poker players win and lose chips, and these chips are valued for their face dollar value. In a tournament, by contrast, players win and lose utility, and in valuing your chips, you must value them according to how many of your skills they will pay for, and how many of your opponents' skills you can devalue by preventing your opponents from using their chips. Chips in a tournament do not represent money and they do not represent "equity" in the prize pool. What chips represent is the very ability to engage in competitive play.

You cannot go into a tournament and play it the way you would play a cash game. In a cash game, when you win a pot, your brain is saying, "Yes! I just made some money!" In a tournament, unless you are somewhere near the very end of the event, you don't win any money when you win a pot; you just have more chips. If you understand chip utility when you win a pot, your brain is saying,

> **WHAT CHIPS REPRESENT IS THE VERY ABILITY TO ENGAGE IN COMPETITIVE PLAY.**

"Yes! More ammo! I can do so many things with these chips! I can see more flops! I can push back at that SOB who keeps raising my blind! I can take shots at the wimps! Call down bluffs on the river!"

If your brain already thinks this way when you win a pot in a tournament, then you have a natural feel for chip utility even if you've never heard the term before.

EMOTIONAL INTELLIGENCE

The math of poker tournaments is not as simple as the math of poker played as a cash game, where a $100 chip equals $100. In a tournament, what is the dollar value of having the capability of calling for information or making a continuation bet? You cannot put any exact number on the value of these functions, as their values will change throughout the tournament based on many factors over which you have no control and which themselves are unquantifiable. What, for example, is the mathematical cost to you of having an aggressive player with a big stack to your immediate left? Can you quantify the value of having a couple of short-stacked timid players at the table? It's impossible to devise numbers for the precise values of such factors because poker tournaments present constantly changing situations and power relationships that are intertwined with the skill levels of all of the players you face.

But this does not mean that you should not attempt to quantify the *utility* value of your chips in a poker tournament. Continually assessing your utility in relation to your opponents' utility during a tournament helps us to visualize a mathematically correct strategy, even if your method of valuation is approximate. In the game of casino blackjack, for example, if I remove an ace from a single deck, the effect on a basic strategy player's edge is -0.61 percent. If I remove a deuce, the effect on that player's edge is +0.28 percent. The most popular card counting system used by professional blackjack players, however, would value the ace removal as -1 and the deuce removal as +1, and these oversimplified card evaluations work very well to provide the expert card counter with an edge over the house. In a sense, I'm suggesting a chip counting system to put a value on your utility—and your opponents' utility—in a poker tournament.

But you're not going to sit there with numbers in your head keeping a plus/minus count at the table as a blackjack player must do to beat the house. I'll provide a very simple numerical guide, but you must always keep in mind that a poker tournament is more about emotions and perceptions than it is about numbers. Once you have an understanding of utility, you will *feel* how the effect of having it or lacking it drives the action, and your emotional intelligence will guide you.

Many players clearly lack emotional intelligence. They cannot play by "feel," but must employ formulaic systems in which they base all of their decisions on their cards, their chips, the action, and their position. Their predictability is their weakness. Their inability to quantify utility in the same sense that they can quantify pot odds makes them terrible tournament players.

The players who are guided by emotional intelligence, however, already know exactly what I'm talking about when I say utility is something you can *feel* at a tournament table. Player by player as you look around the table at your opponents, you can gauge their respective emotional states based on their chip stacks. Some of the short-stacked overly tight players who lack emotional intelligence don't even know yet that they are lacking utility. Their "M" seems fine to them, so they're just waiting for a hand. Their basic strategy came out of a book. An aggressive player with the same size chip stack, by contrast, will be impatiently anticipating an opportunity to do something about his sorry chip status that is restricting his play. As the tight player's "M" slides into his yellow zone, then his orange zone, you can feel his nervousness as he must start looking for more marginal hands to play. You can feel the haughty confidence exuded by the big stacks and the hopelessness of the desperately short. If you know what I'm talking about, then you are probably already making a lot of utility-based decisions. And if you are not, then you should be, because you have the emotional intelligence to be successful at tournaments. If you do not sit at a tournament table and feel these emotions as you assess your opponents, I'll give you some advice: *Hang it up.*

THE FUNDAMENTAL LAW OF CHIP UTILITY

Although we use chips in a tournament in ways that seem similar to chip usage in a cash game, these uses have *very different values* to you in a tournament than in a cash game. That is an important point and it is the key to understanding the differences between optimal tournament strategies and optimal cash game strategies. In a tournament, your chip stack can only increase at your opponents' expense, while in a cash game, you can simply purchase more chips at any time to stay in the game. The escalating blinds in a tournament also require every player to have more chips as the game progresses, so you must keep taking more and more chips from your opponents.

> **A TOURNAMENT IS THEREFORE A GAME WHERE AS YOU INCREASE THE UTILITY VALUE OF YOUR CHIPS, YOU SIMULTANEOUSLY DECREASE THE VALUE OF YOUR OPPONENT'S CHIPS.**

While in a cash game, $1,000 in chips is always worth $1,000, in a tournament, $1,000 in chips has no value whatsoever if I don't turn it into $2,000, then $4,000, then $8,000, then $16,000, and on and on. I need to keep multiplying my chip stack and I can only do so at the expense of my opponents, while they need to multiply their chip stacks at my expense. Any time I succeed in getting closer to my goal by taking my opponents' chips, I foil their chance of success.

If prior to my win they had $1,000 in chips that they knew they had to turn into $2,000 then $4,000, and then more., now they are in a position where they must first turn their $500 into $1,000. I will have increased both the mathematical difficulty of their accomplishing this goal, and the psychological difficulty, as they will now be posing less of a threat to me and every other opponent they face. A tournament is therefore a game where as you increase the utility value of your chips, you simultaneously decrease the value of your opponent's chips. The greater your understanding of this concept, the more successful you will be in tournaments.

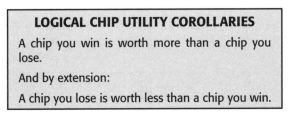

> **THE FUNDAMENTAL LAW OF CHIP UTILITY**
>
> The more chips you have, the more each of your chips is worth.
>
> And, by extension:
>
> The fewer chips you have, the less each of your chips is worth.

All winning tournament strategies are based on this fundamental law. The law of chip utility has numerous logical corollaries, the most important being:

> **LOGICAL CHIP UTILITY COROLLARIES**
>
> A chip you win is worth more than a chip you lose.
>
> And by extension:
>
> A chip you lose is worth less than a chip you win.

Strategies based on the law of chip utility and its corollaries will be loose, aggressive strategies. These are the strategies of the most successful tournament players. They are the opposite of the tighter survival-oriented strategies advised by many tournament "experts." Survival is, of course, important, and every winning tournament strategy must have survival mechanisms. But a player who uses a strategy based on chip utility will understand that loose, aggressive play is more likely to survive with a dominating chip stack than a tighter strategy that overly concerns itself with surviving the current hand or the current blind level.

Let's look at why this is so.

THE SKILL FACTOR

MUCH OF THE VALUE OF SKILL COMES FROM HAVING A BIG ENOUGH STACK TO USE A FULL RANGE OF SKILLS FREELY.

To correctly estimate the value of tournament chips, we must also consider the skill of the player who has them. But skill alone does not give chips their value. Even an incredibly skillful player who is short-stacked will find many of his skills crippled by his lack of chips. He cannot use all of the possible strategic plays in his repertoire; in fact, he is in very much the same position as any short-stacked player with few skills at this point—just looking for a hand to take a stand with. Much of the value of skill comes from having a big enough stack to use a full range of skills freely.

This leads us to two more corollary laws with regards to chip value. In addition to chips having greater value the more you have:

> **1.** The more skill you have, the more your chips are worth, and...
>
> **2.** The more chips you have, the more your skill is worth.

In other words, the more skillful you are as a player, the more you should be willing to take risks to acquire a big chip stack. The value of those chips to you will be huge, while sitting on a short or even an "average" chip stack will be costing you money. Let me emphasize this point:

> The more skill you have, and I'm referring here to both poker skills and tournament skills, the more risks you should be willing to take to acquire a big chip stack.

Note that all utility functions are not equal in value. For example, one of the first utility functions to disappear will be the use of information bets—betting or raising for information to see where you stand in a hand, or calling for information just to see what your opponent was betting on even when you feel you are beat. It takes a lot more chips to use these functions than most other functions because they represent money you put into the pot on which you often do not expect an immediate return. On the other hand, the preflop all-in steal is generally the last function to disappear. This is the last-resort move of the shortest stacks, because it continues to pay off unless they bump into a real hand.

Also, information bets tend to be utility functions that are used by more skillful players. Few amateurs bet for information. Unskillful players tend more toward playing their cards as opposed to playing their opponents and situations. Information bets are made by skillful poker players in both tournaments and cash games. All-in preflop bets are not generally utilized in cash games other than by rank amateurs. This is primarily a tournament move, but it is utilized by both amateurs and pros when short-stacked. The power of the all-in bet is that it immediately removes all skill advantages an opponent may have over you. You are essentially forcing an opponent to either get out of the pot or let the cards decide who wins. When you are short-stacked, this is your most powerful weapon, because no matter what your chip status, utility isn't just something you want to have for yourself—it's something you want to take away from your opponents.

If you read over the list of the ten common utility functions provided earlier in this chapter, you can probably put a personal value on each function to your game, based on how much you feel your game would suffer if you lost that function. But because the skillful player has moves he can make only with a bigger chip stack and he wants to maintain his ability to play with his full range of skills against all of the opponents he faces, skillful or not, he will be putting higher personal values on some of the more advanced plays, like information bets, than an unskillful player will.

If you are a skillful poker player—and I'm referring here to having poker skills that would apply in cash games as well as tournaments—as soon as you understand the implications of chip utility, your overall tournament play will loosen up and your level of aggression will increase considerably. From the very start of a tournament, increasing your chip utility and, by extension, decreasing the utility of your opponents, will become a major consideration of every decision you make. The skillful cash game players who do not fare well in tournaments are generally incognizant of the importance of utility.

CHIP UTILITY AND POT ODDS

Because of the overriding importance of the utility value of chips, the normal mathematics of poker do not apply in tournaments. Decisions based on pot odds, for example, are drastically different in tournaments than they are in cash games, because unlike cash games, chips you win in a tournament are often worth much more than their face value.

If winning a pot means that I will be able to utilize skills I possess that are currently hampered, then I should be willing to risk more on a hand than standard poker pot odds would justify. Many of the best tournament players understand this. I have seen so many of the top tournament pros make what most "solid" cash game players would consider absurdly loose calls that I know that many of the best tournament players are well aware of utility value and are basing their decisions on it.

Gus Hansen, for example, has frequently been criticized for his "bad reads" or his willingness to get all of his chips involved in what many players would consider marginal situations, but not by anyone who understands chip utility. Frankly, I've never seen him make a wrong decision when the utility value of the chips in the pot was added to the pot odds equation. I recall one televised table where he made a call with a very marginal hand, was criticized by the other players at the table for calling an all-in bet with such a marginal hand, and said, "I don't need as much as you guys [to call]." If his opponents are basing their decisions on pot odds, and he's considering utility odds—which are the odds a player should be considering in a tournament—his statement makes perfect sense.

In another notorious call from the WPT's "Bad Boys of Poker" tournament in 2006, Gus called Antonio Esfandiari's all-in bet when Gus had 10-7 suited. Esfandiari seemed shocked that Gus could call such a huge bet with such a marginal hand. This "tournament," however, was a freeroll for the players. It was strictly a made-for-TV event, and while the winner would get paid, second place would get nothing. Technically, it was like a one-winner single-table satellite. Also, at this time, pro players who made WPT final tables were complaining about how "fast" the blind levels were—essentially the TV commentary slowed the dealing procedure so much that very few hands were being played at each blind level. If Gus read Esfandiari's all-in bet as a baby pair—and I think Antonio's bet reeked of small pair—then Gus figured he was in a legitimate race (which he was), and in a fast structured event, and especially in a winner-take-all event, you're making a mistake to avoid races.

1 - THE BIG SECRET: CHIP UTILITY

I've played at a number of tables with Men the Master, and he too will often shock players with his (correct) loose calls in marginal situations. This is true also of David "the Dragon" Pham, John Phan, Nam Le, and many of the other great Vietnamese-American players I've been fortunate enough to sit with. David Pham is a player who simply refuses to play with a short or even an average chip stack. He knows the power of chips and he will acquire them by hook or by crook—or bust out trying to acquire them. He acquires them often enough that his tournament record speaks for itself. His skills at reading weakness in opponents and at representing strength are unparalleled.

I once saw Men the Master get all of his chips involved preflop fairly late in a $1,000 tournament at the Bicycle Club, and the table was stunned to see he had an 8-7 offsuit. Here's how the hand played out:

Men came in with a standard raise from early position. He was below average in chips but far from desperate. The chip leader at the table—who had a massive amount of chips compared to anyone else at the table—reraised enough to put Men just about all in if Men called. Men thought about it for a minute, counting his chips, realizing that it would take 90 percent of his stack to make the call, and he pushed in all of his chips. It actually amazed me that the chip leader took as long as he did to call Men's all in, as the number of extra chips to him was a piddling amount. He was probably getting 10 to 1 pot odds or better and, even if he lost the pot, he would remain a massive chip leader at that table. If ever there was an automatic call with any two cards preflop, this was the time.

This slow, reluctant call illustrates the power of table image. Men the Master's all-in bet combined with his reputation, his indisputable skill, and his relaxed cocky attitude (that convinced me he was sitting there with A-A or K-K) struck such fear into his opponent that he actually was considering laying down his hand despite the huge pot and the insignificant cost of the call. He did finally make the call with his A-Q offsuit and when Men turned over his 8-7 offsuit, many players were literally scratching their heads. Men lost the hand and was eliminated. After he left the table, there was a discussion among a few players about what had transpired.

Some players thought Men was foolish to believe he could push the chip leader out of the pot with an all-in bet when the chip leader already had so many chips in the pot and the cost of the call was so little. But I don't believe for a second that Men believed he would push that guy out of the pot. In fact, I suspect he thought the guy was nuts to take so long to make the call. Some players thought Men must have been steaming as he had recently come from another table with a below average chip stack. They assumed he must have just lost a big pot that put him on tilt. In fact, I was at the same prior table with Men, and both of us were moved to this table together when the prior table broke. He had no reason to be steaming. In fact, I believe his decision was entirely based on utility, and that his risking all of his chips at this point with what amounted to "two live cards" was the correct play.

Why?

Because Men is an extremely skillful tournament player and a big chip stack has huge value to him. Being below average in chips, especially at a table where an aggressive player has a stack big enough to push him around, was simply unacceptable to him. With low utility, his skills were so hampered that the tournament value to him was already extremely low. Winning this pot would not only have increased his utility substantially, it would do so at the same time that it enhanced his table image to truly fearful proportions. His image as a wild player, an intimidating player, and a defensive player, would all soar. The message would definitely go out—you don't reraise Men the Master unless you are prepared to play for all of the chips he has in front of him.

The fact that he didn't win that pot... hey, that's poker. He was less than a 2 to 1 dog in that hand (and I suspect he had a pretty good read on what his opponent had—just two overs) and the value of winning this pot to him made the decision to push close to a no brainer. Most importantly, he had no intention of sitting there with a utility-weakened chip stack waiting for a premium hand to double up on. The blinds and antes were considerable at that point, and the value of doubling up goes down as your chip stack goes down; you want to take these risks when the win will really make a difference.

This is not an isolated unusual example. I saw John Phan call an all-in preflop reraise to his reraise early in a Commerce Casino tournament when Phan had pocket eights. At the time, he was very well-stacked with chips, well above average, and the player who reraised Phan's reraise had Phan outchipped. Phan lost the hand to his opponent's pocket aces and was eliminated. I'm sure Phan put his opponent on having just high cards, probably A-K, and he felt his pocket eights made him the favorite, so the gamble was worth it. Again, he was simply refusing to sit at a table where any player had him outchipped, refusing to be pushed around. He was refusing to back down. He was insisting on having a mountain of chips if he was going to continue in the tournament. If you've ever seen John Phan play when he has a dominating chip stack, then you know that he loves nothing more than squelching his opponents' utility, and he is a master at this. But again, when Phan busted out and walked away, players were commenting on his bad call, wondering aloud if he had been drinking, or was on tilt for some reason. I say, look at his record. As with Men the Master, Phan's tournament record speaks for itself.

Because the concept of pot odds is so widely understood by hold'em players, as well as so misunderstood in the context of tournament play, Chapter Three of this book is titled "Utility Odds," and describes an easy method for overriding pot odds decisions as needed for optimal tournament play. You do not have to make these decisions completely by the seat of your pants. Once you understand utility, the decision-making process is simple.

CHIP UTILITY—THE PROS' SECRET

Calling chip utility a "big secret" is, in a sense, kind of silly, because many successful tournament players already know it. It's not that they know the term "utility," but that they understand utility at a gut level and they play accordingly. It's not like you're going to read this book and find yourself the only player at your table with a top secret weapon. But you'll quickly recognize the other players who know what you know and they'll recognize you as one of them. You'll also recognize which players don't seem to have a clue. And the vast majority of players in any given tournament number among the clueless.

Most of the tournament players who know about the overwhelming importance of chip utility to tournament success didn't learn it from books. Some authors of poker books have mentioned chip utility briefly, but never said, "Stop! Read that paragraph again! That's the secret!" They probably didn't do this because they thought utility was just another idea among many ideas and opinions on how to play. They dropped the secret amidst a dozen other suggestions on things like how to play second pair in a multiway pot. I'm not going to do that. We're going to spend three whole chapters on chip utility until you get it. In these chapters, we're going to completely ignore what you do with the hands you are dealt. Card strategy comes later, and even then the discussions will revolve around utility.

1 - THE BIG SECRET: CHIP UTILITY

The truly bizarre thing about the chip utility secret isn't that a few books have mentioned it without emphasizing (or recognizing) its importance, but that many experts have actually recommended strategies that kill a player's chip utility. You might say their advice creates *chip disutility* for their followers. This is another factor that makes the chip utility secret so valuable. Although many of the top pros understand chip utility, there are also a lot of tournament players making very bad decisions because they've got the big secret *backwards!* Also, most of the tournament players who haven't read any books on how to play tournaments have a natural tendency to play in a way that ruins their chip utility, especially if they have a lot of cash game experience. In any case, the concept of chip utility really is a big secret, something that even a lot of experienced players and many so-called "experts" don't understand. If you have any tendency to believe that you should play your hands in a tournament just as you would play them in a cash game, this chapter should disabuse you of that notion.

You may feel that it's obvious that the value of tournament chips is based on their utility and that anyone who has ever played a few tournaments knows this in his gut. But this book starts with the chip utility concept not only because it is the central idea behind a winning tournament strategy, but also because a lot of what has been written about tournament strategy in the past is based on an idea that is diametrically opposed—the idea that the more chips you have, the less each of your chips is worth.

You may not recall having read in any book on tournament play that the more chips you have the less each of your chips is worth, and if you have not read this idea—which I call the "reverse chip value theory"—you may even find it absurd. But many of poker's math gurus have promulgated this idea in their writings, and numerous other tournament "experts" have assumed this erroneous notion to be true in developing the strategies in their books. Tournament strategies developed with the reverse chip value theory, as I will demonstrate with examples, will advise you to play exactly the opposite of the way you should be playing if you want to win. So, before we get into the strategies you should be using based on the law of chip utility, let's kill the reverse chip value theory once and for all.*

WHY IS EVERYONE PLAYING WRONG?

Twenty years ago, some math heads were trying to figure out the best way to chop up a prize pool equitably among final table players who decided to quit playing and take their respective prizes based on their current chip stacks. How do you solve this problem?

Let's say a tournament is down to the last two players, who are heads-up at the final table. The remaining prizes are $34,000 for the winner, and $18,000 for second place. The player who is the chip leader at this point has $39,000 in chips, while the player in second place has only $13,000 in chips.

If you were to assume that the blinds are so high at this point that both players are simply all in before every flop regardless of cards, making this a coin-flip situation for all intents and purposes, the player in second place has a 25 percent chance of doubling up enough times to take first place, since he holds 25 percent of the total chips in play, and he has a 75 percent chance of taking the second place prize. (If you don't understand the math on this, trust me, it's correct. There wouldn't be any argument among the math heads on this calculation.)

This makes his $13,000 in chips worth $22,000 in prize money. We're simply assigning him 25 percent of the first place money

---

*If you have no interest in the history or theoretical arguments regarding chip utility and the reverse chip value theory, and you just want to know how to play poker tournaments, skip ahead in this chapter to the sub-heading that says "Quantifying Chip Utility."

and 75 percent of the second place money. And, if these two players decided to chop the prize pool based on their chip counts instead of playing the tournament out to the finish, this would generally be regarded as the fair distribution of the prize money. So, the short-stacked player's chips are worth about $1.69 each ($22,000/$13,000).

The chip leader, however, will find that if his results are based entirely on his agreement to go all in on every flop with the shorter stack, regardless of his cards, then his $39,000 in chips have a prize value of $30,000 (the same math, but with his numbers), making them worth only 75 cents each, or less than half the value per chip of the second place player's chips. And if you work out other examples using different sized chip stacks, you'll find that the fewer the chips the second place player has in relation to the first place player, the greater the value of each of the second place player's individual chips. In fact, if he gets down to a single chip, that chip would have a value of more than $18,000, while the chip leader's chips would be worth only about 65 cents each.

Therefore, the math heads erroneously deduced that, in a tournament, where the prizes for each finishing position are based on a percentage payback with first place paying the highest percentage—as just about all multitable tournament payouts today are structured—the more chips a player has, the less each of his chips are worth, and the fewer chips a player has, the more each of his chips are worth.

THE BIG BONER

Here's how the math heads arrived at their mistake. They proposed that the probability of players collecting prize money in a percentage payback tournament is proportionate to the sizes of their chip stacks. Then they showed that if chips are valued according to their proposed "coin-flip" probability of taking the various prize payouts, the more chips a player has, the less each of his chips is worth, and vice versa. And, by extension, a chip you lose is worth more than a chip you win—the exact opposite of the law of chip utility.

How can this be? Frankly, it's because the math heads who worked out this solution to the problem did a poor analysis. Mason Malmuth and David Sklansky were the main proponents of the reverse chip value theory. Their arithmetic is right, but the assumptions underlying their logic are wrong.

In assuming that players have "equal skill" for working out these prize pool distributions, they mean that no player can outplay any other player. The distribution is the same that would be made if these players' odds of collecting the various prizes were based on coin flips. But the fact is, even when two players do have equal skill, the contest ceases to be a coin flip when one player has the chips to use more of his skills, while the other is utility-restricted. The math heads' "fair" method of chopping a prize pool shortchanges the bigger stacks, assuming the big stacks belong to skillful players, because the more utility the bigger stacks have, the less of a coin-flip this contest is.

In the real world, if two tournament pros of equal skill are all that remain at the final table, with the big stack holding 87.5 percent of the chips and the short-stack holding 12.5 percent of the chips, the short stack could not, in fact, expect to take first place 12.5 percent of the time. He could only expect to do this if the big stack agreed to go all in on every hand with him until the finish, making the result a 100 percent luck-based result where neither skill nor utility played any part. In fact, with 87.5 percent of the chips, the big stack would have skill options available to him that would not be available to the short-stack. Even if the short stack insisted on going all-in on every hand himself—which may, in fact, be his optimal strategy—the big stack would still have the option of playing selective hands, a utility function not available to a short-stacked player who can't afford the blind and ante costs.

A player who pushes all in on every round is, in essence, pushing in with any two random cards. A strategy of playing selective cards could easily be devised that can get a substantial edge on a player who is playing random cards. It can be shown mathematically that if one player pushes all in on every round, while the other player calls only when he is a 51 percent favorite or better to win against two random cards, the player who plays these selective hands will win almost 59 percent of the time, while the all-in-on-every-hand player will win only 41 percent of the time. Playing only those starting hands that have an expectation of winning 51 percent of the time or more against two random cards means that you would play close to half of the hands dealt, or all hands of Q-6 offsuit or better.

So, the utility function of playing selective hands in this way provides almost an 18 percent advantage in and of itself (59 percent wins versus 41 percent wins for the short stack). In this case, that 18 percent advantage of the player calling with selective hands only is compounded by the number of times his opponent must double up to beat him. If the player who is pushing all in on every hand starts with only 12.5 percent of the chips, the probability of him surviving three double ups (which would be the number of double ups required for him to win all the chips) when his opponent has an average 18 percent advantage on each hand is only 7 percent! So, the big stack that starts with 87.5 percent of the chips and simply calls with selective "good" cards, as above, actually has a 93 percent chance of winning if his opponent is all-in on every hand in an attempt to beat him. The player playing selective cards has reduced the short stack's coin-flip "equity value" through the use of the simplest of all utility functions—hand selection.

It could be argued that the short-stacked player starting with 12.5 percent of the chips would get even with his opponent after only two double ups, at which time he could abandon his all-in strategy and start playing poker again. But he only has a 17 percent chance of doubling up twice when his opponent has an average advantage of 18 percent against him. This means that if it becomes a "coin-flip" battle between these two "equal skill" players after the short stack has doubled up twice, the short stack's overall probability of winning the tournament is only about 8.5 percent (or half of the 17 percent of the time he manages to double up twice), even though he started with 12.5 percent of the chips.

There was a perfect demonstration of this principle at a televised WPT final table at Bellagio's Five Diamond World Classic in 2004. Paul Phillips faced Dewey Tomko heads-up for the championship, with Phillips holding 86 percent of the chips in play to Tomko's 14 percent. Because of the high blinds and antes, Dewey did what he had to do at this point to build chips and regain utility, and started pushing all-in on every hand. Phillips mucked his marginal cards multiple times and let Dewey take the blinds. Then, Dewey pushed and Phillips found pocket sevens as his hole cards. He called, and eliminated Dewey on that hand. Although Tomko started the heads-up play with 14 percent of the chips on the table, there was no way he had a 14 percent chance of taking first place if he just kept pushing against Phillips' selective-hand strategy. Pocket sevens have better than a 66 percent win rate against two random cards, a fact probably unknown to Phillips at the time. But Phillips was knowledgeable enough about hold'em to know a better-than-random hand when he saw one, and that's all he was waiting for.

But this extreme example of two players with a huge chip discrepancy doesn't even begin to tell the whole utility story. Imagine a final table with five players, where one has $700,000 in chips; another has $400,000; another has $240,000; another has $125,000, and one has only $65,000. Let's say the blinds are

1 - THE BIG SECRET: CHIP UTILITY

$3,000/$6,000. The utility discrepancies among a group of players like this are huge. This is no coin-flip situation. Those bigger stacks have utility options far beyond the value of playing selective cards for a measly 18 percent edge.

And let's take it a step further and consider a tournament in the bubble stage, where 24 players remain and 18 spots are paying. Now you have a couple of players with dominant utility, a handful with full utility, and the rest of the field varying from high levels of moderate utility to low levels of low utility. The notion that this resembles in any way a coin-flip contest is absurd, even if the players did all have equal skill. And the notion that these players would all have equal skill is even more absurd to anyone who has ever made it to the end of a tournament. I see amateur players on final tables all the time. Only in a fantasy world can you devise optimum strategies for players in this endgame portion of the tournament based on coin-flip assumptions.

From my own experience, I can tell you that if I am still alive among the last couple dozen players of a tournament that's paying 18 spots, I feel that I've got the final table locked up even if my chip position is not that great. Even if I'm 20th in chips out of 25 players, I will likely hit at least a midpoint final-table finish, like fourth or fifth. This is due to the fact that so many players voluntarily surrender their utility at this point with their survival-oriented strategies. A tournament at this point is a battle between the utility players and the survival players, and it's not so much a battle as a rout.

The math heads' initial error in logic in developing the reverse chip value theory came from their assumption that in a winner-take-all event, all chips have equal value throughout. The selective-hand example above, however, refutes this erroneous notion. Even in a winner-take-all event, the value of chips must take into account their utility value.

One of the staunchest defenses of the reverse chip value theory can be found in the recently published *Kill Everyone* by Lee Nelson, Tysen Streib and Kim Lee, in a chapter titled "Prize Pools and Equity." The authors assign chips dollar values during the bubble portion of a tournament based on the same old models that neglect utility, and they recommend that players actually play according to this flawed theory long before a few final table players are actually considering chopping the prize pool. Many tournament books have flawed bubble strategies, but I'm mentioning *Kill Everyone* specifically because it has been recently published and garnered a big following. However, many of the strategic tips in the book are good, as they do incorporate utility thinking and psychological aspects of play.

But valuing chips based on bad analyses of how to chop up a prize pool is no way to determine what tournament chips are "worth," especially when it comes to playing the tournament for many hours (sometimes days) in order to get to that final table. And it is an especially poor evaluation for bubble play in a percentage-payback tournament, when the value of utility in a major deep-stack event escalates. Some popular tournament books even apply the reverse chip value theory to strategy decisions long before the bubble portion of a tournament is reached, advising players to use conservative rebuy strategies at the beginning of rebuy events because "the more chips you have, the less each chip is worth," or to avoid taking early risks to build a big stack because the chips you win will be worth less than the chips you would lose if your early aggression fails.

HOW CHIP VALUE THEORY AFFECTS STRATEGY

Belief in the concept of reverse chip value will inevitably lead to overly tight and conservative play. If I believe that the chips I am trying to win are worth less than the chips I must risk to win them, then I must wait for a bigger advantage before putting my chips at risk. For example, if I must bet $2 to win chips valued at $1, then I have to win the bet twice as often as I lose it just to break even, and I must wait for better hands to put my chips in action.

By contrast, if you understand the law of chip utility—that the more chips you have the more each of your chips is worth (because they enable you to finance a bigger set of skill plays)—then looser and more aggressive play will be correct. If I am risking chips that have *less* value than the chips I can win, I can risk my chips with a much smaller advantage over my opponent. For example, if I can win chips valued at $2 for a $1 bet, then I'd have to lose the bet twice as often as I'd win it before it would not be a bet worth making. Getting my chips in action much more frequently, with smaller advantages, would be correct.

Now, I'm not stating here that the chips you add to your stack are always worth twice as much as the chips already in your stack. In many cases, they are worth less than this, though in some cases they are worth quite a bit more than this. The point of this section is to show why belief in the reverse chip value theory will inevitably lead to tighter and more conservative play, while an understanding of chip utility will loosen your play considerably.

THE DEBATE OVER CHIP UTILITY THEORY

In 2007, I published an article on my website (www.pokertournamentformula.com) explaining that a tournament player's chip utility increased as his chip stack increased, making his chips more valuable as his stack size increases. In a response to my article on another poker website, a defender, David Sklansky, of the old school of conventional thinking purported to prove that the value of individual chips in a big stack does not go up as more chips are added to the stack. As "proof," he offered an example in which he proposed that a good player's $100 buy-in in a 32-player tournament was worth $150 and pointed out that her doubling to $200 in tournament chips and again to $400 and again to $800 then $1,600 then finally to $3,200 in tournament chips, could not make her total chips worth more than $4,800, since this would be more than the entire prize pool.

In other words, the argument he provided to disprove the value of chip utility was that if a skilled player wins all of the chips in a tournament, the chips obviously can't have more value than the total prize pool. Math geeks can drive you nuts with inane examples.

There are two major errors in logic in this "proof." First, when we say that a player has a $150 expected value (or EV) on his $100 buy-in, we are saying that this player, because of his skill and overall strategy, expects an *average return* of $150 per $100 buy-in for every tournament like this that he enters. You can't assign that overall expectation on the tournament as the chip utility value of the starting stack, nor can you automatically multiply this overall EV as you multiply your stack.

The reason you can't do this is because your overall $150 EV is derived from your aggressive stack-building strategy; in other words, it's because the player is consistently building his chip stack that he has that $150 EV on his $100 investment. The $150 does not represent chip value, it represents *strategy value*. In incorrectly assigning the player's overall EV as the value of his starting chips, this author errs in his tournament logic.

Granted, the author of this reverse chip value defense, Sklansky, is not known as a tournament player or even as much of a cash game player anymore. But again, this is why understanding chip utility is so powerful in tournaments. The cash game experts and math gurus have simply provided a lot of bad analyses that many players follow.

The second major error in the logic in this "proof" is the reliance on a model that, again, ignores crucial tournament factors. The "proof" has this doubling-up player playing in a tournament vacuum—with no opponents and no steadily-increasing blinds. To illustrate the importance of this mistake, let's consider some situations where a chip increase does not increase utility.

Let's say that a player, who has started with $100 in chips, has increased his chip stack to $200 a few hours into the tournament. Does this doubling of his stack to $200 mean that the chips in his stack are now worth more than the chips in the $100 stack he had when he started the tournament? To answer this question, we must consider whether or not this double up has increased the player's chip utility. How does his chip stack at this point measure up against his opponents' chip stacks, as well as the current blind and ante costs?

If a player doubles his initial chip stack, but the average chip stack at his table has tripled during this time period, then the utility value of his chips has *decreased* since the tournament started, despite his double up. For the chip utility value to increase, the player's stack would have to be big enough to provide a bigger ratio between the size of the stack and the blind/ante costs, and/or a bigger chip lead over the chip stacks of the player's opponents.

So, any model that automatically assigns twice the chip utility value every time a player doubles up is just a badly thought out model. Real chip utility value depends on *when* that double up occurs and how the size of that newly doubled stack relates to the size of competitors' stacks.

If the average chip stack of a player's opponents has also doubled by this point in the tournament, so that our player has merely kept up with the field, while the blinds have doubled or more than doubled during the same time period, the bigger cost of the blinds will in and of themselves have already diminished our player's chip utility prior to his double up. It will have become more difficult and more expensive to steal the blinds or any pot, and more expensive and dangerous to use many of the chip utility functions described at the beginning of this chapter. If a player is losing ground to the blind costs, his chip utility goes down, even if he's keeping up with his competitors, because his skill options are constricted and any move he makes is more likely to jeopardize his tournament survival.

But these tournament factors in no way invalidate the chip utility concept that the more chips you have, the more each chip is worth. While chip utility has the greatest value when a player is not only well stacked in relation to the blinds, but also has built a significant chip lead on his opponents, chip utility has some value even when a player is short-stacked.

For example, let's say that at the point in a tournament when the average chip stack at a table has tripled to $300, our player's chip stack is still just $100. Now, he's in real trouble. No matter how much skill he may possess in comparison to his opponents, his chip utility is seriously diminished. Suddenly, however, he gets that miracle hand that doubles him up to $200. Now, has this increase in chips increased the value of the chips in his stack? Absolutely it has, because he has increased his chip utility. The problem is that his opponents with $300 in chips still have even greater chip utility. They still have more ammunition to outplay him.

AT VIRTUALLY ANY SPECIFIC POINT IN A TOURNAMENT, THE MORE CHIPS YOU HAVE, THE MORE EACH CHIP IS WORTH.

So, even though the individual chips in this $200 stack now have less value than the individual chips in the $100 stack this player had at the very start of the tournament, they have more value than the chips in the $100 stack this player had just before his double up. In that sense—and this is the only sense that matters strategically when you are actually playing—at virtually any specific point in a tournament, the more chips you have, the more each chip is worth. And again, I am assuming here that you are a skillful player who knows how to use your chips for their utility value.

WHAT ABOUT TRIVIAL WINS AND LOSSES?

Very small movements in chips are not really significant when they have minimal utility effect. For example, if I pick up the $25/$50 blinds on the first round of a tournament where all players start with $3,000 in chips, my new $3,075 chip stack doesn't have any significant effect on my utility, nor is the utility of the players who were in the blinds and who now have $2,950 and $2,975 significantly hampered. If I win a $500-chip pot, however, giving me $3,500 in chips, and there is a player who now has somewhere in the neighborhood of only $2,500 in chips, this discrepancy will definitely effect our respective utility, even at an early blind level, especially if we are involved in a pot together.

CAN WE EVER ASSIGN AN EXACT DOLLAR VALUE TO OUR CHIPS?

If you wanted to assign a specific dollar value to a specific player's chips, based on his chip stack's utility in relation to all other players' chip stacks and skill levels, at any moment in a tournament, the calculation would be complex because there are so many tournament factors that affect a player's chip utility value. A poker tournament is a constantly shifting terrain of power relationships. It is generally a mistake to ever try to think of your chips in terms of dollar value. You must think of your chips as ammunition only.

For example, consider what happens to the utility value of the chips of a significant table chip leader if a new player with a much bigger chip stack is suddenly moved to the same table. If the bigger stack is a loose, aggressive player, then that dominating chip stack can cause a decrease in the former chip leader's chip utility, and this decrease can be further exacerbated by the giant stack's seating position in relation to the former chip leader.

Likewise, a player at a table can suddenly double up or triple up and take a big chip lead on a former chip leader; or a chip leader at one table can suddenly be moved to a new table where his chip position is less optimal. There are many factors within a tournament that can instantly affect a player's chip utility even when the size of his chip stack has not changed at all. In fact, a simple change in the blind level can have a big effect on any skillful player's chip utility, not only because it affects his betting costs, but because of the way it can more seriously affect shorter stacked opponents. For example, a blind level change may increase the chip utility of big stacks by decreasing the chip utility of shorter stacks.

Sometimes the opponents' chip stacks get too short for the big-stacked player to use his full range of poker skills against them. Extremely short-stacked players can't afford to play poker and are often limited to looking for all-in shots to take. This will definitely eliminate the bigger stacks' chances to deploy their full skill sets in playing against these players. A player with a big stack must switch to a skill set that is more optimal for play against desperate players. He can no longer use many of his post-flop skills against such players, though the utility value of patience and hand selection for the bigger stack skyrockets, as does the value of risk-taking to eliminate an opponent who is likely taking shots with marginal cards. Likewise, unless his opponents are so short-stacked that they must call any all-in bet with any two cards, the big stack can still use his chips to steal aggressively from them. In other words, some utility functions for the big stack will have diminished, while the utility value of other chip functions has gone up.

CHIP UTILITY AND "GAME THEORY"

Aside from the fact that it's obvious to anyone who's played a few tournaments that having a lot of chips increases your options, and having few chips decreases your options, there is an established mathematical basis for assigning a value to this utility. I did not invent the concept of putting a value on utility. This concept has been well-known to mathematicians for centuries. Ironically, the reverse chip value argument seems at first glance to be supported by a well-known theory in economics called *marginal utility*. This theory was developed during the late 18th century, and basically asserts that the greater the supply of a commodity, the lower the value of any unit of that commodity. For example, if there is a great supply of apples, then the value of a bushel of apples will be less than when apples are in short supply. If there is a great supply of money, then the value of any individual unit of that money will be less than when money is in short supply.

The great Swiss mathematician, Daniel Bernoulli, formulated a widely-accepted theory that even for an individual in society, the concept of utility is of greater importance than intrinsic value. For example, for a poor man to lose $10 could be devastating to him, while a rich man who loses $10 may not even notice that it's missing. Likewise, if a poor man gains $10, it will have much more value to him than it will to a rich man who gains $10. This example provides the easiest-to-comprehend explanation of the logic of utility as employed by economists. The poor man can really use that $10. To the rich man, it's just another bill in his wallet.

We can easily, and erroneously, translate this economic concept to the tournament poker table. We see one player sitting with a mountain of chips in front of him, while the player across the table has a stack so short that the approaching blinds are threatening his survival. Doesn't the threat of the blind costs to the short-stacked player present a situation similar to that of the poor man devastated by the loss of $10?

The problem with applying Bernoulli's theory to the microcosm of a poker tournament is that we can do so only if we ignore the fundamental meaning of *utility*—which is to say, value based on usefulness to the individual.*

A poor man doesn't have to bankrupt the rich man with his $10 in order to meet his goal of surviving. But in a tournament, even the shortest of the short stacks must bankrupt every deep-stacked

---

* Technically, in economic theory, utility can refer to any individual preference, including preferences that are not based on the concept of "using," but that's not relevant to this discussion.

player he faces. In a tournament, both the chip-poor and the chip-rich have an identical goal—to bankrupt each other and everyone else in the game. Bernoulli, by contrast, is assuming that his rich man and poor man can live side by side, the poor man eating his beans and the rich man eating his steak and lobster. Taking two nickel chips from a chip-poor player in a tournament, however, is good for a chip-rich player, if only because it further crushes the short-stacked player's utility, and bankrupting that player along with all others is always the ultimate goal.

Economists and mathematicians have argued about how to quantify the value of utility for as long as the concept has existed. If $10 has a different value to a poor man than it does to a rich man, how do we put a number on the value? It's easy to say that in the real world, as per Bernoulli's theory, the value is inversely proportional to the wealth or poverty of the owner, but can we quantify that value numerically?

The modern founder of "game theory," John von Neumann, expounded at length on Bernoulli's theory of utility, especially as applied to games and gambling. Many poker authors—and especially those with a background in mathematics—are familiar with von Neumann's 1944 masterwork, *Theory of Games and Economic Behavior* (co-authored with economist, Oskar Morgenstern). Ironically, few poker authors have paid much attention to von Neumann's work on the notion of utility. Most have instead concentrated solely on a chapter he wrote titled "Poker and Bluffing." That's too bad, because von Neumann's theories of bluffing at poker are of negligible value to expert players—despite what some of today's poker gurus believe. But we'll deal with bluffing in a later chapter. For now, let's stick with chip utility.

To his credit, von Neumann acknowledged in his book that the notion of utility throws a monkey wrench into game theory. As soon as we have a given quantity of a commodity that has different uses by those involved in the game and by extension differing values, where we can see that one's small loss can mean another's large gain and vice versa—and where there is no logical formulaic approach to putting real numbers on these value differences— game theory comes down to conjecture and guesswork based on assumptions that may or may not have any basis in reality for the participants. In the end, von Neumann threw up his hands in defeat in his attempts to quantify value based on utility.

In *The Mathematics of Poker* (ConJelCo, 2006), Bill Chen and Jerrod Ankenman at least recognize the existence of utility and give a nod to its importance when they say on the first page of their first chapter: "In reality, it is utility that we seek to maximize when playing poker (or in fact, when doing anything). However, the use of utility theory as a basis for analysis presents a difficulty; each individual has his own utility curves and so general analysis becomes extremely difficult. In this book, we will therefore refrain from considering utility and instead use money won inside the game as a proxy for utility."

In analyzing cash games, their arguments make sense, because cash games for most players are about winning cash, and chips not only represent cash, they *are* cash. Poker in a tournament context is quite different, however, because although you are playing in order to win cash, you accomplish this by maximizing your utility and minimizing the utility of your opponents. Each individual player's maximum potential utility is a function of his skill, and chips are simply the tools that enable him to maximize the value of his skill set. To ignore the utility value of chips in analyzing and devising strategies for tournaments—despite the fact that "each individual has his own utility curves," (which is the same reason von Neumann threw up his hands when attempting to incorporate utility into game theory)—is a huge error in logic that will lead, and has led, to major errors in strategic thinking in tournaments.

In Richard Epstein's *Theory of Gambling and Statistical Logic* (Academic Press, 1977), a text that discusses game theory as applied to real world gambling games (while von Neumann primarily created hypothetical games as analogies for economic, political, and business situations), Epstein commented: "This notion of utility is fundamental and must be encompassed by a theory of gambling in order to define and analyze the decision process." In other words, where utility exists as a factor in a game, you cannot develop optimal strategies for that game if you ignore it. And a poker tournament is nothing but one long battle for utility.

So, despite the fact that it is impossible to put precise numerical values on the utility functions of chips, and despite the fact that these values will be different for each player in the tournament based on his range of skills, I am going to incorporate utility theory into my strategic analyses by making broad assumptions about the value of various common skills, the cost of losing these skills as a result of insufficient chips, and the value of curtailing the use of these skills in your opponents.

But, this book is not a treatise on game theory. I'm simply trying to explain where the reverse chip value theory came from, why so many of poker's math gurus embraced it, and why strategies based on that theory are doomed to fail. The most important thing you must know about the reverse chip value theory is that many of your opponents will be playing according to that erroneous logic, and this creates a lot of dead money in the tournament prize pool for those who employ utility-based strategies.

THE MONOPOLY CONNECTION

If you were good at the Parker Brothers' game of Monopoly as a kid, then you have the foundation for being a successful tournament poker player. Unless you were a kid genius, it's unlikely that you used game theory to develop your Monopoly strategies. Somehow, you just figured out what you had to do to win. If you did use game theory to develop your strategies, you would have discovered that in this game, the more properties you own, the more each individual property is worth. The object of the game in Monopoly is to own every property on the board, which inevitably results in bankrupting all other players. Likewise, the object of a poker tournament is to own every chip in the game, bankrupting all other players.

As you may recall, property values in Monopoly increase as you own more. For example, if I own one railroad, then you must pay me $25 each time you land on it. If I own two railroads, you must pay me $50 each time you land on either of them. If I own three railroads, the cost is $100, and if I own all four railroads, you must pay me $200 each time you land on any of them.

The other board properties have similar value structures. It's much more valuable for me to own all of the properties in a group so that I can improve them by investing in houses and hotels, thereby increasing the payment you must make to me if you land on one of my properties. The more I own, and the more I invest in my properties, the more my prior investments are worth.

Some kids never seemed to get it. If I owned three railroads and they owned one, I could often convince them to sell me their railroad by offering some small amount more than they paid for it. They looked at what the railroad they owned was worth to them—just $25 each time I landed on it—instead of what it would be worth to me if I increased my railroad holdings from three to four. The game of Monopoly was created to mimic, more or less, what happens in real-world monopolies. If one person or company in the real world monopolizes any single product or commodity—diamonds, for example—then the value of each unit of that commodity is much greater than when the commodity has widespread ownership among different entities. In a monopoly, assuming there is a demand for the monopolized commodity, the theory of marginal utility often works backwards. Money itself is worth more in the game of Monopoly the more you have, as its utility value—what you can do with it—increases as you amass more of it. What happens in a Monopoly game is that the poor man can no longer traverse the board because the rich man keeps charging him more and more in rental fees. The poor man can no longer buy properties, improve properties, or bargain for favorable trade agreements with his opponents. Unless he runs into a long string of incredible luck that earns him enough money to be competitive again, he is, in a sense, "blinded off." A poker tournament is a variation of a Monopoly game in which chips replace the properties, and the utility value of chips replace the rental values of the properties owned.

The game of Monopoly has been analyzed to death by mathematicians. Statisticians have figured out the frequencies of players landing on each of the properties based on the probabilities of the dice totals and the Chance and Community Chest cards that propel the game forward. And Monopoly is one game where utility can be quantified precisely, because all of the money transactions are spelled out in the rules. There is no bluffing in Monopoly, so the optimal strategies can be devised purely on the math and the probabilities.

QUANTIFYING CHIP UTILITY

Since a poker tournament does not have clearly defined values for chips written into the rules—but rather values that are dependent not only on each individual player's skill but also on the constantly fluctuating power relationships between the players based largely on their respective chip stacks, how do we quantify our chip utility at any given point in a tournament? I use a very simple system of rating my utility as dominant, full, moderate, or low.

Technically, full utility is the minimum acceptable utility throughout most of any deep-stack tournament. Toward the end of many deep-stack events, and toward the middle of many medium-stacked events, no players have full utility due to the high blind/ante costs. This is true even in many of the deepest-stack pro-level tournaments with slow blind structures. (We will discuss how structure affects utility in the next chapter.) But throughout the majority of most deep-stack tournaments, before you get to the money, moderate utility is not really acceptable, for reasons that will be discussed below. Also, in reading my descriptions of dominant, full, moderate and low utility, note that there are gradations to these categories, just as there are gradations in the actual sizes of chip stacks and players' skill sets. For example, you can be close to full utility, or slightly better than low utility.

DOMINANT UTILITY

Dominant utility is a stack size that is equal to at least 100 times the size of the big blind and, at the same time, is at least four times the size of the average stack at your table *and* at least twice the size of the next biggest stack.

With dominant utility, you can run over the table, stealing pots with bets that will be small to you, but would pot-commit many of your opponents. If you have a stack size smaller than 100 big blinds, but still four times the average stack, you will lose some of your dominance because many of your opponents will be too desperate for chips to be pushed around. For example, if your stack size is equivalent to 80 big blinds, and the average stack at your table is equivalent to only 20 big blinds, your chip position is great, but you will have to become more selective in the hands you play against such desperate opponents.

Dominant utility has its greatest potential when most of your opponents feel they have enough chips to wait for trapping hands.

FULL UTILITY

A stack size equivalent to 100 big blinds is *full utility*, because that is the minimum stack size required for unhampered post-flop play, including information bets and more advanced moves on later streets or against more aggressive deep-stacked opponents. You have full utility when you have enough chips to play unhampered "small ball." This means you have enough chips to see a lot of flops with marginal hands, whether in position or not, but especially when in position. And you have enough chips to mix it up post-flop and to make information bets and raises. If you don't know what small-ball poker is, there is a discussion of small ball versus long ball in part two of this book, "Tools."

I consider the small-ball approach a primary strategy in tournaments with slow blind structures, because it provides the highest advantage for skillful players, with more opportunities to use their skills, and the most control over their results. But, unfortunately, you can't play small ball without a big stack. That's just a fact. The shorter your stack in relation to not only the blind/ante costs, but to your table opponents' stacks, the more aggressively you must play and the more risks you must be willing to take. If you are not sufficiently stocked with chips to play small ball, that is a real handicap for a skillful player. We'll be discussing this in depth later, but for now, just remember that if your ability to play small-ball poker is hampered by your chip stack, you have moderate utility at best. And that ain't good.

As for information bets, these always take a big stack. For example, let's say the blinds are $50/$100, and I come in with a raise to $300 from late position with pocket nines. The big blind calls, putting

$650 in the preflop pot. The flop comes down Q-7-4 rainbow and the player in the big blind comes out with a bet of $400, slightly more than half the size of the pot.

BIG BLIND   **ARNOLD**

FLOP

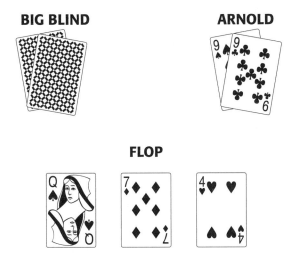

There are a number of possibilities here. First, he could just be doing a resteal, assuming my preflop raise from late position was just an attempt to steal the blinds with no hand to speak of. He may have called my preflop raise fully intending to bet post-flop no matter what came down on the flop. It's also possible that he has a hand himself, maybe even a pocket pair below my nines, and he is simply betting that the flop didn't hit me and I'll have to fold if I didn't hit the queen or I couldn't beat a pair of queens. It's also possible that he called with a hand like K-Q or Q-J or Q-9 suited and he did make top pair on the flop, but with less than the top kicker. With A-Q, he would most likely have reraised me preflop. There are many possible reasons why he may bet here and I don't know what his bet means, though I hate the thought of folding the best hand. I also just as much hate the thought of not taking the pot away from him, if possible, even if he has my hand beat.

1 - THE BIG SECRET: CHIP UTILITY

This is where the information bet is very valuable. By raising him, I will find out right away if he is trying a resteal or betting a hand less than top pair top kicker. Since his post-flop bet was $400, I would have to make it at least $800 to reraise the minimum, and a bigger bet than this would really be optimal. If he hit the queen with a poor kicker, many players would simply call my minimum raise, unable to lay down top pair for just another $400 in chips when there is $1,850 in the pot.

The primary purpose of the information bet is to get information, and a minimum raise may simply get me a call, rather than the information I seek. Also, if he calls the extra $400, I'll have a tough decision on the turn if he bets half the size of the pot again, or even if he checks. With $2,250 in the pot, I'd probably have to lay down my nines if he bets $1,200, and if he checks, do I want to bet $1,200 at this point for what again may be insufficient information? So, the minimum raise to $800 is not a wise play. A raise to $1,200 would be much better for getting me the information I want without risking the cost of a bet on the turn, and would even push him out of many pots when he has my hand beat but simply can't beat A-Q.

That means that with a raise here to $1,200, I would have a total of $1,500 in chips involved in this pot after that bet. If he calls or reraises, I'm done putting chips into this pot. Unless I have some kind of read on this player, the way I'd have to look at that information bet if he remained in the pot is that I asked, and he answered.

Note that I entered the pot preflop with a standard raise to $300 when the blinds were at $50/$100. So, if all I had at the start of this hand was a stack size totaling 30 big blinds ($3,000 in chips), this standard information bet would be completely out of the question, as I would have half of my stack involved in this pot before the turn card even came down. With a stack size totaling only 30 times the big blind, if I truly believed the player was attempting a resteal, or would lay down any hand other than A-Q or better, I might elect to push all in here to take down the pot. But that's dangerous. That's not an information bet. For all I know, this player may have flopped a set of fours.

The logic of the information bet is that you are attempting to get information that you are willing to pay for—not information at any cost. An information bet will often win the pot for you, even when your opponent has a better hand, so for that reason, the value is much higher than just the information.

Information bets generally win good-sized pots when they win. Even if you must ultimately abandon your hand, the information you get from your opponent when you make this bet has a value in itself, saving you lots of chips on later streets, but you must have sufficient chips to be able to pay for that information. A stack size in the neighborhood of 60 big blinds is usually the minimum required to have this utility function. You really don't want to involve more than 25 percent of your stack in a situation where there is a high likelihood that you will have to abandon the pot. Against opponents who tend to bet more than half the size of the pot, or in multiway pots where the pot-size is bigger simply because more players entered preflop, the information bet may require a stack size of 80 to 100 big blinds. In the later stages of many tournaments, after the antes have kicked in, information bets become impossible for all but the deepest stacked players.

COMPETITIVE UTILITY
In a slow-structured tournament, a stack size equivalent to 60 big blinds is a *competitive stack*, because that is the minimum stack required for a lot of post-flop small-ball play, including information bets against most opponents.

1 - THE BIG SECRET: CHIP UTILITY

In *PTF1*, I used the term "competitive" for a stack size of only 30 big blinds, because that book was about fast-structured tournament and in fast tournaments, 30 big blinds is competitive. You can't play small ball in tournaments that have 15- or 20-minute blind levels, nor can you do much fancy post-flop play. The blind costs rise so quickly in fast tournaments, and the play is so aggressive, that you simply cannot see a lot of pots with speculative hands. These types of tournaments must be played very aggressively, with almost all betting done preflop and on the flop, and with many more all-in moves than are optimal in a slow-structured event. You rarely require a stack size of more than 30 big blinds in a fast tournament (or 40 big blinds once the antes have kicked in) to play this way.

Players in slow-structured events who follow traditional survival-oriented strategies, seeing few flops and generally with premium starting cards, tend to feel "fully functional" with a stack size equal to only 30 to 40 big blinds, and most of the advice I've seen in tournament books agrees with this perspective. When you're just not playing all that many hands, and you're rarely taking shots or getting involved in higher-risk plays, you don't need a whole lot of chips.

But as you will see throughout this book, my definition of "fully functional" is very different from a tight player's definition. So, as we get into our strategy discussions, remember that a competitive utility chip stack is equivalent to at least 60 big blinds and a full utility chip stack is equivalent to at least 100 big blinds.

MODERATE UTILITY

A moderate utility chip stack is somewhere in the neighborhood of 30 to 60 big blinds. With moderate utility, you have enough chips to enter a pot with standard raises (three to four times the big blind) without jeopardizing your chip position if you have to abandon your hand post-flop. You can also make standard continuation bets and position bets if an opponent checks to you post-flop. You have enough chips to call when you have strong draws. You can semibluff, push opponents out of pots when they are on draws, and bet for value.

Although you do not have the utility needed to see flops with all of the speculative hands you'd like to play, or to play small ball post-flop at the level you would like to play, you do at least have sufficient utility to be selective in the hands and situations that you get involved in. In other words, moderate utility means you have sufficient chips to play some amount of poker—and you can still threaten your opponents, even the biggest stacks at your table, because you could take a damaging chunk out of anyone. You still have that fear factor going for you. If the biggest stacks at your table have about twice the chips you do, you still have moderate utility because none of them would want to lose half of their chips to you, and essentially reverse chip positions with you.

But remember, moderate utility leaves you at a severe disadvantage to a skillful player with full utility. You must continually take risks to get back to a more competitive stack, and hopefully to full utility.

LOW UTILITY

I consider any stack size of under 30 big blinds as pretty low on the utility scale for a pro-level tournament, especially if the antes have already kicked in. And once you're down to 15 to 25 big blinds, you have got to make a move fast to either double up or bust out trying.

With low utility, you are in real danger. You have sufficient chips to steal the blinds from wimps, but other than for blind steals from late position, most of your preflop bets must be all-in bets in an attempt to either double up or take down pots without any post-flop play. You can still make these bets against normal raisers, who might fold to your reraise preflop because your table image is strong, especially if they entered the pot with a hand like A-J or K-Q or some small or medium pair, and they really don't want to double you up. You also have sufficient chips to attempt post-flop resteals from the blinds. Most of your standard poker play, however, is not an option. You just don't have sufficient chips to play poker post-flop. You are either all-in preflop, or immediately after the flop. And often, if you are not all-in preflop, you enter the pot with the intention of going all-in post-flop regardless of what comes down on the flop.

NO UTILITY

With no utility, you are basically in such a short chip status that any preflop all-in bet you make is likely to be called by a big stack with any marginal hand—sometimes any two cards—in an attempt to finish you off. And, unfortunately, you do not have sufficient chips to wait for premium cards to make your stand. The blind/ante costs are eating you up quickly. All you've got left is one Hail Mary pass, and even if you double up, you will most likely only go from no utility to low utility. You are more than one double up away from any comfort zone. Any stack size under 15 big blinds is knocking on death's door. In his famous poem, "The Hollow Men," T. S. Eliot's final lines are: "This is the way the world ends / Not with a bang but a whimper." Well, maybe that's how it ends for the hollow men, but that's not how it ends for you if you've got guts. Take a stand before you're blinded off.

CHIP UTILITY CLASSIFICATIONS
Stack Size Compared to Big Blinds

Utility Grade	Big Blinds
No Utility Chip Stack	Under 15 Big Blinds
Low Utility Chip Stack	15-30 Big Blinds
Moderate Utility Chip Stack	30-60 Big Blinds
Competitive Utility Chip Stack	60-100 Big Blinds
Full Utility Chip Stack	100+ Big Blinds
Dominant Chip Utility Stack	100+ Big Blinds (and 4x average stack at table)

HOW STYLE AFFECTS UTILITY

Utility is not based entirely on your stack size. There is no simple formula for gauging whether your utility is full, moderate, or low. You can be the big stack at your table with a stack size equivalent to 200 big blinds, and still not have full utility if a loose-aggressive player is severely curtailing your ability to play small-ball poker. In some cases, these players may be skillful experienced players who simply prefer the long-ball "power poker" approach—or who have simply changed gears temporarily to a long-ball style—or they may be unskilled players who are taking the *Kill Phil* approach to eradicating the pros' post-flop skill edge. Of these two types of players, the skillful long-ball player is the one who will hurt your utility the most, as the less skillful all-in specialist will be picking and choosing less frequent hands to get involved with.

Likewise, what might be considered a moderate stack size in relation to the blind/ante costs might only provide low utility if you are facing several deep-stacked players who are continually making outsized bets and raises, whether you regard these players as skillful or not.

PUTTING NUMBERS ON UTILITY

I use a very simple system of quantifying my utility at any point in a tournament. Based on the definitions above of what qualifies as full, moderate, or low utility, I consider full utility—which means the ability to play small-ball poker, engage in lots of post-flop play, and use my chips to obtain information, as 100 percent utility.

If these functions are seriously hampered, then I rate my moderate utility as 50 percent utility at best. In no-limit hold'em tournaments, those full utility functions are hugely important. And if I do not even have moderate utility, I consider low utility to be 10 to 15 percent utility at best. These percentages will be important later.

I mentally adjust my utility from these percentages based on the actual table situation. If players at my table are more aggressive than normal, or a single aggressive player to my left is hampering my play somewhat, I may knock my 100 percent utility down to 80 percent or 75 percent. In some cases, this may be the maximum utility I can have at this table at this time and I must accept that. But if an opportunity arises where I can disarm the player who is hampering my utility, I know it will be worth my taking some risk to do so.

Likewise, I may adjust my moderate utility up or down from the 50 percent benchmark depending on the table situation. Having position on weak players may give me 60 percent or even 70 percent utility. Bad position in regards to aggressive players with deeper stacks may cut my utility to 40 percent or 30 percent.

Basically, I'm pretty loose in my estimations. What I'm really looking for is to have a constantly updated ballpark percentage in my head to guide my strategy decisions.

> The lower I rate my utility, the more aggressively I must play and the more risk I must take to get my utility back. The higher I rate my utility, the more I can relax, play small ball, take shots, and work on my image.

The easiest way to quantify your utility—remembering that it takes 100 big blinds to have full utility—is to simply assign 1 percent utility to each unit of the big blind cost you have in your stack. If your stack size is equivalent to 45 times the size of the big blind, then start with 45 percent utility and mentally shade this number up or down based on specific table conditions and your position in relation to your opponents. Is this an oversimplification? Yes, it is. But it's a useful oversimplification similar to counting the appearance of an ace as -1 when you're counting cards at blackjack. Just because you're oversimplifying doesn't mean you should play blackjack without counting cards. Not if you want to have an edge in the game.

One point I want to make emphatically clear is that when I say that a stack totaling 100 big blinds provides 100 percent utility, I do not mean to imply that with a stack this size you have maxed out the total possible utility. I'm using the figure "100 percent" as a convenience for calculating your level of desperation, not in the traditional way we would think of 100 percent as the maximum. I'm saying that with a chip stack of this size you should be able to engage in all standard poker play, including small-ball play and mixing it up with opponents post-flop.

But a chip stack of this size can still have its utility squelched by any aggressive player who has a chip stack big enough to hurt you, and if numerous opponents at your table have similarly big stacks, you do not have anywhere near maximum utility, not to mention the utility that an aggressive long-ball player would want to be able to bully the table. There is no maximum possible utility until you have bankrupted every player in the tournament, because that is your ultimate goal.

SUMMARY

So far, we've dealt very little with the nuts and bolts of tournament strategy. We're still just looking at the key factor that should drive your tournament decisions—chip utility. Primarily, you've got to start thinking of your chips as ammunition that you want to keep in action, using them to disable your opponents' weapons. And again, you must constantly reassess your utility based on both the size of your chip stack and table conditions. When you play with full utility, you're able to play with a full set of skills if you have them, and playing with a full set of skills gives you a big advantage over anyone playing with a lesser set of skills, whether his skill limitations come from a lack of experience, a lack of talent, or an insufficient number of chips to utilize his skills against you.

In the next chapter, we're going to look at how a tournament's structure—meaning the number of starting chips in relation to the blind structure—affects chip utility. From the utility perspective, all tournaments are not created equal. Your overriding utility-based strategies should be guided by the structure of each tournament you enter.

ANALYZING A TOURNAMENT'S STRUCTURE: THE UTILITY FACTOR

This chapter will look at how tournament structure affects tournament strategy. It's not enough to just understand the concept of utility in a tournament; you must understand how the structure of any specific tournament affects the utility of all players in the event, how this affects their perceptions of their strategic options as the tournament progresses, and how you can optimize your strategy for the structure of any tournament you enter.

In *PTF1*, I introduced the concept of the "Patience Factor" as a gauge for assessing a tournament's speed, which in turn can be used to determine the tournament's "skill level"—with faster events being relatively more luck-based and the slower events relatively more skill-based.

If you have read PTF1, and you are familiar with the patience factor concept—including what it means and how to compute it—you may want to skip over the next few pages (which are excerpted from PTF1). Start reading again on page 95 under the heading: "The Patience Factor in Slow-Structured Events." If you have not read PTF1, then do not skip the next few pages or you will not understand the material that follows.

THE PATIENCE FACTOR

In order to compare tournaments with each other, both to get a handle on the importance of luck versus skill in any particular tournament format, and to figure out the best strategy based on the tournament's speed, we need to quantify the speed of play. We all know that the main event of the WSOP is a slow tournament and that our local Tuesday night $40 buy-in tournament that starts at 7 p.m. and ends around midnight is quite a bit faster. But is there a way to put some numbers on these tournaments that would indicate exactly how slow or how fast they are? As a matter of fact, it's fairly easy to hone in on precise tournament speed if we use the parameters that contribute to a tournament's speed: the number of starting chips and the blind structure.

What we are looking for specifically is what I call the tournament's *"patience factor."* The more patience and flexibility a tournament allows players in selecting the pots they enter and the way they play a hand, the greater a factor skill will be in determining the winners and the more money skilled players will make over time. The more players are forced to take shots with marginal hands just to try to keep up with the blinds, the more luck will play into any player's chance at winning.

WORLD'S MOST PATIENT PLAYER

To simplify the complex problem of quantifying a tournament's speed, I created the World's Most Patient Player, a player who will not enter any pot unless he is dealt two suited aces. Since no deck of cards contains two suited aces, the World's Most Patient Player is fully content to wait forever, never playing a single hand. Obviously, this player is a fiction, but he allows us an easy way to solve the problem of quantifying tournament speed—or the patience factor.

MEASURING THE BLIND-OFF TIME

The first step in determining the patience factor is to estimate how long the World's Most Patient Player would sit without playing a single hand before he was blinded off. We have to make some assumptions based on practical experience in order to come up with an answer to this problem. Let's first assume that this player is playing at ten-handed tables and that he will go through the blinds once every 20 minutes, which is a pretty good assumption for a live ten-handed game. Obviously, 20-minute rounds will not be true for every table in every tournament, but we'll use this assumption anyway for all live tournaments that are played ten-handed, just to get an estimated blind-off time for the World's Most Patient Player (WMPP).

Once we have agreed that a ten-handed round takes 20 minutes, how do we estimate the cost of the blinds (and antes, if any) per hour, so that we can calculate how long it will be until the WMPP is blinded off? For a tournament with 60-minute blind levels, figuring out the cost of the blinds per hour is an easy calculation if we have the tournament's blind schedule. We simply assume that the WMPP will go through the blinds three times (once every 20 minutes) at each blind level, and we reduce his starting chip stack by the cost of the blinds until his stack is depleted.

As an example, let's figure this out for the $1,000 buy-in Seniors No-Limit Hold'em event at the 2005 WSOP, which had 60-minute blind levels. Players in that event started with $1,000 in chips (this has since changed), the first blind level was $25/$25, and the WMPP will go through this blind level three times (at a total cost of $50 once every 20 minutes) in the first hour. Here's a chart that shows the costs of the first four blind levels:

2005 WSOP - SENIORS NO-LIMIT HOLD'EM				
Level	Blinds	Total	x3/hr	Cumulative
1	$25/$25	$50	$150	$150
2	$25/$50	$75	$225	$375
3	$50/$100	$150	$450	$825
4	$100/$200	$300	$900	$1,725

Notice that in the last column (Cumulative), we're totaling the blind costs from the start of the tournament through each succeeding level. The first thing we'll note from this chart is that the WMPP's $1,000 in starting chips will cover the cost of the blinds through the first three levels ($825), but not the blind costs of the fourth blind level. In fact, since the WMPP will have already paid $825 in blind costs by the end of the first three blind levels, he will have only $175 remaining—not even enough to cover the $300 cost of going through the blinds even once at the fourth level.

Since blind levels last one hour each, we know that the WMPP will last three hours, but he will not last through the next 20 minutes. Of course, the exact fraction of those 20 minutes will depend on precisely when he entered the blinds at this level. He could cover a portion of the cost of the big blind ($175 of the $200 blind), but he would bust out on this hand before he got to the small blind. (We'll ignore the possibility that the WMPP will accidentally win on one of his blind hands. The WMPP is so tight that he will immediately muck his cards as soon as he sees that they are not suited aces, so he cannot possibly win a hand, even by accident.)

Let's figure out exactly what percentage of those final 20 minutes the WMPP can cover, on average, with his remaining $175 in chips, by dividing the total cost of the blinds on the final round ($300) by the number of remaining chips the WMPP has at this point ($175). It looks like this:

$$\$175 / \$300 = .58 \text{ or } 58 \text{ percent}$$

Since 58 percent of 20 minutes equals 11.6 minutes, we'll estimate that the WMPP will stay alive in this tournament, on average, approximately 3 hours and 11.6 minutes before he gets blinded off. To express this in decimals, he would be blinded off after 3.19 hours.

Now, let's compare this tournament to another tournament with the same $1,000 in starting chips. Let's use the popular no-limit hold'em tournament held twice daily at the Flamingo Hotel and Casino in Las Vegas that had a buy-in of just $55. (For up-to-date information on both live and online poker tournaments, see my Website www.pokertournamentformula.com.) Players get $1,000 in starting chips, and blinds go up every 20 minutes. The 20-minute blind levels mean that the WMPP will go through each blind level just once. Also, the amounts of the blinds are slightly different from the WSOP event. Here's a chart that shows the costs of the Flamingo tournament's first four blind levels:

FLAMINGO HOTEL & CASINO - NO-LIMIT HOLD'EM			
Level	Blinds	Total	Cumulative
1	$25/$50	$75	$75
2	$50/$100	$150	$225
3	$100/$200	$300	$525
4	$200/$400	$600	$1,125

Again, we can see that with his $1,000 in starting chips, the WMPP has sufficient chips to last through three blind levels (cumulative cost of $525), but he will not make it through the fourth level. Paying $525 in blind costs through the first three levels means that he'll have $475 remaining of his initial $1,000 in chips. But the fourth level blinds cost $600 total, so, again, he won't last 20 minutes at this level. Let's figure out the percentage of those 20 minutes he'll last, on average, based on the $475 in chips he has remaining:

$$\$475/\$600 = .79 \text{ or } 79 \text{ percent,}$$
$$\text{and } 79 \text{ percent of } 20 \text{ minutes} = 15.8 \text{ minutes}$$

Since each of the first three blind levels last 20 minutes, for a total of one hour, the WMPP can expect to be blinded off in this tournament after about 1 hour and 15.8 minutes, or, expressed decimally, in 1.26 hours.

IMPLICATIONS OF THE BLIND-OFF TIME

We now have a measure for comparing the WSOP tournament that starts with $1,000 in chips with this Flamingo tournament that also starts with $1,000 in chips. This "blind-off" time tells us that we'd last 3.19 hours in the WSOP tournament, but only 1.26 hours in the Flamingo tournament, before being blinded off. This difference is due entirely to the different blind structures of these tournaments. The Flamingo blind levels last only 20 minutes, while the WSOP has 60-minute levels. Also, the Flamingo blind levels are higher right from the start. (If you hadn't noticed this before, go and look at the blinds at each level in both of these tournaments.)

But what does this mean in terms of the difference in playing these two tournaments? Nobody is really going to sit for hours without playing a hand. A player in the WSOP tournament would last longer than a player in the Flamingo tournament if indeed neither of these players played a single hand from start to blind-off. But the time difference between 3.19 and 1.26 is less than two hours. Does that time difference matter all that much if you're actually playing?

The answer is yes—that time difference is far from insignificant. Think of the positions two players will be in if they play these two tournaments, and in both cases, never have a playable hand in the first hour. In the Flamingo tournament, as we've seen, the player will have paid $525 in blind costs in the first hour, and couldn't cover the cost of the blinds ($600) for the next round with his remaining $475. In the $1,000 buy-in WSOP tournament, on the other hand, the player will have paid only $150 in blind costs in the first hour, and will have $850 remaining when the cost of the big blind goes up from $25 to $50 for the second hour.

BLIND STRUCTURE MAKES A BIG DIFFERENCE

In other words, a player can afford to be more patient in a tournament with a slower blind structure. But that doesn't even begin to describe how huge the patience difference really is between these two tournaments.

Consider where these players would stand at the end of two hours, assuming both actually played and won $1,000 in that time period. In the WSOP tournament, at the end of two hours, the blinds would be going up to their third level, $50/$100, so that even though the player will have paid $375 in two hours of blind costs to this point, that $1,000 in winnings will have his chip stack at $1,625 two hours into the tournament.

Meanwhile, the Flamingo player's $1,000 in winnings won't even enable him to get through the second hour. He'll be blinded off long before the second hour is up unless he makes a lot more chips than that. Just to survive to the two-hour point, he will have to cover more than $5,600 in blind costs! And after two hours with those 20-minute blind levels and the Flamingo's lightning fast structure, he will find himself entering the seventh blind level, which happens to be $2,000/$4,000.

As you see, even small differences in blind-off times are significant differences. You might think from looking at the blind-off times of these two tournaments (3.19 v. 1.26 hours) that the Flamingo tournament would only be two to three times as fast as the

WSOP event. Not so. This would be true only if the blinds were not going up. Because the blinds are continually escalating, however, differences in blind-off times should not be read as linear differences, but as exponential differences.

In order to help you appreciate this difference, we're going to make a simple mathematical adjustment to the blind-off times to produce a tournament's patience factor. We're simply going to square the blind-off time for comparison purposes. Squaring a number means multiplying the number by itself.

Here's how these tournaments compare after we square the blind-off times to produce the patience factors:

WSOP $1,000 event blind-off = 3.19
Flamingo $55 event blind-off = 1.26

WSOP patience factor = 3.19 x 3.19 = 10.20
Flamingo patience factor = 1.26 x 1.26 = 1.59

Now we can see that these two tournaments are extremely far apart when it comes to how fast they will play out.

The patience factor is simply a tournament's blind-off time squared. That's the entire definition. And that number will tell us a lot of what we need to know to devise a strategy for any fast tournament.*

---

* Note: On my website, www.pokertournamentformula.com, you will find free downloadable Excel spreadsheets that can be used to compute the patience factor of any tournament quickly and easily just by entering the starting chips and blind structure.

THE PATIENCE FACTOR IN SLOW-STRUCTURED EVENTS

If you are playing in events that have blind-off times of three hours or less—meaning patience factors of 9.00 or less, then you should be using the strategies in *PTF1*, not this book. Those are fast tournaments. The strategies in this book are primarily for tournaments with patience factors of 10.00 or higher. I did not address strategies for pro-level tournaments in *PTF1*.

To begin our discussion of pro-level events, let's start by looking at the blind-off times and patience factors of some of the no-limit hold'em events offered at the 2008 WSOP, along with a few other crucial factors that affect utility. [Note that the Seniors $1,000 event used a different structure in 2008 than it did in 2005.]

2008 WSOP EVENTS					
Buy-in	Starting Chips	Starting Big Blind	Starting Chips /Big Blind	Blind-Off Time (hrs)	Patience Factor
$1,000 (seniors)	$2,000	$50	$40	3.26	10.61
$1,500	$3,000	$50	$60	3.86	14.93
$2,000	$4,000	$50	$80	4.37	19.09
$2,500	$5,000	$50	$100	4.85	23.48
$3,000	$6,000	$50	$120	5.20	27.09
$5,000	$10,000	$50	$200	6.28	39.41
$10,000	$20,000	$100	$200	9.43	89.01

In *PTF1*, which discussed strategies for fast tournament structures only, I lumped all of these tournaments together as "pro-level" tournaments, and made no attempt to differentiate between them. In fact, because of the structural differences of these events, they will play out quite differently from each other and smart players will go in knowing they must adjust their strategies accordingly.

Optimal fast tournament strategies are primarily hyper-aggressive, with much more preflop play than post-flop, and many more all ins. Small ball is not much of an option in a fast tournament, because all players lack full utility from the start. With so little utility, the opportunities for sophisticated post-flop poker strategies never come up.

In slow tournament structures, by contrast, utility becomes the major factor in all strategic decisions. And although utility is dependent on many factors—among them your chip position in relation to the chip positions of the players at your table, how loose and/or aggressive those players are, your seating position in relation to those players, your level of skill and even your table image in relation to the opponents you face—one factor that is always crucial in assessing utility is your chip stack in relation to the cost of the blinds. Furthermore, you really want to know how fast your starting utility will dissipate if you do not increase your chip stack. Knowing this will give you an idea of how fast you must play in the early rounds in order to maintain the chip stack you need to retain the greatest possible utility. Players who fail to adjust to the speed of tournaments in which utility dissipates more quickly will be continually passing up better opportunities for worse opportunities later, when they are shorter. In the chart above, note that the fourth column lists the starting chips divided by the starting big blind for each of the seven WSOP tournaments analyzed. Note how low the starting utility is on many of the smaller buy-in events.

If you recall the discussion of information bets in the prior chapter, and my comment that information bets—which are important to skillful players—are among the first of the utility functions to disappear in a slow-structured tournament, I provided an example that showed that at a minimum, it would take a stack size of about 60 big blinds to be comfortable making a post-flop inform-ation bet into a player who bet half the size of the pot after a

> **PLAYERS WHO FAIL TO ADJUST TO THE SPEED OF TOURNAMENTS IN WHICH UTILITY DISSIPATES MORE QUICKLY WILL BE CONTINUALLY PASSING UP BETTER OPPORTUNITIES FOR WORSE OPPORTUNITIES LATER, WHEN THEY ARE SHORTER.**

standard preflop raise. I also stated that a stack size equal to 80 to 100 big blinds might be required to make an information bet into a bigger pot with more aggressive betting. And this is before the turn or river cards are even dealt.

Because of this, I consider a stack size equal to 100 big blinds to be the minimum stack size for a skillful player to able to play with full utility. This is a much higher stack size than is recommended in other books on no-limit hold'em tournaments. Dan Harrington, for example, in *Harrington on Hold'Em II*, says that a player with a stack size of "20 M" (20 x the cost of a round) is a fully functional poker player. In Lee Nelson's *Kill Everyone*, he states that there is no use even calculating your "CSI" (or "chip status index," which is a term he uses for the number of chips in your stack divided by the cost per round) if it is more than 25 to 30. Again, M, or CSI, is simply a player's stack size divided by the cost per round.

In the information bet example discussed earlier, with blinds of $50/$100 and no antes, an M (or CSI) of 20 would be a stack size of $3,000 chips, or just 30 times the big blind. But that post-flop information bet would require a total of $1,500 chips (half of a player's stack if his total stack size was just 30 big blinds) to be put into the pot on this hand, and this is before the turn card has even been dealt! Tight players and less-skilled players who do not play much small ball and do not get involved in a lot of pots tend to greatly underestimate the chips that a skillful player really needs to be fully functional. That's because tight play itself is less than fully functional.

COMPARING SEVEN WSOP EVENTS

Let's look at the seven WSOP events listed above from a chip utility perspective, knowing that it takes a minimum stack size of 100 big blinds to have full utility, and at least 60 big blinds to play at a fairly decent competitive level. Let's look at how close to fully-functional each player is at the start of each of these seven tournaments— that is, how many big blinds each player has in his starting stack, how many he would have after one hour if his stack size remained the same as his starting stack, and how many he would have after two hours if his stack size remained the same as his starting stack.

2008 WSOP EVENTS					
Buy-in	Starting Chips	Starting Big Blind	Starting Chips /Big Blind	After 1 Hr.	After 2 Hrs.
$1,000 (seniors)	$2,000	$50	$40	$20	$10
$1,500	$3,000	$50	$60	$30	$15
$2,000	$4,000	$50	$80	$40	$20
$2,500	$5,000	$50	$100	$50	$25
$3,000	$6,000	$50	$120	$60	$30
$5,000	$10,000	$50	$200	$100	$50
$10,000	$20,000	$100	$200	$200	$100

Note that the players in the $1,000 Seniors event, despite the hour-long blind levels, do not really start this event with anything close to full chip utility. With a total of 40 big blinds to start, which will become 20 big blinds after a single hour of play if they simply maintain their starting stack without increasing it in that first hour, this is not a lot different from a small buy-in fast-format event. The main difference is that because of the slow structure (60-minute blind levels), many players in this event will have a false sense of having a lot of time to play poker.

In the $1,500 event, the players at least enter the tournament with competitive chip stacks (60 big blinds), if not full utility. But again, look at how quickly even that minimally competitive utility is lost.

All of the events with buy-ins below $3,000, in fact, are going to require some pretty aggressive chip collecting in the first hour in order to either obtain or retain at least minimally competitive utility.

STRUCTURE AND TOURNAMENT SPEED

Anyone who regularly enters pro-level events that start out low on utility will have seen skillful players taking risks in the first hour or two that they would never take in the entire first day of a major deep-stack event. The top players have an innate feel for utility, and the speed of play required to get it or maintain it, right from the start.

If you approach all of these WSOP tournaments with no regard for their structures, and play each of them from the start according to the same strategy based on your M or your CSI, you will be making a huge strategic error. In the $1,000 Seniors event, for example, you start out with an M or CSI of about 27—which most M players would view as fully functional and no grave danger. But in this type of tournament that starts with a shorter stack, the period where your M remains "fully functional" is going to be too short for you to be likely to see enough of the premium starting hands you're waiting for to let you build a competitive chip stack. (And I'm assuming here that for your tight playing style, 27 M is full functionality.) In other words, while you think you have time to wait for A-Q, you'll be passing up A-10. Then, when you're shorter, but think you still have time to wait for A-10, you'll be passing up Q-J, and so on.

Again, by failing to adjust to true tournament speed, you'll too often be condemning yourself to shots with junk after having passed up better opportunities. You will also be facing a few players who will be dealt more than their share of premium starting hands, and if you just sit there waiting, you're allowing the cards to decide who will build utility and who will get left behind. That's not poker; that's a crapshoot.

Tournaments where utility either starts low or dissipates fast, or both, must be played more aggressively right from the start than tournaments where utility starts high and takes a long time to dissipate. You simply have to take more risks from the get-go.

In order to devise optimal strategies for individual tournaments based on utility, what we first need is a simple gauge for quantifying a tournament's utility based on its structure. I'll call this gauge the *tournament utility factor*.

THE TOURNAMENT UTILITY FACTOR

In Chapter One, I pointed out that in order to have a minimally competitive chip stack you require a stack size equal to about 60 big blinds. In addition to seeing lots of flops with speculative cards and making information bets—as explained—you also need a stack size of at least this many chips to get deeper into the betting on the turn and river where some of the best chip-collecting opportunities occur for skillful players.

Now let's look at a chart for the WSOP events we've been analyzing that shows what percentage of this minimally competitive utility exists at the start of each tournament. For example, the $1,000 Seniors event starts with $2,000 in chips, the equivalent of 40 big blinds. If we need 60 big blinds for a minimally competitive stack, then this tournament starts out with 40/60, or a 0.67 competitive factor. Note that I'm expressing the percentage in decimal form. 0.67 is the same as 67 percent.

In another column, we'll list each of these tournament's patience factors, and in the final column, we'll multiply each tournament's starting competitive factor by its patience factor (I'll explain why below).

Here's the chart:

2008 WSOP EVENTS					
Buy-in	Starting Chips	Starting Big Blind	Starting Competitive Factor	Patience Factor	Utility Factor
$1,000 (Seniors)	$2,000	$50	0.67	10.61	7.11
$1,500	$3,000	$50	1.00	14.93	14.93
$2,000	$4,000	$50	1.33	19.09	25.45
$2,500	$5,000	$50	1.67	23.48	39.21
$3,000	$6,000	$50	2.00	27.09	54.18
$5,000	$10,000	$50	3.33	39.41	131.37
$10,000	$20,000	$100	3.33	89.01	296.70

The reason we are multiplying the starting competitive factor by the patience factor (in order to obtain the utility factor) is that the patience factor is a gauge for measuring the rate at which our starting chips will disappear. This is precisely the information we need to factor together with the size of our starting chip stack to get an overall utility gauge for the tournament. One immediate question that may come to mind: Why don't we just use the patience factor as a utility gauge? It seems obvious from this chart that a higher patience factor results in a higher utility factor, so why create a new measuring device?

It's because a higher patience factor does not always result in a higher utility factor. In these WSOP events, it works out that way because most have identical blind structures and the only differences between them are the amounts of the starting chips. But that is not always the case. For example, let's look at the Orleans' (Las Vegas) regular Friday night $120 tournaments that were run in 2008. This is a fast small buy-in tournament that starts with

20-minute blind levels that become 30-minute blind levels after the first hour. The patience factor of this tournament is 6.74, quite a bit lower than the 10.61 patience factor of the WSOP $1,000 Seniors event. This is due to the fact that with those significantly shorter blind lengths, you would be blinded off in that Orleans tournament sooner than you would in the WSOP Seniors event. But that Orleans tournament has a utility factor of 11.23, well above the 7.11 utility factor of the WSOP Seniors event.

How can this be so?

The Orleans tournament has $5,000 in starting chips, while the WSOP Seniors event has only $2,000 in starting chips, though both have identical starting blinds of $25/$50. In the Orleans tournament, despite its faster overall structure, players do at least start out with full utility, and that gives the more skillful players a lot more chance to use their skill—and a lot bigger edge—than is the case in the WSOP Seniors event.

When I first started playing bigger buy-in slow-structured tournaments, I realized that the patience factor in itself was not a good guide to tournament quality for skillful play once you have moved beyond fast tournaments. The patience factor works very well for judging fast tournaments because a high patience factor with a fast blind structure can only result from a large number of starting chips in relation to the starting blinds. If a tournament has fifteen or twenty-minute blind levels and a patience factor of more than 5.00, the tournament will have pretty decent starting utility. The utility factor, however, is a much better guide for slow-structured events because, while the patience factor is merely measuring how fast we must make chips in order to remain alive in a tournament, the utility factor tells us what kinds of hands we can play, and what types of plays we can make, based on our personal level of skill.

The utility factor is a useful gauge for several reasons. First, it can be used as a guide to choosing the tournaments that best suit your skills. If you are a small-ball specialist, you might want to avoid tournaments with low utility factors, because they will be long-ball events within an hour or two of the start, if not from the very start. If you excel at final table play and the short-handed play that final tables require, tournaments with high utility factors would provide more opportunities for you to use these skills. Tournaments with low utility factors tend to be all-in luck fests at the final table, and often even before the final table, and the prize pools are often chopped (when allowed by tournament rules) because most players are too short-stacked to engage in meaningful play. The utility factor can also be used to devise an optimal playing strategy for any tournament, as well as for assessing the value of a tournament for a skillful player and the edge that is likely available from it.

Let's look at some general guidelines on what the utility factor means in various pro-level tournaments with blind levels of forty minutes or longer.

RANKING TOURNAMENT VALUE BY STRUCTURE

After computing a utility factor for a tournament, I categorize it by rank, from Rank 0 to Rank 6.

UTILITY FACTOR BELOW 5: RANK 0 TOURNAMENTS

These are tournaments where your starting stack is so short, or the blind structure so fast—or both—that they would not be pro-level events in my opinion. These are crapshoots. If we took the WSOP $1,000 Seniors event and we changed the lengths of the blinds from 60 minutes to 45 minutes, it would still have a utility factor of slightly greater than 5.0. You might occasionally find a utility factor this low on a multitable satellite—though most satellites do not have blind lengths of 40 minutes or more. I've never seen a regular high buy-in multitable tournament with a utility factor this low. If you find one, don't waste your time.

UTILITY FACTOR 6-20: RANK 1 TOURNAMENTS

These are tournaments where you tend to start with a competitive chip stack, but far below full utility. These are excellent pro-level tournaments for amateurs who are trying to move up from fast tournaments because the pros will find many of their skills stifled by the fast structure. You definitely want to build a big stack early or bust out trying. You need to double up early in these events because after the first hour or two, the players who manage to build early stacks will not only be able to dominate their tables, but may also be able to play real poker with each other. If an opponent pushes all-in preflop in the first level, you should call with an awful lot of marginal hands, including any medium pair, A-K, A-Q, maybe even small pairs and A-J, depending on how low the utility factor—and your personal utility—are. Whether you are an experienced pro or a less experienced player, if you don't care much for fast aggressive play early, avoid these events. You're dead money.

UTILITY FACTOR 21-40: RANK 2 TOURNAMENTS

These are tournaments where you will start out with a competitive chip stack, but often less than full utility. If you have full utility at the start of a Rank 2 tournament, you should be able to engage in small-ball play in the first hour or two assuming the players at your table allow it. (There will be a whole chapter on small-ball versus long-ball play in the "Tools" section of this book.) Some pros, especially those who typically play in the major deep-stack events, will feel constricted by their comparatively short starting chip stacks and will be trying to double up early. This could kill the small ball. A less experienced player could do well in these tournaments if he is aggressive. If you don't pick up significant chips in the first hour, you've really got to crank it up in the second hour if you want to remain a vital player. You will be utility-hampered in the next blind level, so do what you have to do. A chance at doubling up early will be worth extra risk. Don't avoid a race with A-K or a medium pair. Go for it.

UTILITY FACTOR 41-60: RANK 3 TOURNAMENTS

These are tournaments where the chip stacks start out pretty healthy and the players are more relaxed through the first two blind levels, though early risks are still required as you definitely need to double up before the third blind level. You won't be quite as desperate in the third blind level as you would be in a Rank 2 tournament, but you will no longer have a competitive chip stack unless you add chips early. If you do not add to your stack considerably by the third blind level, you will be reduced to looking for shots to take, and this will be at a time when a number of other short stacks will be starting to get desperate. So even though the initial stacks seem pretty deep, you definitely want to build chips early if you can. You can't just maintain your stack or you will be falling behind those doubling blind costs. If you are a long-ball specialist and you are not comfortable with small-ball play and a lot of post-flop play, these are excellent tournaments to start learning these skills. There's practice time at the beginning.

UTILITY FACTOR 61-100: RANK 4 TOURNAMENTS

These are deeper-stacked tournaments where the dangerous players finally have the time and the chips to take advantage of their skills. You'll definitely see more small ball and a lot more post-flop play. The urgency to build chips fast is not so pressing, and in the early stages, you may see a lot of small pots that play out to the river. You'll see more preflop limping, and the big blind may even get the occasional walk. There will be a great mixture of small-ball and long-ball play in these events right from the start. These tournaments will get pretty fast about halfway through, when the average stacks fall below the competitive level. By the time you hit the money, most players will be well below the competitive level, with a few deep-stacked players who will be dominating the tables. Your aim is to be among the deep-stacked by that point.

UTILITY FACTOR 101-200: RANK 5 TOURNAMENTS

If you are not adept at small ball and lots of post-flop play, and if you play any kind of a formulaic approach that does not include a lot of reading of hands and situations, you should avoid these events. The long-ball players who play only strong starting cards, and who do most of their betting preflop or on the flop, will need incredibly good luck to survive in these events. The more skilled long-ball specialists who play loose and wild, and who can read weakness in their opponents and pick up big pots by bluffing, will find these events to be excellent money-making opportunities. These are pro-level events in the strictest sense. There will be amateurs in the field, but they will often be lost in the hands.

UTILITY FACTOR 201+: RANK 6 TOURNAMENTS

These are the tournaments that the top pros prefer. In these events, skill reigns supreme. The major WPT events and the WSOP main event are Rank 6 events. Because these tournaments almost always have high buy-ins—$10,000 or more—there shouldn't be too much dead money in these events. But, thanks to aggressive satellite programs, there is often a lot of it. Amateurs who make final tables in these events, or who even make it into the money, have just been damn lucky. They could play a couple of dozen or more of these events and never make the money again.

BUY-IN DOES NOT EQUAL UTILITY

To a certain extent, you pay for utility. Within any tournament series, such as the WSOP events analyzed above, as a general rule, the higher the buy-in, the greater the utility factor. Looking at those seven WSOP events shown earlier, however, you may get the impression that $1,000 tournaments are very much a crapshoot, and that you've got to buy in for $3,000 or more if you want a strong format for skillful play. This is not necessarily the case. Note that the $120 buy-in Orleans tournament described above has a utility factor higher than the $1,000 WSOP Seniors event. The $1,000 WSOP Seniors event, with a utility factor of 7.11, is particularly fast for a tournament at that price point. Let's look at the utility factors of various $1,000 buy-in events that have occurred in recent years where you would have found a lot of pros and semi-pros.

UTILITY FACTORS OF $1,000 BUY-IN TOURNAMENTS (All 2007-2008)		
Event	Utility Factor	Rank
2008 WSOP Series Rio (LV) $1,000 Seniors	7.11	1
Mirage Poker Showdown (WPT Series) $1,000	14.93	1
Grand Tunica WSOP Circuit $1,000	23.15	2
Caesars Palace (LV) WSOP Circuit $1,000	33.30	2
Harrah's Rincon (San Diego) WSOP Circuit $1,000	79.50	4
Venetian (LV) Deep Stack Extravaganza $1,000	120.17	5

All of these tournaments had buy-ins of $1,000, and I computed their utility factors from their starting chips and blind structures. Comparing this data with the chart on page 101 that shows the utility factors of seven different 2008 WSOP events, we see here that the Mirage $1,000 event had a utility factor equal to the WSOP $1,500 event. The Grand Tunica's $1,000 event had a utility factor approximately equal to the WSOP $2,000 event. And Caesars Palace's $1,000 event had a utility factor almost equal to the WSOP $2,500 event. Like the WSOP's $2,500 event, both Grand Tunica's and Caesars' $1,000 events are Rank 2 tournaments. Harrah's Rincon offered a $1,000 event during its WSOP Circuit series with a Rank 4 utility factor. And the Venetian's $1,000 tournament during their Deep Stack Extravaganza series had a utility factor almost equal to the utility factor of the WSOP $5,000 event, as both were Rank 5 tournaments. So, there are definitely $1,000 tournaments available with good utility factors for highly skilled players who are building their bankrolls, as well as for players who are trying to learn strategies for the bigger buy-in deep-stack major events.

During the 2007 WSOP series, the Rio also offered a nightly $1,000 "second-chance" buy-in event that had $3,000 in starting chips with 30-minute blind levels. The utility factor for this tournament was only 5.86 (on the low end of Rank 1). It's no wonder why the Bellagio's daily $1,000 events were totally packed during the 2007 WSOP series, as the Bellagio offered a much more skill-oriented tournament (with a utility factor of 22.60) for the same price. Throughout Las Vegas, just about every day of the week, the Bellagio, Mirage, Venetian, Wynn, Caesars, and even the Orleans offer better tournament formats for skillful players than the Rio's super-fast WSOP second-chance events. Wynn's regular $540 Friday noon tournament had a utility factor of 25.47. And Caesars' daily $200 noon tournament had a utility factor of 28.93. The Venetian's regular $550 Saturday tournament had a utility factor of 69.70 (Rank 4).

I suspect that one of the reasons the annual WSOP series events have such fast blind structures—incidentally, generally much faster than the WSOP Circuit events—is that the annual WSOP Championship series attracts such huge fields, often exceeding 2,000 players per event. The tournament directors have a legitimate concern with speeding up the events so that the fields thin out quickly enough to open up tables for the upcoming events, which will also have huge fields. But this concern does nothing to improve the relatively poor tournament structures of many of the annual WSOP preliminary events.

And despite the poor structures in the smaller buy-in events, many of the top pros play them because the prize pools are humungous, the amount of dead money is through the roof, and most pros know how to crank up their play in fast-structured events, while most amateurs do not. Plus, and this is a huge factor—you get a bracelet if you win.

This is not to say that all tournament pros understand the effects of structure on strategy. Many of those who rarely play fast-structured events enter these events hoping to earn a bracelet, but are not much better off than the amateurs, hoping to hit premium cards early but quickly finding themselves short-stacked and desperate. Some of the most skillful players who come in playing their typical small-ball strategies are amazed to see how quickly their chips disappear if they keep playing speculative hands without hitting something big in the first blind level.

As for the second-chance $1,000 events, since no bracelets are awarded for these tournaments, I have to assume that many of the pros playing them just like to gamble. In fact, these second-chance tournaments are very good "Skill Level 3" events for players who use the *PTF1* strategies for fast tournaments, meaning you should be able to get a 200 percent edge if you use optimal fast tournament strategy.

ADJUSTMENTS TO THE UTILITY FACTOR

If you have read *PTF1*, then you understand how to make adjustments to the patience factor based on various complications such as rebuys and add-ons that alter your starting chip stack, and the shorter blind levels but faster speed of play of online tournaments. Similar adjustments must be made to the patience factor for analyzing slow-structured events before using it to compute the utility factor.

As most of the slow-structured tournaments do not allow rebuys or add-ons, I am not going to waste much ink providing examples. Basically, in slow tournaments, just as in fast ones, you should follow the dictum: Always buy the extra chips, as many as you can, as soon as you can.

In figuring out the patience factor, add as many chips as you can purchase at one time to your starting stack, and use that number of chips as your starting chip stack. If the tournament is an unlimited rebuy event, you will still not be able to purchase more than a specified allotment based on what you have, so do not add more chips to your starting stack than you would be able to purchase at one time.

> **REBUY TOURNAMENTS**
>
> **ALWAYS BUY THE EXTRA CHIPS, AS MANY AS YOU CAN, AS SOON AS YOU CAN.**

If a rebuy or multiple rebuys are allowed off the top, and you intend to purchase these chips, then add these chips to your starting stack. If an add-on is allowed at the end of the rebuy period, regardless of your chip stack, then add these chips to the rebuy chips you have already purchased for your starting chips. Definitely. If you do not intend to make rebuys or add-ons, or you intend to limit yourself to fewer than what is allowed, then you should probably not be playing in a rebuy event. To voluntarily restrict your utility by failing to purchase the chips you are allowed to buy is a mistake. Assuming you intend to purchase as many chips as you can, after computing the patience factor for a rebuy/add-on tournament, reduce it by 20 percent, and use that number for the patience factor. (Read the rebuy chapter in *PTF1* for more information on rebuy logic.)

As for computing the patience factor for online events (as explained in *PTF1*), you must first adjust for the difference in the speed of play. The patience factor, as explained above, assumes full tables (nine or ten-player) and the speed of play in live events—about 30 hands per hour. Online tournaments play much faster—most play at least 50 hands per hour, and some are even faster than that. At 50 hands per hour, a 30-minute online blind level would be equivalent to a 50-minute live blind level in terms of the rounds played per hour. In computing an online patience factor, I suggest that you time the average rounds per hour at the poker site where you intend to play, then adjust the virtual time to be equivalent to the live time before doing the math.

Whether you are adjusting for a rebuy event or an online event—or an online rebuy event!—once you get the patience factor, you compute the utility factor exactly as explained earlier in this chapter. All adjustments are to the patience factor only.

UTILITY FACTOR

Here is a quick reference chart to help you compute the utility factor of a tournament.

UTILITY FACTOR
Quick Reference Chart
(Adjusted to Patience Factor Only)

Utility Factor	Rank	Comments
0-5	0	Not a pro-level event, a crapshoot.
6-20	1	Low utility from start, take early risks to double up, mostly long ball, often a crapshoot by midpoint.
21-40	2	Low utility by second hour, some small ball may be possible in early levels, go for an early double up, very fast in-the-money portion.
41-60	3	About two hours of competitive utility, a bit more small ball possible, pretty damn fast by the money phase, good for aggressive semi-pros, still some play left at final table.
61-100	4	Good utility for smallballers, more trouble for amateurs, players who earn chips can keep utility till the end, becomes mostly long-ball game by the money portion.
101-200	5	Full utility possible all the way to the final table, pros will dominate, small-ball skills will pay well.
201+	6	Full utility start to finish, pros rule, amateurs forget it, high-end poker skills and top tournament skills required.

BEWARE OF WEIRD BLIND STRUCTURES

Always look over a tournament's blind structure for possible problems before buying in. In many cases, a weird blind structure may not be sufficient to keep you from entering a tournament, but in some cases it might, and in other cases it may alert you to a need for strategy adjustments.

For example, most blind structures are faster at the beginning— with blinds typically doubling in the first three levels from $25/$50 to $50/$100 to $100/$200, then slowing down from that point onward. Most players don't complain about these early level doublings of the blinds because all players' chip stacks are at their deepest and everyone feels like they can play poker. A few hours into a tournament, however, blinds rarely double from one level to the next—at least not in pro-level events.

The 2007 Orleans Open had a very unusual blind structure for their tournaments—slower at the beginning, but with one huge jump near the end. The first six blind levels were $25/$25, $25/$50, $50/$100, $75/$150, $100/$200 and $150/$300, and all with no antes. Inexplicably, however, later in the tournament, when going from the 12th blind level to the 13th blind level, the blinds jumped from $1,000/$2,000 to $2,000/$4,000! I had never seen a doubling of the blinds that late in a tournament, and quite a few players complained. I elected to play some of these tournaments anyway. Orleans management said they would fix the blind structure for the Open events in the following year.

Even with more traditional structures, identical utility factors do not always mean identical tournament speeds. For example, some blind structures go from $600/$1,200 to $800/$1,600 to $1,200/$2,400 to $1,600/$3,200 to $2,000/$4,000. Others escalate faster, going from $600/$1,200 to $1,000/$2,000 to

$1,500/$3,000 to $2,000/$4,000. In the first example, there are three blind levels between $600/$1,200 and $2,000/$4,000. In the second example, there are only two blind levels separating $600/$1,200 from $2,000/$4,000. Since these structural differences occur after the blind-off time, neither the patience factor nor the utility factor would reflect this speed difference.

Although it is possible to devise different utility factors for different stages of a tournament, this is unnecessary from a practical perspective. Just mentally note these structural differences in advance so you can adjust your own playing speed, if necessary, when you get to the later stages of a tournament. Shorter stacks will feel the crunch of the faster structures more intensely than big stacks.

Also, look out for phony "deep stack" events. The Bicycle Club provided one of the worst examples of this phenomenon in their 2008 Winnin' o' the Green series. This is an annual series of tournaments, most with small buy-ins in the $200 to $500 range. The three biggest events are the $1,000, the $1,500 and the $2,500 Championship event, and in this case, the biggest buy-in event actually offered a poorer structure for skillful players than the cheaper events.

In the $1,500 event, players started with $3,000 in chips with starting blinds of $25/$25 and hour-long blind levels. In the $2,500 Championship event, players started with $10,000 in chips, but the starting blinds were $50/$100, and the blind levels lasted only 45 minutes. So, if you played in the $1,500 event, you started with a chip stack equivalent to 120 x BB (120 times the big blind), while the starting chip stacks in the $2,500 main event were equivalent to only 100 x BB. Plus the blind levels in the main event were 15 minutes shorter than in the less costly event! That's a drag for players who believe they are paying more to be able to play with more skill.

In previous years, the Winnin' o' the Green main event has always had the best blind structure. I suspect someone at the Bike heard that tournament players are now seeking out deep-stack events (which they are), so they increased the starting chips to $10,000. But it's not really a deep-stack event if you give the players bigger starting stacks but increase the starting blinds and shorten the levels! Heartland Poker Tour does this, but they advertise their tournaments as amateur events and most of the players who compete in the HPT events get in through their satellite system, not through full-price buy-ins.

A similar change of the blind structure was recently put in at Hollywood Park's 2008 Sport of Kings $1,000 main event. On their website, they advertised the event as a "Deepstack No-Limit Hold'em" tournament, with $10,000 in starting chips. The blind schedule on their website for this event showed the typical $25/$50 starting blinds. When I got there to buy-in, however, the blind schedule at the sign-up desk showed that the starting blinds had been changed to $50/$100. Technically, they could have just left the starting blinds at $25/$50 and left the starting chips at $5,000, and it would have been the same event, except that they couldn't have advertised it this year as a "deep-stack" event. I think the Venetian is one of the few venues that understands that deep-stack means deep-stack in relation to the starting blinds. It's silly (and deceptive to unsophisticated players) to add more chips then crank up the starting blinds proportionately, or shorten the blind levels, or both.

SUMMARY

At this point, you should have a pretty good understanding of utility and why it is important, as well as a method of ranking tournaments by comparing their utility factors. The next chapter is going to discuss the relation of utility to pot odds, and provide a simple method for making decisions in tournaments based on the utility odds.

UTILITY ODDS

I know I said there wasn't going to be any complex math to do at the tables; that's my story and I'm sticking to it. Assuming you understand the traditional hold'em concept of pot odds, the math in this chapter will be a piece of cake. You may recall that in Chapter One, I stated that normal pot odds do not apply in tournaments because the traditional way we figure out poker pot odds fails to factor in tournament utility. And sometimes, you do have to make a decision on whether or not to call a bet when you have a strong draw—so I want to provide some guidance on calling according to the utility odds.

POT ODDS: THE WRONG MEASURE

Here's the situation: Let's say it's the first blind level of that $1,000 WSOP Seniors event (or any event with an equivalent structure) and I'm sitting there with my full $2,000 in starting chips, which is a stack equivalent to 40 times the big blind. I'm putting my utility at about 40 percent—not all that great, but we just started and everyone else is in the same boat.

$1,000 WSOP EXAMPLE

With A-K suited, I got involved in a pot with four other players, including the blinds, each of us having put $200 in the pot preflop for a total pot of $1,000 in chips. The flop comes down with three rags, but two of them are in my suit, giving me a nut flush draw. The player in the small blind pushes all in with his remaining

$1,800 in chips. The other three players in the hand fold. I'm sitting there with $1,800 in chips in my stack and a nut flush draw. The pot has exactly $2,800 in chips in it and it would take my whole stack for me to call. So, should I call?

From the traditional pot odds perspective, this would be a bad call. With two cards to come and nine outs, I have about a 35 percent chance to hit my flush in the next two cards, so I need odds of close to 2 to 1 to make this call. But since I have to put $1,800 into the pot to try and win $2,800 in chips, those odds of 28 to 18 are well below 2 to 1. There would have to be closer to $3,500 in chips in the pot to make my call here mathematically correct in terms of conventional poker pot odds.

But that pot odds math fails to take into account the importance of utility in a tournament. Let's look at this problem from the utility perspective. If I fold my hand here, I'll have $1,800 in chips, with the blinds at $25/$50. That means my stack will have the equivalent of 36 big blinds—well below the competitive level (60 big blinds) and on the low end of moderate utility. I'd be rating my utility percentage as somewhere around 36 percent—pretty piss-poor from my perspective—using the simple formula described in Chapter One where each unit of big blind in my stack equals 1 percent utility.

If I call and win this pot, however, my stack size will be $4,600 in chips ($1,800 + $2,800), which is equivalent to 92 big blinds (92 percent utility!), well above the competitive level of 60 percent and very close to full utility. I must also consider other utility-related factors at my table in deciding on whether or not to make this call. How much is that increased utility really worth to me? If winning this pot would give me better than twice the average chip stack at this table, what can I do with it? Can I start playing lots of spec hands, take more position shots and terrorize the shorter stacks? Can I start pushing these tight old cagey codgers around? For me, because of the increased skills I know I could put to use with a big stack, the chance to move from 36 percent utility to 92 percent utility in this situation makes calling this all in with my flush draw a no-brainer, despite the fact that I don't have the traditional pot odds to make this call.

You might argue that I'm putting my whole tournament on the line in the first blind level on a draw where my opponent is a 2 to 1 favorite to bust me. I know that. But I also know that my odds of getting to the money will go up much more than 2 to 1 in my favor in this short-stack event if I hit my flush, making it more than worth it to take the chance on busting out. If I'm not willing to take a risk like this, I shouldn't be entering tournaments with such low starting utility in the first place. In the second blind level, if I haven't increased my chips from this stack of $1,800, I'll have only 18 big blinds in my stack and I'll be close to tasting death. This is a tournament where an early double up is crucial, and when opportunity knocks, you'd damn well better answer the door!

So, even though the pot odds in that $1,000 event are giving me less than 2 to 1, the 36 to 92 percent improvement in utility odds is better than 2 to 1. In a tournament with a short-stack structure like this, I'd be making a huge mistake to pass on this opportunity to double up early. Again, if the next blind level hits ($50/$100) and I'm still sitting there with $1,800 in chips, I'll be reduced to just looking for an all-in shot to keep alive.

When we figure out the pot odds in a cash game, we figure out the ratio of the chips in the pot to the size of the bet we must make. When we figure out the utility odds in a tournament, we figure out the ratio of what our chip stack would be if we add the pot to our stack and compare it to what our chip stack would be if we don't. In a cash game, the size of your chip stack doesn't enter into the equation at all, because you can always get more chips by purchasing them. In a tournament, the size of your chip stack—

with and without the chips in the pot—should be a determining factor in all of your risk/reward decisions, including all of your calling decisions.

WSOP $10,000 MAIN EVENT EXAMPLE

Now, let's change the situation slightly. Let's say I'm in the WSOP $10,000 main event with $20,000 in starting chips with the starting blinds at $50/$100. The situation is similar to the one above, except that there are $2,000 in chips in the preflop pot, and this time it's a short-stacked player who pushes all in for his last $3,600 in chips. The other players in the hand fold, and I have a nut flush draw. My chip stack is at $19,600. Should I call the all-in $3,600 bet on my draw?

The pot odds are essentially the same as in our short-stack example, $5,600 to $3,600, less than 2 to 1 by the same ratio. But do I have the utility odds to call? With $19,600 in chips in my stack (196 big blinds)—well above the minimum level for full utility—I don't really need these chips at this time the same way I needed them in the short-stack $1,000 event. If I call this bet and win, I'll start moving toward dominant utility, which is always good, and if I call this bet and lose, I'll still have full utility, though with fewer chips, which is always bad.

So although the pot odds are the same in both of the above examples, the utility odds are not. In the $1,000 Seniors event, I'm looking for an early double up opportunity and this nut flush draw is it. With full utility in the $10,000 main event, I don't have the same dire need for chips, but that doesn't mean that I should automatically muck my cards because the pot odds are not right. Adding $5,600 in chips to my stack of $19,600 would still be beneficial to my utility—the more chips I have, the more they're worth—especially considering that if I call and lose, I still have full utility. My downside risk is very limited.

From my perspective as a small-ball player, I might feel that risking $3,600 in chips isn't worth it on this draw, especially with the two-hour blind levels. There are a lot of lower-risk ways of earning chips with a big stack. From a long ball perspective, however, I might feel that it's more than worth the risk to shoot my chip stack up to more than $25,000 in chips on a hand where I can't really get hurt all that much.

So, in this situation, I have a real judgment call. The pot odds themselves don't factor in the utility, and utility is what my decision must rest on. The four questions I'd be asking myself are:

1. How close am I to the next blind level? If my stack of 196 big blinds is about to become 98 big blinds because the blinds will be doubling soon, I would lean toward making this call.
2. What are the chip stacks of the other players on my table and are there players who have already increased their chip stacks considerably? If so, I would lean even more toward making this call.
3. Are there aggressive players at my table who are already starting to push the wimps around?
4. Can I already bully players out of pots with my current chip stack, just because there are a lot of survivalists at my table?

How I answer these questions will determine what I decide the utility odds are for this call. The more I feel my "full" utility is being restricted, the more I would lean toward calling.

I can tell you that many loose-aggressive players would make this call with very little thought for that limited downside risk. For one thing, loose-aggressive players are looking for variance because they know it will take good luck to win a tournament, and they want to give themselves more opportunities to get lucky. They also know that they will extract value from terrorizing opponents, who now know their pushes are more likely to be called. This will tend to make their opponents tighten up, which further enhances the loose player's utility even if he loses the hand.

ANOTHER WSOP MAIN EVENT EXAMPLE

What if the situation is identical to the one above in a tournament that starts with $20,000 in chips, except that there are $1,000 chips in the pot in the first blind level, and my opponent pushes in his whole stack of $19,800 in chips. I have a nut flush draw and it would take my whole stack to call. Should I call?

In this case, if I called, I would be risking my whole stack of $19,800 in chips, as well as my tournament life, in order to win $20,800 in chips—a potential win of not much more than even money. With the odds of my flush draw about 2 to 1 against me, and with my utility at 100 percent, I would consider a call here a big mistake, and I think most pros would agree. This case differs from the first example because my utility was so low in that short-stack tournament if I folded (36 percent), and so high if I won (92 percent), that it was worth gambling on. In the second example, I wasn't in such desperate need of utility, but my risk was so limited that the decision on whether to continue in the hand was a judgment call. In this case, however, not only am I not in bad shape from a utility perspective, but the risk is the maximum—all of my chips and my tournament life. In this case, the value isn't there.

UTILITY ODDS REQUIRE JUDGMENT

The nice thing about traditional pot odds is that they are purely based on chip counts and arithmetic. Once you understand them, your decisions are automatic. Utility odds require judgment— they are never so cut and dried. You will have to evaluate gut-level feelings about your utility and the utility of your opponents. And utility itself is based on estimations and approximations. The math heads tend to hate this type of nebulous reasoning. And the players who lack emotional intelligence and rely on following formulas will never understand utility odds. But that's good—let them all live in their pot odds fantasy world where they always know what to do because the book says this and the chart says that and the formula says such-and-such.

The important thing is that you understand utility odds, how to estimate them depending on the overall structure of the tournament you are playing, and what you have to consider when you have to make the tough decisions on whether or not to take a risk. Pot odds and hand values are the wrong measuring devices in a tournament. The top pros go beyond these cash game tools, and so should you.

The next section will look at the tools you bring to the table for carrying out your strategy: playing small ball versus long ball, your ability to read opponents, bluffing, shifting gears, your attitude, and your table image.

PART II: TOOLS

SMALL BALL VS. LONG BALL VS. UTILITY

This chapter will discuss the two major approaches to playing tournaments—small ball and long ball—with specific advice on how and when each approach is appropriate, based not only on your chip utility, but on the utility rank of the tournament. Both strategies are important weapons to have in your arsenal for pro-level tournaments, and even if you favor one form over the other, you should have a good understanding of both forms of play as you will find many opponents who use both approaches and you will often find situations where one form of play is superior to the other.

The terms "small ball" and "long ball" are borrowed from baseball. A team that scores most of its runs as a result of players who hit singles, draw walks, bunt, steal bases, and hit sacrifice flies— scrambling to do whatever it takes to get its runners across the plate—is a small-ball team. A team that scores its runs primarily due to power hitters who smack a lot of extra base hits and hit homeruns is a long-ball team.

SMALL-BALL STRATEGY OVERVIEW

In poker tournaments, a basic small-ball strategy would include seeing a lot of pots cheaply with a wide range of hands in an attempt to either hit a strong and unsuspected hand or to steal the small pots when your opponents seem weak. It's much easier to steal small pots than big pots—and a lot less costly when the steal attempt fails. In other words, small-ball poker consists of a lot of base hits, bunt attempts and frequent stealing.

LONG-BALL STRATEGY OVERVIEW

A basic long-ball strategy would consist of seeing fewer flops, often coming in with big raises and reraises, with the goal of going for big scores with powerful hands, or bluffs that represent powerful hands. The most skillful long-ball players will often see more flops than the tight players who are waiting for premium cards, but the long-ball (sometimes called "power poker") specialist will not attempt to keep the pots small even when his cards do not warrant his big bets. These players live by their reads on opponents and relentlessly put opponents to a test by raising so much that an opponent must go all in or pot-commit himself if he remains in the pot. Longballers are always going for doubles, triples, and home runs.

The most successful baseball teams tend to be adept at both small-ball and long-ball play, and this is true of the most successful tournament pros as well. Many of the top pros swear by a small-ball approach, especially in the early stages of a tournament, but there are times in every tournament when small ball becomes impossible and long ball must be played.

Let's examine each of these strategies separately, as both are common in pro-level tournaments, especially during the first phase, when the survivalists' chips are being served up like little sandwiches to whomever has the appetite to pick them up and take a bite.

SMALL BALL AND UTILITY

If you are entering deep-stack pro-level events (and I would define these as Utility Rank 4, 5, and 6 tournaments), then you really should learn small-ball play. In the faster tournament formats, long ball is much more prevalent and often becomes necessary as an overall approach after the first couple of blind levels.

Small ball is not an easy strategy for beginners to learn, but you have to learn it to thrive in major tournaments these days. It's not easy to learn because it involves many post-flop decisions and judgment calls. But it's also not as difficult as you might think because many of the hands you'll get involved with should be pretty easy to throw away post-flop, at minimal cost.

SMALL BALL HANDS TO PLAY

> **YOU WILL TEND TO EARN MUCH BIGGER POTS WITH A PAIR OF DEUCES IF YOU HIT A SET THAN YOU WILL WITH A PAIR OF ACES IF YOU HIT A SET.**

Assuming you have full utility—a chip stack totaling 100 or more big blinds—what kinds of hands should you play?

I would virtually never throw away any pocket pair preflop—including 2-2 or 3-3—from any position, even under the gun, assuming the preflop pot was not raised more than a standard raise—three to four times the size of the big blind. One thing you must remember about pocket pairs is that smaller pairs have greater implied odds than the big pairs if you hit your set. You will tend to earn much bigger pots with a pair of deuces if you hit a set than you will with a pair of aces if you hit a set. And it's so easy to throw away your pocket deuces if the flop doesn't hit you. Those aces can get you into a lot of trouble.

Given the same conditions, I would usually play all suited connectors, even 3-2 suited or gapped connectors like 5-3 suited. Again, they are so easy to throw away post-flop that they will rarely get you into trouble. But if you hit trips or two pair, or the weird straight, your hand will never be suspected, and the implied odds are through the roof when the flop really hits you hard.

When you play low suited cards, you always run the risk of making your flush against a higher flush. It's not difficult to throw your baby flush away if there are four to your suit on the board and an opponent is betting or coming over the top of you. But with three to a suit on board, it's a lot less likely he has the flush and a lot more likely he won't believe you do, depending on how the hand has played out. The reason you're playing suited connectors, however, instead of just connectors, is precisely because of both the straight and flush possibilities, so if you hit your flush, and there aren't four to your suit on board, you're usually correct to play your hand to the bitter end. I have lost big pots with baby flushes, but the pots I've won with them have far exceeded the few losses.

In addition, given the same conditions as above (a pot raised no more than a standard raise preflop), I would usually play non-suited connectors down to about 6-4 offsuit.

I love finding hole cards like these when the chip stacks are deep and the cost of entering the pot is relatively small, even if raised. When you start playing small ball, you'll often find that these are the hands that earn you your biggest pots in the first few hours of a tournament. If it's a deep stack tournament where small ball remains an option throughout the tournament, these types of hands will continue to be your big moneymakers. And I would only occasionally throw away a suited ace, or any two high cards, and that includes all of the "trouble" hands like K-J and Q-10. I'll usually play J-9, J-8, even J-7, suited or unsuited.

In other words, I want to see lots of flops, whether in position or out of position, and whether the pot has been raised or not. In fact, the "worst" hands, like 6-4, make even more money in pots that are raised preflop because they are even less suspected when the flop really hits you. Hands like this are especially valuable when the preflop pot has been raised and there are lots of callers to the raise. That generally indicates that a lot of the high cards in the deck are in the hands of the players in the pot, and the babies are more likely to come down on the flop. (That's card counting 101!)

Depending on the aggression level of the table, I may play looser in late position than early position, but my basic attitude when I'm well-stocked with chips is this: I've got all these chips for one reason—to use them.

From the button, I'll play any hand in an unraised pot, and most hands in a raised pot, including the "high-low" hands I generally hate like K-6 offsuit and Q-3 offsuit, the hands that are least likely to turn into anything strong and are most capable of getting you into trouble. But I love being on the button. When you play a hand like Q-3, you're really hoping to see a flop like A-3-3 or Q-7-3 in order to pick up a decent pot.

> **MY BASIC ATTITUDE WHEN I'M WELL-STOCKED WITH CHIPS IS: I'VE GOT ALL THESE CHIPS FOR ONE REASON—TO USE THEM.**

Now that's a pretty wide variety of playable hands. Do I always play all of them? No, but I play all of them more often than I muck them preflop. Much depends on how many hands I've been playing lately, which players are in the pot, whether I've taken a number of recent pots or given some up. Also, I will play more of these hands if my chip stack is at least competitive—60 or more big blinds—and fewer if I'm short of a competitive stack, depending on the character of my table (not highly aggressive preflop) and my table image (strong).

I'm also capable of entering the pot by limping, min-raising, making a standard raise, calling a raise, or even reraising, with any of the above hands, just as I'm capable of entering the pot in any of these ways with A-K or a big pocket pair.

RAISING HANDS AND SITUATIONS

I would usually raise or reraise with A-A or K-K, though with A-K, A-Q, or a big pair like Q-Q or J-J, I'll usually just call a normal raise, not reraise. I would generally come in with a small raise with just about any cards if first in the pot, and if I reraise with a big pair like A-A, it would usually be a minimum reraise. I'm not much for defining my hand by my bet size and I'm hoping my opponent will call my reraise because I'm the favorite to win the hand. I like to keep my opponents guessing. I prefer disguised hands to strong hands. If I've got pocket queens and five players see the flop, that's fine with me.

If I've got a big pair, I don't try to limit the number of players in the pot with a big raise. I'd just as soon let anyone in who wants in, then let's see how it plays out. I don't mind tossing my K-K in the muck if an ace comes down on the flop and an opponent is betting like he has it. You rarely make much on these "great" starting cards anyway.

Many players always make oversized raises and reraises with medium and small pairs, and some players even do this with J-J or Q-Q, attempting to pick up the pot preflop without any confrontation. I would come in with the same size raise with Q-Q, A-A, 8-8, 5-5, or 7-6 suited.

I don't like making a big raise with a hand like 9-9 or J-J because the only players who will call you are the players with hands like Q-Q, A-K, and A-Q—or the tricky players who immediately put you on a medium pair and decide to steal the pot from you if any big cards come down on the flop—and since I do this sometimes,

I know other players must be doing it. If you enter the pot preflop with an oversized raise, or reraise with a medium pair and get called, then when the flop comes down with overcards, your continuation bet has to be much bigger since you made the preflop pot so big. You'll often lose a lot of chips unnecessarily.

THERE'S MORE MONEY IN ENGAGING ACTION THAN IN WARDING OFF ACTION.

Why make a big preflop bet with a hand like 9-9? If you're just trying to pick up the blinds, they're not worth it (and if they are worth it, then you are very short-stacked and we're not discussing short-stack strategies here; we're discussing strategies for when you are at least competitive in chips). A medium pocket pair is a premium hand, and if you hit a set with it, it's a dynamite hand. A normal raise will often pick up the blinds preflop anyway, so just make a normal raise. If you get a caller, fine. See how it plays out. Get used to the idea that there's more money in engaging action than in warding off action. If your normal raise gets a call, your opponent most likely has an inferior preflop hand, and if he doesn't hit something on the flop, you'll win more than just the blinds when you make your continuation bet. If you have to give up your 9-9 and a few chips, that's no major catastrophe. It's just a pair of nines. No big deal. Don't invest a lot of chips in it before the flop. What if you run into queens?

KEEPING YOUR CHIPS IN ACTION

There is a general belief among no-limit hold'em tournament players that you should always come in with a raise. Limping, checking and calling are all seen as weak plays. There is more than a modicum of truth to this, but if you start playing a lot of small ball, and you're trying to keep the pots small, there are definitely many situations when limping, checking and calling are just fine. Much depends on the character of your table, your cards, your read on your opponents, and the types of opponents you're up against in any specific pot. If you've developed a strong table image, don't worry about looking weak because you checked, or checked and called. If you're unpredictable, your opponents will always be scared when you're in the pot.

If you come in with a standard raise from middle position with a hand like 7-5 suited and get a couple of late position callers, make your continuation bet when the flop comes down A-K-9, as if that's exactly the flop you were looking for.

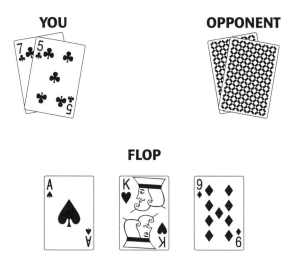

YOU

OPPONENT

FLOP

Bet right out about half the size of the pot. More often than not, you'll take the pot right there. But look at how easy it is to throw away that hand if a player with position comes in with a big reraise. You might take a minute deciding, let him think you've got A-J or something that requires a decision. When you play small ball, your opponents rarely have any idea what you have and there's a fun factor in keeping them wondering by taking your time before throwing your hand away. In other words, it's not hard to play a lot of trashy hands post-flop. You just need enough chips to pay for plays like continuation bets and information bets.

What do you do if your opponent calls your continuation bet in the above situation? Okay, that's where it gets interesting.

MORE SMALL BALL AFTER THE FLOP

Most pros would not usually call here; they would raise. With that straight draw on the board, a smart player who had flopped a set or two pair would usually raise to take it away without giving you a free card on the turn, just in case you were semibluffing on the flop with a straight draw yourself. An experienced player would also often do this if he hit the ace or just the king with a decent kicker. If he has the straight draw, on the other hand, it's an inside straight draw, and he's getting pretty poor odds on his call unless he believes the implied odds or utility odds are really high. Does he think he can extract more chips out of you if a queen, jack, or 10 hits on the turn? So if he calls, you have to ask yourself if he has a made hand or if he's on a draw. Another possibility is that he has nothing himself and he's outplaying you. He knows you have nada, that your continuation bet was a bluff, and he wants to see if he can get another bet out of you on the turn before he puts you to a test.

If he just has an ace or king in hand, and he feels you were making a continuation bet, he may want to see if his call here slows you down. If you check on the turn, he'll feel pretty sure he has the best hand, and he may come in with a big bet himself. He may even do this without an ace or king in hand. He may be a small-ball player himself with a 6-4 suited and no draw, but he thinks you'll wimp out on the turn and he'll be able to take it away from you with any bet.

Then again, if you check on the turn, he may also check. In this case, you might be able to take this pot away from him on the river. Either he is on a draw or he doesn't like his hand enough to invest much more in it. Bad kicker to his ace? Now you've got a river decision.

All of these possibilities make small-ball play difficult when you first start getting involved in pots beyond the flop. The masters of small ball really study their opponents for insights into their betting patterns, the types of hands they play, and any physical mannerisms that might indicate strength or weakness. But the only way you can learn to play at this level is by starting to play at this level. Trust your reads. If you have a feeling you can take a pot away from someone with a raise or a reraise, do it. Test yourself. If you're wrong, you learn something. Go over that hand in your head for signs you should have seen that would have indicated that your move was a mistake.

But the other thing is this: If your opponent calls when you make your continuation bluff at the pot, and you're really unsure about the meaning of his call, and you feel a bet on the turn would take too big of a chunk out of your stack in what may be a dangerous situation, then just shut down your betting and wait for a better opportunity. You don't have to prove to the world that you're just like Stu Ungar and you can take three shots at the pot with a garbage hand. The only person you have to prove anything to is yourself. If you admit to yourself that you're lost in a hand, then give it up. When I say that you should not muck your cards just because the board looks dangerous, I mean that you should put up a fight when you actually have a read on your opponent and you feel he's trying to bully you out of a pot. But if you really are unsure of your opponent's strength, then muck your damn cards.

If your opponent makes what appears to be a value bet on the river, and it's not too expensive, call it, even when you have nothing. It's sometimes worth it just to see what he has. That way you can think through the hand to see if it makes more sense to you. Should you have been able to figure it out? If so, next time you will. If you can't afford to call his river bet, then watch that player carefully for signs of how he plays. Is he a weak player? A tricky player? A calling station?

Remember, your chips are there to use. Using your chips to figure out a hand or a player can give you a good return on investment. Don't sit there hoarding your chips like a wimp. Always keep your chips in action, working to earn you the stack you need to win.

SMALL BALL IN ACTION

Small ball is about keeping your opponents off-balance and guessing, and avoiding getting major amounts of your chips in jeopardy in truly dangerous situations when your utility is high and you don't want the risk. When you play small ball well, you'll almost never show down a hand that's not a winner, and some of your winners will be downright... amusing, at least to the players who were not involved in the pot.

The percentage of times that you actually hit something strong with a speculative hand is small. If you had to actually hit strong hands to make chips, then small ball would be a losing strategy. You just won't get the strong hands often enough. What makes speculative hands profitable are the pots you pick up with bluffs when you feel the chips are pretty much up for grabs. And again, this is where chip utility is crucial to this form of play. You must have not only the skill and the guts to make continuation bluffs, position bluffs, and pseudo-information bluffs (and I'll discuss all of these types of bluffs and more in Chapter Six), you must have sufficient chips, and that means enough chips to abandon the play if you bump into trouble and have to shut down your betting.

You can learn a lot about how to play tournaments just by watching the way strong players play, but small ball is not something you can learn by watching your opponents. Since so few hands are shown down in no-limit hold'em tournaments, you rarely know for sure what cards the winners or losers were playing. Because so many hold'em players are obsessed with big cards, their assumptions about what cards a small-ball player may be in the pot with are often wrong.

About the only time a small-ball player shows down a hand is when he takes down a big pot with a hand no one expected, and these instances are relatively rare. You can't even learn small-ball play by watching televised final tables where the players' hole cards are shown. You will definitely see which players are small-ball players, but you won't learn much about the strategy because they usually show only the more "interesting" hands on TV. You'll see the hands where a smallballer picked up a huge pot with trash cards and a bold bluff, and you'll see the hands where the smallballer with 8-6 offsuit takes a big pot from a player with A-K when the flop comes down A-8-6. But you won't see all of the small pots the small-ball player picks up along the way just by making continuation bets and position bets, or bets that look like value bets on the river.

TV isn't interested in small pots and small pots are the bread and butter of the small-ball player. If you want to learn small ball, you'll just have to start getting involved with more speculative hands, then force yourself to figure out what to do after the flop comes down.

The more small ball you play, the more opportunities you'll find for earning chips whether or not the flop hits you. As R.F. Foster put it more than a hundred years ago in *Practical Poker* (Brentano's, 1905): "Any professional gambler will tell you that most of the money won at Poker is not won on the big hands in big pots… [but] by the continual winning of the small pots in which nobody seems to be particularly interested."

Small ball is nothing new. It's been around since poker was invented and for a very good reason: It works.

LONG BALL

Technically, long ball is an easier strategy to play than small ball if you stick to playing strong hands. Unfortunately, tight-aggressive strategies won't get you into the money very often in tournaments, regardless of the utility factor of the tournaments you play. Card-dependent strategies are very difficult to win with in today's looser, more aggressive tournament environment. Those strategies may have had more validity in the past.

The ultimate long-ball strategy is Blair Rodman's *Kill Phil* strategy, from the book with that title. But when I say that this is an "ultimate" long-ball strategy, I do not mean to imply that *Kill Phil* is the most profitable long-ball strategy. By "ultimate," I mean that it is a strategy based exclusively on a jam (push all in) or fold approach, and pushing all in is about as long ball as you can get. The *Kill Phil* strategy, however, was designed for inexperienced and unskillful poker players who would be better off not making any post-flop decisions. I highly doubt that this strategy would get very far in tournaments today. In fact, *Kill Phil* has sold very well and you virtually never see players using this strategy in major events. I would have to say that enough players have tried it and failed that the verdict is in. So, when I refer to long-ball strategies, I am not referring to jam-or-fold strategies. It's only when the blinds and antes are very high in relation to a player's chip stack that jam-or-fold strategies become optimal strategies for that player. If your chip stack totals only ten big blinds—and especially if the antes have already kicked in—you are either going to jam or fold if you know what you're doing. But that's not long ball; that's a wing and a prayer.

In short-stack slow tournaments, long-ball strategies are a necessity, though loose long-ball strategies will be far more profitable than tight long-ball strategies. The playing strategies described in *PTF1* for fast tournaments are loose long-ball strategies. They are more position-based than card-based and they earn chips by exploiting weak players.

LONG-BALL PHILOSOPHY

Long-ball players should be much more concerned with position than small-ball players. With this style of play, you want to be able to target weak players whom you have seen giving up the lead post-flop. Such players' preflop raises should almost always be called when you have position on them, and reraising preflop is better, even if you have trash cards, as these players are likely to fold preflop. If they do not fold, they will not bet post-flop unless the flop either hits them or they have an overpair to the flop. When they check on the flop, this pot is yours (unless they flopped a monster that they are now slowplaying). Getting involved in big pots—something that small-ball players generally avoid—is often worth the risk for smallballers when the player who opened with the preflop raise is a weak player. All players should keep their eyes open for weak opponents who consistently give up a betting lead. The top players will change gears between small ball and long ball as necessary for the situation.

Unlike small ball, long ball is really about avoiding confrontation and tough decisions by forcing weak opponents out of pots without a lot of back-and-forth posturing and poker playing. You put them to a tough decision before they have a chance to put you to one. Small-ball players often disdain these power poker bullies, but the fact is that the best of the bullies are successful enough to keep at it.

The hands you would most often enter with preflop when playing long ball are medium and big pairs, any two big cards—including all of those "trouble" hands—and suited connectors down to 8-7 suited. But you really can't keep entering as many pots as small-ball players, as you will much more frequently be raising, reraising, and betting into bigger post-flop pots. That takes a lot more chips per hand played.

Because of this, it takes a bigger chip stack to play long ball than small ball. While a small-ball player can feel competitive with a stack size equal to 60 big blinds, a long-ball player would feel constricted by such a small stack. He wants 100 big blinds or more—and the more the better—to have any feeling of comfort at the table. The long-ball player's chip stack will suffer huge fluctuations and, in the early stages of a tournament, he will often find himself alternating between being the short stack at the table and the chip leader. The masters of long ball will often bust out very early in tournaments, but when they get a stack—watch out!

Also, if you play a lot of long ball, you really should be more concerned about having position on your opponents, and you should strive more often to isolate a single opponent in any big pot. You should also look more often to playing against opponents on whom you have a chip advantage. Long-ball strategies are much more based on intimidation than small-ball strategies, which are based on reading opponents, trickery, and trapping. When the pot size is big, players who have been raised (or whose preflop raise has been called) by an aggressive player with a big chip stack will be much less apt to make a continuation bet into a scary flop than when the pot size is small. This is why the long-ball player makes the pot big and isolates weak players.

Inexperienced players generally do much better with a long-ball approach than with a small-ball approach, which is why they are better off avoiding Rank 4, 5, and 6 tournaments where the pros have massive chip utility. There are pros who specialize in long ball, however, and they are very difficult to play against. They are masters of reading weakness in opponents and pushing opponents around. They often seem like maniacs at first, until you notice that they continually extract chips from their opponents and few players seem to have any kind of a handle on them.

As with small ball, you learn to play long ball by playing it. Since almost all tournaments other than Rank 6 tournaments become fast tournaments as they progress, with utility diminishing for all players, you must learn long-ball strategies in order to give yourself any chance of having a strong finish in one of these shorter stacked events.

Also, in the early stages of a Rank 1, 2, or 3 tournament, you will very often be switching back and forth between small-ball and long-ball strategies, even within the same hand. For example, you enter with a speculative hand, then try to crush your opponent if you hit any part of a raggy flop.

MANIPULATING YOUR OPPONENTS' UTILITY

Utility isn't just something you want to have for yourself—it's something you want to take away from your opponents. But you don't necessarily have to take their chips to take their utility, nor must you necessarily have a bigger chip stack than an opponent to start limiting his utility. Long-ball players know that loose-aggressive play does this in and of itself. This is how they earn chips in the early stages of a tournament before they have a big stack to push opponents around.

Also, since most successful long-ball players will enter pots with a pretty wide range of hands, they sometimes do pick up pots with unusual starting cards, just like small-ball players, and this is very disconcerting to opponents. If an opponent can't put you on a hand, you're a difficult player to get involved with. For example, if you win a pot on a showdown with an unusual hand like 9-7 suited, and this was a hand that you raised with, reraised with, or called a raise with, every player at your table will be on notice that you could be in any pot with just about any two cards.

The value of showing down a winner with cards like these is enhanced if you have also shown down a winner with a strong preflop hand—say A-K or a big pocket pair—that you played much the same way. This reinforces the perception that you're not always playing trash. For this reason, if you play an aggressive long-ball style, it's sometimes in your favor to show strong preflop cards when you take down a pot with no showdown. As a general rule, it's not usually wise to show an opponent that he made a good laydown. But if there may be a perception at the table that you are just being a bully when you push a player out of a big pot—and you have recently shown down some pretty unusual hole cards—it's not a bad idea to show that you had pocket aces or you hit a set of jacks in the pot you just won.

DOMINANCE WITH A BIG STACK

If you manage to build a dominating chip stack, then even if you are proficient at small-ball play, sporadically changing gears to long ball will unnerve your opponents. Loose-aggressive play with a big chip stack is even more disconcerting to your opponents than it is when you have a more or less average chip stack. This puts all of your opponents into a position of trying to trap you. This makes them easier to read, as they tighten up while waiting for those trapping opportunities.

What separates the great tournament players from the also-rans is the ability to play a big chip stack masterfully. It's easy to steal when you have a big stack, but you really have to watch out for the traps. When you are bullying your table, playing a lot with no regard for your cards, you want to take the easy pots, but give up any steal attempt quickly if you meet serious resistance from a player you feel will not go away.

If a player who raises preflop is extremely short-stacked, so that his chip utility would only go up minimally if he doubled up, and yours would not be significantly reduced by doubling him up, then you should definitely put him all in or call his all-in shot preflop with *any two cards*. If you end up winning the pot with your trash hand, eliminating this player, it gives a sick feeling to all of the players at your table—like you're on some weird lucky rush that just seems unfair. How could you beat A-Q with 9-4 offsuit? How could you even get involved in a pot with that hand? Is there no justice?

But even if you lose the pot, it intensifies your wild man image, and since you are still the dominating chip stack at your table, it strengthens the resolve of all of your opponents to trap you. Other than the shortest stacks, no one is going to get involved with you now with less than a premium starting hand because they'll feel you're a maniac and if they push, you'll call. You might think that your display of trash cards would cause most players to loosen up their hand requirements against you, but this is generally only true for the desperately short-stacked players who can't damage you much. Players who feel they have any decent amount of chips have little desire to be involved in big pots without big hands. Your willingness to get involved in big pots with a much larger selection of hands is scary. No player wants to bust out of a tournament on a bad ace or K-10 when they have enough chips to wait for a better opportunity.

If a player with a decent-sized chip stack takes a preflop shot at you, you will just about always be up against A-K, A-Q, or a high or medium pair. If this player's chip stack can do you any serious damage, then you should get out of the way unless your cards warrant your play. You definitely don't want to double up this player and increase his utility too much, even if you would remain the chip leader at the table if you lost. In other words, you play differently against opponents who can either hurt your utility or substantially increase their own than against opponents whose chip stacks are too short to make much difference, but whom you can use to enhance your maniac image to terrorize the table.

OFF TO THE RACES

The term "race" usually means a hand in which one of the players is all in preflop—meaning that all five board cards will come down to determine the winner with no other action—and where an underpair is up against two overcards. A classic race would be Q-Q vs. A-K. Races are often referred to as "coin flips" because neither hand has an overwhelming advantage.

Small-ball players tend to avoid races that would bust them or seriously devastate their chip stack, especially in the early stages of a tournament. Longballers often seek out race situations. To win a race and double your chip stack is a home run in anyone's book, but smallballers tend to prefer accumulating chips without so great a risk of busting out.

In slow-structured tournaments, many players try to avoid getting deeply involved in big pots in the early blind levels, so opportunities for doubling up are rare. Long-ball players see races as perfect opportunities for building a big chip lead at a time when the opportunities for winning big pots are few and far between. The long-ball approach is to play a very high variance game in the early stages of a tournament in order to build a huge chip lead or bust out attempting to do so. This enables long-ball players to play a much lower variance game later, when so many of their shorter-stacked opponents are forced into high variance play due to the blind/ante costs. This is not to say that the longballers start avoiding races after they have acquired a big chip lead. But they have put themselves into a position of being able to afford losing races without busting out. A long-ball player with a big chip stack who wins one race and loses the next one is still in the same chip position he was in before these two races. One of his shorter-stacked opponents, however, will be gone, because a short stack cannot afford to lose a single race.

Since the best smallballers often build dominating chip stacks through finesse of play, they don't feel races are necessary, especially in the early stages of a deep-stack tournament. In short-stack tournaments, however, especially Rank 1, 2, and 3 events, when doubling up early is often a necessity for obtaining or maintaining full utility (which smallballers absolutely require if they want to have access to all of their skills), even smallballers will engage in high-risk races when they are utility-hampered. And other than the deepest-stacked (Rank 6) tournaments, most tournaments become all-in race fests at the final table, if not before.

MAKING RACE DECISIONS

So, let's look at the math of races. Whether you are playing a small-ball or a long-ball strategy, or switching back and forth between the two, you should have a handle on the basic probabilities so that you can make important race decisions based on your style of play and your utility.

Most often, the pair has the advantage against the overcards. In an A-K vs. Q-Q race, the A-K has a 43 percent chance of success, while the Q-Q has a 57 percent chance of success. A few factors influence the exact percentages. If the overcards are suited, and the Q-Q does not include a card in that suit, then the overcards' flush possibilities are more favorable. Q-Q is only a 54 percent favorite against A-K suited. If the underpair does not interfere with the overcards' straight possibilities, then the overcards' success rate goes up another notch. A-K suited will perform slightly better (a 48 percent success rate) against 8-8 than against Q-Q because A-K needs a queen to come down in order to make a straight.

Overcards can even be the favorite over an underpair in extreme situations. For example, with J-10 suited vs. 5-5, J-10 suited is a 52 percent favorite. This is due to the fact that in addition to the flush possibilities and hitting a J or 10, J-10 suited has straight possibilities going up or down, and 5-5 interferes with none of them. This type of race is seen only when at least one of the players is desperate for chips, as most players would not go all in, or call an all-in bet, with J-10 suited or 5-5 when both players have fairly decent chip stacks.

The most common overcards in a race are A-K. And the player with A-K most commonly finds himself pitted against one of the higher ranked pairs—Q-Q, J-J, or 10-10—as these pairs are more likely to get involved in races than the smaller pairs. Again, in these races, the pair is usually the favorite, and generally by about 55 to 45 percent. If the player with A-K finds himself up against A-A or K-K, that is not a race. A-K is a big underdog against these hands, especially against A-A.

THE CONVENTIONAL WISDOM ON COIN FLIPS

Many players will not hesitate to get involved in a race any time they have A-K. Regardless of their chip position, or their opponents', they will call any preflop all-in bet with A-K, suited or not. Their logic is that A-K is only a big underdog to A-A and K-K, and players with these monster hands usually won't push all in preflop because even if they're trying to isolate an opponent, they're still trying to get some action. It's depressing to just pick up the blinds when your starting cards are this strong. The all-in preflop bet is often seen as a sign of a small or medium pair in the hands of a player who wants no action because these pairs are difficult to play post-flop. So, the player with A-K assumes—often correctly—that the all-in bettor is not a big favorite and may even be a big underdog if he's just taking a shot with a hand like A-Q or A-J.

One of the problems with races, however, is that you never know for certain that it's a race until you see your opponent's cards. Some (usually less skillful) players do push all in preflop with A-A or K-K, and they are sometimes called by players with A-K or A-Q who assume it is going to be a race. Likewise, players who push all in or call an all in with Q-Q or J-J, expecting a race with A-K, sometimes find themselves facing A-A or K-K. For this reason, many players consider it a mistake to be all in preflop unless you have A-A or K-K, especially against unknown opponents.

It's very difficult to lay down K-K preflop because the only hand that is a preflop favorite to your K-K is A-A. You must bear in mind, however, that an opponent with a single ace in his hand has a 30 percent chance of hitting an ace on the board by the time the river card comes down. When you have K-K and you are considering calling a preflop all in, what it really comes down to is a question of whether or not you should be taking a 30 percent risk of busting out given your current chip utility at this point in the tournament. Most professional gamblers would take a 70 percent edge on a shot to double up without a second thought, and from the utility perspective, this would almost always be a smart play. In the hundreds of tournaments I've played, I have never once laid down K-K preflop when up against a single opponent. I've seen other players do it though, and both times I thought they were morons.

THE MATHEMATICS OF RACING WITH BIG SLICK

How much of a coin flip is it?

To really get a handle on races, let's look more closely at the math. Let's say you are in an event that will take approximately twelve hours before reaching the final table. Let's say you will call any all-in bet preflop if you have A-K, even if your call would put you all in. And let's say that the opportunities to get into these all-in races come up about once every three hours. What are your chances of survival in this tournament if you get into four of these races, and in every race, you find yourself all in against an underpair that is a 55/45 favorite over you?

Your chances of surviving all four races are slightly better than 4 percent, which is to say that if you entered two dozen tournaments in each of which you engaged in up to four of these all-in races, you would bust out on a race in 23 of these tournaments and survive all four races in just one tournament. The math looks like this:

$$0.45^4 = 0.041 = 23 \text{ to } 1$$

This is why the smallballers often hate the amateur long-ball players who are constantly pushing all in preflop. You hate throwing away A-K or A-Q or a big pair preflop, but how many races can you survive? They think, "Can't we just play some poker here?" This is also why some players call big slick "big sucker," because big slick is the underdog in these races, the hand that's behind and has to suck out.

Coming from a professional blackjack background, I also find it curious that poker players call these confrontations "coin flips." I think of a coin flip as a 50/50 shot. But A-K has only a 42.5 percent chance of surviving against J-J. Those jacks actually have a 15 percent edge in this race, and let me tell you, most blackjack players would *kill* for a 15 percent edge. (Card counters rarely see an edge of more than 2 percent at the time they put their chips into their betting spots.) I view getting all of your chips involved as a matter of habit in hands where you are a 15 percent dog as a sure road to ruin. If one of your basic strategy plays is to call any all in any time with big slick, then big slick will frequently send you—as T.J. Cloutier so aptly put it—"walking back to Houston." More amateur tournament players can blame big slick for their poor results than any other hand.

My opinion of big slick is that it's a great hand to see a flop with if you can get in cheap. The power of A-K manifests itself *after* the flop, not before. If the flop doesn't hit you, you can muck it. No big loss. All you're holding is an ace-high hand, nothing to write home about. A pair of deuces has you beat. But if an ace or king come down on the flop and the board does not appear otherwise dangerous to your top pair/top kicker, you've got a hand that will usually make you some money.

THE MATHEMATICS OF RACING WITH A BIG PAIR

Now let's look at racing from the favorite's perspective. You have the big pair and your opponent has A-K. Now what are your chances of surviving four races for all your chips where you are the 55/45 favorite, meaning that you have a high pair that will interfere with big slick's straight draws? Well, your survival chances are a hell of a lot better than big slick's. Here's the math:

$$0.55^4 = 0.0915 = 10 \text{ to } 1$$

Which means that instead of surviving four consecutive races only once out of every 24 tournaments, you'll survive in one out of 11. Definitely an improvement. The problem when you have the big pair, of course—other than accepting the fact that if you get into these races regularly, the odds are still ten to one against your surviving four of these races consecutively—is bumping into a bigger pair instead of overcards. In that case, you're not a 55 percent favorite, but an 80/20 underdog. If you push all in against a preflop raiser with your pocket queens only to discover the initial raiser raised with A-A or K-K, you're in deep trouble. Again, it's that problem that all chronic racers face—you never know it's a race until you see your opponent's cards.

CAN A PROFITABLE RACING STRATEGY BE DEVISED?

What are your chances of surviving four races if half the time you have the overcards and half the time you have the underpair? We can mathematically approximate that situation like this:

$$0.55^2 \times 0.45^2 = 0.06125 = 15 \text{ to } 1$$

Now, you might look at this and say to yourself, "Well, if I can make a final table once out of every 16 tournaments I play, that would be a huge accomplishment! From here on in, that's my strategy. I shall henceforth be known as the Race Master!"

Not so fast, Jack. I didn't say this strategy would put you on the final table. I just said the odds were 15 to 1 against your surviving four races. That's not the same thing. Let's put this into a tournament context. Let's say these are $5,000 tournaments that each start out with a field of 300 players. And let's say your starting chip stack is $10,000 in chips.

At the nine-player final table, the average chip stack will be:

$$\$3,000,000 / 9 = \$333,333$$

Let's oversimplify this for the moment and say that your first double up would bring your chips from $10,000 to $20,000. Your second double up would bring you from $20,000 to $40,000. Your third double up would bring you from $40,000 to $80,000. And your fourth double up would bring you from $80,000 to $160,000. But that still seems pretty good, doesn't it? Although you'd have less than half the chips of the average player at that final table, at least you made it!

But, unfortunately, we've left something out of this equation. In order to continue doubling up like that, you've got to be paying some blind/ante costs along the way. Using the blind structure from the WSOP $5,000 event, in the twelfth hour alone, with the blinds at $1,500/$3,000 and a $400 ante, you'll pay about $25,000 in blind/ante costs (assuming you go through the blinds three times during that one-hour level). And in the eleventh hour, your blind/ante costs will have been about $18,000. In the tenth hour, the blind/ante costs come to about $12,000. That's $55,000 in blind/ante costs in the tenth, eleventh and twelfth blind levels alone.

As for blind levels 7, 8, and 9, your total blind/ante costs come to about $20,000 in chips. And you also had to pay blind/ante costs in the first six levels. And what about those times when those presumed races you entered weren't really races—when your Q-Q bumped into K-K or A-A? Whoops!

Sorry, Race Master. If you think you can play tournaments profitably by surviving some minimum number of double up shots, you're going to find that this strategy leaves something to be desired. You've got to earn an awful lot of chips throughout a tournament just to keep up with the blind/ante costs. This is my main argument against the "easy" long-ball strategies, where a rookie player attempts to make it to the money by playing only a few premium hands with maximum aggression. The math is not in your favor. This is not what a pro-level longballer does. Pick any one of your favorites. How about Carlos Mortensen? Is this how he plays long ball? No. He may be willing to enter a lot of races, but he is also relentlessly brutal in his aggression. He torments his table by putting opponents to constant tests. He never lets his chips rest. And like most of the top pros, Mortensen is also a master of small ball, knows when to get out of the way of danger, and often changes gears in the early chip-building stages of a tournament.

So, when I say a long-ball strategy is easier for a beginner than a small-ball strategy, that doesn't mean it's more profitable. I mean that you will have fewer difficult post-flop decisions because most of the time your opponents will be getting out of your way. But that won't teach you to play poker and it won't help you to win. It will teach you the power of aggression and position and that's important. But you've got to develop your overall game beyond that if you want real success in slow-structured tournaments.

RACES: A UTILITY DECISION

Long-ball players, because they are always trying to hit home runs, generally find races worth the risk more often than smallballers. They are already engaging in a high-risk style of play, and winning a single race can put them in a position to run over a table, which the best longballers are quite adept at doing. For players who have the talent for running over a table and freezing out their opponents, full utility requires a much bigger stack than it does for smallballers. As explained earlier, this is due to the high variance of the long-ball strategy. A long-ball player is not just trying to see a lot of flops and make information bets. Utility to a master longballer means battering the table relentlessly, which can only be done with a monster chip stack.

If you are a skillful small-ball player and you have a lot of chips, meaning you have full utility, and the structure of the tournament you are in is not a threat to your utility in the next couple of hours, races don't make much sense. Small ball is a risk-averse strategy and it can be played profitably as long as the smallballer has full utility, or, at a minimum, a competitive chip stack (provided no long-ball player is making small ball impossible).

But this doesn't mean that only long-ball players should ever engage in races. All tournament players must of necessity engage in some races regardless of their primary style of play, due to factors beyond their control.

Short-stack tournaments, especially Rank 1, 2, and 3 tournaments, generally require a double up within the first or second blind level for small-ball players to maintain competitive utility. Engaging in a race can accomplish this. It is rarely advisable for any skillful player to play with low utility for any length of time, and often an all-in race is the best option for getting up to full (or even moderate) utility, as it is difficult to build any substantial amount of chips with low utility.

Regardless of a tournament's utility factor, races are also often necessary whenever the blind/ante costs are limiting your utility options, whether you're short because of recent chip losses or a long period of being card dead and unable to steal. And, as mentioned above, one or more aggressive deep-stacked opponents can limit your utility by continually making oversize bets and raises, even when you are not technically short-stacked. In effect, because a player like this is limiting your options in the same way as if you were short-stacked, a race to double up may be your best option for regaining utility at your table.

In the later stages of all tournaments other than Rank 6 events, all-in confrontations generally become the only viable mode of play for all players due to the blind/ante costs. When the action has pretty much deteriorated to preflop all-in bets and calls by any player who has an ace, a pair, or any two high cards, you are better off to engage in races than to sit and watch your chips dwindle. You can't play small ball when every other player at your table is playing long ball.

It's important to understand that there are times when it is correct to get all of your chips into a pot even when you feel certain that you are an underdog. Most professional gamblers who do not play tournaments consider it an error to make any negative expectation bet if it can be avoided, so voluntarily putting money into a pot when you are at a significant disadvantage might strike some experienced gamblers as just a bad bet. But a race, even when you have the worst of it, is sometimes the only feasible method of either increasing your utility to a competitive level or putting yourself in position to advance in the tournament in order to win it.

In *Theory of Gambling and Statistical Logic*, Richard Epstein shows that when your objective is to beat an "unfair game" (meaning a gamble where you have the worst of it), "…a 'maximum boldness' strategy is optimal—that is, the gambler should wager the maximum amount permissible consistent with his objective…"

A race is simply a "maximum boldness" strategy and if this is the strategy that will make it most likely that you will accomplish your tournament goal, then you have to do what you have to do. This is true in any type of gambling tournament, not just poker. In a no-limit cash game, voluntarily racing with A-K vs. an underpair would be an error from the purely mathematical perspective. Technically, it's a bad bet. (It may not be an error from the psychological perspective, but we're not discussing no-limit cash game play in this book, so we'll leave these arguments to Doyle Brunson.)

Again, any time you find yourself considering calling an opponent's all-in bet—whether you have A-K preflop or a flush draw post-flop—your decision to engage your chips in a pot in which you believe you are the underdog should always be a *utility-based* decision. You should ask yourself these four questions:

1. Do you currently have full utility?
2. Would winning this race provide you with much increased utility?
3. Would losing this race significantly hurt your utility?
4. Do you have less risky ways, realistically, of getting the utility you need?

If you have full utility, then racing would be a judgment call if the loss would significantly hurt you. Most longballers would take the risk. Many smallballers would not. But if you are below a competitive chip stack in a situation where stealing is difficult because of table conditions, then the race would be very much advised, even if losing the race could bust you out. If the effect on your utility would be negligible because an opponent is so short on chips, then the race might be worth it simply to take a shot at eliminating that opponent and enhancing your image. Is your utility about to suffer due to an impending change in the blind level? You may be competitive now, but less than competitive half an hour from now as a result of the blinds escalating. How would winning or losing this race affect your opponent's utility?

You have to consider all of these factors before you get yourself involved in a race. Race decisions should never be automatic, no matter what your starting cards.

JOHN PHAN—SNAPSHOT OF A LONG-BALL LEGEND

Since playing at tables with John Phan in those two 2006 WSOP events mentioned earlier, I have played a number of other times in California tournaments with him, and I would have to characterize him as the ultimate long-ball player. Keeping the pot small is not something that occurs to him often. In Peter Thomas Fornatale's book, *Winning Secrets of Poker* (Daily Racing Form Press, 2006), the author interviewed Phan and asked him how he got his nickname "Razor." Phan responded, "One of my friends gave it to me. I raise a lot… If I get to a final table in any game, I'll come out firing, raising and raising. I love to raise, that's true. And I love to put other players in a spot where I'm letting them jeopardize all their chips… If I get a chip lead, I'm raising every hand. I don't even look at my cards sometimes…"

Phan is known for his hyper-aggressive, maniacally loose play in the early blind levels, as he seems intent on building a monster stack right from the start or busting out trying. In the first chapter of this book, I mentioned the hand where I saw Phan bust out on his pocket eights after calling an all-in reraise to his reraise. Again, this occurred in one of the early blind levels when his chip status was well above average. This high-risk style has been employed by a number of other long-ball legends. John Bonetti is said to have played this way, as well as the great Stu Ungar. In the July 1, 2007 *WSOP Today* report, a daily four-page report distributed during the Series that contained results of the most recent events, John Phan was quoted as commenting during the $1,500 event: "You gotta get so lucky in the first levels of these tourneys, kid."

I went to the player database at cardplayer.com to look up Phan's record and I saw page after page of tournament cashes, with lots of final tables and five- and six-digit wins, and many first place finishes going back quite a few years.

I became curious about the events he was winning. Since I am of the opinion that long ball is an optimal strategy in short-stack tournaments, while small ball is more of an optimal strategy in deep-stack tournaments, I wondered how his record in deep-stack tournaments compared to his record in short-stack tournaments. I knew he played a lot of the major events, but the page on which the *Card Player* site lists the player's overall record does not list the buy-in amounts for the tournaments, just the tournament title, event number, finishing position, and dollars won.

I decided to make a list of all of John Phan's first, second, and third place finishes in the past four years, then to look up each tournament to find the buy-in amount. I would have liked to have found the starting chip stacks and the blind schedules, so that I could calculate the utility factors of the events, but this data was not available. However, the buy-in amounts do tell us a lot, because as a general rule, the smaller buy-in events are shorter stacked and the major events—$5,000 buy-in or more—are generally deep-stack events. Here's the list I came up with, and again, note that these are just Phan's 1st, 2nd, and 3rd place finishes. He had many other final tables and cashes in lower positions. Just scan down the list of the buy-in amounts.

PHAN'S 1ST, 2ND AND 3RD PLACE FINISHES			
Event (year)	Buy-in	Finish	Amt Won*
WSOP (2007)	$2,500	2nd	$330,000
World Poker Open (2007)	$1,000	1st	$32,000
World Poker Open (2007)	$1,000	3rd	$16,000
WSOP (2006)	$1,000	2nd	$289,000
Mandalay Bay Championship (2006)	$2,500	2nd	$100,000
World Poker Classic (2006)	$3,000	2nd	$179,000
Trump Classic (2005)	$300	3rd	$4,000
Ultimate Poker Challenge (2005)	$5,000	1st	$47,000
Ultimate Poker Challenge (2005)	$500	1st	$21,000
WSOP Circuit Lake Tahoe (2005)	$500	1st	$17,000
Winnin' O' the Green (2005)	$2,500	2nd	$70,000
LA Poker Classic (2005)	$2,500	1st	$300,000
Jack Binion World Poker Open (2005)	$3,000	3rd	$86,000
World Poker Finals (2004)	$1,000	1st	$40,000
Ultimate Poker Challenge (2004)	$1,000	2nd	$4,000
Legends of Poker (2004)	$300	1st	$77,000
Festa al Lago (2004)	$3,000	1st	$190,000
LA Poker Classic (2004)	$300	2nd	$96,000
Jack Binion World Poker Open (2004)	$500	1st	$85,000
Jack Binion World Poker Open (2004)	$500	1st	$161,000

*Amounts won are rounded off.

Some observations: Seven of Phan's ten first place finishes were in tournaments with buy-ins of $1,000 or less. There are no major deep-stack finishes in first, second or third place. The only $5,000 event on this list is that Ultimate Poker Challenge Tournament in 2005 where he did finish in first place. But this was not a major event. There were only 24 entrants in that tournament, which is why first place paid only $47,000.

I doubt that there is a more skillful long-ball player than John Phan anywhere in the world. This record is phenomenal. His total win just in his first, second and third place finishes in this four-year period (2004-2007) comes to more than $2.1 million. His total tournament winnings since 2004, counting all of his cashes, come to about $3.2 million as of early April, 2008. He does have cashes in major events, but no one can touch his record in these short-stack events. There are not many tournament players—including players who specialize in deep-stack events where the biggest prize pools are found—who can say they have averaged $800,000 in cashes per year for four consecutive years. And it's truly astonishing that most of Phan's winnings were earned in the relatively small buy-in events.

So, if you have what it takes to play long ball at the highest levels, far be it from me to try and talk you into small-ball play as a superior strategy. I do believe that small-ball play mixed with long ball is optimal in the deepest stacked tournaments, but there is a hell of a lot of money to be made in smaller buy-in slow events, and there are a lot more short-stack tournaments than deep-stack tournaments available. (Also, if you're good at the shorter stack events, they don't take as big of a bankroll to play.)

THREE TIPS ON GETTING STARTED IN PRO-LEVEL EVENTS

TIP ONE
Regardless of whether you decide to use a small-ball or long-ball style as your primary strategy, you will have to earn a lot of chips by pushing opponents out of pots when you are unlikely to have the best hand. If you have difficulty taking shots at opponents, even when you feel certain they do not have a hand strong enough to stay in a pot with you if you bet with aggression and determination, you have a weakness that you absolutely must deal with if you're going to have any success at all.

If you find yourself regretting not having had the nerve to "pull the trigger" when you felt that you could have picked up a pot if you had just bet on the river—and your opponent picks up the pot instead with his king-high—and this type of situation occurs numerous times in every tournament, here's what's happening: You have the potential to be a dangerous tournament player. You can read your opponents when they're weak, and that's a huge factor in your favor. Your tournament future looks bright save for one unfortunate flaw in your character: You're a wimp. No two ways about it. You are destined to be a time-card-punching, boss-hating, job-despising, working stiff. In your fantasies, you'll be pushing Michael Mizrachi around and teaching Allen Cunningham a lesson or two. But at the tables, you'll be walking away with one poor finish after another, thinking about all those pots you could have picked up if only, if only, if only…

I'm going to suggest an exercise that I advised in *PTF1* for players who have trouble taking shots when they don't have a hand: Play a couple of tournaments in the dark—without looking at your cards. Start to finish. Pretend to look at your cards, but don't really look at them. See how far you can get in the tournament just by taking shots at players who look weak.

You may surprise yourself. You may be much better at reading your opponents than you think. You will definitely be surprised at how much fun it is to play this way, and how satisfying it is each time you take down a pot when you have no idea what your cards are. It's an immense confidence builder and it will teach you to trust your reads better than any other method I know. Unless you are fairly wealthy, you would probably not want to do this in tournaments that have $1,000-plus buy-ins. But if you're regularly playing tournaments that have $1,000-plus buy-ins, and getting nowhere, then spend what you must for the education.

I'm lucky. I live in Vegas and there are hundreds of small buy-in tournaments here every week. Dozens every day. The Venetian has a $150 tournament daily that starts with $7,500 in chips and has 30-minute blind levels. This is a great deep-stack practice tournament for testing moves or playing hands in the dark or whatever. If you have access to small buy-in tournaments, then start playing your hands in those tournaments in the dark. Other than for actually winning lots of money, it's the most fun you can have at a poker table.

TIP TWO

In every tournament you play, when the tournament begins, turn on your wimp radar. Look for players with weaknesses: players who never defend their blinds, players who raise preflop, then fail to make continuation bets, players who have position but don't bet when checked to. Watch for players who fold the small blind preflop in an unraised pot, and players who fold on the button preflop in an unraised pot. Take note of players who regularly fold on the button preflop in a pot that has only been raised 3 x BB or less, when the chip stacks are deep. Anyone may do any of the above at times for various reasons, but you're looking for players who seem to wimp out more frequently than they act with aggression. Stay alert for opportunities to steal pots from these players. And note: In addition to doing this at the start of any tournament, you must also do it every time you change tables. You should also note how players' styles change when they have a big change in their chip stack, either through wins or losses. Get into the habit of using wimp radar continually from the start to the finish of every tournament.

TIP THREE

Start to categorize players from the moment you sit down. Loose? Tight? Passive? Aggressive? Defensive? Weak? Unpredictable? Dangerous? You want to have a handle on every player at your table. You want to feel confident that you know each player's general style—what percentage of hands he plays, how often he plays in late position as opposed to early position, how big his bets and raises are, and so on. Any player whose play you understand is a player you can outplay.

SHIFTING GEARS

One of the secrets to successful loose-aggressive play is frequent gear shifts. You cannot see flop after flop, round after round, hour after hour, pushing the betting without pause, because if you do your opponents will lose respect for your bets. Aggressive players know that there is a lot of value to constantly pushing the envelope, and that most players just don't have the guts to see how much they can get away with. But if your initial aggression earned you a big chip stack, you can blow those chips off just as quickly as you earned them if your opponents start calling you down and pushing back with more marginal hands. Players who would not normally call an all-in bet with nothing more than top pair will call your all-in bet with top pair. The best long-ball players can sense when to turn their aggression off, and they look for signs that indicate that it's time to shift into a lower gear.

FORGET THE "GAP" PRINCIPLE IN TOURNAMENTS

There is a standard hold'em concept known as the "gap principle" that says that it takes a stronger hand to call a raise than to make a raise. In some limit cash games, there is some validity to this principle, but it has little validity in no-limit cash games, and in no-limit tournaments, it's flat-out wrong. Many players, however, who have come to no-limit tournaments from limit cash games regard the gap principle as an immutable law of nature, like gravity, because their favorite gurus—especially those who ascribe to the reverse-chip-value principle—have written that the gap principle is even stronger in tournaments than in cash games. In fact, it's because so many players believe in the gap principle that small-ball players can pick up so many pots with trash hands and aggressive long-ball players can run over tables just by playing position and their chip stacks.

I discussed this topic at some length in *PTF1*, so if you find this difficult to follow, I'd advise you to read that book for a more complete explanation. Suffice it to say that the gap principle is even more worthless in slow-structured tournaments than it is in fast events, because slow-structured tournaments allow smallballers so many more opportunities to play. Essentially, in tournaments, position is stronger than cards, so it doesn't take a stronger hand to call a raise than to make a raise; it just takes a seating position to the left of the raiser. If your opponent checks, you bet. If he bets and it looks doubtful that the raggy flop hit him, or his bet just reeks of weakness, you raise.

If you exercise this power play too often, your gap-obsessed opponents who keep laying down their hands to your raises— believing that you must have a stronger hand to call their raise than they needed to make it!—will start to realize that you cannot always have the better hand and that you must be taking shots based on your position, your chip stack, and your guts.

There is no set formula for when you should turn your aggression off and on. The bigger your chip stack compared to your opponents, the more you can leave it on. But even with a monstrous chip stack, you've got to take breathers. You have to give your opponents enough hope that they'll be able to play that their hope pacifies them once you start up your attacks again. A cornered animal becomes dangerous quickly. Table image changes rapidly at a poker table. Once you've gone into low gear for a while, your opponents will start thinking that you must have just been on a rush of cards with all those pots you took down without a showdown.

HOW TO PLAY A "RUSH" AND HOW TO FIGHT A "RUSH"

Although the concept of a "rush" is based mostly on superstition, there's a strong psychological component, and if you do get a few very strong hands that win pots in showdowns, you should always "play your rush." Again, it's a table image thing, and the field of neuroeconomics has shown that most people are inordinately influenced by events of the recent past. After having shown down a couple of big winners, the players at your table will believe you when you bet, and you should carry this rush fantasy as far as you can. It is a big mistake to fail to play a rush, even though you are not continuing to get great cards and you know that the concept is illogical.

By the same token, if you see a player who is milking his rush, this is a great time to call his bluff and slow him down. Don't let your own neuroeconomics hard-wiring stop you. Most skillful players will play a rush until they are forced to stop. You can make a nice pot off a rushing player, and you can do it with a bold bluff of your own, so you should always look for opportunities to do so.

One of the best times to shift into high gear is immediately after you take a big pot, especially when you show down a strong hand. This is when your bets will get the most respect. Most amateur players decide to rest for a while after picking up a big pot with a monster hand. They avoid getting involved in another pot right away unless they actually pick up another monster. They want to "protect" their chips. This is a huge, huge, huge mistake, and a definite sign of weakness. If you see a player take a big pot after showing a set or better, and then not get involved in a pot within the next five or six hands, this is often a very weak player who can be pushed around. He may even be one who believes rushes are real, but that he just never seems to go on one for very long. He probably wonders why some players seem to go on a lot of rushes that last a long time...

If you are playing a rush, or just being the aggressive bastard at the table, watch for the moment when a number of players at your table are starting to think, "He can't possibly be making that many strong hands," because it's time to shift into low gear for a while. (In fact, it's not unusual for a player to actually make a comment to the effect that, "You sure seem to be raising a hell of a lot.") Time to downshift.

HOW TO PLAY IN LOW GEAR

Shifting into low gear does not mean that you start throwing away playable hands. In fact, if you have the chips to play some speculative hands—suited connectors and small pairs—you should definitely do so, especially if you think your opponents have become suspicious of your relentless aggression. One of the reasons you should play these hands is to see if you can flop a monster, because you are now likely to be called by more marginal hands, and you can reinstate your rush.

But if you don't hit a winner that you can use for this purpose, you have to turn down your aggression and give up some pots to your opponents, even when you are against an opponent you feel is weak and easy to bully. In other words, actually play your cards for a while so that it looks like you're playing your cards. You do not want that player that you have been able to push out of a number of pots to suddenly take a stand against you with a hand as weak as top pair. Once your opponents get fed up with your aggression, they will all be waiting to trap you. You want them waiting to trap you with straights and flushes and sets—not feeling they can trap you with top pair.

By shifting into low gear and giving up some small pots, your image will quickly change from that of a maniac bully to one of a loose player who is difficult to read and who plays with maximum aggression when he has a strong hand. Your opponents don't really know what your cards were when you stole all those pots, which is why they folded to your aggression. By shifting into low gear, they'll rethink their opinion of you. Again, it's that neuroeconomics thing. Within ten to fifteen minutes you can once again turn up your aggression and they will believe you must again be getting premium hands.

Over and over again, however, I have seen loose-aggressive players build an early big stack, then blow it off and bust out early because they never downshifted and their opponents stopped respecting their bets. If you don't slow down occasionally, you'll be viewed as a blind sniper—dangerous and out of control, but pretty easy to pick off for anyone who takes aim.

PLAY IN THE DARK

I mentioned in the prior chapter that it is a good exercise for players to play tournaments "in the dark," without looking at their cards, in order to get a better feel for their skill at reading opponents. Because slow-structured events are more costly, many players might feel hesitant to play a tournament entirely in the dark, and small buy-in fast tournaments are often so aggressive that small-ball play is impossible. I'll suggest a variation of playing blind that I have used in slow-structured tournaments with higher buy-ins: Play in the dark, but with the exception that you look at your cards if you are about to fold.

This way, you don't accidentally muck the nuts, or even a strong hand that you actually do want to play. One caution: Always cup your hands over your cards and act like you're looking at them. You do not want any opponent to think you don't know what your cards are. A second caution: If you take a pot without knowing what your cards are, do not give into the temptation to look at them before mucking. You will likely be curious to see what kind of trash hand you just picked up the pot with, but it really makes no difference. It's unlikely that this peek before mucking will tip off your opponents that you were playing your hand in the dark, because most players just can't imagine doing such a thing, but if you do this over and over, a really sharp player might become suspicious. I always become suspicious when I see a player do this more than once.

If you do peek at your cards after taking a pot, you might sometimes find that you played your hand wrong even though you picked up the pot. You may have flopped a full house, but failed to extract what you could have gotten from opponents had you not quickly pushed them all out of the pot. This will piss you off and convince you that it is a mistake to play in the dark. This is why you must view playing in the dark as an experimental method for learning fundamentals such as position play, aggression, gear-shifting, stealing and reading opponents. It's not a tactic you continue to use once you understand this stuff (well, I still do sometimes, but only in situations where it wouldn't matter if I had a trash hand or a full house). You use playing in the dark to learn about and develop strengths you have independent of your cards. You want to use what you learn from these exercises to take advantage of those situations where you know your cards are not going to win the pot, but you feel you could pick up the pot without having to show down your hand.

I've found in-the-dark play to be an excellent tool for getting a feel for gear-shifting because all of your play is driven by your feel for the current situation. You learn to pick and choose which players to tangle with, when to push and when to back off. And, as I mentioned earlier, it is really fun.

BLUFFS, READS, AND THE PSYCHOLOGY OF THEFT

"Bluffing, in one form or another, permeates the whole game. It is the finesse of Poker. It is the element that gives the game its intense human interest. Without it Poker would be mere chance… A perfect mastery of the Bluff, which includes defense as well as attack, which is not confined to the use of it for vanquishing others, but also embraces the capacity to divine its existence and to frustrate it—such a mastery is never fully attained. Much, very much, may be gained from experience. But in the subtlest forms of this wonderful operation—this manipulation of the unknown, this grappling with the hidden—there is something that mere experience cannot give, any more than it can change a verse-maker into a poet or a dauber into a painter. It is the fine art of play."

—*The Poker Manual*,
by Templar (1895)

"A bluff, provided it be done artistically, with due advantage taken of the favoring circumstances and with just the right shade of insistency to secure the best results, is unquestionably the greatest achievement known in the game of poker."

—*The Science of Draw Poker*,
by David A. Curtis (1901)

"Stealin', stealin', pretty mama don't ya tell on me,

I'm stealin' back to my same old used to be..."

—*Stealin'*,
by Will Shade, recorded by the Memphis Jug Band (1928)

If you are going to be successful in no-limit hold'em tournaments, you are going to steal, and you're going to steal a lot. To give yourself any chance of winning, you must pick up pots when you have the worst hand. That is a fact. No matter how well you play the premium hands you are dealt, you will simply not be dealt enough of these hands to win. Because of what you must accomplish in order to win a tournament—winning all of the chips of all of the players in the event in a relatively short period of time—bluffing is far more important in tournaments than it is in cash games.

In addition to bluffing, you also must be able to recognize when opponents are attempting to bluff you out of pots. Although you must accept the fact that you will occasionally have to lay down the best hand, you cannot afford to give up many pots when your opponent is stealing from you. Unfortunately, it is very difficult to recognize truly good bluffs, and having the ability to pull off a great bluff yourself does not guarantee the ability to detect a great bluff when an opponent makes one. What makes a bluff great—yours or your opponents'—are the subtleties that make it appear to be a bet based on a real hand.

So, in this chapter, we're going to look at bluffing from every angle—when to bluff, how to bluff, and how to detect your opponents' bluffs. We're also going to discuss bad bluffs and how to refrain from making them. Most poker players are terrible at all of these things. Consistently successful tournament pros, on the other hand, are masters at all of these things.

The quote above from Templar's 1895 *Poker Manual* is as true today as it was 100 years ago: *"Much, very much, may be gained from experience."* Some players are more naturally talented at both bluffing and detecting bluffs than others, but you really learn to bluff by bluffing, and you learn to recognize bluffs by calling down suspected bluffers, even when it's scariest to call them down. The more you respond to your intuition when it tells you to do either of these things, the better you'll get. The lessons are often expensive, but if you don't pay for the lessons, you won't get the education.

The Book of Bluffs, by Matt Lessinger (Warner Books, 2005), is probably the best modern source of real-world bluffing strategy in print. I consider it required reading for any player who is struggling with bluffing or calling bluffs. Likewise, John Fox's books—if you can find them—are truly exceptional on this topic. I know I have mentioned John Fox's *Play Poker, Quit Work and Sleep Till Noon* a number of times already, but it truly is in a class by itself as poker books go. His second book, *How to Hustle Home Poker* (Casino Press, 1981), is similarly devoid of fluff and clichés and really digs deep into the psychology of winning at poker. Some old timers I've talked with told me that when Fox's first book came out in 1977, it was viewed by many of the top players as a groundbreaking book on the game that did for poker what Ed Thorp's *Beat the Dealer* did for blackjack.

Fox goes deeply into the subject of "card reading," which was his terminology for what players today call "reading tells." By assessing the strength of his opponents' hands, based on their physical mannerisms, Fox would call suspected bluffers and also know when to bluff. Fox felt that if an opponent appeared to be "acting" as if he were weak, this was "...possibly the most frequently detected tip-off that an opponent is strong." And by contrast, "...the most frequently observed card reading signal of weakness is an opponent trying to act as if he were strong." He provided long lists of precise actions that corresponded to either weakness or strength. If an opponent showed his hand to someone who was not involved in the pot, that hand was probably a winner. If an opponent's hand trembled when betting, which he called the "easiest to spot" of all the tells, that opponent was probably genuinely excited and had a monster hand. If an opponent looked down at his chips before betting, he would almost always have a strong hand.

Many poker players today probably believe that this information about reading tells originated with Mike Caro, but Fox's book was published seven years before Caro's *Book of Tells*. In fact, Caro and Fox were contemporaries and in Fox's second book, Fox includes numerous anecdotes about "The Hustling Adventures of Wild Mike," referring to Mike Caro. And when Caro's *Book of Tells* was published in 1984 (since retitled *Caro's Book of Poker Tells*), Caro not only credited Fox as one of the consultants on the book, but used Fox as one of the models in the photographs that depict the tells he describes.

So, in addition to Matt Lessinger's *Book of Bluffs* and both of Fox's books (if you can find them), I will also recommend *Caro's Book of Poker Tells* as required reading on the psychological strategies of poker. Caro's book builds on Fox's foundation, and is especially helpful because it photo-illustrates the tells described.

STEALING SMALL POTS VS. STEALING BIG POTS

There are two types of stealing in a no-limit hold'em tournament—petty larceny and grand theft. Your success rate with petty larceny will vary greatly, but should average somewhere around 75 to 80 percent. Your success rate with grand theft should be pretty damn close to 100 percent.

PETTY LARCENY

Petty larceny includes theft of the blinds and antes, theft of chips from preflop limpers, or any post-flop theft of a small pot that looks available for a modest bet. The reason petty larceny fails 20 to 25 percent of the time is that the blinds sometimes wake up with strong hands or an opponent limps with a big hand or hits something big on the flop. In most cases, when you know an opponent has a strong hand, you get away from your hand cheaply unless you hit some monster draw on the flop yourself. Petty larceny should not cost you any great amount of your chips on any one hand.

You may lose a good portion of your chips if you repeatedly bump into opponents with hands they won't lay down, but if this happens to you in tournament after tournament, then something is wrong with your approach. Either you look like you're stealing, or you're making your moves too often against the same players, or you are being outplayed by aggressive opponents. Something is not right and you've got to figure it out.

You can't survive in the inevitable card-dead portions of a tournament without petty larceny. In *PTF1*, I estimated that in fast tournaments about 20 percent of all the chips you earn on your way to the final table come from preflop steals. In slow-structured tournaments, this preflop percentage is smaller, especially in the deep-stack events, because players have more chips and will play back at you more often. But the total amount of chips you ultimately earn in slow-structured tournaments from petty larceny should go up to around 30 percent or more. The difference is that you pick up a lot of these small pots by outplaying opponents after the flop, as discussed in the chapter on small ball. If you are continually losing chips on your attempts to steal the blinds, then you are probably not following through post-flop to the extent that you should be. You are going to have to develop your skills at reading opponents and follow your gut instincts. I will discuss this in more detail later in this chapter.

GRAND THEFT

Grand theft is theft of a big pot, usually against a single opponent who has a lot of chips already invested, and whom you know must have a pretty strong hand. Grand theft can rarely be accomplished preflop because any opponent who has a lot of his chips in the pot before the flop is unlikely to lay down his hand if he has a big pair or even A-K. Grand theft is often best accomplished after the river card has come down, though it is sometimes necessary to pull it off after the flop or turn if it seems likely that post-flop betting will pot-commit your opponent.

Grand theft is easier to pull off against skillful experienced players than against amateurs. Amateurs often go broke on top pair or an overpair to the board. A pro will rarely put his tournament survival at risk with top pair or an overpair, assuming he is not short-stacked. If the board appears dangerous, your table image is strong, and the betting action throughout the hand strongly supports the possibility that you have the monster hand you're representing, a pro will consider a "good laydown."

Sometimes, attempts at petty larceny turn into grand theft. You realize your opponent who is calling your bets is on a strong draw—possibly having an overcard or two in addition to a flush or straight draw—and the pot gets bigger than you intended when you made your initial preflop move on it, though you still feel certain that if your opponent fails to hit an out he needs, this pot can be yours. Usually, you would be facing an amateur in this type of situation, as most pros with a draw this strong would be reraising you out of the pot. With an amateur, you must decide if you can reraise him out of the pot—and many amateurs will not lay down a strong draw, even with only one card to come—or if you should keep the pot small till the river then make your move only after it appears that he did not hit one of his outs. Slow-structured deep-stack tournaments simply present many more judgment calls and complications to stealing than you find in faster lower-skill events.

Long-ball players will pull off many more grand thefts than small-ball players, but most smallballers will find opportunities in every tournament for grand theft moves. Often, your success in a tournament will depend on one or two of these moves at crucial times in the latter stages of a tournament. You cannot plan a grand theft move in advance. You just have to keep your eyes open for the opportunities when they present themselves.

FIVE EASY FLEECES

There are five easy bluffs that all tournament players should be making regularly. I'm not going to describe more complicated bluffs because if you can learn these bluffs and really get them down, you'll have a strong enough foundation in the theory of theft and bluffing logic to start getting creative on your own. I'll describe the basic situations, but most of them have variations that can be applied on different streets and against different types of opponents. Start out by making these bluffs in their classic form, then expand on how you use them as you get the feel for how they work, when they work, which players they work against, and when they should be avoided.

If you are a player who never bluffs, or who bluffs very rarely—like once every couple of hours—adding these bluffs to your arsenal of weapons will start you on the road to becoming a veritable larceny machine. You will find continual opportunities to make one of these bluffs—at least two to four times per hour, on average—and they will keep you alive through long streaks of being card-dead.

Some players find stealing very difficult, almost painful. If that's you, then this is something you've got to fix if you're going to get anywhere in tournaments. I suggest you start by getting a decent tournament simulation program, like *Poker Academy* or Wilson Software's *Tournament Hold'em*, and start using these bluffs every chance you get in simulated tournaments. You've got to train yourself to make pot-stealing a natural part of your game. (But pay little attention to your success or lack of success in bluffing at bots. Human opponents are very different from computer-simulated opponents. You're only using these programs to train yourself to bluff regularly, not to try and beat the bots.) When you start trying to bluff in live tournaments, it may feel a lot more dangerous than bluffing the bots in computer-simulated tournaments, but by practicing at home, you'll at least get proficient at recognizing bluffing opportunities when they arise. When you start seeing these opportunities in live tournaments, you've got to make yourself do it despite your fears. You'll start seeing positive results from these bluffs right away and your fear of stealing will slowly disappear. In fact, you'll get hooked on the fun of pulling off good bluffs.

The reason many players don't bluff enough is that they fear complications. If bluffing were as simple as throwing out a bet and picking up the pot, everyone would be doing it all the time. But what if you get called or raised? Now what do you do? Do you continue in the hand with more bluffs, jeopardizing even more of your chips? Or do you just back down and give up the chips you've already invested in the pot? These kinds of questions can be difficult to deal with when you are first learning the art of bluffing, and no matter how proficient you get at bluffing, you will always have to deal with these issues. It's never a smooth ride.

But fear of complications is no reason to not steal. Often there will be no complications, and many times the complications will end up helping you to earn more chips. The more you start playing your opponents instead of playing your cards, the better you will get at dealing with complications—knowing when to get out and when to keep pushing. In fact, you'll know you're achieving bluffing mastery when you start looking forward to complications because of how complications can make your attempts at petty larceny pay off big. So let's look at the five standard bluffing opportunities that all tournament players should be taking advantage of, with discussions of some of the complications that can arise.

1. THE BLIND STEAL

If you are not stealing the blinds regularly when you are in late position—and late position is defined as the button or either of the two seats to the right of the button—you are leaving many chips on the table that you should be adding to your stack. The blind steal is the single most common bluff in all hold'em games—whether in cash games or tournaments, limit or no-limit—for one reason: It works. You do not need a legitimate hand to steal the blinds. You only need late position. Assuming the players in front of you have folded, you simply throw out a standard raise—three to four times the size of the big blind—and that's all there is to it. Add the chips you've won to your stack.

DISCUSSION

The blind steal works great unless, of course, there are complications. Some players are blind defenders, who will call any raise if they have a marginal hand, and will often come out betting on the flop just to test you. Some will reraise you preflop if they have an ace—even a bad ace—or any two high cards like K-J offsuit. But this is the kind of complication you should look forward to, as you will have position on the blind defenders on all three betting rounds from the flop onward if you continue in the hand.

In fact, as discussed at length in *PTF1*, when you take a shot at the blinds, you're actually hoping that one of them wakes up with a hand strong enough to play back at you. This is especially true in the early blind levels of a tournament when the blinds themselves are not much of a prize. Position is power and you are raising the blinds because you want to wield this power post-flop if the blinds do not fold preflop.

In addition to blind defenders who take shots at you with marginal hands, you will also bump into players who wake up with very strong hands in the blinds—A-K, A-Q, big pocket pairs. How do you distinguish these players from the blind defenders? And if your steal attempt is from either of the two seats to the right of the button, you may be called or raised by a player who has post-flop position on you. Because of these complications, some players just never try to steal the blinds. They raise from late position seats only when they have legitimate raising hands, and that's not stealing.

STEALING THE BLINDS FROM THE HIJACK SEAT

In *PTF1*, I labeled the seat to the right of the cutoff seat: "the raising seat." Since then, I've learned that Tommy Angelo, in a book titled *Elements of Poker*, has named this seat the "hijack seat." I really like Tommy's term so I'll use that from now on. This is the easiest position from which to steal the blinds in tournaments. From this seat at a ten-player table, with five players folding in front of you, there are only four to act after you and only two of those players would have position on you after the flop. Entering the pot with a raise from this seat gets a lot more respect than a raise from either of the next two seats that have position on you. When you raise from the hijack seat, blind defenders don't defend as readily as they do when raised from the button or cutoff. In fact, if you get a call from either one of the blinds, you should assume that your opponent has a pretty good hand. If he bets after the flop, you should probably just fold unless you have a read that this player is making a move. (I am assuming, of course, that the flop didn't hit you.)

If you are called when you make your hijack-position raise by one of the players that will act after you post-flop—the button or the cutoff seat—this is more problematic. Calls by these players are not uncommon, as many skillful players, whether they play small ball or long ball, will call standard raises with a wide range of hands from late position. If the caller is an amateur, his call usually indicates that he has a legitimate hand, as he will not be assuming that you were just taking a shot with nothing (though the pros will figure out sooner or later that you take shots from the hijack seat). For the rest of the hand, moreover, this player will have position on you, and you will never be certain of what he's going to do, or whether he's playing his cards or his position.

If your poker skills—and by this I mean your skills at reading and exploiting other players and situations—are superior, then you might reraise a position player who raises behind you. Obviously, this depends on the specific player and any read you might have on that player. If this is an amateur player, you would usually fold to his reraise. If it's a skillful player who is capable of taking position shots, you have a judgment call. If it happens once, and you have a lot of chips and not much invested in the pot, then unless you have a read on your opponent, give it up. If it happens repeatedly, then you're going to have to play back at this opponent, even though he has position on you.

You cannot let an aggressive player push you around just because he has position on you. You'll have to put him to a test with a big reraise, and you may have to do this more than once to get some respect for your bets.

When I say that your hijack seat strategy, given the above preflop conditions, is to raise, I mean that you should make a raise of two to four times the size of the big blind with any "playable" hand. In the small ball chapter, I provided a list of playable hands that included all pairs, all suited connectors, many unsuited connectors, all of the high card "trouble" hands, etc. I'm not much for memorizing lists of hands to play in different positions because these hands change according to the opponents you face. But you pretty much make this raise with a wide range of hands. You will make money with this play more often than not. If you just pick up the blinds, fine. If there is post-flop play and you pick up a bigger pot, great. If you have to abandon your hand as a result of play back by an opponent who appears to have a hand so strong he won't lay it down, fine. You fold. You're going for the long run wins with this play and in the long run you will earn more than you will lose.

Continuing to bet in the hand when you are called—assuming you are playing on a stone cold bluff—is a decision you must make based on your read on your opponent as well as your current utility. Even in slow tournaments, I use all of the same player types I described in *PTF1* to categorize my opponents and their betting styles, plus a few more that are common in the pro-level events. (I'll describe these below.) With low utility, I will either play extremely aggressively in my post-flop steal attempts, pushing all in if necessary, or I will check and fold if I judge my opponent to be in a chip position to call me with any legitimate hand.

You will lose money on blind stealing when you are reraised and must fold your junk hands, or when you continue to bet at an opponent who appears weak but keeps check-calling while he is slowplaying a monster (or just a strong hand he won't lay down). Slowplaying is more common in tournaments with slow structures than in fast events. But even in slow tournaments, most players will reraise when they have strong hands, and you can get out of the way with minimal damage. If you can start to recognize the player types who are capable of tricky plays, as well as the calling stations who will not lay down a pair to save their lives, you will know when to crank up your betting to get rid of an opponent and when to fold it down. Your overall success with position strategy will improve as you come to recognize a few important player types, so you can play against them accordingly.

If you attempt a steal from the hijack seat and you get more than one caller—especially if one of these callers has position on you—this is a very dangerous situation if you raised with a spec hand but hit nothing on the flop. In most cases, if one of the preflop callers is in one of the blinds, and this player comes out betting, and I still have a player yet to act behind me (the cutoff or button player), I will usually just fold. There will be less dangerous opportunities for making chips.

If neither of the blinds is in the pot, or if the blind players check to me post-flop, I will come out with a bet of about half the size of the pot. But I will usually fold to any aggressive play back. Keeping the lead in the betting is generally correct, but in multiway pots, out of position, it is always more dangerous. If I don't take that pot down on the flop, and I have no hand and no strong draw, I will usually shut down my betting. Multiway pots are bigger pots, so I will usually take a stab at them, but the increased risks are great, so I won't go nearly as far in my betting as I would heads-up. It's very difficult to get reads on multiple opponents in the same pot, especially when you are out of position on one or more of them.

Always be extra careful in multiway pots and always be aware of your utility as well as your opponents' utility. Strong players will often make calls with strong draws if the utility odds are right, and their drawing hand—even if they don't hit one of their outs—may actually be a better hand than the trash you're trying to steal with. It will be a lot easier to steal a pot from a loose player on the river, when he can see that any further improvement to his hand is no longer possible.

STEALING THE BLINDS FROM THE CUTOFF SEAT

The seat to the left of the hijack seat (and to the right of the button) is known among poker players as the cutoff seat. In limit games, this is probably the best seat from which to steal the blinds. Enough hold'em players know this, however, that in tournaments, it is more difficult to steal the blinds from the cutoff seat than it is from the hijack seat specifically because every raise from this seat (as well as from the button) tends to be viewed as an attempt to steal. Players are just as suspicious of this move in limit games, but they are not as desperate for chips. The desperation factor in tournaments makes better players less risk-averse and more likely to fight back against anything that looks like a "move."

You also run a greater danger of the button reraising you when you raise from the cutoff seat, because a position player on the button will rarely respect a raise from the cut-off, viewing it as an attempt to steal the button from him (which it is). He'll often try to put a quick end to it by reraising you, especially if you make this move more than once. If the button simply calls your raise, your post-flop play is risky. He may really have a hand, or he may simply represent one, and unless you have some kind of a read on this player, you won't know which is true.

If the button player calls your preflop raise from the cutoff seat, and you wind up heads-up against him, you should automatically bet half the size of the pot on the flop. If your opponent believes you to be an amateur player, he will usually fold if he does not have a decent hand or a strong draw, as he will believe you when you bet. If he believes you are a skillful enough player to follow through on the flop with a continuation bet, then he may put you to the test, especially if he has any legitimate hand himself—like second pair, an underpair to the board, or even two overcards. If your opponent just calls your bet on the flop, and you believe him to be a skillful player capable of making moves, you must decide when the river card comes down if he called on the flop because he is slowplaying a monster (the least likely possibility unless the board presents no dangers to him), or if he's on a draw and may believe the implied odds or utility odds are good enough to stay for another card. In many cases, your opponent is hoping his call on the flop will slow you down on the turn so that he can get the river card for free, or so that he can make a move on you and take the pot with a big bluff when you check to him on the turn.

If I have a big chip stack, and I'm not certain of why my opponent called, I will generally bet again on the turn about half the size of the pot. I have found that despite my fears and all of those dangerous possibilities, this bet on the turn will take down that pot about 90 percent of the time. The way you played this hand simply looks so much like you have a real hand that your opponent will fear that you won't go away if he tries a shot, and he will also not have the pot odds to call this bet on a draw with only one card to come (and most players play the pot odds, not the utility odds).

One caution: You cannot allow either your chip stack or your opponent's chip stack to be placed in serious jeopardy by these bets. If making these bets, or your opponent's call, would mean that either of you will have more than a third of his chips in the pot, then you must either raise all in, or simply check and fold and wait for a better opportunity. Never risk short-stacking yourself on a position play with a "standard" bet or raise. You either go all in or get out of the way. You cannot allow an attempt to steal to force your opponent into a showdown just because he has already invested so many chips in the pot.

NEVER RISK SHORT-STACKING YOURSELF ON A POSITION PLAY WITH A "STANDARD" BET OR RAISE. YOU EITHER GO ALL IN OR GET OUT OF THE WAY.

Despite the risk, when both you and your opponent have sufficient chips to play poker, the basic strategy play is to keep the lead in the betting. If you were the preflop raiser, then you should bet after the flop, and keep betting at each street unless you are reraised.

You will almost never go out on a play like this. Instead, you will almost always bust out when you actually have a strong hand. It is always less risky to play bluffs than it is to play your actual cards. This is because it's easy to abandon your hand on a bluff, but much more difficult to get away from a truly strong hand.

If you bet on the flop with no hand to speak of, simply keeping the lead, and an opponent whom you consider to be an amateur raises, the basic strategy play is to fold. You are probably facing an opponent who has a hand he likes. More amateurs do bluff

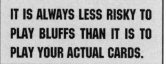

IT IS ALWAYS LESS RISKY TO PLAY BLUFFS THAN IT IS TO PLAY YOUR ACTUAL CARDS.

these days, but they usually give advance clues that they are not total amateurs, and with this type of amateur, you can go ahead and play your read. But if you put this opponent on being a total amateur,

don't test him to see how much he likes his hand. You'll have many less dangerous opportunities to make money.

If you know this player to be an aggressive position player, however, you do have a chance here to make some real money by playing back at him and converting your attempt at petty larceny into a grand theft. You will first have to make the tough decision. Does he really like his hand, or is he just doing what you do—betting that his opponent doesn't have a hand, or at least not a hand strong enough to continue out of position? If you decide the latter case is most likely, then you are making a big mistake if you fold. Your only decision here is whether you should call or reraise.

If you feel fairly certain that the button player is simply making a position move when he raises you after the flop, then your strongest play is to call his raise on the flop, then push all in on the turn before he has a chance to bet at you. If the turn card could be an out that your opponent may have been drawing to—say the third card to a suit on the board—you will have another tough judgment call. If you have no read on the situation, the fact is that much more often than not, your opponent will not have been drawing to that out, and very often, he will be worried that you were drawing to that out. So, unless I have a read to the contrary, I will bet when that possible out hits the board. In this case, I will bet only half to one-third the size of the pot. A bet like that by this point in the hand will be a pretty substantial bet, and it looks like I'm hoping for a call. Unless that dangerous turn card helped my opponent, he will be very reluctant to remain in this pot.

The reason you don't push all in when that scare card comes down is because your opponent may have a strong hand that he just won't abandon to an all-in bet that looks like a bluff, or worse—he may have just made the hand you're representing!

If the turn card is a blank, it's generally not advisable to check on the turn with the intention of check-raising when your opponent bets—especially if there is a strong draw on the board that your opponent may have put you on—as he may very well steal the all-in move from you on the turn if you check to him.

Finally, my advice about the dangers of multiway pots, especially when an opponent has position on you, applies just as much to steal attempts from the cutoff seat as it does to steal attempts from the hijack seat.

STEALING THE BLINDS FROM THE BUTTON

The button is the strongest position at the table. If you get into the pot, you will have position on the flop, turn and river on every other player. This is a huge advantage, so your cards are of minor importance in your decision to enter a pot. As a matter of habit, you should raise from the button if you are the first player in the pot. This will often be viewed as an attempt to steal the blinds (which it is). If one or both blinds are rabid defenders who will automatically call your raises, then you may find it more valuable to call from the button, or min-raise, like you are inviting action (which you are), rather than making a full raise of three to five times the big blind. You can then bet on the flop when the blinds check, or raise if your opponent comes out betting.

Also, it's generally best to mix up your play on the button with raises and calls, simply for camouflage. Occasionally, you might even fold a hand from the button in an unraised pot, but this is always a mistake in a tournament unless you are doing it purely for show, to convince the blinds as well as other players at the table that you primarily play your cards, rather than your position.

Against an opponent who consistently defends his blind, you should experiment with bigger raises, assuming you have the chips. If he calls your raise a couple of times when you bet three times the big blind, make your next bet four times. If he calls this bet, try five times. Most players, even staunch blind defenders, have a threshold above which they won't get involved in a pot out of position unless they have a legitimate hand.

You may also find that, if you simply call from the button, one of the blinds will take a shot at the pot by raising you. This is a pain in the ass because you don't really know whether he has a hand or is just assuming that you don't and that you won't pay to see the flop. I would almost always call this raise unless it was bigger than 5 x BB, with a plan to take the pot if he checks on the flop. But this decision must always be colored by your take on the player. If my opponent is an aggressive shot-taker, I'd give his preflop raise little respect. He's going to have to maintain his aggression out of position after the flop if he wants to take this pot, and even if he bets on the flop, I may raise him if I feel he's just taking another shot to avoid giving up the lead.

Only a relatively small percentage of tournament players are staunch blind defenders, though you'll find more in slow-structured tournaments than in the fast small buy-in events. If you run into complications that leave you confused, then get out of the way and wait for another opportunity. If you continually run into complications to the extent that your attempts to steal the blinds are costing you more than you earn, then you are doing something wrong. The greatest likelihood is that you have a weak table image that your opponents can see through. You have to change that. You need an attitude adjustment. You can't let bullies push you around.

You learn to steal by stealing, and if you're just sitting there playing your cards, you're wasting your money even entering tournaments. You either learn to do this, or quit. You'll need to add all five of the common bluffs described here to your strategy, and blind stealing is absolutely necessary.

Let's go on to number two…

2. THE CONTINUATION BLUFF

You absolutely must make continuation bets in tournaments with slow blind structures if you want to get into the money with any regularity. What is a continuation bet? Often called *keeping the lead*, it is simply a post-flop bet by a player who came in preflop with a raise. The difference between a continuation bet and a continuation bluff is that I consider it a continuation bet when I actually have what may be the best hand. I may have a pocket pair. I may have hit second pair on the flop. I may have A-K but the flop is all rags. I consider it a continuation bluff when the flop does not hit me, I have no legitimate draw, and it's unlikely that I have the best hand. For example: I raise from middle position with 9-8 suited and get one caller, the player on the button. The flop comes down A-J-3, rainbow, not exactly the flop I was looking for. But because I raised preflop, I bet as if I have the ace. The danger here is that my opponent may have the ace, as players who call preflop raises often do have an ace. It is still usually correct to make a continuation bluff in this situation, however, because flops miss players more often than they hit players. Although most players would call a standard raise with a lot of aces from the button, they would also call from the button with a whole lot of other hands that do not contain an ace. So, your best play is to keep the lead with a continuation bluff.

DISCUSSION

Most skillful players make continuation bets as a matter of habit. It is occasionally correct to refrain from a continuation bet just to mix up your play so that when you do make a bet that looks like it could be a continuation bet, your bet will be given more respect. One time when a continuation bluff might be ill-advised would be when the flop doesn't hit you at all—not even giving you a decent draw—and you are against more than one player who called your preflop raise. In this case, I would base my decision on keeping the betting lead on exactly who my opponents were; but the more players in the pot, the less likely your continuation bluff will be to take the pot.

I'm calling the continuation bluff an "easy bluff" because it works more often than not, and without complications, against a single opponent. Unless the flop hits your opponent, you will almost always take the pot with that bet. What is especially nice about the continuation bluff is that it will quite often get you the pot when your opponent actually has a better hand. In the example above where you are betting with Q-J when the flop comes down A-8-3, you will usually take the pot from any player who called your raise with a pair below aces, or with high cards like K-Q or K-J. You may even take it away from a wimpy player who called with a suited bad ace, like A-6 suited, who was hoping to hit a flush or at least a flush draw.

There are always possible complications with a continuation bluff in a pro-level tournament, however, because players will often have the chips to play back at you and the better players—the ones who make continuation bluffs themselves—will often show no respect for what looks like a continuation bet if they have any legitimate hand, like a pocket pair, in which case they will often raise for information.

The most aggressive players may even raise you with no hand, assuming you will have to fold if you were making a continuation bet and you have no ace (or a weak ace) in your hand. Now you're playing poker and you must decide if the raiser has an ace in hand, and if so, if it's a strong enough ace to stay in the hand if you go over the top of him—remember, he didn't reraise you preflop—or if he hit some monster hand (like a set) on the flop, or if he is simply raising you for information, or just making a position play on you. Amateur players won't make moves like this, or information bets, so your continuation bet will take the pot away from many less skillful players who have better hands. With skillful players, you've got some tough decisions.

Generally, if you have no hand and no strong draw, it's better to avoid the complications if you also have no read on your opponent. Just fold to any reraise after your continuation bet. If you have superior skills at both bluffing and reading your opponents, then continue in this hand if you feel the risk is worth the reward. But keep in mind that most tournament amateurs err in being too risk-averse. This is one of those situations that separates the real money-makers from the also-rans in the big buy-in tournaments. The top pros go with their reads. The weaker players are more often afraid to play their reads when danger lurks. My advice to players who are playing in pro-level tournaments, but not making money, is to start playing your reads—those flashes of intuition that just make you feel that an opponent is weak or bluffing or unsure about how strong you are.

You could be a great player, but if you're too chicken to follow through on your reads and find out how good you really are, you'll get nowhere. And if you make mistakes, you'll learn from them. When you make a continuation bet, you should invite complications because these are great opportunities not only for making more chips, but for learning how good you are.

Another complication that can arise with a continuation bluff is that your opponent may simply call your bet on the flop. In this case, with the hand described above, there is no card on the turn that can help you if your opponent has an ace in hand, though you could pick up a straight or flush draw. But would you really be comfortable betting if a 9 or 8 comes down on the turn? Also, how do you interpret that call from your opponent? Does it mean that he has a weak ace or a pair below aces but thinks his hand may still be best? Most pros would not call with such a hand; they would either raise or fold. But you are not always playing against skillful players and calling stations can be difficult to figure out.

Here again, going through the difficult work of testing your skills at reading opponents and bluffing them out of pots will pay off. If you feel your opponent has an ace, maybe even a strong ace like A-Q or A-K, and you feel he will not go away, then you must not put any more chips into that pot. Either check it down to the river, or check and fold if your opponent bets. If you feel you can get your opponent to fold by taking more shots at the pot, and more expensive shots, then you should do so.

So, when I say that you should generally make continuation bluffs because they are easy bluffs to pull off, I mean they are easy when there are no complications. But you can't be so afraid of the complications that you fail to make these bets. As with blind stealing, if you find that you always run into complications with your continuation bluffs, and you lose more chips with these bluffs than you earn with them, then you are probably broadcasting your weakness with tells that you are unaware of.

Continuation bluffs work because they look natural. You raised before the flop, and you're betting after the flop. This is exactly what a player with a strong hand would do. Complications may arise following this bet, but the bet itself is always a good bluff because it fits the logic of the way the hand has been played. If you are not good at bluffing, then continuation bluffs are a great bluff to start with. The best way to start is to refrain from making a continuation bet the first time you've raised preflop and get a flop that doesn't hit you. This instills in your opponents the idea that you are not a continuation bettor. Then you start making continuation bets after that. And force yourself to start following your reads when you face complications. It's the only way to develop the skills you need to make money in pro-level tournaments.

3. THE POSITION BLUFF AFTER AN OPPONENT LIMPS (OR CHECKS)

One or two players limp into the pot. On the button, you raise. If you are making this raise with a hand that would not be considered a raising hand by most hold'em players, then you are making a position bluff. Likewise, if you are involved in a pot with one or more opponents when you have position on them, and all of them check post-flop, and you bet with no hand to speak of, that's a position bluff.

DISCUSSION

Position bluffs should almost always be made against a single opponent, and against a single opponent these bets have a very high rate of success. The greater the number of players in the pot, the more risky position bluffs become. In *PTF1*, I described this bet as the first rule of post-flop position play: He checks. You bet. This strategy is as powerful in tournaments with slow blind structures as it is in tournaments with fast blind structures. Your general attitude about this move should be: Just do it!

This bet works especially well post-flop if you raised or called a raise preflop. That's because it looks natural according to the way the hand has been played. If you raise or call a raise preflop, you are representing a strong hand. A post-flop bet is the logical next step for a player with the strong hand you're representing.

Position bluffs, like continuation bluffs, can have complications. For one, you may be check-raised. For another, you may be called, which puts you in the position of having to decide how to play on the turn and river. When you are check-raised, you must consider the possibility that your opponent may have flopped a set or better. Likewise if you are simply called, your opponent may be on a draw, or trying to milk you with a monster hand.

But as with continuation bluffs, you cannot be so afraid of the possible complications that you fail to make position bluffs. These are among the easiest of the bluffs to pull off, and against a single opponent, a position bluff post-flop (after you raised or called a raise preflop) will have a high rate of success simply because it looks so logical according to the way the hand has been played up to that point.

As with continuation bluffs, my advice to bluffing neophytes is to make post-flop position bluffs any time the bet seems logical, especially when heads-up against a single opponent. You must get this bet into your repertoire of standard bluffs.

4. THE INFORMATION BLUFF

First let's clarify exactly what an "information bet" is, as opposed to an information *bluff*. In its simplest form, it's a bet or raise post-flop when you have a made hand that may be the best hand, but which may have lost its value as a result of the flop. For example, betting or raising with pocket jacks after one or more overcards come down on the flop is an information bet—you're probing to see if your opponent has hit that overcard. If my opponent has position on me, then betting here is simply a continuation bet, although I do have a strong hand despite the danger posed by the flop. If I have position on my opponent, however, and my opponent bets when the flop comes down, then it would take a raise on my part to get that information. He may be simply making a continuation bet and my J-J may be the best hand. My raise is asking for information: Did that high card on the flop really hit you?

An information bluff is a bet placed when I don't have any hand myself, and very likely have a worse hand than my opponent. I place the bet because of the high likelihood that my opponent may be making a continuation bet with no made hand to speak of. I'm asking the question: Can you call a raise after seeing that flop?

DISCUSSION

Technically, when I raise my opponent who appears to be making a continuation bet, I'm representing either that the flop hit me or that my hand is so strong that the flop doesn't scare me. With a standard information bet, I have a made hand myself, which may be the best hand, and I'm trying to find out where I stand. With an information bluff, I have no hand but I'm representing a hand to my opponent to find out where he stands.

The information bluff is a pure bluff because you have no hand yourself. It succeeds when your opponent has made either an information bet himself or a continuation bet or a position bet with a weak or marginal hand, which will often be the case. This is a bluff that you would not attempt against certain tight players who rarely make continuation bets or take position shots. And again, the bluff works best when your bet appears to follow the logic of the betting on that hand and fits your typical betting patterns.

I label this an easy bluff because it's fairly easy to recognize the situations where it may succeed and the types of players it will work against. Again, you must always be aware that this bluff could lead to complications if you are called. If you are raised, the complications are not so complicated. Unless you have a read that your opponent's raise is a bluff, you must fold.

5. THE VALUE BET BLUFF
You'll get value out of this bluff if you play a lot of small ball. It's simply a bet on the river into a pot that your opponent seems to have no interest in. For example, you call a min-raise preflop with 6-8 suited. The flop comes down jack-high with three to a suit, but not your suit. Your opponent checks and you check, thinking he may be checking a flush draw that he won't lay down easily. Basically, you let him have the free card since you are pretty much drawing dead and have no intention of putting any more chips into the pot. The turn card is another blank and you both check again. The river is a king. Your opponent checks. This is the perfect spot for a "value bet" on the river, as if that king hit your hand. Unless your opponent also hit that king—highly unlikely since he did not attempt a value bet on the river himself—or has been slowplaying

a flush from the start, this pot is yours, even though he very likely has a card higher than an eight in his hand and may even have a pair.

DISCUSSION

This bet on the river would be a natural bet for any player with a king in hand to make and, because of the flush possibility that has been a threat on the board since the flop, it's an extremely difficult bet for your opponent to call with ace-high or any underpair. You do not need position on your opponent to make this bet on the river. If you enter the pot with a raise and get called, then elect to not make a continuation bet because of the dangerous cards on the board, this river bet will still take the pot from your opponent most of the time if he cannot beat a pair of kings (or whatever high card may have come down on the river), and he may believe you have been sandbagging a flush all along. Although the possibility exists that the king on the river may have hit your opponent, and he may call you if he's got a decent kicker, the bet will still pay off more often than not. And because it's a bluff disguised as a value bet, it's not an expensive loss when you get called. You don't want to make this a pot-size or larger bet. A bet of half the size of the pot or less is all it takes.

As you get comfortable making value bet bluffs on the river in these types of situations, you'll also start finding opportunities for making these bets on the turn, and even in multiway pots. It's always more dangerous to attempt a bluff against more than one opponent, but multiway pots are generally bigger pots, so there's more value to the bluff when it succeeds.

HOW TO MAKE UP YOUR OWN BLUFFS

Many of the best bluffs cannot be categorized. They come as flashes of inspiration as you are in the midst of a hand. You discover these bluffing opportunities when you are trying to figure out what cards your opponent is holding based on his style of play and the way the hand is playing out. As you do this, you should also be thinking about what hand your opponent is likely to be putting you on based on your table image and the way the hand has been playing out.

Suddenly, a card comes down that you realize would have made a very strong hand for you if you are correct about your opponent's deductions about what hand you might be playing, and it is not a card that you imagine to be among the cards that would help your opponent. In the "value bet bluff" example described above, the appearance of that king on the river, and your opponent's checking to you, created a perfect set-up for that bluff. I included that value bet bluff among the five easy bluffs, because it is one you should be on the lookout for, as you will see opportunities for making it over and over again.

But these types of bluffing opportunities can occur at many times other than on the river. Suddenly a third card to a flush or the kind of straight your opponent could put you on hits the board at a time when you feel certain that your opponent was betting a hand like top pair. You have the perfect set-up. How you play and bet when that scare card comes down must be based on your opponent, your table image, and—as always—the utility issue. What size bet on your part would scare him the most?

If you push all in, he may not believe you unless you are short-stacked and that bet appears to be the bet you would make given the size of the pot. A player who just made a straight or flush usually wants action, so if your chip stack is formidable, an all-in bet here would reek of bluff. But a bet too small, given the size of the pot, may induce your opponent to call simply because the pot is giving him such good odds and you could be making what old timers call a "post oak bluff."

Your opponent's chip stack (and utility) is also a consideration. If he has a deep stack, he will be much more likely to call a bet of half the size of the pot or less, and a bet closer to the size of the pot would scare him more, as your bet would not be outlandish given the size of his chip stack, and it would appear that you are trying to make a bet that he would call. On the other hand, if a bet of half the size of the pot would take a significant chunk out of your opponent's remaining chip stack, then that bet might well look the scariest to him, as it would appear you are trying to get as many of his chips into the pot as possible.

The more you bluff, the more you will get a feel for both the timing and the best bet sizes to get your opponents to go away. I couldn't even count how many times I've bet too much or too little or at the wrong time when attempting to steal, and in almost every instance, I saw that my read on my opponent was correct—he had a hand that he would have laid down had I thought it through and made the right bet—but I didn't take my time to think it through in order to achieve my goal. But that's how you learn, especially when you're starting to get creative with bluffing. The next time a similar situation arises, you'll do it right.

THREE COMMON BLUFFING MYTHS

There may, in fact, be dozens of myths about bluffing, but three really stick out in my mind because I've heard them so often. Believing in these myths can cost you pots and/or get you in a lot of trouble.

1. IT'S TOO EARLY TO BLUFF

You hear this all the time in the early stages of a tournament. With a dangerous-looking board, one player makes a big bet or raise and his opponent reluctantly folds, saying something like, "I think I'm laying down the best hand." The player who takes the pot counters with, "I had you beat. It's too early to bluff." Ninety-nine percent of the time, the player who says this has just stolen the pot.

You also hear this when a player on the button enters the pot with a raise after the table has folded to him preflop. It looks like blind steal, but the blinds muck, with one of them remarking, "I'd like to see a flop with this hand, but I'll give you some respect." And the raiser says, "Hey, man, I had to raise. I had a big hand. It's too early to bluff."

Too early to bluff? That's like saying it's too early to establish a tough aggressive image. Too early to start building a chip stack. Too early to start using reads on weak players. *It's never too early to bluff.*

There is an argument that says it's not worth it to steal the blinds when they're so small in relation to the chip stacks. Bull. When you raise the blinds from late position, you're not just trying to steal the blinds; you're trying to get into a pot where you'll have position on players who may call with marginal hands since they already have chips invested. If all you get for your efforts are the few chips in the blinds, fine. But you're really going for a bigger score, and in the long run, you'll pick up quite a few more chips than the chips in the blinds. You're also getting an early start on establishing an image: I'm an aggressive bastard and I play position and you're going to have to live with it.

Because so many players believe in tight play early, this is the easiest (and cheapest) time to start establishing a loose, tough, unpredictable image. And I absolutely do not buy into the theory that beginners should start out playing tight until they gain a lot of experience. You learn to play by playing. You learn to steal by stealing. You learn to read players by trusting your reads and acting on them. If you suspect a bluff, call it down. Don't fold when

you're unsure. If you think you can fold a player who obviously
has a hand by going over the top of his raise or reraise, do it. I've
said it before and I'll repeat it: You'll never know how good your
reads are if you don't start acting on them.

2. IT TAKES A STU UNGAR TO FIRE THREE SHOTS

This may have been true at some point in the past, but not
anymore. By this time, everyone has heard that the legendary Stu
Ungar was such a fearless bluffer that he would take not just one
shot at the pot, but would fire at the pot on the flop, turn, and
river! Nowadays, a lot of aggressive Internet kids and just players
who have watched a lot of televised final tables make this triple-
shot attack part of their standard bluffing repertoire. This is not
to say that they all have Ungar's skill at reading opponents and
knowing when this relentless bluff attack will succeed. Sometimes
it does succeed because it's so brazen. But when you've got one
of these players at your table and you make a big hand—and it
doesn't have to be anywhere near the nuts—you can milk him for
a lot of chips just by checking and calling.

3. AMATEURS DON'T TAKE SHOTS

That's another myth that probably used to be true. Generally, it's
true that amateurs are more likely to play too tight in tournaments,
passively watching their chip stacks dwindle. But televised poker
tournaments have so glorified the bluff that there is a significant
faction of amateur players who bluff too much, though they really
don't understand the logic of bluffing. How many times have we
now heard Mike Sexton say something like, "You wouldn't expect
an amateur to make a move like that!" A dozen times? More than
a dozen? It's about time you started expecting it. I generally give
players I consider unskillful more credence when they bet—but
I've also called down an awful lot of amateur bluffs. Add to these
TV-trained players a significant number of experienced poker
players who have migrated to no-limit hold'em tournaments from

years of limit play in cash games—where bluffing is much less of a factor—and there are a lot of bad bluffs occurring in tournaments these days. Quite a few unskillful players bust out of tournaments on bad bluffs.

I can't tell you how many times I've seen a player make a terrible bluff at a pot I wasn't involved in, and then watched his opponent just sit there pondering the hand, trying to decide whether or not to call. Mentally, I'm thinking, "What's the matter with you? Call that sucker!" But often he doesn't—he folds and that pleases me, because now I know I have both a bad bluffer at the table and a player who either can't recognize a bad bluff, or (more likely) is too wimpy to play his read.

Because bluffing is so important to tournament success, and because bad bluffs are so common in tournaments, it's important that you not only recognize bad bluffs so that you do not relinquish pots you should be adding to your stack, but also that you do not fall into the habit making bad bluffs yourself.

Where do bad bluffs come from, other than from rookie players trying to mimic players they've seen succeed with bluffs on TV? Again, as with the tight, survival-oriented tournament strategies, we can blame the mathematicians. Let's look at bad bluffs and where they come from.

HOW NOT TO BLUFF

Most players are downright bad at bluffing. Although it's often impossible to detect a great bluff, bad bluffs are plentiful and they're relatively easy to see. If you find that your bluffs are too often called, you're doing something wrong. What makes a bad bluff?

> *"Second Golden Rule of Bluffing: If an opponent makes a*
> *bet which is not in accordance with his usual style of play,*
> *he should always be assumed to be bluffing."*
>
> **—Poker: How to Play and Win**,
> by Maurice Ellinger (1934)

I don't know much about Maurice Ellinger, other than the fact that he authored the above-referenced book about seventy-five years ago and his "Second Golden Rule of Bluffing" describes the essence of calling a bluff succinctly and accurately. A bad bluff is most often a bet that simply does not "look right." It often surprises you because it seems incongruous with the way the hand has been coming down or with your opponent's typical betting patterns.

A TYPICAL BAD BLUFF

This is an actual hand from a $1,000 tournament I played at the Venetian in one of their deep-stack series. It occurred in the first blind level. I made a standard raise preflop from late position with pocket eights and got one caller, the player in the big blind. The flop came down K-10-3 with two spades.

BIG BLIND

ARNOLD

FLOP

My opponent checked. I hated the flop, which not only had two overcards to my pair, but also a potential straight draw and a flush draw. I bet the size of the pot and my opponent called. I figured he probably had one of the draws. The turn was a 7, but not a spade. This put three straight draws on the board in addition to the flush draw, though the only straight draw that concerned me was the draw to the K-10, since I couldn't imagine my opponent staying in the pot with any two cards that would have made the two new straight draws any danger to me. I suppose if he had J-9, he would now have a double belly buster.

Again, he checked, and I made a pot-sized bet, which he called. This pot was getting awfully damn big for me with my pair of eights and no legitimate draws of my own. The river was another 7, but again not a spade, making the board K-10-3-7-7.

BOARD

So, there were no possible straights or flushes out there. But now, my opponent fired out a bet, almost the size of the pot.

That bet took me by surprise, and I sat there a moment thinking: Where did that come from? I was trying to put him on a hand. Was it possible he flopped a set and slowplayed it to the river? Wouldn't the straight and flush draws have concerned him? Wouldn't he have check-raised me either on the flop or—at the latest—on the turn if he'd had a set, or two pair? This was an experienced player whom I'd played against in numerous tournaments in Las Vegas, and I'd never seen him play a hand like this. My read was that he was on a stone cold bluff.

I called and he immediately mucked his cards, saying, "You got me. I missed my flush draw."

Because of the two overcards, he could have taken that pot from me easily on the flop with a check-raise. But on the river? What did he think he was representing? Why would he make a bet that seemed to have come out of nowhere? Granted, if the river card was a spade or a card that could have completed that K-10 straight draw (especially an ace or 9), there's a good chance his bluff would have worked. But everything about that bet on the river just seemed wrong.

The upside of my calling his bluff on the river was that some of the other players at the table started oohing and aahing at my incredibly great call. How could I call that bet with my pair of eights when there were two overcards on the board? If they had been paying attention to the hand as it unfolded, they would likely have seen my call as simply logical. But some players don't pay a lot of attention to hands they're not involved in. They simply notice what the board looks like on the river when there's a big pot, and they see a big bet get called by a player with nothing but an underpair. When it turns out to be a good call, they think the caller is downright scary. That call got me a lot more respect than I deserved. I don't think any other player at that table took a shot at me in the two hours until the table broke.

WHY SO MANY PLAYERS TODAY MAKE BAD BLUFFS

The art of bluffing at poker was set back considerably about 65 years ago when a mathematician purported to find a method of both bluffing and calling bluffs at poker based on "mathematics." To the detriment of amateur players, this mathematical theory of bluffing has seeped into the poker literature, and many players are bluffing by using terrible bastardizations of this mathematician's faulty logic. Let's look at where this nonsense started.

WHY BLUFFING ACCORDING TO "GAME THEORY" IS A MISTAKE

In 1944, a truly revolutionary book was published titled *Theory of Games and Economic Behavior* by John von Neumann and Oskar Morgenstern. In this book, von Neumann introduced the concept of "game theory," which was a new branch of mathematics that used math to devise the best strategies for games. Technically, von Neumann was not interested in games at all, but was using hypothetical game situations to solve problems in other areas, most notably economics, though game theory has been applied to military situations, political situations, and even scientific endeavors like biology and physics.

One of von Neumann's chapters was titled "Poker and Bluffing," and this chapter has resulted in more bad bluffs at the poker tables in the past 65 years than drunkenness, fatigue, and bad-beat tilting combined. This never should have happened because von Neumann wasn't really writing about actual poker games, and only a very small fraction of a percent of the poker players in the world could even understand what he wrote. For your enlightenment, the final part of von Neumann's final solution to the problem of how often to bluff at poker is this:

$$\rho_1^z \begin{cases} = \dfrac{b}{a+b} & \text{for} \quad 0 \le z \le \dfrac{a-b}{a} \\[2em] = 1 & \text{for} \quad \dfrac{a-b}{a} < z \le 1 \end{cases}$$

The "poker" game von Neumann analyzed to come up with this solution, however, did not use a normal 52-card deck. It used a hypothetical 52-card deck in which each card had an assigned numerical value from 1 to 52. The higher the assigned value, the better the card. Each player (and there were only two players in von Neumann's "poker" game) was dealt just one card, and at the showdown, the highest card would win. Following the "deal," the players would bet against each other. From the purely mathematical perspective, all cards numbered from 1 to 26 had below-average value and were more likely to lose, and all cards numbered from 27 to 52 had above average value and were more likely to win.

Von Neumann called this game "poker" because when it came to betting, it would be possible for a player with a lesser valued card to make his opponent fold a stronger hand by betting as if his weaker hand was actually very strong. What is most important here, however, is that von Neumann did not envision this game being played by human beings who actually faced each other across a table. It was an exercise on paper, in which neither player had an act or an image. It was not so much an exercise in psychology as in probability. What von Neumann discovered was that in this hypothetical "poker" game, there was a perfect percentage of times to bluff, and to call bluffs, so that no matter what percentage of the time your opponent bluffed or called bluffs, you would have the best possible result. In fact, if both you and your opponent used the ideal percentages of bluffing and calling, you would break even at the game. But if your opponent used the "wrong" percentages, you would inevitably beat him.

In any case, it's unlikely that any poker players started using von Neumann's solution to perfect bluffing when his book was published in the mid-1940s because his book was written for math geeks and the formula provided above is about as clear as his book ever gets on this subject. It wasn't long, however, before non-mathematicians started interpreting von Neumann's gobbledygook in the popular literature as if von Neumann had been writing about bluffing in actual poker games.

In 1948, one writer, John McDonald, wrote an article for *Fortune* magazine about using von Neumann's findings at the poker tables, and later included this article as a chapter in his popular 1950 book, *Strategy in Poker, Business & War*. Fortunately for poker players, McDonald tells some good poker stories in his book, but he was not much of a poker player himself and he really had no idea of how a player could actually achieve von Neumann's perfect percentage of bluffing and calling bluffs. Unfortunately for poker players, McDonald did understand one extremely important point of von Neumann's strategy—that the bluffing strategy must be based on *random* moves that could not be figured out or predicted by discerning any logical patterns. McDonald planted the seed in players' minds that a mathematically perfect bluffing system existed that was based on unpredictable random moves, and that making completely off-the-wall bets, that were not predictable because there was no logic behind them based on the specific hand in play, was a key factor in bluffing success.

In 1954, McGraw-Hill published a book by a Rand Corporation think-tanker named J.D. Williams, titled *The Compleat Strategist*, subtitled "A Primer on the Theory of Games," that for the first time suggested a vaguely practical method for poker players to apply von Neumann's bluffing strategy. Williams suggested that players could quickly devise randomized strategies based on specific odds by using the cards themselves to produce the bluffing, or bluff-calling, decisions. He pointed out that the odds of an ace appearing were 12 to 1 against and a face card 10 to 3 against, and wrote that by selecting a subset of cards appropriate to the situation, a player could randomize his bluffs and calls to any desired percentage.

Other authors followed with more references to von Neumann's "perfect" bluffing strategy based on unpredictable random bluffs. In 1967, Albert Morehead, one of the most well-known writers on games and gambling forty years ago, and a longtime bridge columnist for the *New York Times*, wrote a popular book titled *The Complete Guide to Winning Poker*, published by Simon & Schuster, which contained a chapter titled "The Mathematical Theory of Games and Its Application to Poker." Morehead provided a much clearer explanation of von Neumann's mathematical bluffing strategy than any prior author, but ultimately concluded that in real world poker games, the perfect percentages for bluffing and calling bluffs were not so cut and dried as in von Neumann's hypothetical two-player poker game, where each player was dealt only one card. "It is virtually impossible to compute them [the percentages] during the play of an actual hand," he determined, though he had no argument with von Neumann's bluffing logic.

By this point, now more than thirty years after von Neumann's book on game theory had been published, many poker players had heard about this math wizard's "perfect" bluffing strategy, and understood only one factor about how it worked: The bluffs must be based on random elements that have nothing to do with the hand in question in order to remain unpredictable.

In 1974, a popular book titled *Winning Poker Systems*, by mathematician Norman Zadeh, in a chapter titled "Rules for General Play," provided the first practical method for players to apply von Neumann's math-based method of bluffing and calling bluffs. His strategies for both bluffing and calling bluffs exclude any consideration of reads you may have on your opponent, or that your opponent may have on you, and instead rely entirely on your estimation of what percentage of the time your opponent would bluff or call bluffs. Somewhat to his discredit, Zadeh never mentions von Neumann as the inventor of this math-based bluffing strategy, though his strategies agree with von Neumann's work on bluffing according to game theory. Overall, however, his methodology was still a bit too vague and theoretical for most players to employ in real life poker games.

In 1977, in his monumental classic, *The Theory of Gambling and Statistical Logic* (Academic Press), Richard Epstein set the record straight on von Neumann's game theory approach to poker analysis: "There are few games that better illustrate elementary probability theory, and, consequently, many works have calculated the probabilities of poker hands and draws. Deriving an optimal strategy, however, is beyond the scope of current game theory." Noting that the game theorists were not analyzing actual poker games but "models" of hypothetical games that contained certain elements of poker, he concluded: "Usually, a detailed analysis of these models furthers the understanding of certain mathematical concepts rather than providing any insight into the real game of poker."

A PRO POKER PLAYER CHIMES IN

That same year, a professional poker player—and one who had a firm grasp on mathematics—spelled out von Neumann's bluffing system in one of the most popular poker books of all time: *Play Poker, Quit Work, and Sleep Till Noon*, by John Fox. Fox provided a number of real world examples of how a player in a draw poker game could use random cards to devise a mathematical strategy for bluffing that would agree with von Neumann's game theory approach. Fox described von Neumann's "saddle point" logic in depth and showed that it was not impossible to use such an approach to bluffing and calling bluffs in real world games.

But as John Fox was also a professional poker player, and not just a math geek and book author, he echoed Epstein's opinion that von Neumann's theories on how and when to bluff would be of little use in real world poker games against experienced skillful players, and indeed would be foolish to attempt to use against such players. According to Fox:

> In real life, poker games are not filled with perfect, unreadable, unemotional opponents. For practical purposes, offensive bluffing should be attempted more as a function of your own image and the actions and emotional states of your opponents rather than because of theoretical considerations of optimal bluffing frequencies... Once you become a master of card reading, you can throw mathematics out the window. This includes the mathematics of theoretical optimal bluffing frequencies.

SKLANSKY'S BAD BLUFFING ADVICE

Other poker authors, however, became entranced with the idea of bluffing according to mathematics. David Sklansky, in *Theory of Poker*, a popular book that came out about ten years after Fox's classic, was so proud of his understanding of the application of game theory to poker that he provided numerous examples that demonstrated that "there are no tricks to this arithmetic." But instead of echoing Fox's warnings that von Neumann's bluffing ideas were not applicable to real world games where you did not face "unreadable, unemotional opponents," he concluded that it was against expert players, that game-theory bluffing was the perfect tool, because, "When you use it, there is no way they can outplay you."

In one example, Sklansky—who like Zadeh failed to cite von Neumann, and also failed to cite John Fox—provided a hand where he was a 4 to 3 underdog and claimed that by choosing key cards to bluff with, he became a 4 to 3 favorite, and that unless his opponent was a psychic, there was no strategy his opponent could possibly use to beat him.

But there *is* a strategy that any expert player could use to beat a player using von Neumann's game theory bluffing method: They can call him when he's bluffing, and lay down their hands when he's not. Pros are very good at reading opponents, including opponents who believe they have perfect "poker faces," *and* very good at making good percentage calls and laydowns.

Von Neumann's bluffing theory would work in the real world only against a poker automaton who has mentally decided to bluff, or call what may be a bluff, based on some arbitrary percentage in his head that he believes is the correct percentage of bluffs and calls to make, based on the pot odds he's getting. But this is not at all the way a professional poker player thinks, nor is it the way that *any* pro plays. A pro bluffs only when he's reasonably certain he can pull it off because his bet looks perfectly convincing for the situation. But because of this idea that von Neumann's fans planted in the poker world, something Sklansly promulgated, that bluffs should be based on random unpredictable factors (such as the appearance of preselected cards), there are many amateurs who attempt various types of random bluffing strategies and get eaten alive by pros. The reason their bluffs fail is simple—their bets just don't "look right."

DON'T BLAME VON NEUMANN

Let's return to that typical bad bluff I described earlier in this chapter where I called the bluffer's big bet on the river with my pocket eights when the board was K-10-3-7-7. Was the player who took that shot at the pot using a von Neumann type strategy? Quite possibly. One of the ways the strategy has been described in books that recommend it is that you remain in the pot on a strong draw and, if you do not hit one of your outs, you bluff if some other "random" card appears from a preselected group of cards that would provide you with the "correct percentage" of times to bluff. Now, there's no way that I could know whether this player actually bluffed at the pot because the 7 that came down on the river was in some preselected group of cards that meant he would bluff. If I knew that, *I* would be psychic! But somehow this player believed that coming out with an inexplicable bet that was totally unpredictable to me would make for a good bluff. But it wasn't. That's just not the way it works.

I've found references to bluffing in many older poker books, but until von Neumann's book, no poker author seemed to think that there was anything but psychology or guts involved in the decisions to bluff or call bluffs. I don't really fault von Neumann for his work on game theory, as I don't believe he ever intended his bluffing strategy to be used in real poker games. It took naïve poker authors with little understanding of bluffing to distort von Neumann's work this way.

REAL WORLD BLUFFING

In fact, bluffing in pro-level games should never be based on "random" cards or random anything. A bluff, if it is to be effective, must be based on the logic of the hand in play, your read on your opponent (including your opponent's emotional state), and on your personal image and style of play. Look at the "Five Easy Fleeces" described at the beginning of this chapter, and you'll find that all but the simple blind steal are not only not "random," they are in fact "predictable" in that they agree with the logical way a hand would be played if strong. When a bluff appears to be the precise amount that you would bet with a strong hand, and is performed with the same style and timing and action that you would use to make that bet when you have made the hand you're representing, you have accomplished a good bluff.

When a bluff appears to come out of nowhere and has your opponent scratching his head as to what hand you could possibly have, or why you would suddenly be representing a stronger hand than you seemed to be playing, you will be called down by skillful players more often than not. If you appeared to be on a draw, and no card appeared on the river that would have completed a hand you could be drawing to, you can't just fire out a big bet and hope your opponent will think you were slowplaying a monster—unless, of course, your opponent has seen you show down a monster in a similarly dangerous situation. Even then, your style and timing had better be exactly right.

PLAYER TYPES IN PRO-LEVEL TOURNAMENTS

I very rarely spot reliable physical tells on opponents. It would be great if most players had quirky mannerisms that revealed the strength of their hands, but if they do, I just don't see them, and I think it's more myth than fact that many of the top players are seeing these types of tells on most players.

I still read players primarily by watching how many hands they play and how aggressively they play, using the same player types I identified in *PTF1* to put them on hands. In that book, I described ten common player types I found in the small buy-in fast tournaments: Ace Masters, Flush Masters, Pair Masters, Cagey

Codgers, Canasta Ladies, Boat People, Show'n'Tellers, Ball-Cap Kids, Wimps and Oafs. If you are familiar with these player types from *PTF1*, you should be happy to know that they all exist in the pro-level tournaments as well. You'll find fewer Ace Masters, Flush Masters, Pair Masters, Canasta Ladies and Oafs, more Boat People and Ball-Cap Kids, and about the same proportion of Cagey Codgers, Show'n'Tellers and Wimps. All of these player types are briefly described in the glossary, but see *PTF1* for full descriptions. In addition, there are a few other types common to the pro-level events that you don't often find in the fast tourneys: the Harringbots, the Killers, the Super Stars, the Hangers-On, and the Groupies. The following sections of this chapter will describe these player types.

THE HARRINGBOTS

These are the players who have read the *Harrington on Hold'em* series and who live by it—a fairly large faction of tournament players in the pro-level events. They play a tight predictable survival-oriented style in the early phases of the tournament, generally find themselves short-stacked after a few hours, then start taking shots en masse when it's too late. They seldom bluff until their "M" dictates it. If they amass any amount of chips it's always a result of being dealt superior hands in ideal situations, such as pocket aces vs. pocket kings and a set vs. top pair. But they pose no problem when they have a big chip stack as they continue to just play their cards. They never become bullies or even try to push weak players around.

Harringbots will slowplay monster hands, so be wary of them if they are in a pot. They are similar to the Cagey Codgers described in *PTF1*, except that they know enough to start taking shots with more marginal hands when short-stacked. During the "mine-field" portion of a tournament (described later in a separate chapter), when the short stacks start dropping like flies, all of the

Harringbots who've been doing nothing but surviving for hours start shoving their chips in pot after pot. A few will get lucky. Most will disappear.

These players make up the biggest proportion of dead money in the pro-level events these days. They have little utility-consciousness and are exceptionally weak players in the early blind levels of the events that have shorter starting stacks and low starting utility.

(Let me make it clear, however, that I do not consider Dan Harrington a Harringbot. If you are a Harringbot, it's time to stop playing according to a recipe in a book.)

THE KILLERS

I named this player type for the jam-or-fold style of play described in Blair Rodman's *Kill Phil*. To be honest, I've never seen the *Kill Phil* strategy being used in a pro-level event. I've seen players in slow-structured tournaments, however, whose only move is all in before the flop when they start to get short-stacked, and I call these players Killers. I also call a player a Killer if he continually overbets the pot preflop and makes frequent all-in bets post-flop. For example, with the blinds at $25/$50, a Killer will typically raise to $400 or more if first in, even if he is well stocked with chips. Some players will do this occasionally with small or medium pocket pairs, especially if any limpers have already entered a pot, but a Killer always enters with outsized bets, regardless of his hand, and if he bets at all after the flop, it's all in. In a sense, Killers are players who play slow-structured tournaments with a style that would be more correct in an online turbo event with three-minute blind levels. Killers generally do not play a lot of hands, so in most cases I believe they are entering with big pairs or hands like A-K or A-Q. With their big bets, they are attempting to avoid the complications of post-flop play by killing the action and taking the pot immediately.

Daniel Negreanu discusses this type of strategy in *Hold'em Wisdom for All Players* as a viable approach for beginners who, if they entered pots with more standard bets and raises, would too often find themselves being outplayed post-flop by more experienced players. There is definitely some truth to this, though the fact is Killers almost never make it to the money. They tend to pick up small pots too infrequently to keep up with the blind costs, and they eventually bump into superior hands that their big bets don't scare away. It's not an approach I would ever recommend, even to a beginner, unless such a player was entering a tournament strictly as a lark with no intention of seriously playing tournaments in the future. With this type of strategy, you will simply never learn to play poker. You've got to get in there and mix it up with your opponents to have any hope of learning how to play at the pro level.

THE SUPER STARS

A Super Star is a player who has made a final table on TV and, in some cases, has also written a book on poker. Some Super Stars deserve their status. Their tournament records are impressive and they are truly dangerous players. Others are no better than mediocre, but they do trade on their Super Star status to whatever extent possible. The main thing you have to be aware of if you have a Super Star at your table is that you must not allow yourself to assign him more skill than he deserves. It's your job to make this player afraid of you.

One benefit to having a Super Star at your table is that other players at your table will often become much wimpier in the way they play for two reasons: one is that they are afraid of getting involved in pots in which the Super Star may be involved, so they play fewer pots. Two, they are afraid of looking bad in front of one of their heroes, so they tighten up even more. If you sense this is happening, you should definitely loosen up your play and really go after the timid players who don't want to "look bad." Make 'em look bad.

You should also look at this as a real opportunity to test yourself. Go out of your way to get involved in pots with the Super Star as much as possible. Take shots at him, and not just wimpy all-in bets where he has to fold. Play small-ball with him if he's up for it. If you're seriously trying to be successful in tournaments, having a top player at your table is your opportunity to see what he's made of and to see what you're made of. You should especially do this if he's trying to use his Super Star status to bully the players at your table. You be the guy who pushes back.

One caution: If you push him out of a pot on a bluff, do not show the bluff. It is rarely wise to show a bluff, especially in the early stages of a tournament, and this would not be the time.

THE HANGERS-ON

A Hanger-On is a player who is a nobody but who tries to trade on the fact that he plays lots of tournaments and "knows" a lot of the Super Stars. The reason he knows them is because he pays big bucks to play in the same events as them. This is a very common player type in the pro-level events, and in the smaller events (up to a few hundred players) you will often have two or three of these players at every table. They all know each other. These guys have the money to play a lot of pro-level tournaments and they occasionally finish in the money just by the luck of the draw. If there is no Super Star at your table, they will drop names incessantly in an attempt to gain some amount of Super Star status for themselves.

Many of these players are also Show'n'Tellers as described in *PTF1*. They love using the lingo and talking about how many outs they had and how they missed their double belly-buster. Their actual skill levels vary, but most play a tight-aggressive style and are pretty readable. Their casual name-dropping ("I hear Gavin's coming in on Saturday for the main event") is a ploy to scare the players at the table who aren't as well-connected, but it always strikes me as a sign of low self-esteem, not exactly the kind of table image that's going to help them steal pots. They generally play too tight in the early stages then start taking shots too late when their chip stacks dwindle. They will occasionally mention their "M" and their "Q." Not a few are by-the-book Harringbots, though some do exhibit a bit more skill and early aggression.

THE GROUPIES

These are players who really shouldn't be playing tournaments at all; they should be watching tournaments on TV. They are out in force during the annual WSOP festivities at the Rio. Believe me, if there are 2,000 players in a tournament, at least 1,500 of them are the deadest of dead money. Despite the fact that there are more pros in the WSOP events than in any other tournaments, there are also more really bad players in these events than you could ever imagine would have the money to buy-in. The WSOP tournaments provide simultaneously the strongest and the weakest fields you will ever encounter in high-buy-in events.

You will see players leaving the table to go take a picture of Johnny Chan, or get an autograph from Phil Hellmuth. They continually talk about how they played at a table with Barry Greenstein, and did you see the way Carlos Mortensen has his chips stacked up? Hurry! Go look! He's right over there on that table in the corner!

The Groupies are not like the Hangers-On who are pretending to be big shots themselves. They are just hero-worshipping fools and they make no pretense of being great poker players, or even decent poker players. They're just thrilled at the prospect of playing in the same events as their television heroes and they consider it a win if they actually get assigned to the same table as a Super Star, where they can bask in the aura of his presence, have their picture taken with him when they bust out, and tell everybody back home about it.

It's almost impossible to figure out what a Groupie has when he's involved in a pot. For this reason, you have to play somewhat carefully around them. If you played a lot of cheap buy-in events when you first started playing tournaments, as I did, you should have a pretty good feel for how to deal with poker oafs. They generally don't play a large number of hands, so they're not that difficult to deal with. Be careful, give them a lot of latitude, and let them beat themselves. You'll usually see most of them disappear as the blinds escalate and the field thins.

Some Groupies do exhibit the traits of Pair Masters, Flush Masters and Ace Masters as discussed in *PTF1*.

LOOKING FOR TELLS ON YOUR OPPONENTS

The best physical reads you get on opponents will often be their immediate reactions upon seeing their hole cards for the first time, seeing the flop, turn or river, or seeing the action of another player in the pot. John Fox suggests that you should never look at your own cards until the action has gotten around to you, and Mike Caro echoes this advice. There are two reasons for this. First, it keeps other players from getting an early read on you; and second, you can take the time to watch your opponents who have to act before you.

I know T.J. Cloutier says he likes to look at his cards immediately, because he likes to know what he's going to do as soon as the action gets to him—and far be it from me to start an argument with T.J. about his style of play—but for those of us who do not have T.J.'s experience, I think the Fox/Caro advice is best.

One physical tell that I've found to have some value is when a player very quickly looks away from the flop, especially if the flop is at all scary, such as having a high pair or three to a suit. That quick look away, which almost seems to say, "I didn't see that," could be indicative of having flopped a monster. Be very careful if this player continues in the hand.

Also, if a player pushes out a big bet and then immediately "freezes," like he's not even there, I've found that this bet is very often a bluff. But be careful with this one—this is one Mike Caro wrote about, and some players may attempt to use this freeze as a reverse tell, trying to look weak and scared. Also, there are some players who always freeze when they bet, as this is their method of keeping a "poker face." It's easy to recognize these players because they are frozen in every pot they play. The freeze is not a tell with them. You'll have to read them using other methods.

Mostly, you want to pay particular attention to the details of your opponent's betting style. How long does he take to bet? Does he have a standard bet size based on the blind level or his position? Does he concern himself with the precise size of his bet, adjusting the number of chips he pushes into the pot before making his move? Does he tend to stare at his opponents, as if looking for reads on them, before making his move? Most players have a rhythm and style to their betting and you want to connect this overall style to the hands they show down when they do show down hands. You want to take notice when a player's typical style or betting pattern changes, then stop and consider what could be different about this hand. Alterations from the norm that just don't jibe with the hand in play, the prior action, or the cards on the board, are more often than not bluffs.

WHEN A PLAYER STARTS TO ACT OUT OF TURN

You should always take notice of any player who starts to act like he's getting ready to bet before the action has gotten to him. This is true both preflop and post-flop. In most cases, a player who does this does not have a strong hand but has a hand he'd like to see a flop with, or—if post-flop—a hand he'd like to see another card with, and he's hoping to slow down the action in front of him. If a player looks at his hole cards preflop and he finds A-A or K-K, he's not going to broadcast the fact that he's planning on entering the pot with a raise or reraise before the action gets to him. Quite the opposite. He's hoping an opponent will come in with a raise so that he can come over the top. A player who broadcasts his intention to bet before it is his turn usually has a small or medium pair, or perhaps suited connectors.

This is another one you have to be careful of if you are playing with inexperienced amateurs or players who are primarily Internet players. Some beginners—and even experienced players who are more accustomed to online play—seem to have no regard whatsoever for what they look like to their opponents. In an online game, they may already have hit their automatic raise button but their opponents don't see the raise until the action has gotten around to them, so they think nothing of "loading up" in live games while waiting for their turn to act. The better online players, however, quickly learn that they are always being observed, and they do not make amateur mistakes that broadcast their intentions.

If you're not paying attention to your opponents, you might even miss this tell, which is usually very reliable. This is straight out of John Fox and it is a perfect example of the Fox/Caro weak equals strong and strong equals weak principle. It can also occur after a player who is in the pot checks, then acts like he's loading up and getting ready to throw a lot of chips into the pot when it appears his opponent may be betting. Again, he's not betting out of turn, but he's providing signals of his intention to check-raise when the action is on another player.

If a player checks to you, then starts to reach for a stack of chips when you appear to be getting ready to bet, it is unlikely that he intends to check-raise. It's more likely that he has a draw and would like to get a free card. And if he does check-raise you, it's usually a semibluff with a draw, not a made hand. Depending on his chip position and yours—as well as his style of play and how he views you—you may be able to bet big enough to get him off his draw.

As with the preflop getting-ready-to-bet act, any player who truly wants to check-raise will not broadcast the move in advance of his opponent putting chips into the pot. The whole purpose of his reaching for chips is to stop you from betting.

You can often bluff a player out of the pot when he acts in this manner—though the bluff will have to be a bet that makes calling with a strong draw too expensive. Sometimes, depending on your chip position and his, your bet will have to be an all-in bet. If you do not bet here, this player may put you to a test with a big bet if he is an aggressive player and he reads your hesitancy to bet as weakness. He may even push all in on you if you make a modest stab at the pot. Make your decision based on the fact that you know your opponent is on a draw—not a made hand—and in most cases, if he pushes in, you should call if you have a legitimate hand yourself.

Some players will also make this out-of-turn reaching for chips move on the river, usually indicating that they have a legitimate hand and they're hoping for a showdown, but they don't like their hand enough to put a lot more chips into the pot. Again, they're just trying to stop the action. A big bet here will usually get rid of them, even when you have no hand yourself—provided, of course, that your big bet agrees with your normal betting pattern and the way the hand has been played. If you have a very strong hand, a value bet will in almost all cases be called.

One thing you must do is stop yourself from trying this out-of-turn reaching-for-chips move if that is something that you do to attempt to keep opponents from betting. It is an amateur move and skillful players will see through it. Some amateur players may fall for it, so for that reason you will sometimes see a pro make this move against an amateur. If a pro tries this move against you, it means he considers you an amateur who is likely to fall for it. Disappoint him once and he will not try it again.

One way you can get mileage out of a bluff with this read, whether you have position on your opponent or not, is to always take your time when it is your turn to act, even if you have no legitimate hand and your most likely action would be to fold preflop or to check and fold post-flop. Act like you're getting your chips ready to bet and give your opponent a chance to consider making this move, because if he makes it, you will know that you are up against an opponent who is most likely on a draw. He does not have a made hand and he is afraid that you do. This is the perfect set-up for a bluff.

WHAT IS A READ?
(THE AMAZING KARNAK)

Why is it that tight players think a stack size of 40 big blinds is sufficient for a poker player to be fully functional, while a loose player—whether he plays small ball or long ball—feels very constrained by a stack size that small? It's because loose players use their chips to communicate, while tight players fail to see chips as communication devices.

Consider the information bet. Loose players make bets for information all the time. They ask questions with their chips and they get answers. An information bet tells you instantly whether an opponent likes his hand, is unsure of his hand, or feels his hand is so bad it's not even worth it to him to answer your question. By using your chips you can learn if a player is on a draw or has a made hand, and how strong he believes his hand is. Loose players use chips to get reads on opponents, and the reads they get are often incredibly accurate.

Tight players, on the other hand, think that getting reads on opponents requires mind-reading. They devote themselves for years to attaining the skills of the Amazing Karnak, thinking that someday they'll just be able to feel that their opponent has pocket queens or whatever. They seem oblivious to the whole complex language of betting.

A loose player who watches a hand in progress can almost always tell you who has the best hand, and very often can tell you quite accurately the strength of each player's hand if not the exact cards each player has. The more you use chips to communicate, the more you will understand the language of chips. If you're struggling with trying to get reads on your opponents, stop trying to read your opponents' minds, and start using your chips to ask questions.

SUMMARY

A no-limit hold'em tournament is an exercise in practical psychology. Your overall success will depend greatly on your ability to figure out your opponents, while keeping them from getting any handle on you. If all you do is learn to pull off the five easy bluffs described in this chapter—and to recognize bad bluffs when you encounter them—you will be miles ahead of most of your opponents.

ATTITUDE: TWISTIN' THE KNIFE WITH A SMILE

TEST QUESTION

How do you play pocket tens when two overcards have come down on the flop and you're up against an aggressive opponent who called your preflop raise? And let's stipulate that you know that he knows that you would probably make a continuation bet even if you didn't like the flop; and not only does he have position on you, he outchips you by 2 to 1.

If you can't answer that question without thinking, you probably need an attitude adjustment. You need to reconsider how you think about your opponents, and do something about how your opponents think about you. So, in this chapter, we're going to answer this tough question once and for all.

ADDING ATTITUDE TO YOUR WEAPONS

As I discussed at length in *PTF1,* cards are secondary to things like position, chip stack, and table image in a no-limit tournament. This is true whether the tournament structure is fast, slow, or somewhere in between. In a no-limit tournament with a slow blind structure, you need to add *attitude* to that list of factors that are more important than cards. To put it bluntly, if you want to be successful, you've got to start by developing a bad attitude—a new way of thinking contemptuously about the opponents you face, as this feeling of contempt cannot help but affect the way your opponents see you.

If you are naturally misanthropic, you probably don't need this advice. Since you already hate everybody, you've got all the bad attitude you need. But most people aren't misanthropes, and many of the most successful poker players are truly nice people. Many have families that mean the world to them, are generous to a fault, would die for their friends, and are deeply concerned about social issues. But at the tables, they are vicious opponents, and the contempt they have cultivated for their opponents contributes greatly to their success.

DEVELOPING THE "RIGHT" ATTITUDE

I come from three decades of blackjack play, and I have to say that having a bad attitude toward your opponents is relatively easy for blackjack players. It's not difficult to envision your opponent—the casino—as a big money-grubbing institution that rakes in piles of loot by selling dreams to the disillusioned and lonely. For the most part, you don't even have to personalize the enemy. Your enemy is a heartless machine set up to siphon money from your hard-earned savings. And if you do personalize the enemy, you tend to think of some smarmy egomaniac billionaire like Donald Trump. Who would not feel good about beating Trump at his own game?

Many successful blackjack pros I know harbor a pretty strong antipathy for the casino industry as a whole. I won't use the word "hatred," because that might be a bit too personal, but the feeling is definitely bordering on hatred for some. Tommy Hyland, the most successful blackjack team organizer in the history of the game, was quoted in Richard Munchkin's *Gambling Wizards* (Huntington Press, 2002) as saying: "If someone told me I could make $10 million a year working for a casino, I wouldn't even consider it. It wouldn't take me five minutes to turn it down... I don't like casinos. I don't like how they ruin people's lives. I don't think the employment they provide is a worthwhile thing for those people. They're taking people that could be contributing to society and making them do a job that has no redeeming social value..."

When I first started playing poker tournaments in 2003, I had some trouble adjusting to the fact that my opponents were no longer the big casino money machines that were so easy to dislike and take money from. I couldn't envision the players who were sitting across the poker tables from me as nameless, faceless institutions. In some cases, my opponents were, like me, professional gamblers, but more often than not, they were working stiffs or retirees or students. I wanted to win, but I was sorry it had to be from them. How do you hate these people? How do you feel good taking their money? I may not be a saint, but neither am I a sociopath.

I even felt uncomfortable taking money from opponents who were playing poker professionally—who made their living gambling—because as a blackjack player I had always thought of fellow pro gamblers as "my people." We were all members of a small brotherhood with a common enemy—the casino. Now, my brotherhood was my enemy!

John Fox, in *How to Hustle Home Poker* (GBC, 1981), says that a top player will "...through a process of self-hypnosis almost begin to *hate* his opponents..." He says that without this killer instinct a player will never get to the top. One of the reasons this bad attitude toward opponents is necessary for success is that you really do make your money by taking advantage of players who are less skillful than you. A nice guy who sympathizes with the weaker opponents he faces will tend not to extract from them as much as he can. The top players, on the other hand, according to Fox, "…will beat the brains out of a weak or inexperienced player."

Stu Ungar, quoted in Nolan Dalla's and Peter Alson's *One of a Kind* (Atria Books, 2005) said pretty much the same thing: "All those guys I used to hang out with, we really loved each other. But when we got to gambling, we took off the gloves. It was like a fistfight. We hated each other, we all wanted to win so bad… See, when I play against a person, I have to find something I don't like about them."

Both Fox and Ungar acknowledge that this bad attitude is not natural, but something that must be cultivated—Fox by going through "a process of self-hypnosis," and Ungar by literally looking for something to dislike about each of his opponents. This was something I really had to work on and that I think most players would have to work on if they weren't just born nasty.

The fact is that if you cannot cultivate a low opinion of your opponents, you'll never be able to make the decisions you have to make in order to win. It's not just going easy on opponents that costs you money, it's that you'll be making actual bad decisions because you are looking at the game as an intellectual challenge or a social event, or anything but what it is, which is, as Ungar put it, "like a fistfight." Success at poker, more than anything else, comes from your ability to instill fear into your opponents, and scaring people is not something that most of us cultivate as a life skill. But if your table image does not scare your opponents, you're wasting your time and money being in the game at all. It's the feeling of contempt that gives you free reign to bully players and push them around and cause them to lose self-esteem at the table by folding to your aggression.

Forget about whether the guy you're up against is a retiree who should be putting his social security check to better use. That guy is trying to take your money. He thinks he's smarter than you, trickier than you, and he wants to prove it. He's challenging you. That college student across the table might be a nice kid who studies hard and cares about the environment and wants to make his mother proud. But at this table he's just a smug little twerp who thinks he's a hotshot. Like everyone else at the table, he's just after your money. That famous pro player who's been on TV and has an endorsement contract with one of the major online poker rooms, and who doesn't even have to pay his own way into tournaments, has to be put in his place. He's living on his reputation and he hasn't met the likes of you yet. You can't beat him if you can't make him fear you. All of these players, whether they know it or not, are involved in this fistfight, and in a tournament, every one of them has a single goal—to knock you out.

When I sit down at a tournament table, I spend the first ten minutes or so looking for things to dislike about each player at my table. This is not always easy. I don't tend to look at someone I don't know and automatically dislike him. There are also some players I've played with in numerous other tournaments whose presence at the table I enjoy because they tend to make humorous comments or may have complimented me on a well-played hand. So, I fake it. I look at each player in turn and mentally assign them all obnoxious qualities that have nothing to do with poker. If an older gentleman is dressed conservatively, I'll mentally harangue him for being a bigot and a tightwad and a self-deluded egomaniac for even fantasizing that he has any chance of beating me out of chips at this table.

In many cases, I know very little about the players I face, but it doesn't take much more than the idea that each player has the arrogance to challenge me to get me in the right frame of mind. I can find initial reasons to dislike opponents for nothing more than the clothes they wear or the way they comb their hair. As the game progresses and I start to get more of a handle on each player individually, I can expand my bad attitude to the personal quirks they have actually displayed. I can also start disliking players for winning pots, especially if they win a pot that I'm involved in.

I'm sure if a team of psychologists could listen in on the workings of my mind while I'm sitting at a tournament table, they'd have me locked up in no time. Sometimes, the disgusting images I mentally produce about my opponents are so grotesque I have to stop myself from laughing out loud. One time, after I had bluffed at a pot on the river—not a big pot and not that big of a bet—when my opponent started to reach for enough chips to reraise, I mentally said to him, "If you dare to put those chips in that pot, I'll take every chip in that pot and—." I'll spare you the details, but the graphic image of what I intended to do with those chips so startled me that I inadvertently snorted a laugh. It was loud enough in that moment of silence that the whole table turned to look at me, including my opponent, who froze with his raising chips in hand and his mouth agape. This unexpected reaction to a laugh I'd never intended to make caused me to laugh even harder, which I attempted to disguise as sniffling by rubbing my nose. My opponent set his chips back onto the felt in front of him and mucked his cards, saying, "Nice hand, sir."

I remembered that one of Mike Caro's surefire tells of a player with a monster hand was an uncontrollable fit of giggling—something I had personally never witnessed at a poker table! In this case, Mike would have been wrong. But I can say for certain that I have won at least one pot solely as a result of my attempting to maintain a bad attitude.

Cultivating a bad attitude toward your opponents does not necessarily mean you have to act mean and surly at the tables. *Au contraire!* Some of the seemingly nicest, friendliest players at the table are the ones you really have to watch out for. These are the guys who love sticking it to you with a smile. These are the players who love to twist the knife a little deeper by showing the bold bluff that pushed you out of the pot. If they get a real handle on an opponent, they can terrorize him by telling him what his cards are before he shows his hand. Nothing scares a player more than an opponent who seems to be reading him like a book. Letting an opponent know that you can read him is one of the nastiest things you can do with a smile. It's downright mean to do things like these to an opponent because you're not only showing him up, you're showing him up in front of the whole table. He won't like you for doing this, but that's just fine. You want him to fear and respect you, not like you.

DANIEL NEGREANU SHOWING DOWN A BLUFF

Probably the best example of a player showing a bluff in order to demoralize an opponent occurred in a televised $10,000 buy-in tournament that was held at the Plaza in Las Vegas in 2004. The field of 68 players—almost all well-known pros—had come down to heads-up play between Daniel Negreanu and Freddy Deeb. Suffice it to say that Negreanu pulled off a beautiful bluff on the river, getting Deeb to fold the best hand.

When this hand started, Deeb had a slight chip lead on Negreanu. When he folded the best hand on the river, Negreanu had better than a 2 to 1 chip lead on him. Deeb was under the impression that he had made a great laydown (he had A-K with a king on the board and in heads-up play, that is a huge hand), but Negreanu decided not to let Deeb bask in self-congratulations. With his typical grin, Negreanu said "Should I show the bluff? It's good for poker, right?" (or words to that effect), and he turned his cards face up to show Deeb he had absolutely nothing. Negreanu's glee at having outplayed Deeb—taking a big chip lead on him in the process—seemed to demoralize Deeb so much that Deeb never recovered from the hand. He looked crushed from that point on until Negreanu finished him off not too many hands later.

I remember thinking, as I watched this on TV, that Negreanu's behavior was one of the meanest, rottenest, most vicious acts of cruelty I had ever seen on a poker table. And Daniel Negreanu immediately became one of my heroes.

Having said all that, let me emphasize that the point is to develop an attitude that instills fear in your opponents, not to advocate showing bluffs or telling your opponents what their cards are—which would probably backfire for most players. Unless you have a massive chip lead on your table, I'm not much for showing bluffs, especially early in a tournament. You will often regret this move as it may make it more difficult for you to pull off bluffs from that point on.

BE CAREFUL ABOUT ANNOUNCING OPPONENTS' CARDS

As for telling an opponent what his cards are, remember that if you're wrong, you not only won't instill fear in your opponents, you'll make them think you're just a dork who thinks he's a hell of a lot smarter than he is. No beginner should ever try this move. If it's obvious to everyone at the table what your opponent has—let's say he reraises you all in when there are four spades on the board and no pair—telling him he has a flush isn't going to make anyone think you're a genius. On the other hand, if he does not have a flush, but he's making this move because he's certain you won't call unless you hold the ace of spades and he's willing to gamble that you don't have it. Then again, announcing his "obvious" hand just makes you look the fool, especially if he decides to show his bluff. I can't tell you how many times players have told me what they put me on when they fold, but I'd say they've been wrong about 95 percent of the time, and as for the 5 percent when they've been right, my cards were pretty obvious. I can tell you that their bad reads on my cards did nothing to make me fear them.

The late great Walter Clyde "Puggy" Pearson, as quoted in Jon Bradshaw's *Fast Company* (Harper & Row, 1975), said: "A gambler's ace is his ability to think clearly under stress. That's very important because, you see, fear is the basis of all mankind. In cards, you psych 'em out, you shark 'em, you put the fear of God in 'em."

Here's Stu Ungar's commentary on Puggy Pearson, again from Nolan Dalla's *One of a Kind*: "With Puggy, it's arrogance. He can really set you off. He really gets under your skin. He'll beat you out of a pot, then look at you like he's fucking Einstein… That smart-assed smile used to drive me crazy."

DEPERSONALIZING THE ENEMY

Many players think of tournament strategy as a mathematical puzzle that has to be figured out. And it is. But to figure out the puzzle, you're going in the wrong direction if you keep trying to figure out the mathematics of the cards. As I stated in the introduction to this book, you have to start focusing on the mathematics of fear. If you think you can get by just playing the hands you are dealt according to some list of hand values and pot odds and the likelihood of hands holding up, you're wrong. This is psychological warfare and you have to think of it as a real war. In World War II, the Americans weren't fighting the Japanese and the Germans; they were fighting the slant-eyes and the krauts. And you can be sure the enemies of America have despicable names for American soldiers that also depersonalize them. Military commanders know that it's hard to kill people you relate to as people. Depersonalizing the enemy may be what leads to war crimes, torture and other atrocities, but it's also what leads to victory.

Note that a bad attitude won't lead to victory all by itself. But you cannot make correct combat decisions in a war without either depersonalizing or to some extent hating your enemy, because ultimately you are always deciding how best to annihilate him.

Professional players will always play better than amateurs because pros are always playing for money that matters. Always. They play for survival and anyone who beats them threatens their survival. Since nobody likes anyone who threatens his survival, it's easy for pros to dislike their competition, whether the competition is amateurs or other pros. But even if you are not playing to survive, you are still playing for real money, and the more seriously you take it, the better your decisions will be. I'm not saying here that you should ever play on scared money. You must always play within the confines of your bankroll. But if your survival truly depends on your winning more than you lose, then poker ceases to be a game and starts to be a real fight; it ceases being gambling, and starts to be a war that must be won.

Any pro player who says he's just "having fun" or "playing for enjoyment" and "doesn't really care about the money" is lying through his teeth. Professional gamblers are viciously competitive and it's always about the money. Money is how we keep score and everyone wants to win. The money in any one tournament itself may not be all that important, but winning the money is extremely important. If you lose more than you win, you're not a professional player; you're just some guy with an expensive hobby.

Tournaments are fun only in the sense that fistfights can be fun. It's never fun to lose a tournament or a fistfight, so until it's over, how much fun it was has yet to be determined. There is a joy to being in the midst of it, an adrenalin rush that can't be compared to anything else. But if you take it seriously and have the proper bad attitude, busting out of a tournament is like getting the wind knocked out of you. You can't even think straight for a while.

But you don't dwell on it for long. You go over the mistakes you made—the pots where you could have won more or lost less had you played your hands differently—and you buy-in to the next event. That's poker.

TEST ANSWER

So, let's get back to the question we opened this chapter with: How do you play pocket tens when two overcards have come down on the flop and you're up against an aggressive opponent who called your preflop raise?

Answer: You play this hand like your opponent has just shot your dog, spit on your mother, and stolen the love of your life. Taking this attitude toward your opponent is the only way you can think clearly enough to make the right decision. You won't let him take an extra nickel from you if you know you can't push him out of the pot and he has you legitimately beat. But you'll gleefully rob him blind if the opportunity presents itself.

TABLE IMAGE: THE FEAR FACTOR

If I had to make a list of the books that I've found most helpful in understanding how to play no-limit hold'em tournaments in the more skill-based events with higher buy-ins and slower blind structures, the book I would put right at the top of that list is John Fox's 1977 classic, *Play Poker, Quit Work and Sleep till Noon.* Players who are familiar with this book may find that to be a strange choice because Fox never discusses tournament play. He only talks about cash games. Nor does he discuss the game of hold'em at all, not even limit hold'em. His entire book is focused on the game of five-card draw—a popular game in the mid-seventies.

What is unique about Fox's book, however, is that he wastes comparatively little ink on the math of the game, and concentrates instead on the psychology of poker—especially the subjects of bluffing, reading players, and table image. Most of his discussions on these topics would apply to any poker game, and even when he gives hand examples from five-card draw, it's easy to think about how the same principles would work in hold'em or other variations of poker.

TABLE IMAGE IN TOURNAMENTS VERSUS CASH GAMES

The psychological aspects of the game take on much greater importance in tournaments than in cash games because of what must be accomplished in order to win a poker tournament. What must be accomplished in a tournament, when you stop to think about it, seems damn near impossible. Let's say you are playing in the Venetian's regular Saturday noon tournament. The buy-in/entry fee is $540 and you start with $10,000 in chips. The blinds start at $25/$50, and each blind level lasts 40 minutes. Because of the deep starting stacks, this is a Rank 5 tournament with a utility factor of 69.70. The field size varies seasonally, but a typical crowd might be 100 players, and the tournament will last about fourteen hours.

What does it take to win this tournament? In fourteen hours, you must increase your starting chip stack from $10,000 in chips to $1 million in chips. That's what the winner will end up with when there are 100 starting players. Can any player expect to be dealt cards good enough in themselves to earn $990,000 in chips in fourteen hours when his starting stack is only $10,000? No. The math is against you. Fourteen hours of play is somewhere around 420 rounds. If you're a tight player who would normally play 8 to 10 percent of your hands, you'll play about 35 to 40 hands in the entire tournament. That's a hell of a lot of chips to earn based on your cards in so few hands. Even if you're a looser player who plays 20 percent of the hands dealt to you, that's only 84 hands in which you have to turn $10,000 in chips into $1,000,000.

So, tournaments are about forced play—about winning pots without great cards. They're about beating your opponents psychologically. And your ability to beat your opponents psychologically—to steal pots without great hands—will be a function of your table image, which means your ability to create fear in your opponents.

JOHN FOX'S THREE ADVANTAGEOUS IMAGE TYPES

John Fox considered three major image types to be advantageous at a poker table—the wild image, the fear-provoking image, and the defensive image. A *wild player* is very difficult to put on a hand. An *intimidating player* can push you out of pots. A *defensive player* will make it more difficult for you to steal. I want to clarify that Fox's definition of "defensive" does not mean "tight." According to Fox, "Most poker books… recommend you attain their version of a good defensive image by calling a few bets now and then even though you know you will very probably be beaten. Like purposely getting caught in almost hopeless 'advertising' purposes, this is not very thrifty… it is almost suicidally stupid… The correct methods for attaining a good defensive image are through the use of artifice, misdirection, and lying."

Fox considered the wild image to be the most valuable of the three because in the cash games, the wild player's primary need is to get players to loosen up. In tournaments, however, there is a completely different dynamic. Due to the overwhelming importance of chip utility for all players, and the restrictions on players' options for maintaining chip utility, the fear-provoking image is by far the most valuable table image.

A cash game player can change his seat at a table if a seat opens up and he dislikes his position in relation to other players, which is not an option in a tournament. A cash game player can also move to another table to escape particularly strong players at his table or to take advantage of particularly weak players at another table, which is not an option in a tournament. A cash game player can also purchase more chips at any time to keep his chip stack competitive with his opponents, and finally, he can cash out and go home, which is one of the cash game player's most powerful options. He can quit a game if he comes ahead and simply wants to leave with a profit, or if he has been on a bad streak and feels his table image has been damaged. Whatever the reason, he can cash out his chips and go home—again, not an option in a tournament.

If a poker game is a fistfight, to build on Stu Ungar's analogy, a tournament is a caged death match where all of the brawlers are locked inside, with the bloodied bodies of the defeated dragged out one by one, until only one fighter is left standing. And it's because the players are locked into the game until death, unable to purchase more chips, that utility rules and there is so much value in scaring your opponents into squelching their own utility.

THE INTIMIDATING IMAGE: HOW TO TIGHTEN UP YOUR OPPONENTS

The most intimidating thing you can do at a tournament table is show down winning hands in big pots. If you can take down a big pot by showing down a set of kings, that will do just fine. But if you can take down a big pot with bottom pair when you call a bet on the river—that's even scarier. If you showdown a weird small-ball straight that earns you a lot of chips, that works too. If you can showdown winning hands two or three times at the same table in the early portion of the tournament, your opponents will be trained to think that you only bet with winning hands, and your bets will get a lot of respect, meaning your opponents will be much more likely to fold even when they have legitimate hands that they would play against other opponents. You do not really need this "rush" to occur at the beginning of a tournament. You can exploit it at any point in a tournament.

The problem with this scenario is that you sometimes will not be dealt strong hands for long periods. Even playing small ball, your speculative hands will often go for long periods without amounting to much, and you'll have to steal to earn chips to stay alive. Picking up pots without showing down strong hands does not build the same kind of intimidating image that showing down strong hands does. And you can't afford to wait for strong hands to start projecting an intimidating image, so you'll have to resort to other methods.

In the discussion on attitude in the prior chapter, I mentioned how intimidating it is to tell a player what his hand is before he shows it down. This is one of the meanest things you can do to a player at a poker table because you're showing him up in front of the whole table. In effect, you're telling him he's so predictable (to you), he may as well be playing with his cards face up. Because it is such a mean thing to do, it is difficult to do unless you have cultivated that bad attitude that's necessary for winning. It's also important to remember that you want people fearing you, not hating you. If they really start to hate you, they may tend to play much better against you. So this kind of play usually has to be done with a good-natured smile and a sense of humor.

I also stressed how dangerous it is to attempt this, because if you are wrong in your assessment of your opponent's cards, you will be seen as a fool—and doubly the fool if you actually lose a big pot to the player whose cards you announced. Your ability to provoke fear at that table will be completely blown and it may be very difficult to get it back.

A safer way to project this ability to read an opponent is by calling his bluff on the river and beating him with any hand less than top pair. For this reason, there is a real value to calling suspected bluffs when your own hand is marginal at best. The more dangerous the board looks, and the weaker your own hand, the more intimidation value you will get from this type of play. The reason it is safer than telling a player what his hand is—when you could be wrong—is that you will not have to show your own hand when you make a bad call. Your opponent and others at your table will believe that you called the bet on the river with a stronger hand than you actually had.

Note that I am not recommending that you turn into a calling station and just start calling with a lot of your weak hands solely for the purpose of trying to catch a bluffer. I'm recommending this play only when you truly suspect that an opponent is bluffing and trying to buy the pot and when you believe your marginal hand is actually best. In addition to occasionally winning a pot for you, these types of loose calls have a huge educational value. In *PTF1*, I urged new players to make the dangerous calls when they felt they were being bluffed because it was the only way to learn. To quote from that book's Chapter 30, titled, "What I Can't Teach You":

> Most books on poker will tell you to start out by playing very conservatively, and only add higher risk plays to your repertoire slowly as you gain experience at the tables…
>
> My advice to you, if you have ambitions to compete with the best, is to start out playing a very high-risk game, and only slowly incorporate more conservative play as you gain the table experience to tell the difference between real danger and just fear. It's the hands where you're not sure what to do that are the best opportunities for learning. If you fold, you learn nothing. The next time that situation arises—and believe me, it will arise again and again—you will once again not know what to do. By contrast, when you don't fold, you

learn right then and there if folding would have been the better play...

If you aren't making a lot of mistakes when you start, you're not doing enough for your own education... In violation of the common poker wisdom, my advice to you is that the less experience and skill you have, the looser and more aggressively you should play in poker tournaments...

If you ask any tournament pro whether he'd rather be at a table with a tight "solid" player or a loose-aggressive player, he'll pick the tight player as an opponent any day of the week. Conservative players are easy to read and easy to beat. Loose-aggressive players, on the other hand—even if they're not very skillful—are difficult to read and always dangerous. Since, as a beginner, you can't be good, at least opt for being dangerous.

I've found this strategy to be every bit as valuable in tournaments with slow blind structures as I did in the fast tournaments I concentrated on in *PTF1*. When you show down your marginal but winning hand, you don't even have to answer when your opponent says, "How could you make that call?" It's worth it for your table image to lose two or three bad calls just to hit one of these seemingly miraculous how-could-you-make-that-call calls.

There are two ways you may be viewed by your opponents when you call down a bluff on a dangerous board with a hand like second or third pair and you win the pot. Some players will think you are a terrible player who simply cannot make a good laydown, and others will think you have superior skills at reading opponents. But regardless of which view they take of you, they will be very hesitant to try to bluff you out of a pot. In fact, if you are an otherwise aggressive player, you will much more often be viewed as a scary player who can read opponents than an unskilled player who cannot read the board.

This type of loose call has very much the same effect as telling a player what his cards are, because it appears that even though you may not have known his exact cards, you knew that he was bluffing and couldn't even beat your miserable second or third pair. That's very scary to your opponents. In a sense, this type of call could be viewed as a "defensive" play, but note that the ultimate effect is one of intimidation, and the long range effect of an intimidating image is to decrease the utility of your opponents. Since you will so often be involved in pots with less than premium hands, an intimidating image that restrains your opponents from trying to bluff you out of pots will keep your chip stack from diminishing unnecessarily.

Always entering pots with raises if first in—even small raises—is another way of creating an intimidating image. And reraising when you have position on an opponent is extremely intimidating due to most players' belief in the "gap principle," which was discussed in Chapter 5 on shifting gears. Generally, you'll know you are succeeding at projecting an intimidating image when you find it easy to steal pots with bets and raises. If you are continually called down, or reraised, you've got some work to do.

THE WILD IMAGE AND BLIND SNIPERS

A wild image is very easy to project if you actually play like a crazy man, but that's a dangerous way to play in a tournament, and it becomes more dangerous as the blinds go up and your opponents become more short-stacked. To pull off a wild image without actually playing stupidly, it takes a real ability to read your opponents. You must know whom to pick on, whom to avoid, when to push, and when to back off.

There are two basic mechanisms players use to project the wild image in a tournament: playing too many hands, and making oversized bets and raises whenever they are involved in a pot. This type of maniac play is most effective during the early "survival" stages of a tournament when the blinds are low and opponents' stacks are deep. The prime danger when playing like a maniac is that you will bump into a player with a hand so strong that he will not lay it down. Most tournaments start with ten-player tables, so there will be strong preflop hands appearing regularly among your opponents.

In any pot you get involved in, your oversized bets and raises will usually isolate a single opponent. If you find yourself facing two or more opponents who continue in the hand post-flop, you must be extremely careful. One of these players may be slowplaying a monster. Because of the image you've created, they know they can let you do the betting for them.

A skillful player will find it easier to lay down a hand like top pair/top kicker than a less skillful player. For this reason, you also have to be cognizant of your opponent's skill level. Also, the more dangerous the board looks to your opponent, the more likely he will be to lay down a strong—but far from the nuts—hand. The best players must be avoided because they will see your act for what it is and will sometimes call you down on the river with a marginal hand like second pair. The better the player, the sooner he will take a stand against you.

In my experience, true maniacs rarely last long in a tournament. Many times I have seen them build a big chip stack during the early "survival" stages, but more often than not they bust out quickly by running into players with real hands who get tired of their nonsense and start calling them down. I think a more controlled wild image is far preferable in a tournament, with more of an emphasis on being loose and unpredictable than actually wild, though most players think of loose, unpredictable players as wild.

ENHANCING YOUR WILD IMAGE

It will enhance your image as a wild player any time you show down an unusual hand that takes the pot, if the way you played the hand was somewhat crazy. For example, let's say that you come in with a raise from an early position with 5-3 suited, get two callers, and the flop comes down A-3-3.

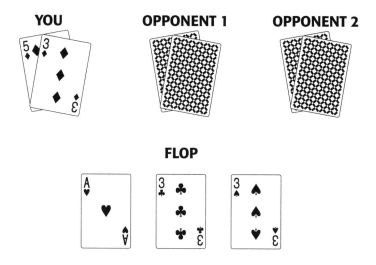

This would not be a bad time to come out betting after the flop, because there is a good chance that one of the players who called your preflop raise has an ace in hand, and it will also appear that you could simply be making a post-flop continuation bet. Unfortunately, both of your opponents fold.

In this situation, showing your 5-3 suited has definite value in strengthening your wild image. From this point on, any time you come in with a preflop raise, your opponents will realize that you could be raising with any two cards. The result of that is that although they may call you more preflop, they will be lost post-flop whenever the flop doesn't hit them hard and you come out betting. The fact that your post-flop bet with your 5-3 suited was made with an unusual, but still very strong, hand will tend to tighten up your opponents post-flop, and will earn you a lot of stolen pots with relatively low risk.

Again, note that this "wild" play is intimidating because unpredictability in itself is intimidating. Every player wants to believe he has a pretty good handle on what cards—or range of cards—his opponent may be playing, and you have just thrown a monkey wrench into the standard process of deduction. But it is not always wise to show a weird winning hand when you take a pot with no callers.

DON'T SHOW EVERY TRASH HAND

Let's say you are in the big blind this time with 5-3 suited, and two limpers enter, giving you a free flop. If the flop again comes down A-3-3, you may decide to come out betting, hoping that at least one of the limpers had an ace—even a bad ace—and will either reraise you or at least call. If your opponents fold, however, there is no value in showing your trip threes. Since you got the flop for free (as opposed to raising in the earlier example), most players would feel that you made a mistake to come out betting with such a strong hand (and maybe you did) and that you should have slowplayed your trips to try to build a bigger pot. The value of showing your 5-3 suited in the prior situation came from the unusual way you got into the pot—raising from an early position—not from the cards themselves.

If you manage to build a truly dominating chip stack, you might look at it as an opportunity to make some aggressive plays with any two cards, and build a wild image simply by playing too many hands. This is a great opportunity for testing your reads on your opponents, and if you get in trouble on a hand, you can back off and still have a lot of chips. A seemingly wild player with a big chip lead is truly a pain in the ass at a tournament table.

But even when you build a massive chip lead in the early portion of a tournament, your wild image must be toned down when the tournament hits that phase I call the "minefield," which is when the short stacks are plentiful and so desperate that their only play is all in before the flop. I will discuss this phase of the tournament at length in a later chapter.

DEFENSIVE PLAY: DON'T TREAD ON ME

You project a defensive table image by not allowing your opponents to push you out of pots too easily. For example, it is generally a good idea to regularly defend your blind against a late position raiser. You must make your opponent understand that your blind is not just his for the taking. It's true that post-flop you will be out of position, but if you always fold unless you have a truly strong preflop hand, you will not only find that your blind will just about always be stolen—usually by the same one or two players seated to your right—but other aggressive players will start to take shots at you post-flop whenever you are involved in a pot, knowing that you are the type of fearful player who prefers to avoid confrontation.

DEFENDING THE BLIND

In defending your blind, it is most often advisable to do so with a resteal move either before or after the flop. That means if you call your opponent's bet preflop, you come out betting after the flop whether it hits you or not. Or, if you reraise preflop, and your opponent calls, bet on the flop whether it hits you or not. Be aware that if you reraise preflop and get called, the pot will be bigger post-flop and will require a much bigger bet from you for an effective resteal. The ultimate resteal—assuming you have the chips to afford it—would be to call the raise from the blind preflop, check on the flop, then check-raise your opponent when he bets.

Note that blind defense is not passive. It is not based on calling, but on very aggressive betting and raising. The success rate with these moves is quite high, as you make them against known thieves who most often do not have premium hands and who are taken by surprise when you seem to come to life with a monster. The utility value of a staunch blind defense is also very high because it stops the thief from taking as many shots at you, often while earning you more chips from the thief than you relinquished to him in multiple thefts.

INFORMATION BET

Another of the most valuable plays you can make as a defensive player is the information bet. Let's say a player in early position limps in, and on the button you find pocket sevens. You come in with a raise, and he calls. The flop comes down with a queen and two rags. He comes out with a pot-sized bet. What do you do?

The wimp would fold in this situation. The moron would call. That queen is a scare card, but unless you have some dynamite read on your opponent and you know he either just paired a queen in hand, flopped a set, or has a pocket pair higher than queens, your best play here would be to raise. Why? For information. Does your opponent really have a queen in his hand? And if so, is his kicker strong enough to stay in the pot against a reraise?

When you think about it, since he limped preflop, it's unlikely he limped with A-Q or Q-Q. And since he didn't reraise you preflop, it's unlikely he has A-A or K-K. If he has a queen in his hand, it is probably Q-J or Q-10 suited, and even if he has your sevens beat with something like 8-8 or 9-9, your reraise will most likely push him out of the pot.

Why is the information bet a "defensive" move? Because you have a made hand that may be the best hand, you have chips already invested in this pot, and your opponent may just be taking a shot. So, you are defending your investment in this hand, not just mucking your cards to avoid confrontation.

CONTINUATION BET

The continuation bet is another type of information bet with which you are defending your preflop investment. Let's say you raised preflop with J-9 suited and you got two callers. The flop comes down K-7-4 rainbow, not hitting your hand at all.

If you are first to act after the flop, you should bet. Keep the lead. It is quite likely that neither of your opponents has a king and your post-flop bet here will take the pot, even against an opponent who has your hand beat. One of your preflop callers may have A-Q; another may have 6-6 or some other underpair. If you check here, then one of these players who has position on you may believe he has the best hand (which he may) and you will have to fold to his bet.

Again, with your continuation bet, you are defending your preflop investment in this pot. This may not be the way you normally think of "defense," but remember the old adage that the best defense is a good offense. Defensive play in tournaments is often aggressive.

AGAINST WEAK PLAYERS

In *PTF1*, I explained that the most basic post-flop position strategy—regardless of your cards—is: He checks. You bet. For example, if you are up against an opponent who raised preflop, then checks to you when the flop comes down, bet! Defend your preflop investment. It doesn't matter what your cards are. If you called the preflop raise with 7-6 suited, and the flop comes down A-K-9, with none of the flop cards in your suit, and your opponent checks when that flop comes down, you bet. Just do it.

Players who do not defend their blinds, who do not defend their made hands, who do not defend their preflop investments, and who do not defend their position, are weak players. Any time you identify a player as non-defensive, you should start pushing that player around. You can take many pots from this player when he has the best hand because he always fears an opponent has a better hand.

Don't think that because an opponent has checked to you post-flop that he must be slowplaying a monster. Usually, he's just a wimp. And you have to take it a step further and identify which players are making defensive moves. You have to start raising them when they make continuation bets or try to resteal from the blinds to find out if they really do have a strong hand or if they're just hoping you don't.

Defensive play is much more important in tournaments with deep stacks and slow blind structures than it is in fast events. Fast tournaments are psychological battles just like slow tournaments, but you win fast tournaments much more with raw aggression than you do with advanced techniques. In fast tournaments, for example, information bets are often too expensive. Even in tournaments with slow structures, these types of options disappear as you lose utility due to the blind costs, your diminishing chip stack, or just a deep-stacked aggressive player or two at your table.

PART III: STRATEGIES

THE FIVE PHASES OF A POKER TOURNAMENT

THE FIVE PHASES

There are five distinct phases to a pro-level no-limit hold'em tournament, and each phase requires a different strategic approach. The changing structure of the event as the blinds and antes escalate and the field diminishes puts the remaining players through predictable intellectual and emotional changes due to their ever-increasing time investment and their perceived likelihood of attaining the goal they are all chasing. The next five chapters of this book are devoted to the subject of how to play in each of the five separate phases. Here is an overview of what is to come.

PHASE 1: STACK BUILDING

Many books on tournament play describe this early phase of a tournament as the "survival" period. I call the first stage "Stack Building" because this is the time for the loose-aggressive players to start transferring chips from the chip stacks of the "survivalists" into their own stacks. In *Making the Final Table*, Erick Lindgren calls this early phase "Chip Accumulation."

Lindgren is in a minority with his perspective, which is the one I share. The main reason you want to build as formidable a chip stack as possible during phase one is because without a decent-sized chip stack, you will be in bad shape when you enter the second phase of the tournament, namely...

PHASE TWO: THE MINEFIELD

It is during this phase of the tournament when the field will be drastically thinned out. I call it the "minefield" because it is a very dangerous time to get involved in pots, yet you must get involved or you will be left behind. It is during this phase that a lot of truly dominating chip stacks will be built. This is when the short-stacked players start pushing all in, sometimes on stone cold bluffs, and the desperate players start calling all ins, often with marginal hands, in a do-or-die attempt to double up. This is a great time to have a dominating chip stack, because you can be selective about your victims and stay out of the way of real danger. It's a terrible time to have an "average" chip stack, especially if you go card dead during this crucial phase. The minefield lasts a hellaciously long time in a deep-stack event, but it is not as wild and dangerous as in a short-stack event. By the time you come out of it—if you survive it—you can almost taste the money. It will take all of the skill you possess to get through the minefield and make it to...

PHASE THREE: THE BUBBLE

The bubble phase is when you finally get to start seriously accumulating chips again and it occurs when the money is just around the corner. Technically, the bubble specifically refers to the unfortunate player who busts out just one shy of the money—for example, in a tournament that pays 36 spots, we would say the player who busts out in 37th place went out on the bubble. The bubble *phase* is when everyone starts worrying about going out on the bubble, and depending on the size of the event, there may be dozens (or even hundreds) of players who will finish out of the money during the bubble phase.

For example, in the 2006 WSOP Main Event, there were 8,773 players and 876 finished in the money. The bubble phase in that event—when players really started to sweat getting knocked out just shy of the money—probably began when there were still over a thousand players remaining. In many ways, phase three is like a reversion to phase one, because the players who have made it through the minefield become so survival-oriented.

Phase three is another great time for chip building. The desperately short stacks will still be in minefield mode, so you've got to watch out for them, but it's pretty easy to pick up pots during the bubble phase if you've got enough chips to scare the medium stacks. They're all terrified they won't make it to…

PHASE FOUR: THE MONEY

In a big event, the players who are still remaining for this phase will number approximately 10 percent of the starting field. The optimal strategy at this time is a combination of the phase two (minefield) and phase three (bubble) strategies. This is because the dangerous minefield aspect has returned—short stacks who were sitting tight just trying to get into the money suddenly start pushing in and dropping like flies once the money is hit—while a lot of medium stacks stay in survival mode trying to make it to the next pay level. It is crucial for you to identify which players at your table are in which mode so that you can play the strategy most likely to succeed with whatever opponent you face.

And it's not just a matter of the chip stacks. The more skillful players with medium stacks will be very dangerous because they are not just trying to get to the next pay level; they're going for the big money and they will take whatever shots and whatever risks are necessary to get there. If you have a medium stack during this phase, you should do the same. Screw the next pay level. Go for the big bucks, because success in phase four leads directly to…

PHASE FIVE: THE FINAL TABLE

To amateurs, making the final table is a successful finish in itself. But many of the top players will tell you that anything short of first place in a tournament is a disappointment and a loss, not a win. Once you start finishing in the money and making final tables with some regularity, you will begin to feel this way. There is such a discrepancy between the first place prize money and every other prize awarded that it actually hurts to get this far in a tournament and not win. In a small event, say 100 players in the whole field, first place will generally pay about thirty times the cost of your buy-in, while ninth place is probably not going to do much more than pay back your buy-in money. And that is a disappointment— all that work to break even.

There are many different tournament payout schedules, though most pay about 10 percent of the starting field. With 200 players, ninth place will generally triple your buy-in, which would be a 200 percent win. With 600 players, you'll get about eight times your buy-in back for a 700 percent win. But you're never shooting for ninth place.

How you play the final table will depend on the structure of the event and your utility when you get there. How are you situated in chips compared to your opponents? How big are the blinds and antes? In a deep-stack event, the final table will often allow small-ball play, though there will usually be a number of players too short-stacked to engage in it. And the optimal strategies change as players are eliminated.

Every tournament has a stack-building phase, a minefield phase, a bubble phase, a money phase, and a final table, though tournaments with different utility factors will play differently in each phase.

In any case, it's stack-building time. The tournament director has taken the mike, and after advising us all to turn off our cell phones and refrain from dropping the f-bomb, he calls out that phrase that's so exciting to tournament players everywhere: "Dealers! Let's get those cards in the air!"

PHASE ONE: STACK BUILDING— TAKE THEIR CHIPS WHILE THEY'RE NAPPING

This chapter will concentrate on the first phase of a pro-level tournament, stack building, which I often think of as "lunch," since it's an excellent time to start building a chip stack by eating up the chips of all the players who are afraid of getting involved with anything other than premium starting cards. The length of the stack-building phase is dependent on the tournament structure. The lower the Utility Rank, the faster you've got to build. In a deep-stack event, this phase fades out slowly, but in a short-stack event, it ends with a lot more of a jolt. There is a foolproof signal for knowing precisely when phase one has absolutely positively come to an end and phase two has begun, but I'll discuss that signal in detail in the next chapter.

If you have been getting nowhere in poker tournaments by following the traditional advice in many books, the first thing you must unlearn is the pervasive idea that the early stages of a tournament are about "survival." Tournament book after tournament book, author after author, expert after expert, has stated that at the beginning of a tournament, when your chip stack is big and the blind costs are relatively small, you should be getting involved only with premium hands, taking few risks, and concentrating on just staying alive.

THE SURVIVAL FALLACY

There is a common saying among the survivalists: "You can't win a tournament in the first hour (or the first hand, or the first blind level, or whatever), but you can definitely lose it." By this, they mean that if you take early risks you can bust out and be gone; while even if you do double up early, you still haven't won anything. There's a long way to go, so why take early big risks? This is one of those platitudes that sounds so patently true that everyone automatically latches onto it. However, I could just as easily point out that you can't win a 15-hour tournament in the tenth hour, but you could lose it. Nor can you win that tournament in the fourteenth hour, but you could lose it. Technically, the only time you can win that tournament is on the very last hand at the final table when you're all in with a chip lead on your opponents.

But does that mean you should wait for that situation to take any risks?

In my opinion, most players do lose tournaments in the early stages by failing to take the risks they should be taking. They just don't know they've already lost it because they're still sitting there. In fact, let me go out on a limb and state that this is why most players are tournament failures. They sit there waiting for hands and powerful opportunities—which more often than not do not materialize—and three or four blind levels into the tournament they find themselves with severely limited chip utility, by which point a few aggressive players at their table have already built chip stacks big enough to push the wimps around and kill their dreams. Early aggression is much less risky, in fact, than aggression later in a tournament, because so many players are thinking survival in the early stages of a tournament, while in the later stages of a tournament, the majority of players are feeling desperate. Right from the start of every tournament, the top players are thinking attack and confrontation.

In the past few years, a number of books have been published that refute the tight survival-oriented strategies that have dominated tournament thinking for decades. Erick Lindgren's *Making the Final Table* (2005), my own *Poker Tournament Formula* (2006), Daniel Negreanu's *Hold'em Wisdom for All Players* (2007), and *Kill Everyone* (2007) by Lee Nelson, Tysen Streib and Kim Lee, all assert that loose strategies are superior to the traditional tight strategies that most players have been following for years in no-limit hold'em tournaments. I'm going to begin this discussion of the first phase of tournaments by describing an actual hand I witnessed.

MARK SEIF GONE WILD

This hand occurred in a $1,500 event during the 2008 Wynn Classic. This tournament provided $5,000 in starting chips with hour-long blind levels. The starting blinds were $25/$50. The utility factor was 37.50 (Rank 2). With 100 big blinds in starting chips, all players started out with full utility, although that utility goes away pretty quickly in a Rank 2 tournament. By the second blind level, any player who had not increased his starting chips by 20 percent would not even be competitive.

In the first blind level, Mark Seif came in with a standard raise from under the gun. Though I had never played at a table with him before, I immediately put him on a big hand based purely on commentary I had heard him make on televised poker shows. I assumed him to be a pretty tight and predictable player and an under-the-gun raise from him had to mean a big hand. He was quickly reraised, however, by the player to his left—who was also in early position—so I put this player on having some kind of a monster hand as well, assuming this player's opinion of Mark Seif was anything like mine.

In middle position, I looked down to find 8-6 offsuit, a small-ball hand I would generally love to play in a raised pot, but not this one. I had sufficient utility to make this call, and I had position on both players, but if I threw in a call to the reraise, it would not be a small pot any more. In addition, I was concerned that Seif might go over the top of the raiser if he had A-A or K-K. I mucked my 8-6 offsuit.

All the other players folded and when the betting got back around to Mark Seif, he called the raise. Because he just called instead of reraising, I assumed he did not have aces, and probably not kings, because with either of those hands I suspect he would have reraised or even pushed all in.

The flop came down 4-5-7 with two spades. Needless to say, I was sick at having mucked my 8-6 offsuit, as I would have flopped the nuts. I was even sicker when Seif came out with a nearly pot-sized bet, his opponent pushed all in, and Seif, remarking something like, "I can't be too far behind," called the all in! This is the kind of hand a small-ball player dreams of!

SEIF'S "BIG" HAND

When Seif and his opponent turned over their cards, however, I was shocked to see that Mark Seif had a 6♠ 2♠, and had flopped an open-end straight draw and a baby flush draw. His opponent had pocket queens, which didn't surprise me.

In fact, if I had stayed in the hand, Seif would have been a lot further behind in the hand than he'd thought, as his open-end straight draw would have been pretty much dead. I already would have had the low end beat, and he had only three outs for high end. Plus, if he hit the high end, he would simply split the pot with me. Also, the 8 in my hand had been the 8♠, so even his flush draw had one less out than he supposed.

As it turned out, however, a spade came down on the turn, and Seif doubled up. Had I been in that pot, he would have tripled up and I would have been gone. I really had to go over this hand later to figure out if I'd played it wrong from the small ball perspective. Just because I would have busted out on it if I'd played it does not mean I played correctly. The fact that I would have flopped the nuts with a very strong advantage on two players, making me the favorite to triple up, was thought provoking. I knew the reasoning behind my decision, however, and ultimately I decided that I would play my hand the same way again, and just muck my 8-6 offsuit preflop. With a raise and a reraise in front of me, and my feeling that the initial raiser might go over the top if I just called, I think I made the right decision getting out of the way. (Of course, if it was Mark Seif who made that under-the-gun raise next time, I might very well elect to call!)

This hand, however, really altered my opinion of Mark Seif. My assumption that he would be a tight and predictable player did an immediate about-face. Raising from under the gun with 6-2 suited is not a play that is in many players' repertoires. This is a small-ball play that even a lot of loose smallballers might pass on. Then, his call of a reraise preflop with that hand, knowing that he'd be out of position post-flop—whew! That's loose!

His betting out on the flop definitely made sense. Any player with that strong of a draw would come out with a bet here, and if his opponent had reraised preflop with a hand like A-K, Seif could expect to take down this pot without complications. But I also suspect Seif would have come out betting here even if the flop had not hit him so hard. Most smallballers would do a continuation bet on a flop like this, assuming it could not have hit their opponent, and Seif may also have attempted to trade on his reputation as a pro. But when his opponent went over the top of him all in, despite the fact that Seif had to know he was behind in the hand at that moment, he was definitely willing to put his tournament life on the line with his draws, even though it was the first blind level, and he didn't have that much invested in the pot. If he'd folded, he would still have had about $4,000 in chips—about 80 times the big blind—so he didn't need that double up to remain a viable player, at least not from the traditional perspective.

Many players—even with that strong draw—would simply get away from their hand and wait for a better opportunity to make chips. Drawing hands—no matter how strong—often spell death in a tournament. If his opponent had pushed in on A♠ K♠, definitely a possibility, more than half of Seif's outs would have been gone and he would have been drawing only to his straight. In calling the all-in bet, he was assuming his baby flush—if he made it—would hold up.

ANALYZING THE HAND

There are a lot of different ways to look at this hand from the perspectives of both small-ball and long-ball strategies, as well as from the perspectives of utility and table image. Raising from under the gun with 6-2 suited is a classic small-ball play, as it disguises the hand very effectively when you can afford the chips. It was also classic small ball to call the preflop reraise from out of position. With a hand like 6-2 suited and a deep stack, position is not a big factor. Either the flop hits you hard or you go away, and calling that reraise just works to enhance the disguising of the hand. Also, I should point out that the preflop reraise was not a big reraise. The player with Q-Q reraised the minimum, which gave Seif slightly better than 3 to 1 odds to call with his trash hand. Now some smallballers might be tempted to fold a hand like 6-2 suited against a reraise, but the better players would not.

If you're going to play small ball, you can't be timid about it when you've got the chips to play. When you're getting 3 to 1 or better preflop with a hand that is totally disguised from your opponent, this is exactly the type of situation you're looking for when you play small ball.

But once Seif called that preflop reraise and then bet out on the flop on his drawing hand, the pot was no longer small. In a tournament where players start out with $5,000 in chips, a pot with somewhere in the neighborhood of $1,500 in chips in it is a big pot, especially considering that the turn and river cards have yet to be dealt. (I don't recall the exact betting action in this hand. Seif's preflop raise was something like $200 [4 x BB] and the reraiser made it $400. When he called, that would have put $875 in the pot with the blinds. Seif's post-flop bet was something like $700, which would make the pot $1,575 when the action got to the player with Q-Q. Some of these bets may be slightly different, but you get the picture.)

I find no fault with the player who pushed all in on his Q-Q. With that many chips in the pot, he didn't have the utility to make an information raise, and he had no way of knowing if Seif's post-flop bet was just a continuation bet, a semibluff, or a bet on a pocket overpair like 9-9 or 8-8. He probably did feel he had the best hand, as Seif would likely have gone over the top of his preflop reraise if he had K-K or A-A. He probably thought he had nothing to fear but a set. Seif's disguise had worked perfectly in this situation.

And Seif's call of his opponent's all in on a draw was definitely the correct play in this Rank 2 tournament. This is a tournament where utility disappears quickly and any players who know what they're doing will be going for an early double up. In all tournaments ranked 1, 2, or 3, high-risk early play is correct if you have the skill to use the big chip stack you're gambling to acquire. By calling this all in with his draw, Mark Seif showed that he was willing to go all in on what was essentially a coin-flip in the first blind level of this tournament. With an open-end straight draw and a flush draw, Seif actually had the advantage since he had so many outs against an overpair. This was a coin-flip where he was the 55/45 favorite, despite being behind on the flop. But it was not his small edge that made his call correct. What made the call correct was what a win could do for his utility.

Whether or not Seif's call would be the correct play at the same point in a deep-stack tournament where players start with $20,000 in chips, assuming he had only $1,000 invested, might be open to debate, especially considering that his flush draw was to such a baby flush. I do believe Seif had his opponent read as being on a big pocket pair. That was definitely my read on him with his preflop reraise and over-the-top all in post-flop. But in a deep-stack tournament, we don't know how the hand would have played out. I think it's unlikely that either player would have gone broke on it, not with one player having just an overpair, and the other a strong (but still a coin-flip) draw. Tournament structure always has a huge effect on players' strategic decisions.

One move in this hand that is interesting to consider was the preflop min-reraise by the player with Q-Q. A min-reraise will almost never get a preflop raiser off of his hand (including a smallballer with 6-2 suited!), and in a short-stack (Rank 2) tournament like this one, a small raise like that will really just build the pot. That's dangerous because the play will quickly revert from small ball to long ball from that point forward, which is exactly what happened. But that min-reraise can also be seen as an information raise. The player was asking Seif if he had A-A or K-K, and Seif's call answered no. That's not a bad question to ask an under-the-gun raiser when you've got Q-Q. It was also enough of a reraise to get rid of any bad aces or kings behind him—or potential smallballers like me with 8-6 offsuit. In a tournament where you're looking for an early double up because utility dissipates so quickly, a min-raise with

Q-Q can also be viewed as a worthwhile high-risk gamble that isolated the under-the-gun raiser, whom the reraiser probably put on a medium pair or a high-card hand like A-K or A-Q.

Unfortunately for the player with Q-Q, the flop looked safe for his hand except for the flush draw. His all-in bet would have made drawing to the flush alone too expensive in terms of pot odds, unless Seif had the A♠ K♠. It was his misfortune that Seif had not only the flush draw but an open-end straight draw as well. Also, this was not a deep-stack tournament where a pro might forego a race in the early stages. If both players had started the hand with $20,000 in chips, the player with Q-Q would very likely have gotten Seif to fold preflop with a much bigger reraise. If Seif had remained in the hand against a bigger reraise, then came out betting on that flop, the player with Q-Q probably could have gotten Seif to fold his strong draw with a bet quite a bit less than all in. And if Seif went over the top, trading on his Super Star status, Q-Q may very well have folded, fearing he might be up against A-A, K-K, or a set. But this was a short-stack tournament, and sometimes the cards just screw you.

RISK AND REWARD IN PRO-LEVEL SHORT-STACK TOURNAMENTS

As you may have noticed from the discussion above, in the shorter-stacked pro-level tournaments, which I would define as Rank 1, 2, or 3 tournaments, small-ball play often becomes long ball simply because players do not have sufficient chips to engage in a lot of post-flop play. The hand described above, which took place in a Rank 2 tournament, occurred during the first blind level ($25/$50) when both players had somewhere around their $5,000-chip starting stacks (100 big blinds). Because the pot had been raised and reraised preflop, however, a simple information bet had already become too expensive after a single post-flop bet by a player (Mark Seif) who could have been just making a continuation bet with a hand like A-K.

SMALL-BALL PLAY OFTEN BECOMES LONG BALL SIMPLY BECAUSE PLAYERS DO NOT HAVE SUFFICIENT CHIPS TO ENGAGE IN A LOT OF POST-FLOP PLAY.

Any slow-structured tournament in which players start out with chip stacks equivalent to 100 big blinds or less is a "short-stack" tournament. (You might recall from Chapter Two that even the $3,000 WSOP event that started with 120 big blinds is a Rank 3 tournament, still a short-stack event from the utility perspective.) This is especially true if the big blind doubles at the second blind level, then doubles again at the third blind level, which is very common in slow-structured events in which the most common first three blind levels are $25/$50, $50/$100, then $100/$200. After this point in most tournaments, the blind raises become gentler. A deep-stack tournament, by contrast, is one in which you can get through the first couple hours of play without any pressing need to double up. Deep-stack tournaments and short-stack tournaments are entirely different types of events, even when the blind structures are otherwise identical.

Again, players who play a more conservative strategy, waiting for premium cards to enter pots and engaging in very little post-flop play unless they hit strong hands, do not need a chip stack of much more than 40 to 50 big blinds to be "fully functional" for their style, because this tight playing style, in itself, is less than fully functional. Such players would likely muck a hand like 6-2 suited, even if they were on the button and only limpers were in the pot, because they would consider it such a trash hand that it would be a waste of chips to play. If you flop the baby flush, you'll get killed by the bigger flush—this is the way tight players think. Avoid trouble.

Many won't even play hands like K-J or Q-10, because if they hit one of their cards, they could be out-kicked.

The top tournament players, whether they play small ball or long ball, don't think this way, especially in a short-stack tournament. If you're in a short-stack tournament and you hit the bottom end of a straight or a baby flush, you're probably going all the way with your hand. If another player hits the top end of the straight or a bigger flush, so be it. In a deep stack tournament, you might be able to get away from a strong but dangerous hand, but not early on in a Rank 1 to 3 event. You just don't have the time or the chips to wait for better opportunities.

I once called a raise in a multiway pot with 3-2 suited from the button. The flop came down 4-3-2 rainbow. A player in early position came in with a pot-sized bet, and he was raised by a player in middle position. I pushed all in. What the hell. Bottom two pair. I figured they both had overpairs. Unfortunately, the player who raised had A-5 suited and had flopped a straight. That hand busted me out. Did I play it wrong? Not from my perspective. It was a short-stack event. The hand was a cooler, that's all.

The whole reason you call a raise with a hand like 3-2 suited is because you're hoping to see a flop like that. If you're not going to play your hand after you get that flop, you shouldn't be playing small ball in the first place. No one at that stage in the tournament had the chips to play much poker, including me, and I regarded that flop as my best shot at getting an early chip lead on the table. The potential increase in utility made it worth the risk of busting out.

No matter what style of play you engage in, you're going to see heartbreak hands. Your set will be beaten by a bigger set. Your nut full house will run into quads. Limiting yourself to playing "premium" cards doesn't diminish the percentage of heartbreakers you'll bump into.

In phase one of a deep-stack tournament, it's often a mistake to overplay top pair or an overpair to the board. Players do flop two pair and sets and straights and nut flush draws, hands they just won't lay down very easily. But in a Rank 1 to 3 event, you often have to go with your top pair or overpair in the early stages unless the board presents clear dangers and/or you've already built a comfortable chip lead. Sure, you should play your reads on your opponent, and get out of the way if you feel you're beat. But when you don't have a read, you've got to play the structure, and a short-stack tournament calls for aggressive play when you feel your hand is best.

So, in considering phase one strategy, we're going to pay special attention to tournament structure. I'll first discuss phase one strategy in a short-stack (Rank 1 to 3) event. Then I'll discuss phase one strategy in a deep-stack (Rank 4 to 6) event. And bear in mind that a Rank 1 tournament is often quite a bit faster than a Rank 3 tournament, even though I'm grouping them together as "short-stack" events. Likewise, a Rank 6 tournament is much slower than a Rank 4 tournament, though I'm calling both "deep-stack" events. The tournament structure, however, is really secondary to your personal utility and the character of your table. I'll assume you can mentally adjust my commentary for the precise tournament structure you're playing. Remember that your primary consideration should be getting and maintaining full utility—dominant utility if you can get it—or as close to full utility as you can get.

SHORT-STACK PHASE ONE STRATEGY: 7 GUIDELINES

Here are some general strategy guidelines for phase one of a Rank 1 to 3 tournament. And remember these are guidelines only. Feel free to adjust your strategy for the specific opponents you face.

GUIDELINE 1

Assuming you have at least a competitive stack, take advantage of a table with a lot of preflop limping by playing a lot of hands, especially in late position. But don't always limp yourself. Come in with a raise now and then on any speculative hand from middle position, and play it like you mean it. If the table is more aggressive, then play all of your small and medium pairs in pots where the preflop raise is not more than 3 x BB, plus cards that are both suited and connected, including most of your suited gapped connectors (one gap). Stay away from high-low hands unless they are suited, and don't play unsuited gapped connectors below 7-5 offsuit except in unraised pots.

GUIDELINE 2

If your stack is less than competitive, then you must curtail most of your small-ball play, especially in raised pots. You must earn some chips before the next blind level by hook or by crook. And if you're card-dead, it will have to be by crook. Be alert for any opportunity to make chips. You have to pick out the weak players and target them, and remember your utility odds—it's worth taking a big risk to build up your utility to a more comfortable level. Don't sit there waiting for good cards.

GUIDELINE 3

On any speculative hand, get away from your hand fast post-flop (especially in multiway pots) if you don't:

- hit a very strong hand on the flop
- hit a monster draw on the flop, or
- feel that your opponent is weak and cannot continue in the hand if you make him pay.

If your stack is less than competitive and any of the above are true, bet or raise big—and make it all in if a big raise would either pot-commit you or leave you in a state of low utility if you lose the hand.

GUIDELINE 4

You absolutely cannot blow off chips on drawing hands when your utility is not, at the very least, on the high side of competitive. Drawing hands are murder. Calling with straight and flush draws is one of the fastest ways possible to short-stack yourself. If your draw is that strong, and you are considering calling a bet because the utility odds are great, then push all in and be done with it. Otherwise, lay it down. One of the problems with spec hands is that you often will have drawing hands after the flop. That's great when you have a mountain of chips. But when you can *feel* those calling chips leaving your stack for that pot you crave, you're misplaying your hand. It should never be painful to throw chips into the pot on a call. Either push in all your chips or muck your cards.

With full utility, you might consider a call on a strong draw if the call will not make too big of a dent in your stack, and you don't think you can take the pot right there with a reraise.

GUIDELINE 5

If you go below 40 big blinds, and you've got an aggressive long-ball player at your table, look at him as an opportunity to steal a big pot. Whatever it takes, you've got to get involved in a pot with this guy—maybe call him when he enters with a raise, or limp in front of him, whatever—you've got to get him to put a bunch of chips into the pot, then push all in on him after the flop no matter what comes down. And pay no regard to your actual cards or to what comes down on the flop when you make this move.

This is purely a utility move. You don't even have to look at your cards. Just pretend to look. But make that move. Just do it. Catch your breath later. And don't make the mistake of pushing in on him preflop. If he's a loose player and he's got A-K or A-Q or any half-assed pocket pair, he'll call your all in preflop. A preflop all in always looks weak to a loose-aggressive player.

If you wait until the flop comes down to make your move, that looks scary. Chances are great he won't hit the flop and he'll have to give it to you. There's also the off-chance that the flop will hit you hard—no matter what your garbage cards are—in which case you can milk this aggressive player for a lot more chips than his preflop raise.

GUIDELINE 6

If you go below 30 big blinds in Phase One of a Rank 1-3 tournament, you've got to switch to a long-ball style. No more spec hands. Get very aggressive and if you have any kind of a decent hand, push in on any opponent whom you think you have beat or who you think cannot call an all in. The only exception to this is when your starting cards are A-A or K-K, in which case you are going to slowplay by limping or calling a raise preflop in order to get as many chips into the pot as possible, knowing full well that despite whatever dangers appear, you will play this hand to the death and go for as many chips as you can possibly get out of any opponents who challenge you. If you bust out, so be it. Because of your poor utility, it's worth the risk at this point to go for max variance.

To have a stack size of fewer than 30 big blinds in the early stages of a Rank 1 or 2 tournament is truly a sad state of affairs. When that next blind level hits, you'll be in utility hell. If you're card dead, tough beans. You've got to do something now while you still have enough chips to scare your opponents, or to make a really decent stack if you get called and double up. Don't worry about busting out if you're below 30 big blinds this early on. If the next blind level will hit within the next half hour, you're almost dead anyway. Do what you have to do to give yourself a shot.

GUIDELINE 7

Read the deep-stack strategy suggestions below because some of them will also apply in short-stack tournaments depending on the specific hands, specific opponents in the pot, or specific situations.

DEEP-STACK PHASE ONE STRATEGY: 6 GUIDELINES

Here are some general strategy guidelines for the early stages of a Rank 4 to 6 tournament:

GUIDELINE 1

Assuming you have full utility, you should seize every opportunity to get your chips into action. Read over the lists of playable hands in the description of small-ball play in Chapter Four, but don't bother trying to memorize a list of playable hands. If your cards are suited or vaguely connected or you've got any pair at all, or a couple of high cards, or good position, or any excuse whatsoever to play—get your chips into the pot. Don't worry about blowing off a chunk of your stack at this time, provided you remain competitive. Get your chips in there and look for opportunities to pick up pots, whether from strong hands, strong situations, or weak opponents.

It's important that you establish the image of a player at this time, not of just another tight guy waiting for a hand.

GUIDELINE 2

If you find that in tournament after tournament when you try to play a lot of hands, all you ever do is blow off chips and shrink your starting stack, then you're basing your play too much on your cards. Study the five easy bluffs in Chapter Six and start applying them. Also, study the "Three Tips on Getting Started" at the end of Chapter Four. If you are using long-ball plays and your stack is going up and down radically, that's to be expected with this style of play.

A long-ball player will often find himself going from chip leader to short stack and back to chip leader again in the early blind levels as he attempts to build his monster stack. If you lose half your chips in the first half-hour with aggressive moves that don't pay off, you must accept that as the norm for this hyper-aggressive strategy, and just keep going. You are either going to build a mountain or bust out trying. When you play for variance, variance is what you get.

GUIDELINE 3

If your table has a lot of seemingly cautious players—small preflop raises, lots of limping, lots of checking and calling, not much post-flop play—you have to ascertain which players are survival-oriented and which are the smallballers who will be more dangerous. You figure this out by paying attention to the hands that are shown down and, since there will probably be too few showdowns to make a reliable judgment on this basis alone, by observing how many hands the various players at your table are playing.

The survivalists enter far fewer pots and will be the easier players to read. You'll be able to put them on hands much more often and more accurately. The smallballers will be a pain in the ass to put on a hand. And you will be an equal pain in the ass to them.

GUIDELINE 4

If your table is aggressive from the get-go—not much limping, preflop raises of 5 x BB or more, lots of reraising, lots of post-flop action, big pots developing right from the start—you have to ascertain which players are loose-aggressive players and which are actually more conservative longballers who just happen to be making strong hands.

It takes a bit more time to separate the loose-aggressives from the conservatives than it takes to separate the smallballers from the survivalists because if any hands are shown down, they will tend to be strong hands. Aggressive shot-takers don't play that many more hands than a player who's just having a lucky run of cards might get, at least not until they've built up their chip stacks considerably. But you should be able to figure them out within 20 to 30 minutes. The smarter ones will change gears to keep you guessing, but then they'll go on another tear. In general, the longballers who are just playing their cards will be easy to read.

The loose-aggressive players will keep you off balance. You have to make the loose-aggressive players wary of you so that you do not become one of their targets. If you can milk one of these guys for a good-sized pot on any unusual hand, you will be left alone, because long ball maniacs don't like smallballers any more than smallballers like long ball maniacs. If you can call a loose-aggressive player on the river with second pair and take the pot, they'll all back off. If you're just not getting any trapping opportunities, then you may have to pull a grand theft bluff. You're going to have to incur some risk at a table like this if you want some respect. So do it. It's far riskier to become the target of players who think they can push you around.

GUIDELINE 5

The survival players like the deep-stack events because they offer much more time to wait for premium hands before getting any great amount of chips involved in a pot. The loose-aggressive players—whether smallballers or longballers—like deep-stack events because they provide more time for establishing a table image and for getting reads on opponents. While the survivalists feel they don't have to take chances on risky hands, the loose players feel they don't have to take chances on risky reads. Some aggressive players feel that they must come out gangbusters from the start in order establish the image they want. Very often, this is their downfall. They do get trapped by failing to see that the calling station they were trying to push around actually flopped a set.

If you are going to be using a long-ball style in a deep-stack event, give yourself whatever time it takes to size up your opponents before attempting to batter them into submission.

GUIDELINE 6

Change gears often. You want to move from small ball to long ball to short periods of rest frequently in order to keep your opponents guessing. If you pick up a couple of big pots with actual strong hands that get shown down, then definitely play your rush. See if you can take down another pot or two (or three or four) with nothing more than your scary table image. But at the first sign of trouble, slow down. Take a breather. Then get back into your standard small ball mode.

Look at a lot of flops. Mix it up post-flop. Play your reads but don't go crazy. Keep your opponents off-balance. You want them to feel like they never quite know what you're going to do.

ON TO PHASE TWO

Anyway, phase one is over. Hopefully, you've built a pretty good chip stack during this phase, because you're going to need all the utility you can get for phase two, a phase I call the "minefield."

PHASE TWO: THE MINEFIELD

The second phase of a tournament, the minefield, is the portion of the tournament in which the field gets drastically thinned out. This is when the short-stacked players start pushing all in, sometimes on stone cold bluffs, and the desperate players start calling all ins, often with marginal hands, in a do-or-die attempt to double up. You know you're in the minefield phase of a tournament when you start hearing the dealers call out with increasing frequency, "Seat open! Table nine!" "Seat open! Table twenty!" The short stacks are dropping like flies. I call this phase of the tournament the minefield because it is a very dangerous time to get involved in pots, because you have no control over the size of the pot with so many all-in bets both pre- and post-flop. Yet you must get involved or you will get left behind.

It is during this phase when the truly dominating chip stacks will be built for the fight to get into the money.

WAITING FOR THE CARPATHIAN

In tournaments with a lot of amateur players, such as the 2,000+ field WSOP events, you will always have a lot of players during the minefield portion who are "waiting for the Carpathian," which is how I think of the players who sit there watching their chips disappear in blind/ante costs while they're stubbornly waiting for a miracle hand that isn't going to show up. If you recall the story of the Titanic, once the ship hit an iceberg and sent out an SOS, the closest ship to respond was the Carpathian, which was about three hours away. Unfortunately, the Titanic's passengers had only about an hour before they would find themselves in the freezing cold waters of the Atlantic. There are a lot of mistakes you can make during the minefield portion of a tournament, but waiting for the Carpathian is the biggest mistake of all.

USING THE STACKS AT BLIND-OFF TIME AS A TELL

In the first section of this chapter, I'm going to discuss the structural features of a tournament that not only cause the minefield phase to start, but affect the intensity of the phase, the length of the phase, and dictate the optimal strategies for playing in this dangerous portion of the tournament. In discussing the optimal strategies, I'll introduce the concept of "attack dynamics" to guide you in your decisions to enter pots during this phase, and especially your decisions to get involved in big pots, including all ins. Then I'll discuss how you play during this phase when you have a big stack, an average stack, and a short stack. These strategic playing decisions will, of course, be utility-based.

The nice thing about the minefield phase is that the time of its start is very predictable, which helps you set up strategically for it. It begins during the blind level that corresponds to the tournament's blind-off time. There is an explanation of how to use a tournament's blind structure to calculate its blind-off time in the second chapter of this book, "Analyzing a Tournament's Structure: the Utility Factor." The blind-off time, you may recall, is a factor used to calculate a tournament's patience factor, which is then used to calculate its utility factor. But the raw blind-off time is a highly useful number in itself because it so accurately signals when you will be entering the dangerous minefield phase of any tournament.

Here are the blind-off times for the seven 2008 WSOP events we analyzed in Chapter Two:

2008 WSOP EVENTS		
Buy-in	Blind-Off Time (hours)	Minefield Starts
$1,000 (Seniors)	3.26	blind level 4
$1,500	3.86	blind level 4
$2,000	4.37	blind level 5
$2,500	4.85	blind level 5
$3,000	5.20	blind level 6
$5,000	6.28	blind level 7
$10,00	9.43	blind level 5

From this data, knowing that all of the WSOP preliminary events have one-hour blind levels, it's easy to see that the minefield portion of the tournament will begin during the fourth blind level in the $1,000 and $1,500 events; during the fifth blind level in the $2,000 and $2,500 events; during the sixth blind level in the $3,000 event; during the seventh blind level in the $5,000 event; and during the fifth blind level in the $10,000 event (since the $10,000 event has two-hour blind levels).

The earlier the blind-off time occurs in a tournament, the more perilous the minefield will be. The later it occurs, the longer this phase will be stretched out. It's easy to understand why. When a tournament begins, all players have equal chip stacks, and during the early blind levels, a large portion of the chips in front of any player represent his starting chip stack. In a short-stack tournament like the WSOP $1,000 Seniors event, there will be many tight players who have played very few hands for the first three hours simply because the cards weren't coming to them, and they will suddenly find themselves entering the fourth blind level in desperate chip shape.

But in the $10,000 main event, there will be very few players who have seen no hands to play in the nine hours before blind-off time. Even the tightest, most survival-oriented players will usually have been dealt good enough cards to have gotten involved in some pots in all those hours.

THE STORY TOLD BY THE STACKS

Moreover, one thing we know beyond any doubt in a tournament is that any player who is still alive upon the arrival of blind-off time has earned as many chips as are sitting in front of him. We know this because the blind-off time tells us that at this point in the tournament, every player still alive will have already paid blinds and antes equal to his starting chip stack.

In the $1,000 Seniors event, for example, at the blind-off time halfway through the fourth blind level, every player still alive will have paid $2,000 in chips just in blind/ante costs. If one player is sitting there at blind-off time with a stack equal to his starting stack, then he has earned $2,000 in chips up to this point. (Obviously, we can't say *exactly* what he has earned. Some tables may play a little more than thirty rounds per hour, some may play slightly fewer, but this estimate of what this player has earned in his first three and a half hours of play will be good enough for our purposes.)

I like looking around my table when we hit a tournament's blind-off time, because I can see how much each player has won, in total, up to that point, and that tells a story in itself. Even at the tightest and most conservative table, it is very rare to have a lot of more-or-less equal-sized stacks once the blind-off time has passed. Players at the same table just don't win chips at the same rate. There will generally be two to three dominating stacks, two to three pretty desperate stacks, and four to six stacks somewhere in between.

It's true that in some cases, the big stacks may simply represent the players who were dealt the greatest number of lucky hands. And some of the best players may already have busted out or be sitting on desperately short stacks. But in most cases, the bigger stacks will belong to the most aggressive and skillful players, and the short stacks will usually belong to the tight players. If you have not witnessed how the players at your table got into their current chip positions, the way these players handle their stacks in the next 15 to 20 minutes will tell you everything you need to know. The way I like to look at a tournament is that phase two is when the real tournament begins. Each player's buy-in provided him with enough chips to last x-number of hours, but that's all. It's my job to see how many chips I can win in that time period, because after that, everyone left is just playing with their winnings.

IT STARTS GETTING DANGEROUS!

If this is a short-stack event, phase two is gonna get hairy! That's because, in a short-stack event, the average chip stacks will already be short—or verging on short—in relation to the blind/ante costs once you enter this phase. So, half the table or more will be looking for a shot to take or a hand to take a stand with.

This may sound like a field day for the big stacks, but it's not. A lot of the chip leaders that built impressive stacks during phase one are going to go down. It's not easy for any player to make it through the minefield phase of a tournament. It's definitely better to be a big stack than a short stack at this time, but it's not easy to steal pots from opponents who are truly desperate. And it's impossible to play small ball when a table full of desperate opponents keep pushing all in on you.

This is another reason why the top players—and especially the smallballers—prefer the deep-stack events. The average stacks in a deep-stack tournament are generally in much better shape when blind-off time is hit, which makes for a kinder, gentler minefield. It's still a minefield, but by this point the biggest stacks can more easily negotiate the dangerous terrain. In a short-stack tournament, the minefield hits you with surprising suddenness, like a cyclone, then slowly fades away as players bust out and double up and the chips are redistributed to the survivors. In a deep-stack event, on the other hand, you ease slowly into the minefield phase, and the cards decide which of the desperate few will go home and which will earn the chips they need to stay in the fray.

Some of the big stacks that go down during the minefield phase will go down due to bad beats and coolers through no fault of their own. Others can blame their own bad calls, and play that's just too loose and aggressive for this portion of the tournament. They continue to play as if they haven't even noticed that the tournament has entered a new phase where danger lurks in every pot.

All players have to change gears during the minefield phase. The shorter your stack, the more aggressively you must play and the more risks you must be willing to take to get back to a competitive stack. The bigger your stack, the more you've got to be aware of whom you're getting involved with in the pots you enter. But even with a big stack, you cannot wimp out at this point in an attempt to preserve your chips and avoid all risk. You have to be willing to gamble throughout this phase of the tournament because you have to keep your stack growing.

Regardless of your stack size, during the minefield phase having reads on your opponents and understanding their playing styles will continue to pay off. With a big stack, you have to be able to identify which players you can push around and which you can't, who's just taking a shot, and who has a real hand.

Gauging the desperation level of opponents—and how they will play when desperate—is not always easy. Players who understand utility will take risks with a moderate stack that they would not have taken a blind level earlier. And you can expect constant all ins from the Harringbots whose M's are entering their orange zones. The difference between the good players and the Harringbots at this point is that the latter will have waited too long to get aggressive, and will stop their aggression well short of the stack required for even competitive utility, while any good player who finds himself short in the minefield phase will keep hammering away for a much bigger stack.

Individual tables within a tournament can have very different minefield phases. A table with a few loose-aggressive players who have managed early double ups and triple-ups, and where multiple players have already busted out and fresh blood and more chips have already been brought in, will enter the minefield phase earlier than a conservative table where the original ten players are still jockeying for position when blind-off time hits. This is due to the fact that when loose-aggressive players are driving the action on a table, the chip discrepancies get bigger earlier and desperate players appear sooner.

YOU'LL KNOW WHEN THE MINEFIELD HITS
But you shouldn't have any trouble identifying when the minefield phase has begun at your table. The average stacks will be starting to sweat because they lack utility and are finding it increasingly difficult to play poker. Even if the average stacks have 40 big blinds, the big stacks will be breathing down everyone's necks with outsize raises, and the short stacks will just keep pushing in. Early in a tournament, you can play some poker if most of the stack

sizes at your table are around 40 big blinds. But if there are only a few of you with 40 big blinds, and a few short stacks with only 10 to 15 big blinds, and a few big stacks with 100+ big blinds, then you have to face the fact that you no longer have even the amount of functionality you once had with your medium stack.

BUMPING INTO SHORTS STACKS

If you come in with a standard raise during the minefield phase and bump into a short stack who likes his hand, he will not just call your raise. He will push all in on you and you have to be prepared for this during this phase. For example, let's say that with $8,000 in chips, you raised the $200 big blind to $600 with your A-Q. The short stack pushes all in with his $3,000 in chips. Do you really want to call an all in for $2,400 more? If your A-Q doesn't hold up, you'll go down to $5,000 in chips.

Is A-Q worth the risk?

In most cases, the answer is yes, because of how low your utility is at this still early stage of the tournament. You've got to play some high-risk poker at this time when you are this short on chips. Your actual decision would always depend on the opponent you face, other players who may be in the pot, and the character of your table, but in most cases, I would consider it a big mistake to not gamble on A-Q in this circumstance. What hand do you think you're waiting for?

SHORT- AND DEEP-STACK TOURNAMENTS

In discussing strategy in the minefield phase, I'm not going to separate short-stack (Rank 1-3) tournament strategy and deep-stack (Rank 4-6) tournament strategy, as I did for the phase one. The deep-stack tournament minefield will be somewhat less crazy than the short-stack tournament minefield, but the strategy considerations are much the same, and the key to your strategy decisions are in what I call the "attack dynamics."

The attack dynamics provide a logical basis for entering pots based on your stack size in relation to your opponents'. With this logic as a guide, we'll then look at the important strategy considerations for big stacks, average stacks, and short stacks separately, based on their utility.

ATTACK DYNAMICS

The minefield basic attack strategy is really very simple, though it is contrary to a lot of the traditional thinking on tournament strategy, because it is based on utility, not survival. It can be graphically reduced to a triangular chart that shows which players you should launch your attacks against, based on your stack size.

MINEFIELD ATTACK DYNAMICS

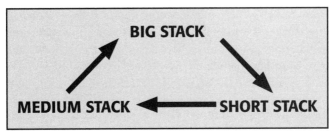

In other words, if you are a medium stack, you primarily want to attack the big stacks. If you are a big stack, you primarily want to attack the short stacks. And if you are a short stack, you primarily want to attack the medium stacks. Note that this strategy is meant to guide your attacks when you do not have premium starting cards or a powerful hand post-flop. (When you have a truly strong hand, you can and should go up against any player who is willing to get involved with you.) The attack dynamics should be viewed primarily as a guide to whom you should launch your stealing attacks against, and you should never stop stealing in a tournament, even during the minefield phase. If you go card-dead during the minefield, stealing is all you may be able to do to keep yourself alive.

You may note that the attack dynamics are contrary to the traditional tournament thinking, which has been that all players should avoid the big stacks since the big stacks can bust you out of a tournament in a single hand. Yet, this chart shows that the medium stacks should be attacking the big stacks during the minefield phase of a tournament. Why is this so?

PLAYING A MEDIUM STACK DURING THE MINEFIELD

Obviously, if you're dealt a big pair or A-K, you're going to tangle with any player who comes along. But because these great starting hands are so rare, and because you're going to have to make a lot of chips during the minefield phase of a tournament in order to get anywhere near the money, you have to be thinking continually about picking up pots when you do not have any hand to speak of.

When you have a medium stack, the logic behind attacking the big stacks is that you should be going after the players you can really hurt. If you have anywhere close to half the chips of the big stack, you will make his call to your all-in bet a tough decision, even if he has a legitimate hand.

Note that I'm talking here about making an all-in move on the big stack, not trying to play normal poker with him. Once you have entered the minefield, forget about normal poker if you have a medium chip stack. Remember the example above in the initial description of the minefield about how difficult it is to try to play poker against a short stack. You come in with a normal raise with a pretty decent hand and the short stack pushes all in on you. Now you have a preflop decision for half your chip stack with A-Q or A-J or 7-7.

You'll run into the same type of problem if you try to play normal poker against a big stack at this time. Here's how it works:

The blinds are $200/$400 with a $50 ante. With ten players at the table, there's $1,100 in the pot before the cards are dealt. You have $10,000 in chips—a stack size equivalent to 25 big blinds, which is about the average stack in this tournament that started out with $5,000 in chips and half the field is already gone. In middle position, you find A-Q suited when the table folds around to you. You put in a standard raise to 3 x BB—$1,200 chips. That puts $2,300 into the pot. The big stack on the button, who has about $30,000 in chips, says "Raise," and throws in $3,000. The blinds fold.

Do you call, fold, or reraise?

Look at the situation: With $5,300 chips now in the pot, you're getting 3 to 1 odds to call the $1,800 reraise. A-Q suited is a strong hand, and with those odds, you'd like to see the flop. Technically, that reraise is not an overbet, assuming the raiser has a strong ace or a big or even a medium pair that he feels is likely the best hand preflop, since he'll have position on you post-flop if you call.

But here's your dilemma: The pot now has $5,300 in it, more than half as much as your remaining $8,800 in chips. A simple call to this $1,800 reraise would put $7,100 in chips into the pot, leaving you with only $7,000 in your stack. This means that you won't be able to get away from your hand post-flop if you make top pair— regardless of any dangers the board may present, as your only legitimate post-flop bet would be all in. And if the flop doesn't hit you, you can't afford a continuation bet to see if you can pick up the pot. If you flop a straight or flush draw, a semibluff would have to be an all-in bet. If you make top pair but three to a suit other than your suit come down, you can't afford an information bet to see where you stand. So, calling that preflop reraise leaves you with very little post-flop utility.

What about reraising all in? If you think the big stack is just trying to bully you out of the pot with no legitimate hand, and you really think you can push him out of the pot, this should be your move. If you push all in, however, that would put $14,100 into the pot, and it would be $7,000 for him to call. He'd be getting 2 to 1 and may make that call with a lot of hands, especially if he's a loose player. Even if he loses this pot, he'd still have $20,000 in chips, double the average. So, your decision on whether to push in now or after the flop will have to come from your read on this player based on how he has been playing, and on whether you feel you get more utility value from your chips pushing now or post-flop.

All of these complications probably have you wondering why you would want to attack the big stacks during the minefield when you have a medium stack. Good question. The answer is that you do not attack by playing normal poker. Unless you've got a hand you're willing to go to the mat with preflop, you don't come in with a normal raise. Plus, recall that minefield attack dynamics apply to launching attacks when you do *not* have a legitimate raising hand.

The fact is you're just not going to be dealt A-Q or better all that often. For example, if you decide that you're willing to go to the mat preflop with A-K or A-Q, suited or not, or any A-A, K-K, Q-Q, or J-J, you would expect to see only one of these hands, on average, only *once* (or, technically, 1.15 times) during a one-hour blind level, assuming 30 rounds per hour. You can't sit there waiting for the Carpathian. Your ship is going down.

If you sit through the three cycles of this blind level (that costs $1,100 in blinds and antes per cycle) without getting a playable hand, your $10,000 in chips will be down to $6,700 in chips when you enter the $300/$600 blind level, leaving you with only 11 big blinds, or four rounds of play when you consider the $75 ante at that level.

Unless your miracle cards come in (and occasionally they will), you've got to steal your way to the next blind level if you're going to make it with any chips to speak of, and the players you want to target are the big stacks. Your cards are immaterial at this point. You've got to make a move on the big stack before he can make a move on you. You want to target a player who has you outchipped by somewhere between 2 to 1 and 3 to 1, someone whose stack you could really dent. If he has you outchipped by 4 to 1, he may be too big to tangle with. Essentially, you're just looking for the right opportunity. You're looking for a loose player who is liable to enter with a raise with a wide variety of hands. You would also like to be heads-up with this player, not in a multiway pot. It's best if you make your all-in move *after* the flop, not before. Again, if he has a playable hand and he really is a loose player, he may call you if you push in preflop.

Your chances of success in stealing from a loose player are much better after the flop, when it will look as if you really have something and his possibilities of making something out of his hand have been diminished. Your bluff bet has to be all in, and it has to look real. You have to call a raise preflop, then bet out or check-raise or whatever works post-flop. Your bet will usually be given respect, and you will pick up a nice bunch of chips, including your opponent's raising chips in addition to the blinds and antes. And you may need to make these moves on big-stacked opponents a couple of times per blind level, depending on your actual chip stack, the stacks of your opponents, and how card-dead you really are.

You cannot make a move like this on a player who has an average-size stack like you, because he will be much more likely to be entering the pot preflop with a much stronger hand—a hand he is willing to go the distance with. And you should not try to make moves on the short stacks when you have no cards, because you should always go after the opponents who feel they have something to lose. A short-stacked player will likely call you with any ace, any high cards, any single high card suited, any baby pair. All of these hands are better than your trash.

GETTING A REAL HAND

What if you are dealt a miracle hand at this time? You've got to make it pay, and that means you will have to court danger. Forget the attack dynamics when you have a real premium hand. If you're dealt aces, kings, or queens, do not raise more than a min-raise. You absolutely must get a caller, and hopefully a reraise. If you feel that a min-raise would be too out of character for your betting style, then limp. Forget about the dangers of limping with a big pair, letting multiple spec hands into the pot. You are going to go the distance with your hand and you want as much money in the pot as you can get into it. You've got to gamble. The reward—utility—is worth the risk. If there's a raise in front of you, then reraise the minimum. You'll almost positively get a call from the raiser since the odds for calling will be too good with the blinds and antes in there. On the flop, you have to be willing to go all in no matter what comes down, and you're going to do whatever you can to get as many of your opponent's chips into the pot as possible.

With any strong starting cards other than a big pair—A-K, A-Q, A-J, A-10, K-Q, or any medium or small pair, come in with a standard raise. If you are reraised, no matter what the reraise is—even if it puts you all in—call. You may be an "average" stack at your table, but from the utility perspective you need a double up desperately to get back to a competitive stack, and this is your shot. Although you may not be counted among the desperately short stacks at your table, you have to realize that the minefield lasts a long time—many blind levels—and you're going to be swallowed up by it if you don't gamble when you've got enough chips to make a double up meaningful.

Here's one thing you must keep in mind, however, when you have a medium stack: Never make a standard raise during the minefield phase of a tournament with a hand you are not prepared to play to the death. Many tight players would argue in favor of folding that A-Q suited in the example described earlier, where the big stack on the button reraised your $1,200 raise to $3,000.

A-Q DURING THE MINEFIELD PHASE

Here are some of the tight-guy arguments in favor of folding A-Q:

TIGHT-GUY ARGUMENTS IN FAVOR OF FOLDING A-Q

> **NEVER MAKE A STANDARD RAISE DURING THE MINEFIELD PHASE OF A TOURNAMENT WITH A HAND YOU ARE NOT PREPARED TO PLAY TO THE DEATH.**

You will have cut your losses on the hand to $1,200, leaving you with $8,800, just a bit below average and still a viable stack with the big blind at $400.

You don't really have a hand yet. All you've got is an ace with a second-best kicker. As for pushing all in, isn't there a no-limit hold'em "commandment" that says you should never get all of your chips into a pot before the flop with a queen in your hand?

You're avoiding a risky confrontation with a player who not only has you outchipped, but has position on you as well.

ARGUMENTS AGAINST FOLDING A-Q

You're surrendering 12 percent of your chips—which will leave you below average at a dangerous point in the tournament—when you have a much stronger than average hand.

The reraiser could very likely be making a move on you with a marginal hand. That likelihood goes up if the reraiser has a monster stack and late position.

Folding would send a message not only to this player but to the table that your preflop raises don't mean much since you'll fold to a standard reraise. You'll appear to be a player who's either making moves with marginal hands, or a downright wimp who will crumble in the face of heat.

WHY YOU DON'T FOLD

But the most important reason not to fold, and to go all the way with your hand instead, is that you are desperate for *utility*. You cannot play poker with an advantage without sufficient chips to use your skills. The chips in front of you are all but valueless but for the ray of hope that they provide at this moment: They can gain you a stack, if you're willing to gamble with them, that will be well above average at a time when you need it most.

So, how do you play this hand? You call the raise, then push in on the flop regardless of what comes down.

PLAYING A SHORT STACK DURING THE MINEFIELD

According to the attack dynamics graphic, if you are a short stack you want to launch your attacks against the medium stacks during the minefield. Again, I'm assuming that you do not have a premium hand, and you are looking for shots to take. As a short stack, you have to face the fact that you will be unlikely to make it through this blind level with much more than a chip and a chair, if that, and you have got to turn on some real aggression fast. The reasons why you should be targeting the medium stacks is that you cannot hurt the big stacks enough to dissuade them from calling your shots, and the other short stacks will be happy to call your all in if they have a hand with even a prayer of winning. Again, when you have garbage cards and you're hoping to steal a pot, you should always go after the opponents who feel they have something to lose.

If you take a shot at a big stack, he may call your all in in the dark just to see if he can knock you out. So, with premium cards, you can definitely go after a big stack since his starting hand requirements will be well below those of a medium stack. But if you're just trying to steal with trash to keep yourself alive, follow the attack dynamics.

Against an average stack, your all in poses a real problem. If you can take anywhere near half the stack of an opponent, he'll need a very strong hand to call you. A loose player with an average stack would probably call you with A-J or A-10, maybe K-Q, or a pair as low as 7-7 or 6-6, but most players who are worried about staying alive in this dangerous phase of the tournament would want a stronger hand than those to risk half their chips.

Technically, you're looking for a player whose medium stack would become a short stack if he called your bet and lost. One of the things in your favor is that most tournament players are ignorant of the logic of attack dynamics. The medium stacks especially try to avoid confrontations with big stacks and target short stacks when they want to try to steal with marginal cards. You can often capitalize on their mistake. If you have a medium stack to your right during the minefield phase of a tournament, there is a good chance that he will take shots at your blinds with very marginal hands. Even a normally tight player who is concerned about his diminishing M will do this. So long as his bet isn't all in and you have enough chips for a substantial reraise if you push in, he cannot call you without a pretty decent hand himself.

If you happen to be dealt a premium hand, then you should play it much the same as a medium stack should—do whatever you can to get as many chips into the pot as possible, even if that means limping with aces. You have to play this hand with whatever amount of risk is necessary to get the pot as big as you can possibly get it. This is not the time to limit the field. The standard hold'em logic says that with a big pair you would prefer to see a flop with as few players as possible, ideally isolating a single opponent to give yourself the best chance at having your hand hold up. But when short-stacked, you are not trying to maximize the odds of surviving this hand, you are trying to maximize the odds of regaining competitive utility. Gamble.

If you are dealt a "playable" hand that is not premium, such as any ace, any suited high card, any two high cards suited or not, or any decent suited connectors, you should automatically push all in preflop if you are the first player into the pot, regardless of your position. If you have 6-5 suited under the gun, you push. Same thing with J-9 offsuit or A-3 offsuit or a whole lot of other marginal hands. Read over the list of hands I provided for small-ball play during the deeper-stacked portion of the tournament. If you manage to steal the blinds and antes, fine. But just the blinds and antes on one round aren't going to help you much. You still have

> **WHEN SHORT-STACKED, YOU ARE NOT TRYING TO MAXIMIZE THE ODDS OF SURVIVING THIS HAND, YOU ARE TRYING TO MAXIMIZE THE ODDS OF REGAINING COMPETITIVE UTILITY.**

no utility. Make this move again the first opportunity you get.

You shouldn't be afraid of getting called here. It's time to gamble. You really need a double up badly and since you are a short stack, you usually will be called if you keep this up relentlessly. If you have a strong table image and you are good at stealing, you may be surprised at how many times you can steal the preflop pot without a caller. You may even be able to steal your way back up to an average stack, in which case you should switch to the medium stack minefield strategy and start targeting the big stacks.

PLAYING A BIG STACK DURING THE MINEFIELD

Playing a big stack during the minefield phase is much more complex than playing a medium or short stack. Of course, the medium and short stacks would give anything to have your problem.

If you are a natural long-ball player and you know how to bully a table once you get a big stack, you've got to slow down once the minefield hits. Desperate players cannot be pushed around as easily as players who think they're in fine shape and don't need to take risks.

Note that optimal attack dynamics dictate that you should be targeting the short stacks at this time. There are a number of reasons for this. First and foremost, they cannot hurt you as much as a medium stack can. Second, they will often be playing more marginal hands than the medium stacks. And third, most tournament players, regardless of the size of their chip stacks, try to avoid confrontations with the big stack. They know they cannot push you out of a pot with a reraise, so they will tend to stay out of your way. Also, in many cases the short stacks are the tightest players. If you have been playing at the same table with these players for an hour or more, you will know which ones became short waiting for hands, letting their chip stacks get eaten up by the blinds and antes. As long as they're waiting for the Carpathian, it's your duty as the table iceberg to sink them before the Carpathian arrives.

Going after the short stacks is easy. There are no tough decisions since a short stack will likely be all in before the flop if he plays his hand. If he doesn't understand he's in a jam-or-fold situation, then he's a tournament moron. Some amount of hand selectivity on your part would be wise, especially when a double up would significantly improve a short stack's utility. You don't want to give him an easy shot at getting back to average. You're going to find yourself in more confrontations that get shown down, so keep that in mind. You especially do not want to double up a short stack if he is a skillful player. Always play the man and the situation, not just your stack.

On the other hand, if a short stack's double up will not mean much to him utility-wise (whether because he is so short that a double up will still leave him short or because he is a poor player who plays his cards without a thought for utility), and a loss to this player would not significantly hurt your utility, then you should call this player's all in with *any two cards*, and this is especially true if you raised and he pushed in on you. Maintaining a wild image with a big stack will keep other players from taking shots at you even if you lose this hand. If you recall the discussion in Chapter Eight on table image, there is no better image a big stack can have during the minefield phase of a tournament than that of a maniac. The smarter players will understand why you are calling a short stack with a trash hand, but most players who are looking for a shot to take don't really want an all-in confrontation with anything less than superior cards in their own hands. Players who are looking for an easy pot to pick up will find this type of loose play very scary.

Professional gamblers call this type of play—where you are obviously getting involved in a bet as an underdog—"advertising" or "being a sport." Pros do this in all sorts of prop bet situations just to show they're willing to gamble. The purpose of advertising is to get you action when you do have the best of it. But in a tournament, this type of advertising serves two purposes. It will definitely get you action because you'll be seen as a gambler, but it will also throw a scare into players who are considering trying to bluff you. Players generally try to bluff tight players, not players who like action and want to gamble.

BIG STACK VERSUS AVERAGE STACK

When playing against an average chip stack, you have to be very careful not to get trapped. You will usually be able to steal with a simple reraise from an average-stacked player who entered the pot with a standard raise, but you must decide before you make this move if this player is one who will play his hand to the death. If you have a premium hand yourself, then you should push all in on him preflop if he comes in with a raise. Put the tough decision on him. If he folds, then you know he's a tournament moron who shouldn't have entered the pot with a standard raise in the first place, given his crippled utility. But again, you do this when you have a premium hand, not with any two cards or any "playable" hand.

I'm not going to define "premium" here. I'll leave that to your discretion. Again, I'm not much for memorizing lists of hands to play in different circumstances, and if you are in the habit of memorizing such lists, I'd suggest you shake it and focus on more important aspects of the game. In a situation like this, so much depends on the actual chip discrepancies between you and your opponent, how you view his level of skill and the consequent utility benefit of a bigger stack to him should he win this pot, how loose or tight or tricky or wimpy you might feel he is under pressure, and how strong your table image is at present. You have to feel out the specific situation and play your hand at a gut level. Do you think you have a hand that is likely to be stronger than a lot of hands he might push in with or call an all in with? Do you think you can get him to fold even if his hand is stronger than yours? Or do you think it best to save your chips, let him have this one, and wait for a better opportunity?

But don't turn into a wimp yourself against players with average chip stacks. Most are not making intelligent utility-based decisions in tournaments, and the "smart" ones who have read all the books usually have a much more survival-oriented approach where they know just enough of the wrong math to get themselves in trouble. And if you are playing utility while they're playing survival, they're in deep trouble.

THE BITCH SLAP

Consider the example I provided at the beginning of this chapter in which a player with $10,000 in chips comes in with a raise to $1,200, then finds himself reraised to $3,000 by the big stack on the button. Again, this standard reraise in and of itself destroys most post-flop utility this player may have if he calls. His chip stack will be smaller than the pot. In that example, the average-stacked player had a stack equivalent to 25 big blinds (which by my definition is godawful short, and even a Harringbot would have himself in the "orange zone" with this stack considering the antes in the pot). This same play, however, that destroys an average-stacked player's utility, can be pulled when the player with the average stack has much greater utility than just 25 big blinds.

For example, let's say this is a deeper-stack event, where players start out with $10,000 in chips. We'll leave the blind level the same, $200/$400 with a $50 ante, which puts $1,100 into the preflop pot. Now let's say our player has $22,000 in chips when the average is slightly less than $20,000. He feels he's in pretty good shape. The big stack on the button, however, is sitting there with $50,000 in chips, not an unusual amount for a big stack during the fifth blind level of a tournament where players started with $10,000 in chips.

Now, the average-stacked player enters the pot from the cutoff seat with A-Q suited and a bet of 5 x BB. This would be a fairly standard raise from a late position seat considering the antes. This puts $3,100 into the pot. The big stack on the button then reraises to $7,000, which would be a fairly standard reraise from a player who had a big pair or A-K, especially considering that the big stack is sitting on $50,000 in chips.

That raise to $7,000 puts $10,100 into the pot, and if the average-stacked player calls the extra $5,000 in chips, the pot will have $15,100 in it, and the average stacked player will have only $15,000 left in his stack—again, less than the amount in the pot—when the flop comes down. In other words, a raise of $5,000 from a player who has $50,000 has crippled the post-flop utility of a player who entered the hand with a chip stack of 55 x BB (or 20 M, Harrington's "green zone").

Technically, 55 x BB is a bit shy of what I consider to be even a competitive chip stack, and it's not anywhere near full utility. But most tournament players are quite ignorant of these concepts and they just see a big stack pushing players around without considering that the big stack is simply playing the math of the situation. I've witnessed this type of move by a big stack hundreds of times in tournaments and I make it myself whenever the opportunity is right for it.

It's easy to figure the math when the situation arises. You simply calculate how much of a raise will put more into the pot than your opponent will have left in his stack if he calls. Then you make that bet. I don't know what other players call this move, but in my head, I call it a "bitch slap," which may be sexist and politically incorrect, but does convey to me the feeling of what I'm doing when I make this move.

It works best against an experienced opponent who will stop and think about what has happened to the pot size, as well as what his chip stack will be if he calls, and unless he's on a monster hand himself, he will almost always fold. If he calls or reraises, then follow your instincts. If you have trash cards, you'll obviously have to fold to any reraise. This player will not go away. If he just calls, you have position, so play poker with him post-flop based on what comes down and what he does. You're still outchipping him by almost 3 to 1, so give him respect if he deserves it.

During the minefield portion of a tournament, these types of situations will arise again and again at most tables because the chip discrepancies at this time tend to be very substantial. If you are the big stack, you should definitely play against an average stack when you feel you can bitch-slap your opponent into submission. It doesn't really take that big of a chunk of your chip stack to make the move, and your success rate should be extremely high if you pick your spots and your opponents wisely.

BIG STACK VERSUS BIG STACK

As for deciding whether or not to play against another big stack during the minefield portion of a tournament, you should base this decision on poker factors, such as your cards, the type of opponent, your table image and your position in relation to him, and the amount of current action in the pot. You don't need to challenge a player who can devastate your chip stack at this time, but you shouldn't shy away from calling standard raises from other big stacks when you have playable hands or a good read on this player and you feel you can play poker with him. Playing against another big stack provides a terrific opportunity to use all of your poker skills to build a really dominant stack. But this isn't the opponent you're going out of your way to gamble with when you've got a big stack yourself.

Attack dynamics would pit you against the short stacks whenever you have a playable hand, and this should be your basic approach. Medium and big stacks present real dangers that shouldn't be ignored. Most players who enter the minefield phase of a tournament with a big stack don't come out the other end with a big stack if they come out the other end at all. If you focus on utility—yours and your opponents'—with a goal of increasing your own utility with as little risk as possible, while squelching the utility of your opponents, you'll make good decisions. If you lose your stack, it should be due to coolers and bad beats, not bad decisions.

WHEN A DESPERATE PLAYER PUSHES ALL IN

In *PTF1*, in a short chapter titled "The Wolf Pack Instinct," I advised players with premium starting cards not to reraise in order to isolate a desperate player who moves all in preflop, but to simply call the all in to allow as many other players into the pot as possible in order to reduce the chances of the desperate player surviving. It's a lot easier for any player to beat one player than it is to beat a whole lot of players. In general, I do believe in allowing other players into the pot to try to knock out the desperate, but there are a few qualifiers to that general advice.

If you are short-stacked at all yourself and you find yourself with premium or even semi-premium starting cards (say a medium pair or just two high cards, maybe even a bad ace, depending on how short-stacked you are) after a desperate player has moved all in, you would be making a big mistake if you didn't push over the top with an all-in bet of your own in order to try and isolate the desperate player. When you are short-stacked, you must do what you must do to pick up chips, and a desperately short-stacked player may very well be pushing in on marginal cards. Your own utility always comes first, and improving your personal chances of taking this pot by pushing other players out should be foremost in your decision-making process.

ISOLATING WHEN YOU'RE NOT UTILITY CONSTRICTED

As for players who are not utility-constricted, it is a mistake to raise in order to isolate a desperate player, especially if your premium hand is not a big pair but a hand like A-K or A-Q. And this mistake is even worse if other callers have already entered the pot and you push all the other callers out. I once called a desperate all in along with three other callers, then a big stack went all in over the top and pushed everyone out of the pot except for the desperate player who was already all in. The desperate player turned over his cards to reveal pocket 6-6 and the big stack's big slick never improved. The desperate player literally quintupled up on that hand because of all the prior calls to his all in. Two of the players who initially called but were pushed out of the pot said they had mucked cards higher than six that would have paired the board. What made this particularly irksome was that the desperate player who quintupled up was an aggressive and skillful player whom everyone at that table would have loved to see gone.

GANGING UP ON A SKILLFUL PLAYER

It is much more important to gang up on a skillful all-in player than it is on a mediocre player. I don't really care if a mediocre player doubles up or triples up because some player with A-K pushed all other potential callers out of the pot. A mediocre player will likely redistribute his chips to the better players anyway. But when a dangerous player is desperate and all in, as many players as possible should be allowed into the pot for the kill.

If you have a hand like A-A or K-K, maybe even Q-Q, isolating the desperate player is not that bad of a move, but don't push over the top to isolate with pairs smaller than these. If you go over the top with your J-J or a lesser pair, you might find the desperate player has a high card bigger than your pair, which he may pair on the flop. Your over-the-top bet may have pushed other potential callers out of the pot who had the same high card but with a better kicker. Again, this is even more of a mistake if there are already other callers in the pot before you move in, since the desperate player can now win a very substantial pot and will only have to beat one opponent, and it's more of a mistake still if the desperate player is a skillful player who can really use chips when he has them.

READY FOR THE NEXT PHASE

Whatever your chip stack, if you make it through the minefield, you are now entering the third phase of the tournament, the bubble.

PHASE THREE: THE BUBBLE—A BUFFET OF CHIP SANDWICHES

In this chapter, we're going to concentrate on the third phase of a poker tournament, the bubble, a phase that I often think of as "dinner," in the same sense that the first phase of a tournament is "lunch." It's a great time for eating up the chips of survival-oriented players. The bubble phase occurs when the money is just around the corner. Suddenly, everyone remaining in the tournament starts worrying about going out before they hit the money. In many ways, because the players who make it through the minefield become so survival-oriented, it's like a reversion to phase one.

MAKING CHIPS OR MAKING THE MONEY?

The bubble phase is another great time for chip building, and it couldn't come at a better time. The desperately short stacks will still be in minefield mode, so you've got to watch out for them, but it's pretty easy to pick up pots during the bubble phase if you've got enough chips to scare the medium stacks. They're all terrified they won't make it to the money when they're oh-so-close. They voluntarily surrender whatever utility their limited stacks might have afforded them.

Technically, the optimal bubble phase strategy should not differ appreciably from the minefield phase, because players' chip discrepancies will remain similar to what they were during the minefield phase. There will still be big stacks, average stacks and short stacks. The main difference will be that the big stacks will be a bit bigger and the average stacks will be somewhat shorter in relation to the blind/ante costs. But based on the stack discrepancies, you would expect minefield psychology to persist and attack dynamics to be the same.

But, nothing could be further from the truth. A poker tournament is not so much a game of math as it is a game of emotions and perceptions, and when players perceive that they're close to the money, their emotions run rampant and cloud their decision-making processes.

Also, there are a lot of bad mathematical analyses in tournament books about what it means to be "on the bubble." These analyses are usually based on the reverse-chip-value theory, and they neglect chip utility in favor of survival. It's no wonder that so many players tighten up at this time.

If you're in a tournament that started with 400 players, and the top 45 finishes are paying, just about all players will start paying close attention to the exact number of players remaining by the time there are sixty-some players left. And many of the more conservative players will start tightening up even sooner than this if they feel they already have enough chips to make it to the money by just sitting and waiting. The medium stacks will start requiring very premium hands before they'll get involved in pots—if they get involved at all. Even some of the bigger stacks will slow down, trying to avoid taking what they view as unnecessary chances.

This is one of the biggest mistakes a player can make in a tournament, because in most tournaments, just squeaking into the low end of the money means you'll get your buy-in money back plus some piddling profit. For example, if this is a $1,000 buy-in tournament, it wouldn't be unusual for the bottom-end money finishes to pay $1,100. Moreover, it's most common for this same bottom payout to be awarded to quite a few finishing positions before the next pay level is hit. With 45 spots paying, all finishing positions from 45 to 37 might pay $1,100; then all finishing positions from 36 to 28 might pay $1,300, and so on.

If you are paying $1,000 to enter a tournament, and it's so important to you to get your buy-in back that you will alter your strategy as you get nearer to the money to ensure your survival to that pay point, then you cannot afford to be entering $1,000 tournaments. The reason for this is that you will not get into the money often enough in these low-end finishes to give yourself an overall winning record.

So, if you look at your chip stack as the bubble nears and you think, "I could definitely make it into the money if I just sit on these chips until the shorter stacks bust out," and you follow through with this plan, you'll never make money in tournaments. You either have to aim for the top payouts or you should give it up right now. If you start thinking about what the "dollar value" of your chips is, you're already dead money. You aren't playing smart tournament poker at any point in a tournament if you voluntarily squelch your own chip utility.

> **IF YOU JUST SIT ON YOUR CHIPS UNTIL THE SHORTER STACKS BUST OUT, YOU'LL NEVER MAKE MONEY IN TOURNAMENTS.**

Now, if you are a hobbyist, and you got into a $10,000 tournament on a $1,000 satellite, and this is a tournament that you never would have entered had you not gotten in on a satellite, then I can understand it if you feel that just making it into the money is a big accomplishment. Getting a 10 for 1 payout on your initial investment isn't bad. But one of the reasons the pro players are so happy with the boom in poker tournaments is that there has been a huge boom in satellite entries into the big events, and many satellite players enter with this survive-to-the-money outlook. What you have is a situation where utility players are going up against survival players, and the utility players kick ass.

THE BUBBLE IN RANK 1-3 (SHORT-STACK) EVENTS

In short-stack tournaments (Rank 1-3), the bubble phase will often begin with the "average" chip stacks very short—often under 20 x BB. Any player with an average chip stack at this time who tightens up his play is a tournament moron who deserves to bust out at the bottom end of the payouts. Ironically, in these short-stack events, a lot of "average" stacks that try to sit on their chips through the bubble don't make it to the money. With the blinds and antes so high, and so many players playing so cautiously, a chip stack of 15 to 20 x BB gets toasted pretty quickly, especially if there is a blind level change before the money is hit.

What happens if you attempt to wait it out is that the other survivalists with bigger stacks than yours will see that you have decided to sit on your chips, and as your stack dwindles, they will play fewer and fewer hands as they wait for you to be blinded off. And I'm not saying that this is intelligent play on their parts. They too will almost always be heading for a low-end finish. I'm just saying they will do this.

The desperately short, of course, will be pushing all in as necessary, but some of these players will not be called and will pick up the blinds and antes, buying them more time, some will be called by bigger stacks and double up, and some will bust out. But it's unlikely that enough of them will bust out to put all of the players who started this phase with average stacks into the money.

The bubble phase of a tournament can last an ungodly long time due to the overly cautious play of so many medium and short stacks.

Generally, only the deepest stacks will have decent utility at this point in a Rank 1 to 3 tournament and it may not be full utility according to our benchmark definition of 100 x BB. But if you have one of the bigger stacks, you can often have sufficient utility to play post-flop when you get involved with other big stacks, and aggressive players who are going for the win should be doing this. And since most of the players at any given table will be in the sit-and-wait mode, the big stacks will be adding to their chip leads by picking up the blinds and antes with uncalled raises—and those blinds and antes are often quite high by this point in the tournament.

THE BUBBLE IN RANK 4-6 (DEEP-STACK) EVENTS

In deep-stack tournaments (Rank 4-6), the average chip stacks will be in significantly better shape when the bubble phase begins. Depending on exactly how deep starting stacks were and the number of players in the starting field, average chip stacks may be anywhere from 25 to 50 x BB when the bubble phase begins. You might assume that it would be somewhat more likely in these events for a player with an average chip stack to make it into the money by sitting tight on his chips, but in fact, a lot more players with average chip stacks will be trying to do this. This makes it easier for both the big stacks and the short stacks to pick up pots. If a short stack has anywhere near a third of the chips of a survival-oriented average stack, the average-stacked player is unlikely to get involved with him.

As in the Rank 1-3 events, the bubble phase of a Rank 4-6 tournament can last an ungodly long time due to the overly cautious play of so many medium and short stacks.

PLAYING A SHORT STACK DURING THE BUBBLE

Play in this portion of the tournament is pretty straightforward if you are a short stack. You're in much better shape during the bubble phase than you were during the minefield phase, because so many medium stacks are terrified of busting out on the bubble. This is a great time to steal from the players at your table who have more-or-less average stacks—provided you can dodge the big stacks. If you're lucky, the big stacks will be to your right and the medium stacks to your left. If you're not so lucky, you may have a difficult time surviving unless you pick up some big hands or the big stacks to your left are pretty wimpy.

JAM OR FOLD

Your short-stack bubble strategy is easy. You make preflop all-in bets with any playable hand. (You can limp if you have A-A or K-K. If you're really short, you might even limp with Q-Q, J-J, and even 10-10, but understand in advance you are going all the way with the hand.) Don't ask me what "playable" is because it depends on too many factors and again, I don't believe in memorizing lists of hands to play.* Just don't get anal about the hands you need to play. It's more important to get in there with enough chips to make a double up meaningful than it is to wait for a hand that's a little more likely to hold up. Think of your utility odds.

---

*One great source for thinking about which hands are playable when you're in jam-or-fold mode is the *Full Tilt Poker Strategy Guide—Tournament Edition* (Warner Books, 2007). Study Andy Bloch's article titled "No-Limit Hold'em: Play Before the Flop."

What if you have a very loose big stack to your left who you feel will call your all in with any two cards? If you want to make your all in knowing you have the best of it against two random cards, what hands would you push with? You're the favorite with any pair, any ace, any king, any suited queen, any unsuited queen down to Q-5 offsuit, suited jacks down to J-6 suited, unsuited jacks down to J-8 offsuit, suited tens down to 10-7 suited, and unsuited tens down to 10-9. Close to half the possible starting hands you could be dealt will beat two random cards more often than not.

What if the big stack is on the button when you're in the big blind, but you feel he's not that loose of a player? He doesn't steal much, but he may make a move to put you all in if he had a fairly decent "playable" hand that would rank in the top 25 percent of hands. This means he'd raise you all in with any pair down to 2-2, most suited aces, most hands that consist of two high cards, suited connectors down to 10-8 suited, suited kings down to K-8 suited and suited queens down to Q-9 suited. Now what hands would you call with if you wanted to have a better than 50 percent chance of winning the pot? You'd have the best of it with any pair down to 6-6, any suited ace down to A-9 suited, and any unsuited ace down to A-10 offsuit.

If it's a truly tight player who raises, however, and you think he'd only raise with a hand in the top 10 percent of hands, then if you want to have better than a 50 percent chance of holding up if you call, you need any pair from A-A down to 10-10, A-K or A-Q suited. The list is short against a real rock, but at this point in a tournament if a survivalist suddenly gets aggressive with a hand, watch out.

TWO LIVE CARDS

If you are going up against a loose deep-stacked player who will be all in against you with any two cards, and you're considering calling, you'd do better to play high card hands as opposed to little pairs or small and medium suited connectors. Against this loose player, you'll win more often with K-Q suited than you will with any pair below 7-7.

But against the tight player who will only push in on you with a hand in the top 10 percent of hands, your jam-or-fold hand selection changes. For example, 3-3 outperforms K-Q suited, and 2-2 outperforms K-J suited and A-10 offsuit. A lowly 5-4 suited outperforms K-10 offsuit and A-9 offsuit. Why is this so? The reason is that if the tight player is only pushing in on the top 10 percent of hands, then you will too often find yourself dominated if you play a high-card hand yourself that is not truly premium.

This phenomenon is well known to no-limit hold'em players, who call it "playing two live cards." If I'm up against A-K when I have K-Q, my chance of winning the hand is only about 25 percent. With 8-7 suited versus A-K, however, my chance of winning is about 42 percent because I have two live cards instead of just one. It's not all that much worse than being on the bad end of a typical "race."

So, the important thing to remember when you consider entering a race for all of your chips is the type of player you're racing with. Many players who are desperate for a double up make the mistake of just looking for high cards. Against a tight player, you're often better off taking your shot with medium suited connectors.

In many situations, and especially when you are short-stacked, calling an all-in bet with two live cards, or even reraising all in when you put your opponent on high cards, is the mathematically correct play.

Let's say that I have $12,000 in chips—a short stack in this phase of the tournament, with the blinds at $600/$1,200 and a $100 ante. I go into the big blind and, after putting in my $1,200 and my $100 ante, I have $10,700 left in my stack. The table folds around to the player on the button, a loose-aggressive bully with a big stack who has been pushing players around with oversized bets and raises for the past hour. He raises the bet to $11,900—just enough to put me all in, and the player with an average chip stack in the small blind folds. I look down to find 7-6 suited, a spec hand that would not normally be considered a hand to call an all-in bet with. But let's do the math…

There is $2,800 in the pot in blinds and antes when the bully raises enough to put me all in. His $11,900 bet puts $14,700 in the pot. Since I already have $1,200 in there (my big blind), it's $10,700 more for me to call. Essentially, by calling here, I'm risking $10,700 to win $14,700.

If I believe that my opponent is raising with no pair in his hand, even though he may have two overcards to my hand, should I call this all in?

Let's say he has A-K, making him a 58 to 42 favorite over my 7-6 suited. Because the potential win of $14,700 would give me $4,000 more than my bet of $10,700, this hand is a virtual coin-flip. But consider the utility value to me if I win this pot. Rather than trying to survive in this dangerous phase of the tournament with only $10,700 in chips (less than 9 x BB), winning this bet would give me $25,400 in chips (almost 22 x BB), which would be a very badly needed first step toward recovering some semblance of utility. Furthermore, if I win this pot, I really will be back to having an average stack if this is a Rank 1 or 2 tournament, which means I can threaten not only the other average stacks but some of the big stacks as well.

Playing two live cards is not just something you would consider during the bubble phase of a Rank 1-3 tournament. You should consider this type of play any time you need to double up at any point in any Rank of tournament. You will often see top players play two live cards during the early portion of the minefield phase, especially in a tournament where all players start with less than full utility.

You have to be careful to target the right players when playing what you hope are two live cards. Loose-aggressive shot-takers are good targets, especially when they have position and a lot of chips, because this is when they are most likely to make moves. An average-stacked player who doesn't play many hands and is not a big thief who suddenly enters a pot with an oversized bet is often a player who has a medium pair—9-9, 10-10, J-J, or even Q-Q. He simply wants to pick up the blinds and antes without seeing a flop. This would not be a good situation to get involved with two live cards. An overpair to your cards would give this player closer to an 80 percent win expectation, rather than 60 percent.

Again, I enjoy studying Andy Bloch's charts, but I'm not one for memorizing lists because every situation is unique and every opponent is unique. If you understand how the math works based on the type of player who makes a move on you, or on whom you intend to make a move, you can adjust your strategy appropriately. Live cards that are suited and closely connected will perform better than cards that are not suited or connected. Also, bear in mind that Andy's charts only provide the mathematical odds of a hand winning against a certain type of player. They do not include the utility value of winning, which is something that changes the risk/ reward equation. If you are so short-stacked that doubling your chip stack quadruples your utility, then the gamble is often worth it with almost any two cards.

There are also various ways to play two live cards. You can call all-in bets, make all-in bets, or reraise a standard raise when you know the initial raiser will likely call because of the pot odds. When you're short-stacked during the bubble phase, face the facts: You are in trouble and there's a good chance you won't make it to the money unless you are at a particularly wimpy table, you are exceptionally good at stealing even when short, or you hit a lucky hand or two and pick up some much-needed chips. You simply have to play a hand before you get too short-stacked for a double up to help you much. You have to gamble, to take whatever risks are necessary to double up, triple up, or quadruple up. You can't wait for premium cards and you can't wait too long for stealing opportunities, since the blinds and antes are eating you up.

PLAYING AN AVERAGE STACK DURING THE BUBBLE

The problem with having an average stack in the bubble phase of a short-stack event is that you will usually be short-stacked from a utility perspective even if you are not technically one of the short stacks at your table (or in the tournament field). If you are playing in a tournament that uses a time clock display screen that shows not only the time remaining in the blind level but the total players remaining in the event, some of these displays also show the current average chip stack. That's a good number to keep mindful of, because you can see where you stand overall in relation to the whole field, and you can also tell how desperate the bubble phase is going to be. If the average chip stack is less than 20 big blinds, there will be no small ball and very little post-flop play, except among the big stacks, who can and will continue to play poker with each other. But for you, standard raises with any hand you are not prepared to go the distance with are not generally advised.

So your playing strategy with an average chip stack in this phase is very similar to the short stack's strategy. With fewer than 20 x BB in your stack, you will primarily be making all-in bets preflop. With more than 20 x BB, you may occasionally see a flop, but you will usually either jam or fold after the flop if there is any action at all. You just don't have the chips to play poker.

One major difference between the short stacks and the average stacks in this phase of the tournament is that the short stacks are usually aware of the fact that they must earn chips if they are going to make it into the money, while many average stacks seem to believe that they can just float into the bottom end of the money payouts by not playing. If you have an average stack, you should be quick to target any other average stacked players whom you feel are just trying to hold onto their chips. But watch out. Any pro with an average stack at this point will be itching to turn on the aggression.

You've played a long time to get to this point in the tournament, so don't give up now. You've got a real shot at making it if you don't wimp out and settle for some dinky low-end payout. Don't let all the work you've done to get here go to waste. If you are down to the last 50 players in a 400-player tournament that pays 45 spots, do you really want to settle for just getting your $1,000 back, plus $100 or $200 more, when the top spot is going to get somewhere in the neighborhood of $130,000? Forget about just making it into the money and shoot for the top. Make your work count for something. Right now, the money is not important. You have to get more utility. The value of utility skyrockets when there are big chip discrepancies, especially as the big money looms closer. (I will explain why this is so later in this section.)

The fact that you've made it to this point should in itself give you confidence in your abilities. The real differences between what the big stacks have accomplished by this point in a tournament and what the average stacks and short stacks have accomplished is not all that great. The amount paid in blind/ante costs to this point are the same for all players who remain and since the blind-off time passed many hours ago, all of these costs since then have been paid with chips won.

Consider a tournament where 200 players each start with $5,000 in chips, which puts the total chips in the tournament at $1 million. I'll use the structure for the most recent Los Angeles Poker Classic $2,500 event for this example. There are 60-minute blind levels starting at $25/$50. It's a Rank 3 tournament, so it's a bit fast toward the end, but not as crazy as a Rank 1 or 2 event. With 200 players, the top 18 finishers would be paid. This is a two-day event. Let's say it takes 12 hours to get to the money, which would be somewhere in the neighborhood of reality with this number of players in this event. After 12 hours of play, all remaining players will have paid $65,850 in blind/ante costs (based on 10-player tables and 30 rounds per hour). Let's say that at this point in the tournament there is one player with $100,000 in chips, one with $50,000 in chips, and another with $25,000 in chips at the same table. (The actual average chip stack when the field gets down to 18 players will be $55,555; so, late in the bubble phase, when there are 20 players remaining, $50,000 in chips would be the exact average.)

As each of these players will have paid the same $65,000+ in blind/ante costs, then what each of these players have actually earned in chips to get to this point, after subtracting the initial $5,000 in chips they each started with, are $161,000 for the player with the $100,000 stack, $111,000 for the player with the player with the $50,000 stack, and $86,000 for the player with the $25,000 stack.

That means the player with the short stack who currently has only half as many chips as the player with the average stack has actually earned almost 80 percent as many chips through the course of the tournament as the player who has twice his amount of chips. In fact, both of these players have paid more in blinds and antes than they currently have sitting in front of them in chips! And the chip leader among these three, who has four times as many chips as the short stack, hasn't really earned even twice as many through the course of the tournament.

There are many different factors that can account for these current chip discrepancies, since the actual earned chips of each of these players are not as far apart as they appear. A single double up by one player or a big loss on a bad beat by another—factors beyond either player's control—could account for the whole difference between the two of them.

These differences could also be caused by real differences in skill if two players had pretty much equal luck in catching cards. One player may be a master at picking up those small pots that his opponents seem uninterested in, or he may know how to extract the maximum chips from his opponents on his few powerful hands, while making a few more good laydowns when he knew he was beat.

One thing I can tell you, however, is that the skillful players who play with a loose-aggressive style—whether their primary style could be characterized as small ball, long ball, or a mixture of what seems right to them for the situation—are going to get to this point in a tournament a lot more often than the tighter more conservative players who are primarily playing their cards rather than their opponents, and they are going to be getting there with a lot more chips on average. When you have a strategy that gets your chips into action with an edge more frequently, you will continually build bigger stacks than players who get their chips into action with an edge less frequently.

Gambling earnings are always a function of total action times edge. And remember that an "edge" in a poker tournament does not always mean an edge on your cards. You can have an edge over an opponent as a result of your table image, the size of your

> **WHEN YOU GET YOUR CHIPS INTO ACTION WITH AN EDGE MORE FREQUENTLY, YOU WILL CONTINUALLY BUILD BIGGER STACKS THAN PLAYERS WHO GET THEIR CHIPS INTO ACTION WITH AN EDGE LESS FREQUENTLY.**

chip stack, your read on your opponent, or just your superior position.

The top players are all aware of the fact that chip discrepancies among the skillful pros at this point in a tournament can often be caused by luck factors, because all of them have had big stacks, average stacks and short stacks at this point in various tournaments, just as all of them have busted out of more tournaments before this point than not. This is why they don't give up now and settle for some easy slide into the low-end of the money.

The thing that you should be focused on now is that even though you have an average stack compared to the other players in the tournament, you're short on utility at a time when you have an excellent opportunity for changing that situation. Since so many players are tightening up at this time, you have to exploit this situation as much as you can. Big stacks will be worried about getting involved with you. Average stacks in the hands of survivalists will be terrified of getting involved without premium hands. And even some of the short stacks will be playing with extreme wariness. You really want to turn on the aggression now, and mostly watch out for the pros who are thinking the same way, no matter what their stack size.

TWO LIVE CARDS WITH AN AVERAGE STACK

Let's say that I have $48,000 in chips—an average stack of 24 x BB with the blinds at $1,000/$2,000, with a $300 ante. The table folds around to me in the cutoff seat and with a 7-6 suited I enter with a slightly bigger than standard raise to $9,000 (4½ x BB). I'm really just hoping to pick up the blinds and antes with my big raise, but I figure my hand is easy to get away from post-flop if there are any callers or I bump into preflop or post-flop resistance from one of the blinds.

Technically, I consider it a mistake to try playing standard poker during a long ball portion of a tournament, and especially without sufficient chips to play small ball. But it's also true that players should never stop making unpredictable plays. Raising with a hand that most players would not consider a raising hand, even when all you have in your chip stack is 24 x BB, is not always a mistake, especially from a late position seat. It's important to make unexpected moves throughout a tournament to keep your opponents off-balance in their reads on you. Although I consider 24 x BB a pretty desperate chip stack, it's not as bad as 10 x BB. Poker is a game of perceptions and most players would respect this raise as indicative of a strong starting hand if the average chip stack at the table was around 25 x BB. Coming in with this raise looks a lot more like a powerful hand than pushing all in.

Unfortunately, the deep-stacked bully on the button, who has $110,000 in chips, makes it $11,000 more, reraising to $20,000. Both blinds fold, and the decision comes back to me. Calling $11,000 more in chips seems like a very bad idea with a spec hand, when all I have in my stack after my initial raise is $39,000, but this player has been bullying opponents out of pots for the past hour with oversized bets and raises and I really believe he's just taking a chip shot at me with his position. So, what if I push all in?

This may seem suicidal to many players, but because of the two-live cards principle and my lack of utility at this point in the tournament, there are a lot of arguments in favor of this move. First, let's consider the pot. With $6,000 in the pot in blinds and antes, $9,000 from my initial raise and $20,000 added by the button player, the pot is $35,000 by the time it gets back around to me. If I push all in here with my remaining $39,000 in chips, making the pot $74,000, the deep-stacked bully will only have to call $28,000 more, giving him better than 2 to 1 odds on his call. He would probably call with a lot of fairly decent hands, putting a total of $102,000 into the pot.

But if he is making this raise with a hand like A-Q or 9-9 or some lesser hand, he may very likely fold, because he may put me on A-A or K-K to be able to put my tournament on the line with an all-in reraise. If he doesn't call, he'll still have $90,000 in chips, and still be a big stack at the table; while if he calls and loses, he'll have only $62,000 in chips—much closer to average.

But, let's say he has A-K and he makes the call. Essentially, I'm playing two live cards. When I pushed in, if I assumed the bully would call, then I was placing a bet of $39,000 to win $63,000. Is this a good bet? If he has A-K, then he is a 58 to 42 percent favorite to win over my 7-6 suited. If I lose $39,000 with a probability of 0.58, but win $63,000 with a probability of 0.42 (because the potential win of $63,000 is $24,000 more in chips than my bet of $39,000), I actually have a big advantage on this hand. (It's about a 10 percent advantage, which is big to a blackjack player, though to a poker player it's just the good end of a coin-flip!)

More importantly, what would this "coin-flip" do for my utility? With the blinds at $1,000/$2,000, my chip stack of $39,000 (less than 20 x BB) if I fold is very bad from a utility perspective (especially with the $300 antes in there) in this dangerous phase of the tournament. By contrast, with $102,000 in chips (more than 50 x BB) if I get called by the button player and win, I would immediately become one of the big stacks at my table, and at the same time I'd be taking a nice chunk out of a deep-stacked bully who's seated to my left and limiting my utility.

So, two-live-card plays are not just for desperately short stacks. Always think through the situation whenever you have a hand that may provide a two-live-cards play that could dramatically alter your chip status. Your thought process should consider these four questions:

1. What do I think this player has?
2. What would my utility be if I fold?
3. What would my utility be if he folds to my all-in raise?
4. What would my utility be if he calls my all in and I win?

If you think your opponent most likely has overcards but no made pair, and your utility would be pretty damn poor if you fold and pretty damn good if you push and win, then you should get your money into the pot. In this case, in addition to the utility odds you're getting if the bully calls your preflop all in, there is the added value from the possibility of the bully folding preflop since the all-in over-the-top reraise may appear to represent a monster starting hand given the preflop betting and my chip status. My only worry would be if he had a pocket pair premium enough to call my all-in over-the-top bet. But in my utility-weak status, with no clear read to that effect, it's correct for me to gamble.

PLAYING A BIG STACK DURING THE BUBBLE

It's very easy to read the survival players during this phase of a tournament; they simply stop playing. But it's extremely difficult to read the aggressive players, whether they are short on chips, or have average or big stacks. Because the play becomes so cautious for the majority of players in this phase, the better players generally turn on the aggression.

It is not difficult to blow off your chips at this point of the tournament if you make bad decisions. With a big stack, you can afford some time to reassess your opponents when you first feel the bubble consciousness taking over. Before you start making moves on opponents with fewer chips, figure out which ones are going to be all-in maniacs, which are just going to be trying to survive, which ones are looking at this time as a great opportunity to acquire a big chip stack, and which ones are going to be tricky players. Again, players do change the way they play when the minefield ends and bubble consciousness signals the start of the new "survival" phase for conservative players.

If you have a really monster stack in relation to your opponents and you attempt blind ruthless aggression—which often works very well in the first phase of a tournament when so many players are thinking survival—you will definitely blow off a lot of chips during the bubble phase. In that sense, the bubble phase is similar to the minefield phase. It's like "minefield lite." Short stacks will have to call you down when they have decent hands because they have to play, and the smarter average stacks who know they have to make chips at this time will see what you are doing and will continually engage you in pots when you have the worst of it.

With a big chip stack, your main job is to pick up the easy pots with your own aggressive play. But that doesn't mean you take no risks. If you sit on your chip stack until the money is hit, you'll be leaving a lot of pots on the table you could have picked up. The short stacks are desperate and many will be taking shots with very marginal hands. If you've got a pretty decent hand, even a hand like A-J or A-9 suited or K-Q or 8-8, call their all ins. It's not your job to double them up by calling with trash hands, but their pushing requirements will be pretty low.

It's often impossible to detect a player who's taking a two-live-cards shot, but this should never worry you. Although a play like this may be the right move for him, you're always on the long end of this bet, so if you've got a good hand and you can afford the loss, let him take his chances. And yes, it can be mathematically correct for both of you to be in the pot. He would often be making a mistake if he did not go for increased utility, and you would be making a mistake if you did not try to stop him when you had the mathematical edge on the bet and the chips to afford the gamble.

Do be careful when playing pros who have average stacks. You can bitch-slap a wimp who thinks he knows how to play poker, but pros may go over the top of you if it looks too much like you're making a move.

Other big stacks at the table will generally give you a wide berth, as you should them, and you don't want to get too deeply involved with other big stacks unless you have a very powerful hand or a great shot to make a nice pot with a good read on your opponent. If you try to completely avoid play with the other big stacks, however, some of the more aggressive of them will know that you are thinking this way, and they will take advantage of your survival instinct, especially if they have position on you. If your preflop raises are continually reraised by another big stack, he's betting that your bubble instincts will force you into survival mode. You may have to play back at a player like this, even with a marginal hand and no read. You should never let any player push you around, no matter what phase of the tournament it is, and you need to continue to build your stack at this time.

By the same token, you will sometimes have conservative players with big chip stacks who will be very hesitant to get involved in pots without premium hands, and if you have a player like this at your table, you should make yourself a thorn in his side. Push him out of every pot you can.

Your biggest utility advantage over your lesser-chipped opponents at this time is that you really can be selective in the cards you play, the pots you get involved in, and the opponents you go up against. If you just take your time, feel out what's happening, and keep getting your chips into pots when you feel you have the cards, the position, or the table image to take it down, you'll tend to build your stack during this phase of the tournament. Just pick on the survivalists if you don't get the cards to tangle with the players who want to mix it up. Even in a Rank 1-3 event where the average stacks will be pretty short in this phase, this is one of the easiest phases of a tournament in which to make money when you have a scary chip stack.

WHAT COMES AFTER THE "DINNER" PHASE?

Is it time for dessert?

You come out of the bubble phase when all players remaining are going to get paid. Your dessert may be half an Oreo cookie with the filling scraped off, or a banana split with all the trimmings. Let's look at the next phase of the tournament: phase four, *the money*.

PHASE FOUR: THE MONEY— EXPLOITING MASS RELIEF

This chapter will concentrate on the fourth phase of a tournament—a phase that just about everyone refers to as "in the money." You'll definitely know when you reach this phase, as will everyone else still alive in the tournament. Generally, just before the money phase, the bubble play is completed with "hand-for-hand" play until the unlucky bubble player bites the dust, one shy of the money.

"Hand-for-hand" means that if there is more than one table of players, each table will play one hand and then stop until all other tables complete their hands, before the next hand starts. The reason for this is to keep the shortest stacks from taking forever to play their hands, in the hope that while they're stalling, a player at one of the other tables will bust out, putting them into the money by default. By playing hand-for-hand, each table plays the exact same number of rounds as every other table, so there's no point in any player stalling the game.

Quite often, when there is only one bubble player left in the field, the tournament director will survey all remaining players to see if anyone has any objection to taking an amount off of the first place prize equal to the tournament buy-in and giving it to the next player who busts out. If all players agree to this arrangement, then there is no hand-for-hand play, as all remaining players are technically now in the money. More often than not all players agree to this plan, though occasionally a player objects. If any single player objects, there is no arguing about it, and the hand-for-hand play continues until the bubble player is eliminated. Expect a cheer to go up once the bubble player busts out. Now you're in the money.

THE THINNING OF THE HERD

Technically, overall conditions on the tables will have not changed appreciably since the bubble phase, or even since the minefield phase. There will still be a couple of big stacks, a couple of short stacks, and a handful of more-or-less average stacks at each table. The attack dynamics should still be the same as during the minefield phase. But again, money changes everything. While getting close to the money changed the emotional character of the tables when moving from the minefield to the bubble, actually being in the money brings about another radical change.

Suddenly, all those short and average stacks who spent much of the bubble phase waiting for premium cards breathe a collective sigh of relief and start throwing their chips into pot after pot like they've been dying to start rammin' and jammin'. What's happening is that they've already achieved their main goal—getting their buy-in money back in addition to the right to say, "I cashed." Plus, the next pay level barely raises the cash-out amount and they know that it doesn't come until another whole group of players have been eliminated. (If the starting field was a few hundred players, pay levels would go up in groups of nine.) That next pay level seems so far away.

Having just survived the agonizingly slow bubble period, topped off by the excruciatingly torpid hand-for-hand play, where it always seems that at least one table has some dork that needs to have a clock called on him, the elimination of nine more players hardly seems worth waiting for, not for a measly $100 or whatever. Hey, I cashed! That's what's important!

So, incredibly, the next nine players will probably be gone in less time than it took to play a single round of hand-for-hand at the end of the bubble phase. I mean players just fall like lemmings off a cliff once the money is hit.

The funny thing is that the beginning of the money phase is actually one of the few times in a tournament when it would be advisable for a player who has chips to just sit and wait for premium hands. The action gets so loose and wild that it's almost impossible to put any player on a hand at this time. And most of this action is the short-stacked ex-survivalists taking shots at each other. I have been on a few tables where this sudden rush to play did not occur when the money was hit, but as a general rule, you should expect this type of loosening up. The whole character of the table seems to change from tight to loose.

I think of this early part of the money phase as a thinning of the herd. A few of the survivalists will make hands and put together some amount of a chip stack, while a lot more of them will go down, happy that they made it into the money, knowing that Nam Le and Dutch Boyd and a number of other recognizable pros they happened to see in the event busted out before getting to the money. "Hey, dude, I outlasted Dutch Boyd!"

The thinning of the herd doesn't take that long except in events with huge initial fields, like the WSOP no-limit hold'em events, where hundreds of players make it into the money. In more normal tournament fields, you will fairly quickly get down to a few tables where a lot of players seem to have chips, and if some player is short-stacked or gets short-stacked, he either comes back fast or disappears. Suddenly, it seems like you can play poker again. There is an immense collective sense of relief once the herd thins and everyone left knows that he's accomplished his first goal, and that's where the opportunity lies.

THE MONEY PHASE IN RANK 1-3 EVENTS

In the shorter-stacked Rank 1-3 tournaments, the big stacks will tend to rule once the herd thins out. The average stacks are just too short to play much poker at this point so they play very much like the short stacks, with mostly all-in preflop bets. The big stacks will pick up the blinds and antes consistently until some average or short-stacked player has a hand he wants to take a stand with.

This is a pretty easy time to steal pots if you have an average stack as the big stacks will generally believe you when you push and the few remaining short stacks are looking for real hands to take a stand with. It will appear that some of the average stacks may be waiting to move up to the next pay level if the next pay level is close. But with the shortest stacks mostly gone, and most of the average stacks now in jam-or-fold mode, most of these players are not so much waiting for the next pay level as they are waiting for jamming cards. A lot of players have difficulty pushing in their chips with less-than-premium hands, so there's quite a bit of tight play, making a great situation for the big stacks, as well as for the average stacks who have good stealing moves.

In a Rank 1 tournament, where the average chip stacks in this phase may be very short in relation to the blinds and antes, there may be a short or average stack pushing in on most rounds, usually picking up the pot without confrontation. The most desperate players will be pushing in or calling any all in with any ace or any pair. It won't take too long in a short stack tournament to get through this phase and onto the final table—it will sometimes happen within a blind level, and it can be very fast if there is a blind level change shortly after the money is hit. Rank 2 and 3 tournaments, where there tend to be a few more competitive chip stacks, will take a bit more time.

If you have a big stack, you can't do any fancy bullying at this time because most of the players will not provide opportunities for you to bully them. They're either all in or they're out. But you can definitely keep building your stack with easy steals of small pots, and occasionally you'll get to play some poker with another big stack. You should definitely look for opportunities to call all-in bets from the shortest stacks when you have any decent hand—any ace, any two high cards, any pair. This is 100 percent a long-ball game from here on out in a Rank 1-3 event, and you can't just sit there waiting for big pairs.

One of the reasons you built your big stack was to be able to afford selective calls on all-in shots from desperately short stacks at this point in the tournament. Because of the blinds and antes, the pots will be pretty decent when a short stack gets his chips in there and the hands they'll be pushing with will not often be premium hands. You can afford to gamble and they can't afford not to.

THE MONEY PHASE IN RANK 4-6 EVENTS

In these tournaments, once the herd thins out, there's a lot more poker to play. There won't really be much of a small-ball game except perhaps in the Rank 6 events, but there will definitely be normal raises, and some cautious post-flop back-and-forth play. Because the average stacks will be bigger, there will definitely be a few players sitting tight, just waiting for premium cards and trying to stay alive to the next pay level.

If you are a big stack at your table, you must take charge, especially if any other big stack at your table is not taking charge. Be a bully. Believe me, your opponents are afraid to mess with you, and if you do not take advantage of this situation, you are making a huge tactical mistake. You've got those chips, so use them. You are terrifying to the players at your table since you can squash any of their big money dreams on a single hand, and you can put any player who gets into a pot with you to a test for his tournament life—while none of them can do this to you. You must let the players at your table know that all play from here on goes through you. You'll decide how big the pot is and if they want to play with you, fine. Bring it on. If there are one or more other big stacks at your table who have the same idea, then you are going to get to play some real poker and see what you're made of. The shorter stacks will love watching two big stacks jousting with each other, so give them a show. You have reached a point in the tournament where image and utility have equal importance and you can't let either of them go.

Note here that I'm talking about a power struggle between two big stacks who are both trying to take control of the table, not about one big stack who is trying to take control while the other has the nuts and isn't going to go away. Just because you get some play back from a deep-stacked opponent on a hand does not mean he's trying to control the table or you. He may really have a hand and you do not want to get yourself in trouble with stupid posturing. I have seen a lot of big stacks go down late in a tournament by failing to recognize that another big-stacked opponent really did have the hand he was representing, and many times I felt it was obvious that he was not just bluffing. To work all those hours to put together a dominating chip stack and then blow it off on one bad read—that's sad.

If there is still a short stack or two at your table, be careful of them unless they are so short that they cannot affect your utility and a double up for them would be insignificant. These players will be looking to push in on any ace, any pair, any two high cards, and sometimes just on guts. You can't read a short stack so don't give him an opportunity to push you out of a pot—or force you to call due to the pot odds—if you come in with a standard raise in front of him with some garbage hand. Attack dynamics still apply, but targeting a short stack means putting him to a test before he puts you to a test. If you don't have the cards to tangle with him, you push in on him. Don't make a standard raise.

If you are an average stack, you cannot let the big stack control you. You do have enough chips to push him out of a pot with an all-in over-the-top bet, and you have to let him know that despite his taking charge of the rest of the table, he'd better be damn careful around you. Be very careful that you do not set yourself up for bitch-slap moves, however, by entering the pot in front of a bully who may want to teach you a lesson. Be very aware of your position in relation to this player on every round. And remember, sometimes he really will have A-A or K-K.

THE SEABISCUIT MOVE

It's during the money phase of a tournament when you're first liable to see a player type (and a move or series of moves) that I call the "Seabiscuit." If you read the book or saw the movie, you'll recall that America's most famous race horse didn't just run fast—he had a strategy for winning. Briefly, he paced himself with the field throughout the race, then poured it on at the end when the field was slowing down. Horse race fans call a horse that does this a "pace stalker."

There are definitely pace stalkers in poker tournaments. It is virtually impossible to just keep up with the field in a poker tournament from the start to the finish. There is just too much variance that results from winning and losing big pots sporadically throughout. But there are players who have stealing down to an art form who become pace stalkers by default during the money phase, when they are card dead, but well-chipped enough to make their moves against the right players at the right times in order to not fall back in chips while the short stacks and average stacks are slowly busting out. These pace stalkers can turn into Seabiscuits.

If you saw the movie, *When We Were Kings*, which documented the 1974 Muhammad Ali-George Foreman fight in Zaire, the famous "rumble in the jungle," you may recall that Ali used a similar strategy against Foreman in that fight. For the first seven rounds, he threw comparatively few punches, mostly ineffective right hand leads, allowing Foreman to connect many more times than he did. One of the tactics Ali used was to allow Foreman to back him onto the ropes in almost every round. He didn't dance away from trouble as was his usual style in the ring. He kept backing up and it looked like he couldn't get away. Foreman was often flailing away like a madman while Ali—who never really lost his footing or appeared to be in real trouble—uncharacteristically seemed to be passively taking the punishment. In essence, Foreman was doing all the work. Ali was just keeping pace. Then, in the eighth round, when Foreman was physically spent and his guard was down, Ali came on like gangbusters. He suddenly seemed like a different fighter. With a combination left hook and smashing right to the face, Ali knocked out Foreman, who never saw it coming. When reporters later asked Ali about being "on the ropes" so much throughout the fight, Ali had a name for his strategy. He called it his "rope a dope" strategy. It was Seabiscuit all the way.

In a poker tournament, in order for a player to pull off a Seabiscuit, the conditions have to be right. It works best when players have finally gotten into the money after a long battle, and there is a sense of relief at having made it. The always perilous minefield phase, followed by the slow torture of the bubble play, are mentally exhausting. When the remaining players at a table are all sharing a sense of relief at having made it through the nerve-wracking battle to survive, their collective guards are down and the stage is set for Seabiscuit to turn on the juice.

For a player to successfully pull off a Seabiscuit play, certain other conditions must also be met. He cannot be so short-stacked that any moves he makes will be seen as desperation plays and given no respect. He has to be close enough to the field in chips that he's seen as a viable player, though he doesn't appear to be a serious threat. His current table image has to be fairly solid. He cannot have been caught stealing recently, and he cannot have been entering an inordinate number of pots. A good thief who has been pace stalking through the money portion and whose current table image is not in any way wild or extremely loose is in perfect position to pull a Seabiscuit move.

A Seabiscuit move can be a single brazen steal of a big pot that moves a player from being an also-ran to a serious contender. Often, however, it is a series of relentless power plays on numerous pots that take the table by surprise. In simple poker terms, this player has shifted gears, something that all experienced skillful players do throughout a tournament. But it is the timing of this gear shift, and the uncharacteristic aggression of the player doing it, which make everyone at the table think he must just be catching a lot of great cards, that make it a perfect Seabiscuit move. What he's doing is shifting into high gear right when all of his opponents have shifted into low. It makes for a devastatingly powerful attack.

Seabiscuit moves can be made at times other than when players first get into the money. You can pull a Seabiscuit any time there is a sense of relief at your table, provided your current table image and chip status meet the other requirements. For example, if a deep-stacked bully who has been running over everyone for a long time suddenly busts out on a series of hands, or just gets moved to another table, and everyone left is breathing a collective sigh of relief, the stage is set for the right player to pull off a Seabiscuit.

It can also be used when players who are already in the money hit a new pay level, and especially when players first make it to the final table. The sense of relief at having made it to the final table is always huge. For a great example of a Seabiscuit play in a poker tournament, think of Jerry Yang at the final table of the 2007 WSOP main event.

ESPN broadcast all sixteen hours of the event live, narrated by Phil Gordon. An unknown Laotian player from San Diego named Jerry Yang, who was described at the start of the broadcast as a conservative player, dominated the table from the very start. He came into the event on a short stack in eighth place (out of nine), and within half an hour had taken over the chip lead. It was an absolutely masterful display of dominance over players who were waiting for big hands, hoping to not go out early, and afraid to get involved.

Gordon was at first critical of Yang, though I suspect if it had been Scotty Nguyen or Hoyt Corkins or some other known aggressive pro taking charge the way Yang did, Gordon may have been praising him. At one point, Yang came into the pot from the button with a standard raise, and well-known pro Lee Watkinson pushed all in on him from the small blind. After a minute or more of agonizing over what to do, Yang called the all in. Watkinson showed A-6 offsuit. Yang had called with A-9 offsuit. I thought Yang (who works as a psychologist) had made one of the most astonishing reads and one of the gutsiest calls I had ever seen. Yang was a player who trusted his read to the death, and he was justly rewarded for his courage. This hand knocked out Watkinson in eighth place (and Watkinson was considered the favorite to win the event!).

Meanwhile, Phil Gordon criticized Yang for this call, based on conventional tight-guy theory. How could he call such a huge bet with A-9 offsuit? But from the utility perspective, Yang's call was 100 percent correct. The utility value of not only doubling up but at the same time taking out one of the world's top tournament pros is huge for an amateur player whose post-flop skills are limited by his relative lack of experience. Watkinson's all-in reraise was a huge overbet, and Yang read it correctly as being indicative of a weak hand. Following that showdown, Yang had a virtual license to steal. No player would dare take a shot at him. If they didn't have the nuts, they just gave up their chips. He stole the blinds and antes so often it was comical.

Yang also continually entered pots preflop with raises of anywhere from 2 x BB to 10 x BB. Gordon continually criticized Yang for the changing sizes of these raises, saying that the pros at the table would be able to define Yang's hands based on the size of his raise. Again, I felt Gordon missed the point. Yang completely befuddled his opponents. He almost never showed down a hand, but instead used his chips to keep pushing over the top of reraisers, forcing them to fold, so none of his opponents had any idea what his hands were based on his bet sizes. Indeed, throughout the event, Gordon repeatedly acknowledged that he had no idea what hands Yang was playing. Toward the end of the event, once Yang was clearly in line for the win, Gordon finally admitted that his initial criticisms of Yang's play had probably been off base.

By the time it got down to heads-up play, Yang had $103 million in chips. His opponent, Tuan Lam, a Canadian Internet pro, had $23 million and was completely at a loss as to how to play back at Yang, just as every other player at that table had been. Ultimately, Yang busted seven of his eight final table opponents, just as Jamie Gold had done the prior year. But Gold had entered the final table in 2006 with a monstrous chip lead while Yang had entered on a short stack.

Because it takes a certain type of table image and chip status to pull off a Seabiscuit, you can't just make a plan in advance to pull a Seabiscuit as soon as you get into the money. You might plan in advance to pull a Seabiscuit should the perfect opportunity present itself at any point in a tournament, but you may never get that opportunity. You can, and should, always be looking for opportunities to change gears in attempts to take your opponents by surprise, but real Seabiscuit opportunities usually take place after the money is hit, or the final table is made, when all of the conditions are right. There are very few other situations in a tournament when a whole tableful of players collectively shifts into low gear, and that's what you're looking for. Players who are recuperating from battle are off-guard and weak, and can be pushed around easily.

GUARDING AGAINST SEABISCUIT

This is one of the more difficult moves to guard against because the player making it is trading on his solid reputation and viable chip status, both of which seem to rule out sudden maniac aggression. The beauty of the move is that you really can't see it coming. Solid players do suddenly get dealt great hands, and most will play aggressively when dealt those hands and will not be bullied out of pots when they believe they have the best hand. If a player makes a single big pot steal with a Seabiscuit move, he may decide right there to change gears back to his solid style in relief at having pulled it off. You won't even know a move was made. But if a player turns on relentless aggression in pot after pot, he can run over the table unless someone puts a stop to him.

One thing you should be aware of any time you are at a table where there is a collective sense of relief is that the stage is set for Seabiscuit. If you are in position to make the move due to your current table image and chip status, go for it. But in addition to having the perfect set-up, you really do have to throw caution to the wind, suddenly turn yourself into a John Phan or a Carlos Mortensen, and go for broke. You must play your guts to the max.

If you are not in a position to make a Seabiscuit move yourself, watch out for it. When the money is hit, these moves are more common than you think, especially when there is a really smart experienced player at your table who always has his feelers out for weakness. And once a player embarks on a Seabiscuit, he goes on an emotional rush and won't shut down his aggression easily. Your best defense against this move is to never let yourself feel relieved just because you made it to the money, or the final table, or because the table bully just disappeared. As long as you are still engaged in battle, there is no time for relief.

When the money is hit and the tournament director announces a congratulations to all remaining players, and the dorks start pulling out their cell phones to call Mom and tell her their brilliant play has finally paid off, and players all around you are high-fiving each other and saying, "Yes! We made it!" you should be like Tonto in the old joke about the Lone Ranger. "What you mean *we*, paleface?"

The thing about Seabiscuit, the racehorse, is that he truly had the energy and stamina to outrun his competitors with an inexplicable burst of speed after having kept up with them through 90 percent of the race. The thing about Muhammad Ali is that he really could let George Foreman pummel him for seven rounds, then find the strength to knock out a bull with two punches. And the thing about a player who is capable of a Seabiscuit move is that he's got the wits, heart, and mental stamina to put on a show when his competitors are napping.

Keep your bad attitude during these standard vulnerable phases that occur in every tournament, and stay aware of changing conditions that could enable a Seabiscuit. Then just play your hyper-aware, tough-as-nails game. If your current table image and chip position don't allow you to pull off a Seabiscuit, then watch for it. If you sense some "solid" player is suddenly trying to run over the in-the-money revelers, you be the player who stops him, regardless of your stack size. Put him in his place.

SHORT-HANDED PLAY

It's generally in the money phase of a tournament when you first have to start dealing with short-handed play. Most tournaments' payout schedules pay about 10 percent of the field, but the exact number is usually a multiple of nine that comes closest to this result. For example, a tournament with 250 players would likely pay 27 spots (the last three 9-handed tables remaining), as would a tournament with 290 players. There are differences between payout schedules as to the precise number of spots paid and where the breaking points occur for adding more payout spots, but the general idea is the same.

A tournament that starts out with 250 players will usually start with ten-handed play at 25 tables, but as the field gets smaller, most tournaments—and especially those with higher buy-ins— change to nine-handed play at some point. If a poker room cannot accommodate all of the players who want to buy-in to an event, many will even start out with eleven-handed tables until the field gets small enough to go down to ten. So, throughout most of a tournament, you can expect to be playing nine- or ten-handed, occasionally eleven- or eight-handed. But all of these tables would be considered full-ring games, and strategically, play would be about the same.

There is always an attempt to keep the tables balanced—with as close to nine or ten players per table as possible—and if multiple players bust out from one table, a player or players will be moved to that table from other tables to accomplish this end. For example, if one table has six players due to three players busting out on one hand, one player may be moved to this table from each of two nine-handed tables, so that all three tables will have eight players.

Technically, the fewer the number of players at a table, the looser your requirements should be for entering a pot, because the strength of the "average" hand goes down in synch with the number of hands being dealt at a table. As an extreme example of this principle, a pocket pair will be dealt, on average, once every seventeen hands. At a ten-handed table, that means the chances are better than 50-50 that at least one player will be dealt a pocket pair on a given round. If two players are playing heads-up, however, we would expect at least one of them to be dealt a pocket pair about every eight or nine rounds of play. Any pocket pair is therefore a more powerful hand when playing heads-up than it is at a ten-handed table.

If we define short-handed play as playing with seven or fewer players, then in a multitable tournament that started with ten-handed tables, this condition would not present itself until the field got down to 31 players. At that point, you would have three tables of eight players each, and one of seven. In tournaments where there are nine players per table as the norm, you would start playing short-handed somewhat earlier. You would see your first seven-handed table when you got down to a field of 47 players—made up of five eight-handed tables and one seven-handed. As with the ten-handed game, however, play would go down to two tables of five each before the final table was reached.

This means that during the money phase, whether the regular tournament is played nine- or ten-handed, you will absolutely have to play short-handed (down to five players per table) before you get to the final table. So let's look at a few guidelines on how to play with 5 to 7 players at your table.

First of all, although it is almost always a mistake in a no-limit tournament to wait for premium hands before entering a pot, the fewer the number of players at your table, the more this mistake is magnified. Players who are not used to short-handed play will tend to put too much value on premium cards and will enter too few pots. You will see right away who these players are and you should exploit their mistake by stealing from them as relentlessly as you can. They will be easy to read because when they stay in a pot they have either a pretty strong hand or a very strong draw.

SHORT-HANDED STRATEGY CONSIDERATIONS BASED ON THE MATH

Most players put too much emphasis on the math in tournaments and too little on psychology, and this is especially true when playing short-handed. When playing short-handed, you should be even more inclined to bluff and steal, playing your opponents rather than your cards.

Still, you should have a basic understanding of the mathematical differences between full-table and short-handed play, as many of your skillful opponents will understand these differences, and your less-skillful opponents will not.

I am of the general opinion that it is rarely correct to limp into a pot if you are the first player to enter, even in the early small-ball stages of a tournament. I'll often call preflop limpers, however, because I tend to view them as weak players and I like the idea of having position on them no matter what my cards are. Limping into a pot at a short-handed table, however, is a much bigger mistake—unless you are limping to disguise a very powerful hand like A-A—because you will so much more often be raised by a player who has position on you. Limping with a baby pair or a spec hand like 8-7 suited is just wrong when the table is down to five or six players. Either muck your cards or raise to disguise your hand.

Spec hands, in fact, should usually be mucked at a short-handed table, unless you are entering the pot because your opponent in the hand is a player whom you intend to exploit post-flop. In that case, you might enter the pot with any two cards. But without a weak player in the hand to take advantage of, you should be aware of whether or not you actually have sufficient chips to play spec hands for their potential value. Post-flop drawing hands when you are short on chips are usually more expensive than they're worth. Because most pots at a short-handed table are raised preflop, there will be fewer multiway pots, which is also detrimental to spec hands because you will rarely be getting the right odds to call with draws post-flop.

Against experienced opponents, post-flop play will be aggressive. Big cards usually rule, but again, you can't let yourself turn into a card-obsessed wimp. At a short-handed table, more pots will be picked up by the players who are betting aggressively than by the players who have the best hands.

Legitimate hands that would be pretty weak at a nine- or ten-handed table are much stronger at a five- or six-handed table. If you flop second pair with an ace or king kicker, you should probably raise if an opponent bets the flop. You might do this automatically at a full table as well if you have full utility, but your chip status is often more precarious at a short-handed table this late in a tournament, especially in a Rank 1-3 event. You may not be able to afford an information bet, so that your decision really comes down to whether you should push all in or fold. The shorter your chip stack, the more you should lean toward pushing, especially if you feel your opponent is just making a continuation bet. Short-handed play requires a lot of gutsy moves.

If you really make a strong hand—say you flop a set—slowplaying is often the best way to make the most of your monster hand, and this is especially true if you are playing against an aggressive opponent who you know will take the lead in the betting if you let him. At a full table, I would rarely slowplay a set because the hand is so invisible and there is usually more to be made by betting and hoping an opponent will stay in the pot with you. If there was a dangerous straight or flush draw on the board at a full table, I would normally play a set very aggressively, making any opponent pay dearly to stay in the pot and try to beat me.

Short-handed, however, the likelihood of being outdrawn when I flop a set is lower—since there are fewer multiway pots and fewer spec hands in play—and the risk is usually outweighed by the utility benefit of the huge pot I might collect at this crucial point in the tournament. I will bet at the pot if I am first to act, but I will not bet more than my opponent would consider a standard continuation bet, and if I am raised, I will just call. Maybe my opponent will think I'm on the draw. If a third card to the straight or flush comes down, I will probably push in, and if my opponent has what I am representing, so be it.

Top pair is a very strong hand in a short-handed game, and I would tend to play it with maximum aggression even without the top kicker. If I have K-Q versus A-K and the flop comes down with a king and two rags, I'm toast. I will probably not be able to get away from my hand as easily as I could at a full table. Your short-handed opponents are so much more likely to bluff, or to feel confident with any second or third pair, or even with an ace in hand or two overcards to the board, that laying down top pair with a decent kicker is usually a mistake.

Check-raising with top pair is another move I'll sometimes make at a short-handed table. I just about never check-raise at a full table in a tournament, but when short-handed, and up against an aggressive opponent that I feel will bet if I don't, I will use this move. If I have top pair and the board presents dangers, I'll check-raise all in.

Restealing from the blinds is also an excellent short-handed play, even when you have no hand. I give almost no respect to late position raisers in a short-handed game if I have any kind of legitimate hand. If I am in one of the blinds with utter trash cards, I will usually throw my hand away to a raise, especially a big raise. But I'll definitely look for a resteal opportunity to get my chips back.

If I hit a pair on a raggy flop, I'll bet very aggressively to get overcards to fold. And if I actually have an overpair to the flop, I may be a goner if any player has that hand beat because I'm likely to be all in.

You do have to keep in mind that even when the table is short-handed, there will be players who are dealt pocket A-A and K-K and Q-Q, and there will be players who make nut straights and nut flushes and other powerful hands. You have to let your instincts guide you when playing short-handed, but you also have to keep in mind that these powerful starting cards and post-flop monster hands are a lot less likely.

Again, I don't believe in memorizing lists of hands to play and how to play them for pro-level tournaments, so I'm not going to provide such a list. I guarantee you the best players are not playing memorized lists of hands. I love looking at these types of lists that show the probabilities of hands holding up or drawing out and

13 - PHASE FOUR: THE MONEY

I believe there is real value to having a good grasp on the math of the game. But when I look at the statistics for hands on short-handed tables versus full ring games, it's not to find a list of hands to memorize for different situations; it's to get an overall feel for the game so that I can recognize which players are probably making mistakes by playing too tight or not aggressively enough.

From my perspective, the biggest mistake you can make when playing short-handed is to fail to change gears to a looser and more aggressive style. This is a terrible time to let your chips dwindle. You want to arrive at the final table with as deep a stack as possible. Watching half your stack disappear during the short-handed portion of the money phase because you failed to realize that you could enter the pot with a wider variety of hands, or that hitting second pair on the flop was worth betting on, is a costly mistake.

Now let's go on to the most important phase of a tournament, phase five, the final table.

PHASE FIVE: THE FINAL TABLE— LAST CHANCE TO SCREW UP

This chapter will focus on the fifth phase of a tournament—the final table. Many of the topics covered in previous chapters are applicable to final table play and I'm not going to rehash all of that stuff. But a few points specific to final tables must be made.

POWER PLAYS AND TRAPPERS

There are usually one or two weak players who have lucked their way to the final table, but as for the rest of your opponents, you generally find that a lot of the cream has risen to the top. Definitely be aware of any "solid" pace stalker who suddenly turns into Seabiscuit. Bet-sizing is more critical now than ever, as the chip discrepancies will be bigger than ever, the blinds and antes higher than ever, and the big stacks will be waiting like crocodiles in a swamp for average-stacked players to come wading in, thinking this is just a friendly game of poker.

The shorter stacks—which may include a lot of the average stacks—will often have to get by on power moves, and this is especially true in the Rank 1-3 events where even the big stacks will not have a lot of utility. Any skillful player who is checking and calling should be assumed to be trapping. Any less-skillful player who is checking and calling will not last long at this table unless he is trapping.

If you have not read *PTF1*, you should read chapters 4 and 5 in that book—"Rock, Paper, Scissors" and "Basic Position Strategy." Those chapters describe the power relationships in a no-limit hold'em tournament and the importance of position. A lot of the psychology of a final table is described in those chapters, as almost all final tables turn into fast-structured tournaments at some point, and many do so quite early. The psychology of a final table starts with the standard rock-paper-scissors power relationship when there are eight to ten players at the table, then slides into looser short-handed play where position becomes less important and chip stacks dominate, but finally becomes just a battle of wills, where the most aggressive player with the biggest stack has the edge, but often the cards decide differently.

SHORT-HANDED PLAY WITH FEWER THAN FIVE PLAYERS

Obviously, the discussion of short-handed play in the previous chapter is crucial to the final table. In that chapter, however, I only discussed short-handed play down to five or six players. Once you get to four-handed play, the under-the-gun player is actually in a strong post-flop position, since this preflop position corresponds to what would be the cutoff seat in a full ring game—one seat to the right of the button. Since preflop raising is more common in short-handed games, and legitimate pot-entering hand requirements are looser, this means that one of the two players who are not in the blinds will be raising on almost every round. If the cutoff seat raises and the button has any ace—even a bad ace—or any two high cards, any pair, or just a feeling that the cutoff seat is trying to steal the button a bit too often, the button will likely reraise. And the blinds themselves, knowing that the position players will be taking a lot more shots, will be much more likely to defend.

The level of craziness, pre- and post-flop, will depend on the players and their chip stacks. An aggressive player who is also a staunch blind defender will easily run over the table if the other players do not change gears for the looser playing environment. With more than one really aggressive player at the table, you will often see raising wars, both pre- and post-flop, and if hands are shown down, you may be astonished at how weak both players were throughout their game of chicken. This type of battling will continue as you get down to three players, then two players playing heads-up. In these very short-handed situations, the most aggressive players will in almost all cases steal the top finishing positions from more conservative players who are playing a more card-based game.

As for lists of hands that you should play based on the number of players remaining, your seating position, your chip position and the action in front of you, forget it. If you're still worrying about cards, you've missed the whole point of this book. If you want a decision on whether you should enter a pot, call a raise, reraise, or fold, after considering the fact that you're mathematically correct to be playing a looser and more aggressive game, look at your opponents, muster up every drop of bad attitude you can find within you, and let your attitude be your guide. You think that's too vague? Then your attitude's too vague. Work on it.

MY OWN FINAL TABLE EXPERIENCES

If you've read *PTF1*, then you know that in that book I did not include a chapter on final table play and for a very good reason. Although I played hundreds of those fast format tournaments where the average buy-ins were usually between $40 and $200, and I made dozens of final tables, there just wasn't ever much play at the final tables. Players are typically so short-stacked in fast events relative to the blind/ante costs that by the time you hit the final table, the only strategic decisions are whether to push all in, call an all in, or fold. The fact is that in those tournaments, I rarely saw a final table played to completion. In almost every case, before an actual winner was determined by the cards, there was a mutual agreement to chop up the prize pool based on chip count. So, in *PTF1*, in lieu of a chapter on final table play, I included a brief chapter on chopping up a prize pool.

After that book was published in the summer of 2006, I began entering smaller buy-in events at the 2006 WSOP to research slower-structured tournaments. I actually managed to cash in a $1,000 event, but I could see that there were important differences between fast tournaments and slow ones, and even between slow tournaments with different structures. When it comes to tournament strategy, structure dictates, and failing to adjust your strategy to the structure is a costly error. I also watched a lot of the WSOP final tables that year, very interested in this aspect of tournament play as I'd engaged in so little of it. I started playing some of the smaller buy-in local Vegas slow-structured tournaments in order to develop some initial thoughts on how the slower structures affected optimal strategy, formulated an attack plan, and decided to go after the slow-structured tournaments using the same crash-course methodology I had used to figure out fast tournaments—just get in there and start playing.

Living in Vegas where so many tournaments and pro-level tournament series are held, and just a few hours drive from Los Angeles, where so many more are held, I decided to start by concentrating on live multitable tournaments (MTTs) only—no online tournaments—that had "modest" buy-ins between $300 and $5,000, seeking out the best structures within these buy-in limits based on blind lengths and chip counts.

MY TOURNAMENT RECORD

From January 2007 through early April 2008, I played exactly 111 tournaments that met the above criteria. I also played a number of tournaments outside my focus of concentration, including a few with lower buy-ins, a couple of pot-limit Omaha tournaments, one short-handed event, and various single and multitable satellites. But one thing I really liked about these slow-structured tournaments was that I finally got to play some final tables.

When I go to the *Card Player* website and I look up my name in their player database (and I don't play under the name Arnold Snyder), they show that I've made twelve final tables in the past 16 months in their Player-of-the-Year (POY) rated tournaments. To qualify as a POY event, a tournament must be open to the general public (events such as invitation-only, ladies-only, or seniors-only events do not qualify); there must be a buy-in of $300 or more; there must be at least 60 players in the event; and the overall payouts in the tournament series must be over $1 million. Eight of my twelve final tables were in 2007, and of the 5,114 players in the *Card Player* database for that year, only seven players have more than eight final tables. And even though I played none of the major $10K+ events, where the most POY points are awarded, I still ranked in the top 5 percent among all those players.

More importantly to me as a professional gambler, I made money and had a high win rate. ("Win rate" is return on investment expressed as a percentage. If I invest $1,000 in buy-ins, and I get a return of $2,200, then I have won $1,200 for my $1,000 invested, a win rate of 120 percent.) I finished in the money in approximately one out of every 5.3 tournaments I entered, for an overall win rate of 121 percent.

In thinking over the final tables I've played to get a handle on how to write this chapter, I keep coming back to how I learned to play final tables, and I learned to play them by making mistakes.

Nothing teaches like experience and the experience of loss is the best teacher of all. In going over my notes from tournaments past, which contain almost nothing but my mistakes—the ones that really bugged me—I found two real doozies that occurred at final tables. One of these mistakes I made more than once, and I've seen other players make variations on both of them numerous times. I think if you can learn to avoid just these two mistakes at a final table, including all of their variations, you'll have a shot at final table success.

So, instead of writing a chapter on how to play a final table, I'm going to start this chapter over from a different perspective. Let's call it…

HOW NOT TO PLAY A FINAL TABLE

This first mistake is one I made over and over again before I figured it out. And since figuring it out, I've seen dozens of other players make it, including some very skillful and talented players and, in some cases, well-known ones. There are also many variations on this mistake, and I had to make every variation of it before I could see that it was always the same mistake in slightly different circumstances. Other than for playing tight, this may be the most common mistake being made at final tables. I call this:

MISTAKE #1: GIVING "FREE CARDS" BY PUSHING ALL IN

I was at the final table of a $550 buy-in WSOP Circuit event. We were down to six players and I was short-stacked—not the shortest stack at the table, but way too short for comfort. The blinds were $2,000/$4,000 with a $1,000 ante. I had $65,000 in chips. The table folded around to the chip leader in the cutoff seat, who had well over $200,000 in chips. He entered the pot with a bet of $25,000. The button folded and I looked down to find pocket tens.

Because the raiser was not only in the cutoff seat but also had a big chip stack, I didn't have a lot of respect for his overbet. But he was also an amateur player that I had been at a different table with for a number of hours, and I knew he didn't raise with trash hands, though he frequently overbet the pot. In fact, I'd seen how he'd acquired a lot of his chips and it was on a series of incredibly lucky hands that went his way.

So, I decided to take a stand. Just calling his $25,000 bet—another $23,000 to me since I already had $2,000 in the small blind, would pretty much pot-commit me, and a minimum reraise would take so many of my $65,000 in chips that it would be silly. I decided to push all in.

He called quickly and turned his cards face up—pocket sixes—making me with my pocket tens an 80 percent favorite to double up. Unfortunately, a 6 came down on the river, his set of sixes cracked my tens, and I ended up with a sixth place finish.

As I stood up to bow out, one of the players said, "Oh, man, bad beat!" And, technically, it was; but still, the fact was I had played the hand wrong. I made a mistake and I paid the price.

How should I have played my hand?

ANALYSIS

I was absolutely correct in my decision to take a stand with this hand. I had very little utility and I desperately needed to increase my chip stack. But my execution was terrible. There was no doubt in my mind that my opponent would call my all in preflop. Even though he was an amateur player, I knew he wasn't raising preflop on air and when I pushed in there were $102,000 chips in the pot and it was only $40,000 more for him to call. If he lost this pot, he would still be the chip leader at the table. As he had been getting lucky for hours, I'm sure he would have called my all in with any two high cards, any ace in hand, or any other hand with which he would have made that oversized preflop raise.

Knowing he would not fold to my preflop all in, I was putting my tournament life on the line while giving him five cards to beat me. And he did not, in fact, beat me until that river card hit the felt.

Consider how this hand would have played out if I had simply decided to call his raise preflop and then push in after the flop regardless of what came down on the flop. Three overcards to his sixes came down, including a king. In the small blind, I had to play first, so if I pushed in my last $40,000 in chips post-flop, is there any way he would have called that bet with his pocket sixes? No. A very loose pro who didn't believe my bet may have called with a pair of sixes, but with my preflop call to his big raise and my all-in push of $40,000 chips on the flop, that amateur would have put me on a hand superior to 6-6, and I would have increased my chip stack from $65,000 to $102,000 on that hand—still a short stack, but a lot more viable and still in the hunt.

It's true that I desperately needed to build my stack and utility and my decision to go all the way with this hand was justified. For example, if my opponent had pushed in preflop, it would have been a mistake for me not to call for all my chips with pocket tens. In fact, it would also have been correct for me to push all in on him like I did if I knew he had pocket sixes! What made my all-in move a mistake was that I didn't know I was such a strong favorite in the hand. In fact, I was guessing it would be a race, and hoping it would not be against an overpair to my tens.

Finally, consider how I would have played my pocket tens if this player had limped into the pot by just calling the $4,000 big blind.

In this case, I would have been correct to push all in with my $65,000 in chips, not because I would have wanted the limper to call the extra $61,000, but because I'd be hoping to take that $16,000 pot right there without giving him any cards at all to try and beat me. Had he limped into the pot, I would have had the chip utility to use my all in for the full power that move should have. The fact that I would have pushed in on him had I known he had sixes is irrelevant. Pocket tens are not pocket aces. Tens are just too vulnerable to getting beat by overcards.

So, how should I have played this hand? I should have played it the same way as I would play it if I was trying to resteal with trash cards. I should have called his raise preflop, then pushed all in on the flop. An all-in resteal move against an amateur player wins a huge percentage of the time—maybe 90 percent or more. And for me to have odds like that to add $37,000 in chips to my stack of $65,000, when all I have is pocket tens that are very vulnerable to a suck-out in a race situation, made it a mistake not to take the easy chips since they would significantly improve my stack size and my utility in themselves. I was definitely thinking utility when I made my all-in move, but it would have been smarter for me to pick up the easy $37,000 than trying to get the $40,000 more on a hand that could easily bust me.

When I pushed all in preflop, I surrendered my post-flop utility. The reason you push in preflop on an opponent is to put him to a test by taking his away his utility. If you know an opponent will call your all in because of his stack size and the odds he's getting, then you're not putting him to a test, you're relinquishing your own post-flop utility and giving him two free cards. The $40,000 in chips I had in excess of his $25,000 raise had no preflop utility. I knew he would call my all-in bet. But those $40,000 in chips would have had sufficient post-flop utility to win me that pot. In fact, an amateur player like my opponent would likely have folded even pocket J-J or Q-Q to my all-in bet with that king on the board.

The mistake I made by pushing all in preflop was that I never gave my opponent an opportunity to fold. I just gave him two extra cards to try and beat me and, in this case, those two extra cards were all he needed.

It could be argued that my opponent may have made a preflop raise like that with A-K, and when the king came down on the flop, my all-in bet would have spelled my doom anyway. That's true. But since I knew that my preflop all-in bet would not get rid of him no matter what he raised with, that point is moot. The fact is, flops do not hit a hand as often as they miss it, so I should have given him an opportunity to miss before I pushed the rest of my chips into the pot.

KEY UTILITY DECISION

Because of my low utility at that point, my pushing all in on my pockets tens preflop, even knowing I would be called, was very close to a correct decision. And like I say, if he had pushed all in on me, it would have been correct for me to call, while if I had known he had 6-6, it would have been correct for me to push. But what it really comes down to is the voluntary relinquishing of utility preflop, when I could have retained it. It is almost always a mistake to give up your utility in a hand.

This type of mistake is not limited to final tables, but you see it more often at final tables because the play is so much more aggressive and every hand and decision seem so much more important. What annoyed me the most about that hand was that I had already learned this lesson during the bubble phase of a $5,000 WSOP Circuit event. With 180+ players in the field and 18 spots paying, it was the second day of the event and we were down to fewer than 30 players. I was in decent chip shape and had a good handle on most of the players at my table.

$5,000 CIRCUIT EVENT HAND

An aggressive player with one of the bigger chip stacks at the table entered the pot with a standard raise from under the gun. I had played in a number of other tournaments with this player, including a few hours during this tournament in some of the early blind levels the previous day. I knew him to be loose and tricky, gutsy and hard to read. In middle position, I looked down to find big slick. With little hesitation, I pushed all in.

The rest of the table folded and when it got back to the under-the-gun raiser, he called my all in with his pocket queens. To my delight, an ace came down on the flop, immediately making me a huge favorite in the hand. Unfortunately, a queen came down on the turn, and I went out shy of the money.

> ONE OF THE WEAKEST PLAYS YOU CAN MAKE IS TO PUSH ALL IN BEFORE THE FLOP AGAINST A LOOSE-AGGRESSIVE PLAYER WHO SIGNIFICANTLY OUTCHIPS YOU WHEN YOU DON'T EVEN HAVE A PAIR IN YOUR HAND.

Same mistake, slightly different context. I was not so short on chips that I couldn't have just called that preflop raise to see what the flop brought. Before the flop, A-K is just two high cards. Big slick doesn't beat a pair of deuces if it doesn't improve. But pushing in with big slick on a loose-aggressive player with a big chip stack who raised from under the gun is idiotic. Unless the raiser is so short on chips that I'm trying to get all of his chips into the pot, this is an amateur move. One of the strongest plays you can make in a no-limit hold'em tournament is to push all in. But one of the weakest plays you can make is to push all in before the flop against a loose-aggressive player who significantly outchips you when you don't even have a pair in your hand.

ANALYSIS

Again, I relinquished my post-flop utility and gave an opponent two extra cards to beat me—which he did. It's true that I was looking for every opportunity to increase my chip stack and my utility, but since I was above-average in chips at my table, I didn't need to take that big of a risk. It's not like my opponent had been hampering my utility or running over the table, and he didn't have position on me. You shouldn't just gamble it up when you can actually use skill to better control your outcome.

My big mistake was that I based my decision on my cards and immediately fell back into fast tournament habits. If I had looked at my hole cards and found 7-4 offsuit, instead of big slick, but decided it was time to steal a pot from this opponent, I would never have tried it with an all in preflop. It would have been a much stronger play with much lower risk to call my opponent's preflop raise, then go over the top of him when he bet on the flop.

This was another hand I could have won a good-sized pot with had I retained my utility. And if no ace or king came down on the flop, I could have made a decision at that point on whether I wanted to play back at my opponent or just fold with minimal damage and a still viable chip stack. Any time you are in need of utility, you should use every bit of the utility you have to acquire more.

I see many players making this mistake in every tournament I play. And at final tables, this mistake is one of the most common ways for players to bust out. Because final table play can be so emotionally intense due to the huge prize money that's so close, many players push all in preflop when they should be taking their time and considering all of their options.

> ### How Not to Play a Final Table: Rule #1:
>
> Don't fail to give an opponent an opportunity to fold after the flop. Always use whatever utility you have to get more utility. Many preflop all ins are card-based amateur plays that should be avoided in pro-level tournaments.

Here's another final table mistake that again has to do with pushing all in at an inappropriate time. I call this one "utility blindness."

MISTAKE #2: UTILITY BLINDNESS

This hand occurred in a Rank 5, deep-stack, $1,000 event. There were 222 starting players. It was the second day and we had been on the final table for more than three hours. We were down to four players. The blinds were at the seventeenth level, $10,000/$20,000 with a $4,000 ante—so there were $46,000 in chips in the pot before the cards were even dealt. When we started four-handed play, two players had a bit more chips and slightly more utility, but no player had a huge chip edge. Even the two of us with shorter stacks could put a real hurt on either of the bigger stacks, and any all-in pot between a short stack and a big stack that went to the shorter stack would cause them to reverse positions. As one of the shorter stacks, I was pretty much in jam-or-fold mode. The two bigger stacks occasionally played a bit of poker with each other, but neither of them were getting too reckless. There were big differences in the payouts that we were all aware of—with first place paying $66,000 and fourth place paying $19,000—and it had been a long hard fight for all of us to get here. No one wanted to blow it on a stupid mistake.

With the blinds and antes so high, however, none of us could sit long waiting for a hand. A standard raise to $60,000 put $106,000 in the pot, and a call to the raise made the pot $166,000. Most post-flop bets, therefore, were all in. A number of pots were folded around to the blinds who played cautiously against each other. For a while we jockeyed for position like this, then hit a point where all four of us had nearly equal chip stacks, with all of us in possession of somewhere between $500,000 and $600,000 in chips. Aware that the next blind level would be $15,000/$30,000 with a $5,000 ante, it appeared that lucky cards were going to decide this event, as none of us could afford to not play with the cost of sitting there so high.

So, we cut a deal whereby we would play the tournament out to the finish, but three players would get just under the second place money, and the winner would get just eight thousand more than the other three. That gave everyone a sense of relief, as we all felt that we could now start playing poker beyond the combination of cautiousness and kamikaze all ins that had been going on for some time. And the extra $8,000 was worth playing for.

Very shortly after cutting this deal, two players busted out. The chip leader took out the first player, and I took out the second. We were down to heads-up play and he had me outchipped by about $1.4 million to $800,000. I had viewed him as the toughest opponent at the table almost since the final table had started and it didn't surprise me that he was in the position he was now in. (Additionally, I had watched this player at a final table in one of the 2006 WSOP events where he took third place, so I considered him a pro.)

On the first heads-up hand, I found A-9, and I came in with a standard raise. He reraised. Now A-9 is a strong hand heads-up, and I felt that he had judged my raise to be a position play since I'd have position on him after the flop. So I pushed all in.

Mistake.

He called. He had A-J, and one hand after getting to heads-up play, I ended up taking second place.

ANALYSIS

Three hands earlier, my all in would have been an appropriate move. But with two players busting out, and the two of us now having all of the chips, we had enough utility to play poker again. It's true that A-9 is a strong hand heads-up, but I had no actual read on my opponent when he reraised. And there was also a chance I could have taken that pot away from him simply with aggressive position play on the flop, turn, or river. No ace, jack, or 9 came down on the board, and he beat me on the basis of nothing more than a better kicker. With position on him, and enough chips to do serious damage to him, that pot could easily have gone to me had I played my cards right.

My mistake this time was that I had failed to stop and reassess our chip positions and utility, and I was still mentally in jam-or-fold mode. He had less than a 2 to 1 chip advantage on me, and with the big blind at $20,000, and $800,000 in chips in my stack, there was a lot of poker left to play. I blew the opportunity to see what I could do heads-up against him.

When two players out of only four remaining bust out on a final table, it's very different from two players busting out of full tables earlier in the tournament. Any time multiple players bust out within the same blind level at a final table, there will be a big shift in the table's overall utility. And the later these bust-outs occur at a final table, the bigger the utility change. I had seen this happen at final tables when eight players turned into five within the same blind level, and even when nine went down to six. I'd watched other players fail to adjust many times, and mentally noted their mistake.

If you have played a lot of single-table satellites and sit-n-gos, you probably have developed a good instinct for short-handed and heads-up play. But if most of your tournament play has been in multitable events, especially fast-structured multitable events, the sudden dramatic utility changes that can take place at the final table of a deep-stack event may take you by surprise.

That leads us to:

How Not to Play a Final Table: Rule #2:

Do not fail to reassess your utility, and the utility of your opponents, any time there is a change in the number of players at a final table, and especially when more than one player has busted out within the same blind level.

CASHING OUT

A highly successful sports bettor told me that the difference in talent between the top NFL superstars and the more run-of-the-mill NFL pros is extremely small. At the NFL level of play, all of the players are so far above the rest of humanity in football skill, and by comparison so close in skill to each other, that it's not unusual for the worst players to have golden games where they outperform the best players. The actual differences between the overall career records of the superstars and the rest of the players come down to the best players' obsession for perfection. In their relentless determination to press for every increment of edge, they simply manage to accumulate those golden games a lot more often than the others.

In Chapter Twelve, I showed that the difference between what the big stacks have accomplished by late in a tournament and what the average stacks and short stacks have accomplished is relatively small. And although luck may be a factor in these differences in any given tournament, the superior performance of the top players over the long run comes down to the same relentless drive for perfection that's behind the success of the top NFL pros. What it comes down to is the top tournament pros consistently making one or two fewer mistakes per tournament, or finding one or two more opportunities to earn chips, than their closest competition.

Most players who show up at any given tournament are clueless about how to play tournaments. They think they always bust out of tournaments or become crippled due to bad beats or coolers, or because they just weren't dealt enough premium hands. But in most cases, if you were to review all of their play in all of the tournaments they entered, you'd find that the unfortunate hands that caused their downfalls shouldn't have knocked them out—not if they had earned the chips they should have earned in many other prior hands, or not missed out on so many opportunities to steal pots, or avoided blowing off chips in pots where they should have realized they were beat.

You should expect to run into bad beats and coolers in every tournament you play. It's what you do in all of the other hands throughout the tournament that gives you the chips you need to survive the inevitable bad beats, keeping you in the competition for the money. In a tournament, any opportunity missed could be the opportunity that would have changed your result from loser to winner. I encourage you to think obsessively about every tournament hand you play in which you could have increased your utility, avoided losing utility, or simply played better with the utility you had.

If you understand the principles in this book, all it will take for you to succeed is the heart and will to do what you have to.

I'll see you at the tables.

PART IV
FOR HARD CORE
PLAYERS ONLY

APPENDIX A: BANKROLLING YOUR PLAY

INTRODUCTION

In *PTF1*, I provide a simple formula for figuring out standard deviation for tournament players and if you are considering playing tournaments at the pro level, I would suggest you get that book. You don't need to run computer simulations to figure this stuff out and you don't need any advanced math. All you need is a calculator. If you can use a computer spreadsheet, you can set it up to do the math for you when you enter the variables.

Some of the material in this chapter will be foreign to poker players who have not read *PTF1*, because I've estimated bankroll requirements using methods that would only be familiar to those who have taken college level statistics courses. In my opinion, professional gamblers need to understand this math, or they will condemn themselves to years of going broke repeatedly, no matter how skillful they are. But you do not need to go back to college to understand this stuff. Just read *PTF1*. Since I provided a fairly comprehensive treatment of bankroll requirements for tournament players in that book, I will not reproduce all of that here. But as I put it in *PTF1*, Chapter 28, "How Much Money Do You Need?":*

---

* Some five months after *PTF1* was published, another poker book was published that does deal seriously and intelligently—and in much greater depth for cash

APPENDIX A: BANKROLLING

It's the rare blackjack book these days that doesn't provide at least some information on such topics as standard deviation, the Gambler's Ruin formula, risk-averse betting strategies, the Kelly criterion, and various related topics, in addition to simplified charts of data that card counters can use to estimate their bankroll requirements.

Most poker books, by contrast, stick to strategic advice exclusively. Blackjack players learn early how to manage their bankrolls; poker players learn early how to hit up their friends when they go broke.

QUICK, EASY GUIDE TO STANDARD DEVIATION

Statisticians use the "standard deviation" formula to estimate fluctuations. It's not that difficult to apply the formula to poker tournaments if we use a specific tournament's payout structure and make some assumptions about expected results, and in *PTF1*, I describe exactly how to do this for poker tournaments. Let's define what the term standard deviation means to a statistician, using a simple coin-flip example.

---

game players—with the topic of bankroll requirements. This book is *The Mathematics of Poker* (ConJelCo, 2006), by Bill Chen and Jerrod Ankenman. This book is to poker what Peter Griffin's *The Theory of Blackjack* is to twenty-one. Unfortunately, like Griffin's book, much of the material in the Chen/Ankenman book is not readily accessible to a player who has not taken some college level courses in probability and statistics. I still urge any serious poker player to get this book, just as I have always recommended Griffin's book to all serious blackjack players. The Chen/Ankenman book provides discussions on a wide range of topics I haven't seen elsewhere for serious players.

If I flip a coin 1,000 times, and I bet $1 on each flip, winning a dollar each time the coin comes up heads but losing the dollar each time the coin comes up tails, I would expect to break even, assuming the coin and the flipper are honest. If you try flipping a coin 1,000 times and recording the actual results, however, you'd be highly unlikely to come up with exactly 500 wins and 500 losses.

Statisticians use the term *standard deviation* to explain normal variations from an expected result. For instance, if you flip an honest coin 10 times, betting $1 per flip on heads, your expected result is to break even with five heads and five tails. If, however, you came up with 7 tails and 3 heads, so that you lost $4 on these coin-flips, this would not be an indication that something was wrong. In 10 coin flips, having 7 tails come up would be considered a *normal fluctuation*. If, on the other hand, you flipped a coin 10,000 times, and it came up 7,000 tails and only 3,000 heads, giving you a $4,000 loss, any mathematician would call it a very *abnormal fluctuation*, and advise you that something was fishy with either the flipper or the coin. Even though the ratio of heads to tails has remained 7 to 3, the large number of flips makes such a highly skewed result suspect.

When we are considering even-money bets (bet $1 to either win $1 or lose $1), on a coin flip, we can figure out the standard deviation on our win/loss result for any number of flips simply by taking the square root of the number of flips. It is not difficult to figure this out on any pocket calculator that has a square root key. The square root of 100 is 10, so the standard deviation on our win/loss results in 100 coin flips betting $1 a flip is $10. The square root of 1,000 is approximately 31.62, so the standard deviation on the results of 1,000 coin-flips is $31.62.

Once you understand what the square root of a number means to a statistician, you will understand why it can be perfectly normal for you to lose $4 with $1 bets on 10 flips of an honest coin, but nearly impossible for you to lose $4,000 with $1 bets on 10,000 flips of that same coin.

The standard deviation on 10 $1 bets equals the square root of 10, which equals $3.16.

The standard deviation on 10,000 $1 bets equals the square root of 10,000, which equals $100.

So, to have a loss of $4 in ten flips of the coin is to be just over one standard deviation ($3.16) away from our break-even expectation. But to lose $4,000 in 10,000 flips of the coin, where one standard deviation (S.D.) is $100, is to be 40 standard deviations away from our expectation. This is in the realm of the mathematically impossible.

How impossible is it?

Statistically, we expect to be within one standard deviation of our expectation 68 percent of the time. We will be within two standard deviations of our expectation 95 percent of the time. We will be within three standard deviations 99.7 percent of the time. Suffice it to say that if we get a coin flip result that is 40 standard deviations from our expectation, either the coin or the flipper is crooked. You have a much better chance of winning a state lottery than you do of flipping 7,000 heads in 10,000 trials with an honest coin.

The results on a poker tournament bet (or buy-in) involve complexities that are not involved in a simple $1 bet on a coin flip, but it's not rocket science either to do these calculations. You can do them on any pocket calculator. So, if you're interested in the math, use the method explained in *PTF1*. If you don't care about the math itself, then just use the chart provided toward the end of this chapter.

HOW MUCH BANKROLL IS NEEDED?

As a professional gambler, the first thing I think of when I see a profitable gambling opportunity is this: How much of a bankroll do I need? All gambling is a high-risk investment, and the risk is caused by what mathematicians call variance—which is essentially just a $2 word for luck. Even with a strong advantage, a player can go broke playing poker tournaments unless he has enough of a bankroll to ride out his inevitable negative swings.

You can't prevent suck-outs, coolers, runs of bad cards, or bad beats. But, believe it or not, there are mathematical limits on both good and bad luck, and a professional gambler can actually control his own destiny—ensuring himself of long run profits if he simply bets within the limits of his bankroll. Managing your money well will turn these miserable events into nothing but small downward blips on the ever-rising upward trend of your gambling career. Managing your money well will also maximize your return on investment.

Near the end of this chapter, you will find a convenient one-page chart that shows bankroll requirements for tournament players based on tournament buy-in costs and the number of players entered. If you don't care anything about the math or how this chart was devised, then you don't need to read *PTF1*. Just use the chart. I am of the opinion, however, that professional gamblers should get a handle on the mathematics behind their gambling investments, and *PTF1* provides information on how that chart came to be, and exactly what the numbers mean.

Coming as I do from a blackjack background, it strikes me as downright weird that charts like the one in this chapter do not exist in other books on poker tournaments. With the current poker tournament boom, all serious tournament players should be thinking in terms of bankrolling their play. The fluctuations in poker tournaments are pretty hairy, and it's not all that difficult to put some numbers on these things.

One way to look at the bankroll requirement for entering any specific tournament is to simply say, "This tournament has a total buy-in and entry fee of $1,060, therefore the total bankroll requirement is $1,060. Since I cannot lose more than $1,060, that's all I need."

This simplistic view is fine if you intend to play only one tournament, and never play another. Or if all you intend to play is a tournament every once in a while as entertainment, then your total bankroll requirement is $1,060 "every once in a while." No-brainer. But that's not how it is for many tournament players. They play lots of tournaments—sometimes 100 or more per year. And if they're only entering a few dozen tournaments each year, the tournaments are expensive. They are spending an amount of money that is dear to them, and they are counting on a return on their investment.

Any experienced tournament pro can tell you that the bankroll fluctuations for tournament players can be drastic. To illustrate this, I've charted the results of the 111 slow-structured no-limit hold'em tournaments I played, starting in January, 2007, through the present (May 1, 2008), while using the strategies (and developing the strategies) in this book. The tournament buy-ins ranged from $300 to $5,000, had field sizes ranging from 30 to 3,150 (obviously a WSOP event!), and formed a roughly equal mix of Rank 2 through Rank 5 tournaments. You'll note that the line is definitely an upward trend, but it is also pretty jagged.

Here's the chart:

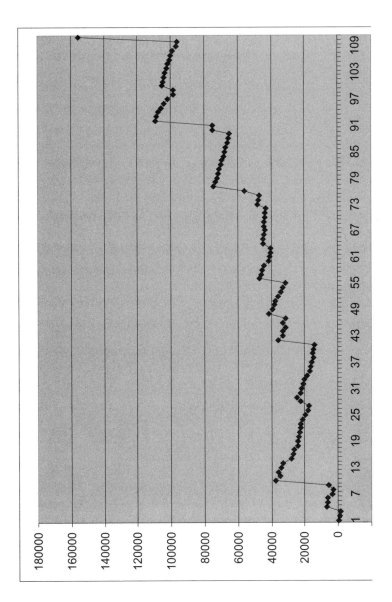

APPENDIX A: BANKROLLING

The vertical numbers on the left represent the amount of money won (or lost), while the numbers going left to right, represent the events entered (a total of 111 as shown in the chart). Cashes are shown by, generally, sharp upward movement in the chart, while busting out before the money, are reflected by short downward blips.

In the chart above, I'm showing 21 finishes in the money out of these 111 tournaments, finishing in the money on average once for every 5.3 events I entered. The upward trend is driven primarily by a relatively small handful of cashes, as I failed to cash in 90 of these 111 tournaments, and only half a dozen or so of my cashes were significant. My overall win rate in these 111 tournaments was about 121 percent. I was fortunate during this run of tournament play that my big cashes, as well as my small cashes, were fairly evenly distributed. This kept me from ever going into a real nosedive.

You'll notice a number of runs of bad flux in the chart. My longest series of events played without cashing was 15, and I had another run of 13 consecutive events with no cash. But if you look at my results from tournament #10 through tournament #41, despite four minor cashes in that period, I lost more than $24,000 in that series of 30 tournaments. So, I'm not trying to say this has been a cakewalk by any means. Fortunately, all of my serious drawdowns occurred after I was far enough into the black that I was playing on money previously won.

Does this mean that if you follow the strategies in this book you can expect to match my results in your first 100 tournaments? No. Actually, I would hope you would fare better than I did, since I played these tournaments as part of my learning process. I wish I'd had all of the information in this book when I started this project!

But I also feel like I'd better include the kind of warning you always see on those TV ads for weight-loss programs: Your results may differ!

For one thing, there is no way in the space of one book to disclose every trick in my repertoire. For another, I have no idea how good you may be at reading opponents or misleading opponents. What I have told you about bluffs and reads in this book is absolutely accurate, but there is no way to fit everything I'd like to tell you into these pages. If you don't get out there and come up with some of your own methods for reading players and stealing pots, you'll never achieve your potential anyway. Also, I don't know if you can learn the psychological strategies of poker without playing hands in the dark—which is the method I used during some of these tournaments—and some players I've talked to about this have told me they could just never do that.

As a professional gambler, I'm looking to play as many tournaments as I can play, knowing that I have an expectation of earning money in each of them, but also aware that I will lose my buy-ins and entry fees most of the time. What interests me as a professional gambler, however, is how bad the negative fluctuations could get. (If I had started out this project on tournament #11 in the graph above, by the time I got to tournament #41, in the hole more than $24,000 for my efforts in 30 consecutive tournaments, I may have quit in despair before hitting that nice win on tournament #41!)

Various factors affect your bankroll requirements for tournament play. You need to know the buy-in/entry fees, the payout schedules, the number of players entered in the events, and your approximate advantage over the field (assuming you have an advantage). Some of these numbers may be hard to come up with, which may be why so many poker writers have ignored the issue. My feeling is that it's better to come up with a ballpark estimate than it is to have no estimate whatsoever.

HOW MUCH OF AN ADVANTAGE DOES A TOP TOURNAMENT PRO HAVE?

In talking with various experienced players, I kept hearing the estimate that the top tournament pros have an advantage in the neighborhood of 200 to 300 percent. In the hundreds of small buy-in tournaments I entered a few years ago, which led to the writing of *PTF1*, I kept track of all buy-in/entry costs and cash-outs. My own advantage in these events came to well over 200 percent, so I don't feel this estimate was out of line for the top players in the bigger buy-in pro-level events. In fact, it was hearing these kinds of numbers that piqued my interest in poker tournaments in the first place.

Other players have argued, however, that there are always some pros who show an advantage this high in a given year, but that the fluctuations in tournaments are so great that these big win years are just flukes. They win a lot playing tournaments one year, but lose a lot playing tournaments in other years, and their overall advantages are really not that big.

There are various websites that track tournament players' winnings, using rating systems that award points to players. There are many arguments about which "Player of the Year" rating system is best. Some feel that total dollars won should be the major criterion. I disagree with this because such a system would rate Jamie Gold and Jerry Yang at the very top in the years they won the WSOP main event, while neither of their overall tournament records has been all that remarkable. Others think that only major event winnings should be tracked, meaning primarily tournaments that have buy-ins of $5,000 or more, arguing that these are the events that attract the toughest fields of pros. I disagree with this approach as well because a player like John Phan, who excels at the faster events that favor masters of long ball, would not rate very high, though his dollar winnings and overall record are so exceptional.

Also, as I have been moving up in my tournament skills and results, one of the most striking things to me about the WSOP and WPT events is how exceptionally weak the overall fields are. The Bellagio $540 weekday tournament—in which the small (30 to 80 player) field consists of 75 percent local pros and semi-pros who play the tournament regularly, is a much tougher field than you will typically find in most WPT or WSOP events with much higher buy-ins.

I personally prefer *Card Player's* approach, because they award points in any tournaments that have buy-ins of $300 or more, provided there are at least 60 players in the event, and the event is part of a series that will have a total prize pool of at least one million dollars. The number of points awarded in any given tournament is based on the buy-in cost, the number of players, and the finishing position. There are many arguments about how to weight these factors—for example, should the number of players in an event count more than the buy-in cost—but I have no major arguments with *Card Player's* method of weighting.

ANALYZING PLAYER OF THE YEAR RESULTS

I decided to use their player database to look at the records of some of the top players over a period of time to see if these players simply had fluke years where they won a lot, while having unexceptional results most other years, or if they appeared to be consistent winners, year after year. To decide who the "top players" were, I let *Card Player* decide for me. Since they pick a Player of the Year every year based on that player's overall points in that year only, I would look at the records of the players who were chosen as Player of the Year in each of the last four years—2007, 2006, 2005, and 2004. For each of these players, I would look at their record in the year they were chosen Player of the Year, as well as their records in each of the most recent three years when they did not win, total up their non-POY year winnings, and compute their three-year average win in their non-POY years.

If profitable years are flukes, then a player who captures *Card Player's* Player of the Year award in one year should not have consistently high average winnings in the other three years around that same time period. The four players whose data I extracted from the *Card Player* database in this survey were: David "the Dragon" Pham, the 2007 Player of the Year (POY); Michael Mizrachi, the 2006 POY; Men "the Master" Nguyen, the 2005 POY; and Daniel Negreanu, the 2004 POY.

Here's what the *Card Player* data shows (and all dollar amounts are rounded to the nearest thousand):

	FOUR POY'S FOUR-YEAR AVERAGE			
Year	POY	POY $ Won	Avg $ Won per Year Other 3 Years	4 Year Average
2007	Pham	$1,814,000	$997,000	$1,201,000
2006	Mizrachi	$2,329,000	$1,072,000	$1,387,000
2005	Nguyen	$974,000	$504,000	$622,000
2004	Negreanu	$4,466,000	$1,046,000	$1,901,000

In all cases, we can see that in the year each of these players won *Card Player's* coveted POY award, their winnings in that year exceeded their average winnings in the other three years surveyed. The most extreme example is Daniel Negreanu who won almost $4.5 million in 2004, but whose winnings averaged just over $1 million in each of the three other years.

Three of these four players—Pham, Mizrachi, and Negreanu—all averaged about a million dollars per year in tournament winnings in each of the three years surveyed when they did *not* win the POY award. Men the Master averaged about half a million per year in winnings on his three non-POY years. Exactly what any of these players' overall advantages are is impossible to say since *Card Player* doesn't publish the total amounts that players spend to enter tournaments, and it's virtually impossible to even guesstimate this amount.

Tournament players who play the "Circuit," meaning they travel in order to follow the major events—most of which are WPT or WSOP Circuit series—can pay hundreds of thousands of dollars in buy-ins and entry fees, but it's impossible to estimate what any individual player might be paying in these costs. Some pros do not travel to all of the far-flung destinations—such as Australia, Paris or Aruba—where big buy-in events are held, but stick to tournaments that are closer to home, wherever their home may be. Some who play a lot of preliminary events do not play certain types of events—such as limit hold'em, Omaha high-low, seven-card stud, heads-up, short-handed and H.O.R.S.E.—but stick primarily to "standard" no-limit hold'em games. Some of the top players play mostly the main events and few preliminary events, if any. Some are excellent satellite players and cut their buy-in expenses by getting into some percentage of their annual big tournaments through satellites. And many of the big-name pros have some of their buy-in costs covered by commercial sponsors (often big online poker sites). So, again, it's impossible to put any hard numbers on what an "average" tournament pro might spend in buy-in and entry fee costs. I would say for an unsponsored player, it's probably somewhere between $200,000 and $500,000 per year, depending on willingness to travel and types of events played.

APPENDIX A: BANKROLLING

So, for three of these players whose tournament results I surveyed—Pham, Mizrachi, and Negreanu—if we assume all paid $500,000 in buy-in costs, then their $1 million average return on their non-POY year winnings would indicate an advantage of about 100 percent in these years. During each of their POY years, making this same assumption, Pham won at the rate of about 260 percent in 2007; Mizrachi won at the rate of about 365 percent in 2006; and Negreanu won at the rate of about 525 percent in 2004. All of their 4-year averages would be indicative of overall advantages between 120 percent and 190 percent.

If Men the Master was paying $500,000 per year in buy-in costs, then on his non-POY years, he was just breaking even, and during his POY year, he netted $474,000 for a 95 percent advantage in that year.

But assuming all of these players spent $500,000 in buy-ins every year could be a very erroneous assumption. For example, if Men the Master had buy-in/entry fees of only $200,000 per year, then his average winnings of over $500,000 per year in his non-POY years would indicate a net win of more than $300,000 per year, for an advantage of 150 percent. And on his POY year, his net win of $774,000 would be an advantage of 387 percent for that year. His average win of over $600,000 per year for the four-year period would be indicative of an overall 211 percent advantage for this four-year time period.

Also, most pro players who are familiar with Men the Master's long term record would find it ludicrous to say that in 2005 he just had a lucky year. He has actually placed first in *Card Player's* POY standings four times since 1997—more POY awards than any other tournament player in the time since *Card Player* started tracking tournament players' records! Not only that, but he has also won six WSOP bracelets, his lifetime winnings are over $8 million, and as I write this (April, 2008), he is currently in sixth place in *Card*

Player's POY standings with more than $500,000 in winnings this year already. Men the Master is a one-man tournament wrecking crew.

Likewise, if we assumed Negreanu, Mizrachi, and Pham, all paid only $300,000 per year in buy-ins, then their non-POY year winnings would all be averaging over 200 percent per year, and in their POY years their advantages would literally be through the roof—Pham's at over 500 percent; Mizrachi's at 676 percent; and Negreanu's at 1,388 percent!

I believe it would probably be wrong to assume that all of these players have paid $500,000 per year in buy-in/entry fees every year for these four years. (Players I've talked to who focus on the bigger events on the circuit pay about $300,000 per year in buy-ins and entry fees, though their travel expenses can also be extremely high). So I tend to believe that the best tournament players probably enjoy advantages in the neighborhood of 200 percent and more, especially in big events (like WSOP tournaments) where there are weak fields. They also do have fluke years where they win far in excess of their normal advantage, as well as fluke years where they underperform. Any player who is averaging $1 million per year in tournament winnings, however, cannot possibly be playing with an advantage of much less than 100 percent.

Out of curiosity, I surveyed David "the Dragon" Pham's results to see if his winnings were coming from the big money events. I was astonished to find that almost $800,000 of his winnings in this time period came from tournaments that had buy-ins of $1,000 or less, including many $300 and $500 events! (This is another reason why I believe players who want to get into the big events and compete with the top players should start in these smaller buy-in events that do not require a huge bankroll. Pham's record, like John Phan's, shows that there is a lot of money to be made in these smaller buy-in pro-level tournaments.)

More than $2 million of David Pham's winnings came from tournaments with buy-ins from $1,500 to $3,000. And more than $2.75 million came from major events with buy-ins of $5,000 or more. David Pham excels at every level of tournament he enters, and is one of the players whose talents I most respect.

THE "WEAK FIELD" EFFECT

One factor that will greatly affect your percent advantage in any tournament is the strength of the field you are playing against. One of the reasons that the pros flock to the annual WSOP series of tournaments is that these tournaments provide the weakest fields of players that can be found in high buy-in events. There are so many poker groupies and players who managed to get into events on satellites that the dead money in all of these events that have more than 1,000 players is through the roof. The top pros, who might have a 200 percent advantage in typical tournament fields with 200 to 300 players, probably enjoy advantages of 400 percent or more in these events with monster fields.

This weak-field effect can also be found in other tournaments that attract large numbers of the general public who simply want the chance to play against the top players they watch on TV. WSOP Circuit events and WPT series events often have a significant weak field effect. The bigger fields do cause greater fluctuations and have greater bankroll requirements, but the higher edge for the pros compensates for some of this.

Ironically, this weak field effect also gives the amateurs a greater shot at the money. In the early stages of a tournament that has a significantly weak field, many tables will consist mostly of amateurs playing against each other. Inevitably, some of these amateurs will build big chip stacks. Many pros actually hate these early blind levels because it's so difficult to put an amateur on a hand or to use any skillful moves to take pots away from them. For example, amateurs are likely to call all-in bets in the early levels of a major event on drawing hands—something most pros would never do. If the amateur got into this $10,000 event through some $100 online satellite, his perspective on risk will be much different from a pro's perspective. To him, this isn't how he makes his living; it's just a crazy vacation in Vegas, and if he doesn't hit his draw he can go play three-card-poker and tell everyone at home how he got busted by Men the Master.

Pros who enter tournaments with less popular formats—such as H.O.R.S.E. tournaments or heads-up tournaments or short-handed tournaments—where the fields are often smaller and have a greater ratio of pros to amateurs, will generally have a much smaller overall advantage. The legendary Johnny Moss once commented that the pro players were always trying to find fish to play against because playing against each other was like "taking in each other's wash." An amateur in a H.O.R.S.E. event would have little chance of surviving to the money. But the pros themselves also have less of a chance of making big money than they do in weaker fields.

When a pro player enters a tournament, he is generally looking around the field of players to determine how much dead money there is in the event. If he believes that 80 percent of the players are pretty clueless, he knows his edge is great because most of those players' buy-in money will be divvied up among the 20 percent of pros in the event. A good portion of the pros, in fact, will not get in on the money distribution, and some of the amateurs will. But any time you are looking for tournaments to enter, you should look for weak fields first and foremost if your goal is to make money. The pros who enter H.O.R.S.E. events know what they are up against, and they enter these events for the challenge of playing against the best players, not because these are the events where they have the biggest edge or the highest dollar expectation.

APPENDIX A: BANKROLLING

One of the reasons I believe most players who are new to tournaments should start with the small buy-in fast tournaments (and I'm talking about the daily or weekly tournaments that most poker rooms now sponsor with buy-ins from $20 to $200 that I focused on in *PTF1*) is that these tournaments tend to have the weakest fields. If you can't beat these weak-field events with a very solid win rate, then you should probably not start entering the tournaments with tougher fields.

SNYDER'S BANKROLL FUDGE FORMULA

My method for determining the minimum bankroll requirement for a specific tournament, assuming a skillful tournament player has an approximate 150 to 200 percent advantage, is to multiply the total cost of the tournament by the square root of the number of players. Then double this number. I devised this method to mimic results obtained by calculating the standard deviation a player this skilled would encounter in various tournament structures with various numbers of players (as per the standard deviation formula in *PTF1*.). I regard the bankroll requirement as calculated by the method I'm proposing to be the minimum bankroll requirement. The recommended bankroll with this method should get a player this skilled through most of his worst negative fluctuations.

For example, if there are 200 players in a tournament, and the buy-in is $1,060, then your minimum bankroll requirement for playing this tournament is the square root of 200 (which is 14.14) x $1,060 x 2 = $29,977. So, if you've got a total playing bankroll in the neighborhood of $30,000 or more, and you are playing with an edge of about 200 percent, you should be able to withstand the bad flux you'll encounter in these $1,000 tournaments.

A few qualifiers—I am basing this advice on three assumptions:

That you intend to play a lot of tournaments.

That you are a skillful player. I'm assuming that you have a very strong advantage over your opponents, providing you with a 150 percent win rate or more.

That you are going to reevaluate your bankroll position frequently. If your bankroll has early negative flux, you'll have to limit yourself to cheaper tournaments or tournaments with fewer players, until your bankroll recovers.

The chart at the end of this chapter is based on the flux you may expect to encounter in 100 tournaments. I chose 100 tournaments for my estimates because if a player has a 150 percent advantage or more, he should have enough cashes within 100 tournaments to replenish his bankroll from any losing streaks, and to keep him going until his wins bring him up to his long-run expectation. There is always a rare but real mathematical possibility that any player can hit an inordinate bad streak, but professional gamblers work within more normal probabilities. My chart estimates are based on withstanding fluctuations up to about two standard deviations. That's why I recommend frequent reevaluation of your bankroll and the tournaments you can afford. You would make it through the fluctuations 95 percent of the time without reevaluating, but frequent reassessments will protect you should you be one of the unlucky players whose negative results go beyond two standard deviations.

SKILL LEVEL ADJUSTMENTS
And don't be tempted to adjust the bankroll requirement downward based on your presumption that you possess a greater level of skill. Even if you think you have an advantage much greater than 200 percent because you're playing against complete poker morons, your fluctuations won't change that much. The number of players, whether they're smart players or not, is a major factor in the

number of hours a tournament lasts, and this directly affects the number of confrontations you must survive. You may be a 2 to 1 favorite half a dozen times in your confrontations with lesser players, but that only means that you'd expect to win four of these battles, and lose two. Either one of those losing confrontations could cripple you, or bust you out. And the fact is—you could lose all six confrontations and it would be a meaningless blip of standard deviation to a mathematician. This stuff happens all the time. It's not like you're having thousands of these confrontations in every tournament, all at affordable chip amounts, so that your actual percentage of success will stay close to expectation. Your overall win or loss in any given tournament will result from a relative handful of very high-risk confrontations.

If you are a player of lesser skill, but still a winning tournament player, then you probably ought to have twice the bankroll this method estimates if you want to assure yourself of survival. And again, should your bankroll go into a nose-dive, be willing to start entering tournaments with either smaller buy-ins or smaller fields of players, until you rebuild your bank.

Most of the tournaments in live poker rooms will have fields of 50 to 300 players. Internet tournaments, however, will often have much larger fields. Look at how the size of the field affects the bankroll requirements for entry. Let's compare the bankroll requirements for entering a $1,060 tournament with 60 players, 200 players, and 1,000 players. For this comparison, note that the square root of 60 =7.75, and the square root of 1,000 = 31.62.

Again, here is the formula: Cost of tournament x square root of the total number of players, multiplied by 2.

SNYDER'S BANKROLL FUDGE FORMULA						
# Players	Sq.Rt.		Players Cost			Min. Bankroll Req.
60	7.75	x	$1,060	x 2 =		$16,430
200	14.14	x	$1,060	x 2 =		$29,977
1,000	31.62	x	$1,060	x 2 =		$67,034

Technically, your actual win rate may be much higher in the tournament with 1,000 players due to the weak field effect, but again I would advise against lowering this bankroll requirement a whole lot. Also, if the tournament with only 60 players is dominated by the local Vegas pros and semi-pros, you will likely have a strong-field effect that would diminish your overall advantage. In that case, I would double the bankroll requirement.

In the fast small buy-in tournaments where I first started tournament play, I made the final table in about one in five tournaments. In the graph of my initial 75 small buy-in tournaments provided in *PTF1*, the average number of players in these tournaments was 143. In the 100 slow-structured higher-buy-in tournaments I graphed in this chapter, the average number of players was 473 (skewed upward by the big WSOP events I played in 2007), and again I finished in the money in about one out of five events entered.

I keep track of this stuff and so should you. I'm sure this comes from my blackjack background—card counters, because their edge is so small, must keep track of results rigorously. I think fewer poker players do this, but in high flux tournament play, I think it makes sense to track your results. I also paid very close attention to which types of tournaments—based on buy-in, field size, and structure—I did better or worse in, especially while learning, so I could look for weaknesses in my game.

APPENDIX A: BANKROLLING

Ideally, many other tournament-specific factors would enter into these bankroll calculations. Some of these factors are impossible to put numbers on—including the various skill levels of all your opponents relative to your own skill. Other factors that might alter the formula would include the total number of chips in play, the exact blind structure, the number of finishers in the money, and the precise payout structure for the winners. Consider the fudge formula a general guide, and understand that you should look at the estimated bankroll requirement as the *minimum* amount required to get through most bad swings for a dedicated and skillful tournament player who plays lots of tournaments with no intention of stopping any time soon.

The chart on the following page will give you a pretty good ballpark estimate of the minimum bankroll requirements for just about any tournament you're likely to encounter. In using the chart, note that the "cost" includes not only the entry fee and buy-in, but any rebuys and add-ons you are prepared to make. If you want a formula for analyzing a tournament with a specific number of players and cost that is not included in the chart, you may use the method provided in *PTF1* or just interpolate the minimum bankroll requirement from the data that is provided in the chart.

For example, if a tournament costs $750, and there will be 400 players, there is no entry in the chart for this situation. So, I would look at the chart entry just above these numbers, and I'd see that with a $1,000 cost and 500 players, the bankroll requirement is $44,721. Then I'd note the entry just below these numbers, and I'd see that with a $500 cost and 300 players, the bankroll requirement is $17,321. If I average these two numbers (add them together and then divide by two), I get a bankroll requirement of $31,021. The actual number I'd come up with if I took the square root of 400, then multiplied by $750, then again by 2, is $30,000, a negligible difference. Again, these are ballpark estimates.

Minimum* Bankroll Requirement Based on Tournament Cost and the Number of Players in Tournament

Number of Players

COST	40	60	80	100	150	200	250	300	500	750	1,000	2,000	5,000
$25	$316	$387	$447	$500	$612	$707	$791	$866	$1,118	$1,369	$1,581	$2,236	$3,536
$50	$632	$775	$894	$1,000	$1,225	$1,414	$1,581	$1,732	$2,236	$2,739	$3,162	$4,472	$7,071
$75	$949	$1,162	$1,342	$1,500	$1,837	$2,121	$2,372	$2,598	$3,354	$4,108	$4,743	$6,708	$10,607
$100	$1,265	$1,549	$1,789	$2,000	$2,449	$2,828	$3,162	$3,464	$4,472	$5,477	$6,325	$8,944	$14,142
$150	$1,897	$2,324	$2,683	$3,000	$3,674	$4,243	$4,743	$5,196	$6,708	$8,216	$9,487	$13,416	$21,213
$200	$2,530	$3,098	$3,578	$4,000	$4,899	$5,657	$6,325	$6,928	$8,944	$10,954	$12,649	$17,889	$28,284
$300	$3,795	$4,648	$5,367	$6,000	$7,348	$8,485	$9,487	$10,392	$13,416	$16,432	$18,974	$26,833	$42,426
$400	$5,060	$6,197	$7,155	$8,000	$9,798	$11,314	$12,649	$13,856	$17,889	$21,909	$25,298	$35,777	$56,569
$500	$6,325	$7,746	$8,944	$10,000	$12,247	$14,142	$15,811	$17,321	$22,361	$27,386	$31,623	$44,721	$70,711
$1,000	$12,649	$15,492	$17,889	$20,000	$24,495	$28,284	$31,623	$34,641	$44,721	$54,772	$63,246	$89,443	$141,421
$1,500	$18,974	$23,238	$26,833	$30,000	$36,742	$42,426	$47,434	$51,962	$67,082	$82,158	$94,868	$134,164	$212,132
$2,000	$25,298	$30,984	$35,777	$40,000	$48,990	$56,569	$63,246	$69,282	$89,443	$109,545	$126,491	$178,885	$282,843
$2,500	$31,623	$38,730	$44,721	$50,000	$61,237	$70,711	$79,057	$86,603	$111,803	$136,931	$158,114	$223,607	$353,553
$3,000	$37,947	$46,476	$53,666	$60,000	$73,485	$84,853	$94,868	$103,923	$134,164	$164,317	$189,737	$268,328	$424,264
$5,000	$63,246	$77,460	$89,443	$100,000	$122,474	$141,421	$158,114	$173,205	$223,607	$273,861	$316,228	$447,214	$707,107
$10,000	$126,491	$154,919	$178,885	$200,000	$244,949	$282,843	$316,228	$346,410	$447,214	$547,723	$632,456	$894,427	$1,414,214
$25,000	$316,228	$387,298	$447,214	$500,000	$612,372	$707,107	$790,569	$866,025	$1,118,054	$1,369,306	$1,581,139	$2,236,068	$3,535,534

*Add 10 percent more for rebuy tournaments.

APPENDIX A: BANKROLLING

One of the most practical uses of the chart is simply in determining if the fluctuations you are experiencing are within the realm of normal luck. If you experience a downswing greater than the chart entry for the type of tournaments you play in, then it may be time to begin questioning your strategy or skill. For example, if you regularly play $500 tournaments, where the number of players averages about 80, and you are down more than $9,000 in 100 or fewer of these tournaments (the bankroll chart shows a minimum bankroll requirement of $8,944 for $500 tournaments with this field size), then I would seriously start to question your skill relative to the other players in this event. You may be a winning player on an unusually bad streak, but it's more likely that you're overestimating your skill level, or underestimating the skill levels of your opponents. I'm sure you have 100 bad beat stories to go with all those losses, but I also suspect you are making some serious errors in your play.

It is possible that your poor results really are caused by nothing but inordinate negative flux. That's poker. If you've got the bankroll to continue playing these events without affecting your lifestyle, then keep at it. But if you continue to lose at this rate, face the fact that your opponents are outplaying you and consider experimenting with some strategy changes, or looking for weaker fields.

APPENDIX B: SATELLITES: ARE THEY WORTH IT?

SATELLITES AND RISK OF RUIN

With contributions by Math Boy

Let's look at how you should estimate the dollar value of a poker tournament satellite, including the factors that make a satellite a good investment, and how skill at satellites can lower the bankroll you need to enter poker tournaments by lowering the risk of ruin (RoR) for any given bankroll.

First, a definition: A *satellite* is a tournament that does not award money to the winners, but instead awards an entry to a tournament that has a bigger buy-in cost. In some satellites, a small amount of money is awarded in addition to a seat or seats into a bigger event, but this money is a secondary prize, awarded either to cover the winners' travel expenses or to "round out" the prize pool. It is the seat in the bigger tournament that is the main prize. There are some satellite pros who play satellites primarily for money, not seats into a bigger event. Many satellites, especially for big multi-tournament events, award tournament chips rather than seats in specific events, and these chips can be sold to other players who are buying into the big events. The primary focus in this chapter, however, will be on using satellites to lower your entry costs into main events.

A single-table satellite will usually start with ten players, and will typically award one winner a seat in a tournament that has a buy-in of about ten times the cost of the satellite. Some single-table satellites award seats to the top two finishers. A *supersatellite* is a multitable satellite that will award multiple seats into a major tournament, with the exact number dependent on the number of entrants in the satellite.

THE "HOUSE EDGE" ON POKER TOURNAMENT SATELLITES

The first thing we need to consider when analyzing a satellite's value is the house edge. By this, I mean the percentage of the total cost of the satellite that the players are paying to the house for hosting the satellite. Figuring out the house commission is pretty straightforward. We need only two factors: the total combined dollar cost to all of the entrants, and the total dollar value of the satellite prize pool.

For example, a popular World Poker Tour (WPT) single-table satellite has a buy-in of $125. One of the ten entrants will win two $500 tournament chips plus $120 in cash. The other nine entrants receive nothing. A player who wins two $500 tournament chips may use those chips to enter two $500 events, a single $1,000 event, or as partial payment into an event that has a buy-in greater than $1,000.

In this particular WPT satellite example, the house collects $125 x 10 = $1,250, while paying out $500 + $500 (two chips) + $120 (cash) = $1,120. So, the house profits $1,250 - $1,120 = $130 every time they run this satellite. The house edge from the players' perspective is: $130 / $1,250 = 10.40 percent. Which is to say, the house keeps 10.4 percent of all the money they collect from the satellite entrants.

At the 2006 Mirage Poker Showdown, a WPT series of tournaments with a $10,000 main event, there were seven different single-table satellite formats. All were ten-player/one-winner formats. The least expensive had a $60 buy-in, with the winner receiving a single $500 chip plus $50 cash. The most expensive had a $1,060 buy-in, with the winner receiving twenty $500 chips (a total of $10,000 in chips) plus $340 in cash. The chart below shows the buy-ins of these seven satellites with their payouts, the house commission (in $), and the house edge (in %).

MIRAGE POKER SHOWDOWN (WPT) SINGLE TABLE SATELLITES, ONE WINNER FORMAT					
Buy-in	Payout in Chips	Payout in Cash	Total Payout	House Commission $	House Percent
$60	$500	$50	$550	$50	8.33%
$125	$1,000	$120	$1,120	$130	10.40%
$175	$1,500	$120	$1,620	$130	7.43%
$225	$2,000	$120	$2,120	$130	5.78%
$275	$2,500	$120	$2,620	$130	4.73%
$810	$7,500	$340	$7,840	$260	3.21%
$1,060	$10,000	$340	$10,340	$260	2.45%

One obvious trend is that, in general, the greater the buy-in cost, the lower the house edge. The only exception among this group of satellites was that the house edge on the least expensive ($60 buy-in) satellite was smaller than the house edge on the second cheapest ($125 buy-in) satellite.

SATELLITE VALUE FOR THE AVERAGE PLAYER

As a satellite player, what does the house edge mean to you? Consider your result in these satellites if you play with an average level of skill that gives you neither an advantage nor a disadvantage against the field. Some may be better players than you, and some worse, but in the long run, you will average one satellite win for every ten satellites you play.

This chart shows the value (in $ and %) of each of these seven WPT satellites for an "average" player:

PLAYER WINS 1 OUT OF 10 SATELLITES ENTERED		
Buy-in	**$ Value**	**Player Advantage in %**
$60	-$5.00	-8.33%
$125	-$13.00	-10.40%
$175	-$13.00	-7.43%
$225	-$13.00	-5.78%
$275	-$13.00	-4.73%
$810	-$26.00	-3.21%
$1,060	-$26.00	-2.45%

Let's first note that in all cases, the dollar value is negative. Average players will lose money in satellites over the long run. Computing the dollar value is simple. Consider the $60 satellite. If you play ten of these satellites, you will invest $60 x 10 = $600 in these ten plays. If you win one, you get paid $500 (chip) + $50 (cash) = $550 in dollar value. Collecting $550 for every $600 you invest is a loss of $50 for every ten satellites you play, which is an average loss of

$5 per satellite. So, the dollar value of this satellite to the average player is -$5.00.

Likewise, the "Player Advantage in %" is negative for the average player in all of these satellites, as we would expect. Again, the computation is simple. If I lose $5 for every $60 I invest, then my result (in %) is: -5/60 = -0.0833, which is -8.33 percent. You might also note that if you look at the prior chart, which shows the house edge on these satellites, the player advantage for an average player is always the negative of the house edge.

From the professional players' perspective, this means that to play satellites with average skill is a waste of money. In the long run, it will cost the average player more to enter tournaments via satellite than it would cost him to simply buy-in to the big events directly.

A player who is short on funds might argue that he would never pay $10,000 to enter a major tournament, but that he is willing to gamble $1,060 on a long shot to get into such an event. In fact, this is a good argument if you accept the fact that you are gambling on a negative expectation game. One of the reasons that tournaments have become so valuable to professional players is that so many amateurs are willing to gamble at a disadvantage on satellite entries.

SATELLITE VALUE FOR THE BETTER-THAN-AVERAGE PLAYER

Now let's look at how satellite skill affects the value of satellites to the player. Let's say you can win 1 out of every 9 of these ten-player satellites that you enter. How would this affect both the dollar value and your advantage (in %) in these same seven WPT satellites?

APPENDIX B: SATELLITES

PLAYER WINS 1 OUT OF 9 SATELLITES ENTERED		
Buy-in	Dollar Value	Player Advantage in %
$60	$1.11	1.85%
$125	-$0.56	-0.44%
$175	$5.00	2.86%
$225	$10.56	4.69%
$275	$16.11	5.86%
$810	$61.11	7.54%
$1,060	$88.89	8.39%

Big difference. The cheapest satellites are still not worth the trouble, due to the high house edge. Few players at this modest level of satellite skill should be interested in entering the $60 satellite, as the $1.11 value is a pretty low payout for a lot of work. And the $125 satellite (which you may recall has a higher house edge) is still a negative expectation gamble. The player who can win 1 in 9 of these has a notably superior result to the average player who can win only 1 in 10, as the more skillful player will be losing only 56 cents per satellite played, as opposed to losing $13.00 Still, in the long run, the player who expects to win just 1 in 9 of the $125 satellites would be paying less to enter the bigger tournaments if he skipped the satellites and just paid the full buy-in price of the event.

With the $1,060 satellite, the one-in-nine player advantage is 8.39 percent, which is a dollar value of $88.89. For many players, this modest level of satellite skill might make these satellites worth the effort.

THE SATELLITE PROFESSIONALS

As your satellite skill increases, the value of playing satellites goes up dramatically. A more talented satellite pro can do quite well in ten-player/one-winner satellites if he can win just 1 of every 8 satellites he enters.

Here's how he would do in these seven WPT satellites with this level of skill:

PLAYER WINS 1 OUT OF 8 SATELLITES ENTERED		
Buy-in	Dollar Value	Player Advantage in %
$60	$8.75	14.58%
$125	$15.00	12.00%
$175	$27.50	15.71%
$225	$40.00	17.78%
$275	$52.50	19.09%
$810	$170.00	20.99%
$1,060	$232.50	21.93%

At this skill level, there may be sufficient dollar value to warrant playing these satellites at any buy-in level. With the smaller buy-in satellites, you must decide if the expected dollar return is sufficient to spend, on average, about an hour of your time in satellite play. Many of us wouldn't work for $8.75 an hour, which is the dollar value of the $60 satellite for the one-win-in-eight player. But we must also consider that for every satellite we play, we gain more satellite experience, and this should translate sooner or later to greater satellite skill. As in all other forms of poker, you can't increase your satellite skills without playing them. And this becomes more important as the dollar value increases with the satellite cost. For example, with a dollar value of $232.50, the $1,060 satellite will gain you entry into a $10,000 event, on average, for a cost of just over $8,000. That's a substantial discount.

THE TOP-OF-THE-LINE SATELLITE PROS

The top satellite pros win, on average, about 1 out of every 6 to 7 ten-player/one-winner satellites they enter. They accomplish this with a combination of skill at fast-play strategies, skill at short-handed play, and skill at choosing weak fields of competitors. No pro wants to enter a satellite and find himself facing a table full of other pros. The value of satellites to a pro is as much a function of his competitors' lack of skill as it is of his own skill.

Let's compare the dollar values of these seven WPT single-table satellites for players who expect to win 1 of every 10, 9, 8, 7, 6, and 5 satellites they play:

$ VALUE PER SATELLITE IF PLAYER WINS ONCE PER:					
Buy-in	**10**	**9**	**8**	**7**	**6**	**5**
$60	-$5.00	$1.11	$8.75	$18.57	$31.67	$50.00
$125	-$13.00	-$0.56	$15.00	$35.00	$61.67	$99.00
$175	-$13.00	$5.00	$27.50	$56.43	$95.00	$149.00
$225	-$13.00	$10.56	$40.00	$77.86	$128.33	$199.00
$275	-$13.00	$16.11	$52.50	$99.29	$161.67	$249.00
$810	-$26.00	$61.11	$170.00	$310.00	$496.67	$758.00
$1,060	-$26.00	$88.89	$232.50	$417.14	$663.33	$1,008.00

Let's also look at the various players' advantages in percent for these frequencies of wins:

PLAYER ADVANTAGE (%), IF PLAYER WINS ONCE PER:						
Buy-in	10	9	8	7	6	5
$60	-8.33%	1.85%	14.58%	30.95%	52.78%	83.33%
$125	-10.40%	-0.44%	12.00%	28.00%	49.33%	79.20%
$175	-7.43%	2.86%	15.71%	32.24%	54.29%	85.14%
$225	-5.78%	4.69%	17.78%	34.60%	57.04%	88.44%
$275	-4.73%	5.86%	19.09%	36.10%	58.79%	90.55%
$810	-3.21%	7.54%	20.99%	38.27%	61.32%	93.58%
$1,060	-2.45%	8.39%	21.93%	39.35%	62.58%	95.09%

The final column in both charts, which shows the player's expectation if he is skillful enough to win 1 out of every 5 of the satellites he plays, is more theoretical than realistic. This may be possible for a skillful satellite player who always manages to face a very weak field, but most satellite players today are not this weak. Many more players are aware of the necessity of taking risks in satellites as the field diminishes and the blinds increase than they used to be.

Nevertheless, we can see from the charts that a satellite player who is skillful enough to win 1 out of every 6 or 7 of these satellites will have an advantage in the neighborhood of 30 to 60 percent, and that is a big enough edge to interest any professional gambler.

OTHER SATELLITE FORMATS

Not all satellites are single-player one-winner formats. The two-winner format is also quite common. Typically, a player might pay $200 plus the house fee to win 1 of 2 seats into a $1,000 event. With this format, the average player would expect to win 2 out of every 10 satellites entered, as opposed to 1 in 10. Likewise, a win of 2 in 8 with the two-winner format would be equivalent to winning 1 in 8 with the single-winner format. And the top satellite pros would expect to win 2 out of every 6 or 7 played in the two-winner format.

The two-winner format is generally advantageous for both the players and the poker room. Satellites played down to two winners finish faster than satellites played down to one winner. This means that more satellites can be played prior to a big event, with twice as many main event entries generated per satellite. The two-winner format also reduces fluctuations for the players.

If you're good with spreadsheets, you can easily set up a spreadsheet to calculate the dollar return and house/player advantages for the two-winner format based on the buy-in costs and payouts.

Multitable satellites, often called super-satellites or mega-satellites, are also very common, especially for major events. For example, the WSOP typically has a $1,060 super-satellite for the $10,000 main event. One seat to the main event is awarded for every ten satellite entries. Here's a chart that shows the dollar values and player advantages based on the frequency of player wins:

WSOP MEGA SATELLITE, $1,060 BUY-IN, 1 Seat Awarded per 10 Entrants Dollar Value and Player Advantage if Player Wins Once per:					
10	**9**	**8**	**7**	**6**	**5**
$ Value -$60.00	$51.11	$190.00	$368.57	$606.67	$940.00
Adv. (%) -5.66%	4.82%	17.92%	34.77%	57.23%	88.68%

Note that the house edge on this event is 5.66 percent. These multitable satellites are a good value for a player on a budget who can only afford to enter one satellite for a shot at the main event. And this is especially true if the player is a good multitable tournament player, but not really all that skilled at single-table satellite play. (And there are many players who are skilled at multitable tournaments who do not fare well in single-table satellites, primarily because of a lack of experience with making the speed adjustments necessary for short-handed play.)

For a skillful single-table satellite player, however, super satellites have less value than single-table satellites. The higher-priced single-table satellites often have a lower house edge, and they play out much faster. Big multitable satellites often take many hours to determine the winners, as opposed to the typical 60 to 90 minutes a single-table satellite lasts. Time is money.

USING SATELLITES TO LOWER THE BUY-IN COSTS OF MAJOR TOURNAMENTS

Let's say you've been playing a lot of small buy-in tournaments and your tournament skills have increased to the point where you want to start playing bigger events where you can make more money. You don't feel ready for the major $5,000 and $10,000 events that the top pros dominate, so you want to start playing in $1,000 events as a stepping stone to the majors. Let's also assume that you've been beating the small buy-in tournaments at a rate of well over 200 percent, and you believe you would have an advantage of at least 100 percent in these bigger $1,000 events. You've been building your bankroll with these small buy-in tournaments, and your plan is to start using the money you've won to advance. The main question you have: Is your bankroll really big enough to withstand the greater fluctuations you'll encounter in these $1,000 events?

If you do not have a sufficient bankroll to enter $1,000 events at this time, that does not necessarily mean that you must resign yourself to smaller buy-in tournaments. In fact, if you are a skillful satellite player, you can start entering $1,000 tournaments via satellites with a smaller bankroll. As the charts above show, satellites can very effectively lower the buy-in costs of bigger events. And a lower buy-in cost means a smaller bankroll is required. But how much smaller?

Before we can figure out how much satellite skill can lower your bankroll requirements, let's quickly review what your bankroll requirements would be for a given type of tournament if you pay the full buy-in cost.

Let's say you would like to play one hundred $1,000 tournaments in the next year. If you live in Las Vegas, this is easily accomplished, as Bellagio has two $1,000 buy-in tournaments every week. $1,000 events are also popular preliminary events for WSOP Circuit series, WPT events, and many other special tournament series that poker rooms run throughout the year. In order to estimate the bankroll requirements for entering a hundred $1,000 events, assuming a player has a 100 percent advantage on the field, let's use a real-world example.

At the recent WSOP Circuit Events that were hosted by Harrah's Rincon in San Diego, the $1,000 event on February 13, 2007, had a total of 89 players who paid $1,060 for a seat. Nine spots were paid. This was the payout structure:

HARRAH'S RINCON IN SAN DIEGO $1,000 EVENT ON FEBRUARY 13, 2007	
Place	Payout
1st	$31,079
2nd	$17,266
3rd	$9,496
4th	$6,906
5th	$6,043
6th	$5,180
7th	$4,317
8th	$3,453
9th	$2,590

Now, we have something to work with. Obviously, every $1,000 tournament you enter will not have this payout structure, but for our purposes, we're going to assume that you want to know the bankroll requirements for entering 100 of these specific tournaments. Since we already said that you estimate that you have a 100 percent advantage in these events, we next have to make some assumptions as to how that 100 percent advantage will be realized.

When we say that you have a 100 percent advantage, we mean that for every $1,000 you pay to get into these tournaments in the long run, you will cash out $2,000. That cash out will pay you back your $1,000 buy-in and provide a $1,000 profit, which is a 100 percent advantage. From looking at the payout schedule, we can see that there is no payout of exactly $2,120 (twice the buy-in/entry) for any finishing position. Even 9th place pays $2,590, which is a 144 percent profit. In order to realize a 100 percent advantage, we will accomplish this by having many finishes with no return, but also a number of finishes that return greatly in excess of 100 percent.

Assuming you play 100 of these tournaments, let's create a win record that would provide an advantage in the neighborhood of 100 percent overall. To do this, I'll assume that you finish in the money 16 times, or about once every 6 to 7 tournaments. Here's a set of finishes that includes 3 first places, 3 second places, 3 third places, 2 fourths, 2 fifths, 1 sixth, 1 seventh, 1 eighth, and 84 finishes out of the money, and would earn you 100.35 percent on your total investment:

WINNING RECORD EXAMPLE: 100% ADVANTAGE 100 Tournaments Played			
Finish	Payout	# Cashes	Total
1st	$31,079	3	$93,237
2nd	$17,266	3	$51,798
3rd	$9,496	3	$28,488
4th	$6,906	2	$13,812
5th	$6,043	2	$12,086
6th	$5,180	1	$5,180
7th	$4,317	1	$4,317
8th	$3,453	1	$3,453
9th	$2,590	0	$0
10th-	$0	0	$0

Total Cashed: $212,371
Total Invested: $106,000
Total Win: $106,371
Win Percentage: 100.35%

That's close enough to 100 percent for our purposes. Obviously, no player could estimate that these will be his exact finishes in 100 tournaments. We're just creating a set of finishes that would return approximately 100 percent profit to the player. There are many other ways that a 100 percent advantage could be realized. There could be fewer than 16 money finishes, but more with the higher payouts, or there could be more than 16 money finishes, but fewer with the big payouts and more low-end finishes. The above set of payouts is just one way that a player with a 100 percent advantage might realize this profit.

In fact, despite the assumed 100 percent advantage, over the course of these 100 tournaments, a player in real life would be highly unlikely to show a result this close to an actual 100 percent profit. His real-world result in a series of 100 consecutive tournaments would be subject to standard deviation. He may have an exceptionally good run of tournaments, or an exceptionally bad run, just due to normal fluctuations in the cards and the situations he encounters.

Using the method described in *PTF1*, and applying it to the player with the 100 percent advantage in the $1,060 tournaments described above, we find that although our expectation is to win (profit, after subtracting our buy-in/entry fees) a total of $106,371 over the course of 100 tournaments, one standard deviation on that result is $62,853. So, if we finish two standard deviations below our actual expectation (and 2 SDs = $125,706), we could actually finish these 100 tournaments with a loss of $19,000, despite our 100 percent advantage!

This may sound impossible, but keep in mind that we only expect to win $106,000 and that $93,000 of our total return comes from just three first place finishes. A few bad beats and cold decks at crucial times at the final table, or before we get to the final table, can wreak havoc with our overall results. Since we could conceivably suffer a net loss of $19,000 over the course of these 100 tournaments, and still be within the realm of what a statistician would consider a "normal" fluctuation, we might conclude that a bankroll of $20,000 would be sufficient to finance our play, though we could conceivably lose it all. In fact, a bankroll of $20,000 would usually be more than sufficient to finance this level of play, assuming we are correct about our 100 percent edge. The standard deviation on our expected results does give us a pretty good idea of the kinds of fluctuations that are possible due to bad luck in tournaments of this level over this period of time.

Technically, your $20,000 bankroll would probably be very safe if you cut back on the cost of the tournaments you entered if you started experiencing significant negative results. In other words, if you finish out of the money in the first ten tournaments you enter—and this is entirely possible—then you really would be wise to start entering $500 tournaments until you hit a few wins (or just one good win) to build your bankroll back up. Fluctuations of greater than two standard deviations happen all the time. (Cutting back on the size of your bets after bankroll reductions is a method of "Kelly Betting," another term that would be known to any serious blackjack player, but few poker players. I'll discuss Kelly betting approaches for tournament players in more detail later in this chapter.)

If you are familiar with the statistical concept of standard deviation as discussed in Appendix A, you should recall that a statistician expects a fluctuation of greater than two standard deviations 5 percent of the time. Which is to say that if 20 players were playing these tournaments with a 100 percent advantage, 19 of them would expect to finish 100 tournaments within two standard deviations of their expectation, but one of them would expect to experience a fluctuation of greater than two standard deviations from his expectation.

A fluctuation of three standard deviations is extremely rare, as results this far from expectation have only about a 1/300 chance of occurrence, so it's not really necessary to maintain a bankroll to withstand this much of a fluctuation. But to be safe, just based on the standard deviation, I'd advise a bankroll closer to $30,000 for these $1,000 events, assuming you have a 100 percent advantage.

DIFFERENT LEVELS OF AGGRESSION

Let's consider the fact that we've created our hypothetical 100 percent advantage in this tournament by devising a specific set of in-the-money finishes that would result in this win rate. In the real world, there are many different ways a player could end up with a 100 percent advantage. He could be a very aggressive player who had fewer cashes but more top-end finishes, or he could be a more conservative player who had a greater number of cashes, but more low-end finishes. Might not the bankroll requirements for these player types differ from each other?

Let's analyze and compare the requirements for these different player types.

THE MORE AGGRESSIVE HYPOTHETICAL TOURNAMENT PLAYER

To provide this player with a 100 percent advantage, let's say he finishes in the money only 10 times in 100 tournaments (instead of 16 times as in our prior example), but with more high-end finishes. Here's the aggressive player's chart:

WINNING RECORD EXAMPLE: 100% ADVANTAGE Aggressive Player's Chart: 100 Tournaments Played			
Finish	Payout	# Cashes	Total
1st	$31,079	4	$124,316
2nd	$17,266	4	$69,064
3rd	$9,496	2	$18,992
4th	$6,906	0	$0
5th	$6,043	0	$0
6th	$5,180	0	$0
7th	$4,317	0	$0
8th	$3,453	0	$0
9th	$2,590	0	$0
10th-	$0	0	$0

Total Cashed: $212,372
Total Invested: $106,000
Total Win: $106,372
Win Percentage: 100.35%

Conveniently, this very different set of cashes provides this aggressive player with the same 100.35 percent win rate as the player in our first example.

THE MORE CONSERVATIVE HYPOTHETICAL TOURNAMENT PLAYER

For further comparison, let's also create a sample player who has more final table finishes (25, instead of 16 or 10), with more low-end finishes, but still, with a 100 percent win rate. Here's this more conservative player's chart:

WINNING RECORD EXAMPLE: 100% ADVANTAGE Conservative Player's Chart: 100 Tournaments Played			
Finish	Payout	# Cashes	Total
1st	$31,079	2	$62,158
2nd	$17,266	2	$34,532
3rd	$9,496	3	$28,488
4th	$6,906	3	$20,718
5th	$6,043	3	$18,129
6th	$5,180	3	$15,540
7th	$4,317	4	$17,268
8th	$3,453	3	$10,359
9th	$2,590	2	$5,180
10th-	$0	0	$0

Total Cashed: $212,372
Total Invested: $106,000
Total Win: $106,372
Win Percentage: 100.35%

In order to compare the bankroll requirements of these three different player types, who all have the same overall win rate in the same tournament, let's use a different statistical method of analysis, the Gambler's Ruin Formula, or, as gamblers today more often call it, Risk of Ruin (or RoR).

First, here's an explanation of what we're trying to figure out. A player wants to play tournaments that have a specified buy-in/ entry cost, say, $1,060. He knows from the above discussion on standard deviation that he could conceivably lose his bankroll due to negative fluctuations, even if he has a 100 percent overall advantage. The player wants to minimize his risk, so he wants to know how much of a bankroll he'd need to insure himself of a 90 percent chance of success, or 95 percent chance of success, or even 99 percent chance of success. Also, if the player could maintain his 100 percent win rate while using either a more aggressive or more conservative strategy, how would this affect his chance of success?

The Risk of Ruin Formula that was used to analyze the three sample players described above was first published by Math Boy and Dunbar in the Fall 1999 issue of *Blackjack Forum*. The article is titled, "Risk of Ruin for Video Poker and Other Skewed Up Games." This article is available on my website, www. blackjackforumonline.com, in the free online library, so I'm not going to reproduce the Risk of Ruin formula here.

Let's just look at the RoR data on our three player types. Remember, the conservative player makes it to the final table 25 times in 100 tournaments, but wins the fewest top-end prizes. The middle-of-the-road player has 16 money finishes out of 100 tournaments, with more at the top-end. The aggressive player has only 10 money finishes, but takes four firsts, four seconds, and two third-place payouts. These are their bankroll requirements for various levels of risk:

RoR	RISK OF RUIN: THREE PLAYER TYPES Bankroll Requirements		
	Conservative Bankroll	Middle-of- Road Bankroll	Aggressive Bankroll
1%	$37,213	$45,449	$55,853
5%	$24,208	$29,565	$36,333
10%	$18,607	$22,724	$27,926

I want to emphasize here that the "conservative" and "aggressive" styles I've created are for purposes of analysis—they are not meant to be realistic. With regards to the aggressive player, it's unlikely that a player who was skillful enough to always make the top three when he finished in the money (with 80 percent of those finishes in the top two) would never finish in any other final table position. Even the most aggressive and skillful players will suffer bad beats and cold decks and hit lower payouts occasionally. It's really more likely that such a player would have a range of money finishes at all levels, even if he had more than his share of the top prizes. The problem I faced in creating this player, however, was that I was attempting to maintain that 100 percent win rate for purposes of risk of ruin comparison, and if I start scattering a more realistic set of smaller wins among his finishes, his win rate will climb dramatically, as it tends to do in real life with the best aggressive players.

The conservative player's results were similarly skewed. It is highly unlikely that a player with so few top-end finishes would be able to hit the money often enough to have a 100 percent win rate. But the purpose of the example is simply to show that playing style does have an effect on a player's bankroll requirement, all other things being equal. If we look at the middle-of-the road player's bankroll requirement for a 5 percent RoR (95 percent chance of success), we see he needs a bankroll in the neighborhood of $30,000. The conservative player might get away with a bankroll of about $5,000 less than this, but the aggressive player might need $5,000 more.

These numbers may surprise many tournament players who have not read *PTF1*, as there is widespread ignorance among poker players with regards to bankroll requirements. On one of the WPT shows, for example, a sidebar feature showed professional poker players being asked for advice on bankroll requirements for tournament players, and wound up providing the specific recommendation that tournament players should have a bankroll of ten times their buy-in cost. Don't we wish.... In fact, that is potentially disastrous advice for serious poker tournament players.

One other thing we must note here is that this sample tournament we're analyzing had a prize pool based on a total of 89 players. In fact, if you are entering $1,000 tournaments with 300 players, or 2,000+ players as in some of the 2006 WSOP $1,000 events, the top prizes will be much bigger, and so will your fluctuations and bankroll requirements. We don't want you to think that a $30,000 bankroll is sufficient for all $1,000 tournaments. Again, I'll refer you to the detailed discussion in Appendix A as well as in *PTF1* on how field size affects bankroll requirements.

Now let's look at how we can use satellites to lower this bankroll requirement.

LOWER BUY-IN COSTS MEAN LOWER BANKROLL REQUIREMENTS

Since we're discussing a specific $1,000 WSOP Circuit Event, let's look at one of the actual satellites that was being offered at Harrah's Rincon that allowed a player to win entry into this event. They ran ten-player satellites that cost $240, and the satellites paid two winners. Each winner received two $500 chips and $100 cash. So, if you were one of the two satellite winners, you'd have been able to cover your $1,060 buy-in/entry to the $1,000 tournament, and still have $40 cash to put in your pocket.

Here's a chart that shows this satellite's dollar value and player advantage, based on a player's expectation of winning twice out of every 10, 9, 8, 7, 6, and 5 satellites entered:

SATELLITE $ VALUE & PLAYER ADVANTAGE Winning Twice Per X Satellites WSOP Circuit Satellite, $240 Buy-in, Two Winners Each Get $1,000 (chips) plus $100 cash Dollar Value and Player Advantage If Player Wins Twice per:						
	10	**9**	**8**	**7**	**6**	**5**
$ Value	-$20.00	$4.44	$35.00	$74.29	$126.67	$200.00
Advan-tage (%)	-8.33%	1.85%	14.58%	30.95%	52.78%	83.33%

Now, let's say the same three hypothetical tournament players (conservative, middle-of-the-road, and aggressive), all with the same 100 percent advantage in the $1,000 events, are also skillful satellite players, and they each decide that they will always enter these $1,000 events through satellites. And, let's assume their levels of satellite skill provide all of them with an expectation of winning twice for every seven (or, essentially, 1 for every 3.5) two-winner satellites they enter. How does this affect the actual cost to them of entering the $1,000 events? Here's the math:

Three-and-a-half of these satellites will cost $240 x 3.5 = $840. For that $840 expense, the player gets $1,000 in chips plus $100 in cash. Since the buy-in/entry for the $1,000 event is $1,060, the player can buy-in to the $1,000 tourney and pocket the extra $40 cash, leaving him with a total buy-in/entry cost of $800 even, a discount of $260 from the full tournament price.

This lowered cost per tournament drastically reduces the risk of ruin for each player. You might guess off the top of your head that paying $800 per tournament on average, as opposed to $1,060, might cut your bankroll requirements proportionately. Since 800 divided by 1,060 equals 75.5 percent, you might be tempted to take the 1 percent RoR bankroll requirement of $45,449 for the middle of the road player, and multiply it by 75.5 percent, for a bankroll requirement of $34,300. But, in fact, the effect of the

APPENDIX B: SATELLITES

satellite discount entry is quite a bit stronger than that. What you must also consider is that although you are entering these $1,060 tournaments for only $800, the prize pool does not change. This means that the same win record will increase your percent advantage in the tournament itself from 100 to 165 percent. This increased percent advantage will lower the bankroll requirement for a 1 percent risk of ruin for the middle of the road player from $45,000 to $30,000.

(Unfortunately, figuring out the RoR for entering these tournaments through satellites is not quite as simple as just using $800 as the entry fee. The situation is similar to a parlay bet at a sports book. The satellite has its own flux, and that must be included with the flux on the main tournament in order to correctly calculate overall flux and risk of ruin.)

Let's look at the RoR bankroll requirements assuming these three players always enter these $1,060 tournaments through these $240 two-winner satellites, with each winning 2 out of every 7 of the satellites:

	RISK OF RUIN: THREE PLAYER TYPES Bankroll Requirements for $1,060 Satellites		
RoR	Conservative Bankroll	Middle-of-Road Bankroll	Aggressive Bankroll
1%	$19,358	$30,380	$42,905
5%	$12,592	$19,762	$27,910
10%	$9,679	$15,190	$21,452

WHAT RISK OF RUIN SHOULD A PLAYER CONSIDER SAFE?

Many players might say off the top of their heads that they'd be comfortable with a 90 percent chance of tournament success. But bear in mind that ruin means ruin. If you have a $30,000 bankroll, and you find yourself in that unlucky 10 percent of players who would expect to lose it all if playing at this risk level, then you are flat broke. So, if this $30,000 represents your life savings, that would be a foolhardy way to play. If it represents money that is easily replaceable (say by cashing in a few CDs when they mature), then it may not be a bad gamble.

Most professional gamblers prefer to use a "Kelly betting" system. Those of you who have read any of my blackjack books know what this is. If you are not familiar with the term, it essentially means that you always bet proportionately to your bankroll in order to ensure that you never go broke. For example, if a player was playing these $1,000 tournaments with a 5 percent RoR, he could do so with a $30,000 bankroll. If this same player decided in advance that he would enter tournaments with smaller buy-ins than $1,000 if he lost a significant portion of his bankroll (until he built it back up), then his actual RoR would be quite a bit lower than 5 percent.

In an ideal world, a player would create a chart of optimal entry fees to pay, based on his current bankroll, that would virtually eliminate any Risk of Ruin. For example, if he lost 40 percent of his starting bank, he would play in $600 events. If he lost 50 percent of his bankroll, he would play in $500 events. With a 75 percent loss, he would play in $250 events, etc. Unfortunately, in the real world, we can't always find tournaments priced to our needs. If I lose 10 percent of my bankroll, can I find a $900 tournament?

For any poker tournament player on a limited bankroll, however, it makes sense to follow such a plan as closely as possible. If your bankroll drops by 10 percent from the amount sufficient for $1,000 tournaments, you have to decide if you are willing to accept the increased risk of ruin inherent in continuing to play $1,000 events, or if you had better drop to $500 events, if that is all that's available below the $1,000 buy-in level.

Also, be honest with yourself about the actual size of your tournament bankroll. Your playing bankroll should not include your rent money, car payments, living expenses, credit card or installment loan payments, or the like.

FREQUENTLY ASKED QUESTIONS

Question: If I've already played a few satellites without winning, should I still buy-in to the main event if there are no more satellites?

Answer: If you have the bankroll to enter the main event at full price, and you have the skill to make money in these types of events, then by all means, buy-in for the full price. If the reason you are playing satellites is to cut your costs because you can't afford to play the bigger events, then do not buy-in for the full price. Just keep developing your satellite skills and play in the big events only when you win your seat through a satellite.

Question: If I'm just an amateur but I really want to get into a WPT main event just to play with the pros and take my shot at fame and fortune, but that $10,000 buy-in is a bit steep for my wallet, should I set a limit to the number of satellites I'll play in an attempt to enter the event?

Answer: If you are not a skillful satellite player and you are simply attempting to enter a major event cheaply on a long shot gamble, then you should definitely decide beforehand exactly how much you're willing to spend on satellites, and quit if you hit your limit.

Question: If I'm skillful at both satellites and regular tournaments, should I limit the number of satellites I'll play for any one event?

Answer: For a skillful player, it's a different situation. First of all, if you fully intend to enter the main event regardless of your satellite result, then there is the practical consideration of time. If an event starts at 2 p.m., and satellites start at 8 a.m., it may not be in your best interest to play satellites for six hours prior to starting a tournament that might go 12 to 14 more hours.

Some pros always play a satellite or two before major events, even when they can afford the full buy-in price, because the satellites are a good value and can be used to lower their overall tournament expenses. If a pro can win 1 out of 7 $1,000 satellites in order to enter $10,000 tournaments, and if he plays just one satellite before each major event, then six times he'll be paying $11,000 for his seat, and once he'll pay just $1,000. If he plays 21 of these $10,000 tournaments per year, his three satellite wins will lower his overall tournament cost (and raise his overall profit) by $9,000.

If time constraints and guarding against fatigue aren't part of the equation, and you have an edge at satellite play, there is no reason to limit the number of satellites you'll play to enter any one event. During big multi-event tournaments like the WSOP, there are satellite pros who virtually camp out in the satellite area, playing one satellite after another, day after day. On some days, they may play ten satellites without a single win, then they'll win three or four the next day. They use the tournament chips they win to buy-in to the events they want to play, and sell the rest to players for full value. Obviously, these pros pay no attention whatsoever to limiting the number of satellites they'll play for any one event. Nor should they. They're in it for the long run, and if they have the skill to beat the satellite fields and the house edge, they'll come out ahead in the long run.

CONCLUSION

If you are serious about playing in major tournaments with big buy-ins, there is a huge value to developing satellite skills. At the 2006 WSOP, I overheard one player commenting to another that he was surprised at how many of the big name pros were entering satellites, since they could so easily afford the full buy-ins. If you look at the value of satellites as shown in the charts provided in this article, you can see why many pros are attracted to satellites. If you play a lot of major events, and a lot of satellites to enter these events, you can substantially lower your overall annual tournament costs while increasing your percentage return. I don't care how much money you have. If you're paying $10,000 for an event that you could get into for $8,000, you may be a great poker player, but you're not that great at financial planning.

NOTES AND ACKNOWLEDGMENTS

Risk of ruin is a statistical measure that blackjack players would be familiar with, but that is almost completely absent from the poker literature. There is an excellent explanation of RoR in Dr. Allan Wilson's classic text, *The Casino Gambler's Guide* (1965). But neither Wilson's description of risk of ruin, nor any of the descriptions that have been published in many blackjack texts since then, allow for the formula's use in a game where there are multiple possible payouts, ranging from a loss of the bet (buy-in), to a modest win (low-end finish) to a very large payout compared to the size of the initial bet.

The first published discussion of RoR that I know of for games with multiple payout possibilities was an article by Russian mathematician Evgeny Sorokin that appeared in the March 1999 issue of Dan Paymar's *Video Poker Times* newsletter. In response to Sorokin's article, professional gamblers Math Boy and Dunbar developed an Excel spreadsheet method of applying Sorokin's generalized risk equation to virtually any game with a skewed payout structure, and I published their method in the Fall 1999 issue of *Blackjack Forum*, in their article, "Risk of Ruin for Video Poker and Other Skewed Up Games." Math Boy has helped me to adjust their method for analyzing poker tournaments or any other gambling tournaments. (You'll also find a discussion of risk of ruin in *The Mathematics of Poker* by Bill Chen and Jerrod Ankenman, though they do not deal with the topic of this section—using satellites to lower your RoR.)

I am especially indebted to Math Boy for creating an Excel spreadsheet for me that would not only estimate a tournament's standard deviation and risk of ruin, but would automatically recalculate these values based on entering the tournament via satellite, at any satellite cost, and with any selected percentage of satellite wins. The spreadsheet is not currently user-friendly for anyone who is not familiar with some of Excel's advanced statistical functions, but I have been twisting Math Boy's arm to get a simpler version, similar to his Patience Factor Calculator that is available for free download on my website, www.pokertournamentformula. com.

A number of players have asked me where I came up with the standard deviation formula that appears in *PTF1*, as they had never seen a method for calculating standard deviation for a game with a tournament payout structure. My method was simply to modify a formula originally created by Doug Reul, which first appeared as the "Volatility Index" in one of Dan Paymar's 1996 issues of *Video Poker Times*, and can currently be found in his book, *Video Poker—Precision Play.*

The information in this section first appeared in slightly different form in the Winter 2007 issue of *Blackjack Forum Online.* You can find the original version, as well as Math Boy's Patience Factor Calculator and hopefully, in the near future, his RoR and Satellite Analyzer online at www.pokertournamentformula.com

APPENDIX C: "TRUE M" VERSUS HARRINGTON'S M

I must address some of the flaws in the concept of "M" as put forth by Dan Harrington in *Harrington on Hold'em II* (*HOH II*), not only as a measure of player viability in poker tournaments, but also as a tool for strategy decisions. *PTF1* has been criticized by some poker writers who contend that my strategies for fast tournaments must be wrong, since they violate strategies based on Harrington's M. I'm sure this book will fall under the same criticisms. Because the *HOH* series has been so popular, I know that many serious players swear by it as the no-limit hold'em tournament bible, and many of these players still can't figure out why they are getting nowhere in terms of tournament success.

So, I will explain exactly where Harrington made his errors, why Harrington's strategies are incorrect not only for fast tournaments, but for tournaments with slow blind structures as well, and why poker tournament structure, which Harrington ignores, is a key factor in devising optimal tournament strategies.

Some of the players who are using the strategies from *PTF1*, and acknowledge that structure is a crucial factor in any poker tournament, tell me they still calculate M at the tables because they believe it provides a more accurate assessment of a player's current chip stack status than the simpler way I propose—gauging your current stack as a multiple of the big blind. But M, in fact, is a less accurate guide, and I will explain why. There is a way to calculate what I call "True M" that would provide the information that Harrington's M is purported to provide, but I do not believe there is any real strategic value in calculating this number, so I will explain the reason for that too.

Let me say right off that I like the *Harrington on Hold'em* series, and that I recommend these books to players. Volume III is essentially a series of 50 different hands and situations presented as problems that must be solved. It's an excellent training format for players who are trying to learn how to play various hands based on position, betting patterns, and the cards on board. Volume I of the series was the first book I know of to describe the aggressive and super-aggressive playing styles that are employed by many of today's top players. Harrington does not expound on these looser, more aggressive styles at any length, but he does recognize them as valid approaches and does not claim that conservative play is a superior approach. He acknowledges that his own style is conservative but also claims that he employs more of the aggressive strategies as the tournament progresses and the chip stacks get shorter in relation to the blinds. Harrington introduces the concept of "M" in Volume II of his series, and this is also an important book for tournament players to read. So, let me explain the issues I have with his thinking.

THE BASICS OF HARRINGTON'S M STRATEGY

Harrington uses a zone system to categorize a player's current chip position. In the "green zone," a player's chip stack is said to be healthy enough for the player to use a full range of poker skills. As a player's chip stack diminishes, the player goes through the yellow zone, the orange zone, the red zone, and finally the dead zone. The zones are identified by a simple rating number Harrington calls

"M." According to Harrington, the M concept has been around for years. He credits backgammon/poker pro Paul Magriel as one of the originators of the concept. As I have never seen anything written by Magriel on this topic, I do not know if he would be in agreement with Harrington's treatment of M. So, my comments are specifically limited to M as presented in *HOH II*.

WHAT IS "M"?

In *HOH II*, on page 125, Dan Harrington defines M as: "...the ratio of your stack to the current total of blinds and antes." For example, if your chip stack totals $3,000, and the blinds are $100/$200 (with no ante), then you find your M by dividing 3,000/300 = 10.

On page 126, Harrington expounds on the meaning of M to a tournament player: "What M tells you is the number of rounds of the table that you can survive before being blinded off, assuming you play no pots in the meantime." In other words, Harrington describes M as a player's *survival indicator*. If your M = 5, then Harrington is saying you will survive for five more rounds of the table (five circuits of the blinds) if you do not play a hand. At a 10-handed table, this would mean you have about 50 hands until you would be blinded off. All of Harrington's zone strategies are based on this understanding of how to calculate M, and what M means to your current chances of tournament survival.

Amateur tournament players tend to tighten up their play as their chip stacks diminish, becoming overly protective of their remaining chips. This is due to the natural survival instinct of players. They know they cannot purchase more chips if they lose their whole stack, so they try to hold on to the precious few chips that are keeping them alive. If they have read a few books on the subject of tournament play, they may also have been influenced by the unfortunate writings of other authors who for many years have promulgated the misguided reverse-chip-value theory that says the fewer chips you have in a tournament, the more each chip is worth.

But in *HOH II*, Harrington explains that as your M diminishes, which is to say as your stack size becomes smaller in relation to the cost of the blinds and antes, "…the blinds are starting to catch you, so you have to loosen your play… you have to start making moves with hands weaker than those a conservative player would elect to play." I agree with Harrington on this point, and I also concur with his explanation of why looser play is correct as a player's chip stack gets shorter: "Another way of looking at M is to see it as a measure of just how likely you are to get a better hand in a better situation, *with a reasonable amount of money left.*" (Italics his.)

In other words, Harrington devised his looser pot-entering strategy, which begins when your M falls below 20, and goes through four zones as it continues to shrink, based on the likelihood of your being dealt better cards to make chips with than your present starting hand. For example, with an M of 15 (Harrington's yellow zone), if a player is dealt an A-10 offsuit in early position, Harrington's yellow zone strategy would advise the player to enter the pot with a raise. This play is not advised in Harrington's green zone strategy (with an M > 20) because he considers A-10 offsuit to be too weak of a hand to play from early position, since your bigger chip stack means you will be likely to catch a better pot-entering opportunity if you wait. The desperation of your reduced chip stack in the yellow zone, however, has made it necessary for you to take a risk with this hand because with the number of hands remaining before you will be blinded off, you are unlikely "…to get a better hand in a better situation, *with a reasonable amount of money left.*"

Again, I fully agree with the logic of loosening starting hand requirements as a player's chip stack gets short. In fact, the strategies in *PTF1* are based in part on the same logic. But despite the similarity of some of the logic behind our strategies, there are big differences between our specific strategies for any specific size of chip stack. For starters, my strategy for entering a pot with what I categorize as a "competitive stack" (a stack size more or less comparable to Harrington's "green zone") is far looser and more aggressive than his. And my short-stack strategies are downright maniacal compared to Harrington's strategies for his yellow, orange, and red zones.

There are two major reasons why our strategies are so different, even though we agree on the logic that looser play is required as stacks get shorter. Again, the first is a fundamental difference in our overriding tournament theory, which I will deal with later in this section. The second reason, which I will deal with now, is a serious flaw in Harrington's method of calculating and interpreting M. Again, what Harrington specifically assumes, as per *HOH II*, is that: "What M tells you is the number of rounds of the table that you can survive before being blinded off, assuming you play no pots in the meantime."

But that's simply not correct. The only way M, as defined by Harrington, could indicate the number of rounds a player could survive is by ignoring the tournament structure.

WHY TOURNAMENT STRUCTURE MATTERS IN DEVISING OPTIMAL STRATEGY

Let's look at some sample poker tournaments to show how structure matters, and how it affects the underlying meaning of M, or "the number of rounds of the table that you can survive before being blinded off, assuming you play no pots in the meantime." Let's say the blinds are $50/$100, and you have $3,000 in chips. What is your M, according to Harrington?

$$M = 3,000/150 = 20$$

So, according to the explanation of M provided in *HOH II*, you could survive 20 more rounds of the table before being blinded off, assuming you play no pots in the meantime. This is not correct, however, because the actual number of rounds you can survive before being blinded off is entirely dependent on the tournament's blind structure.

For example, what if this tournament has 60-minute blind levels? Would you survive 20 rounds with the blinds at $50/$100 if you entered no pots? No way. Assuming this is a ten-handed table, you would go through the blinds about once every twenty minutes, which is to say, you would only play *three rounds* at this $50/$100 level. Then the blinds would go up.

If we use the blind structure from the 2007 WSOP Circuit events played at Caesars Palace in Las Vegas, after 60 minutes the blinds would go from $50/$100 to $100/$200, then to $100/$200 with a $25 ante 60 minutes after that. What is the actual number of rounds you would survive without entering a pot in this tournament from this point? Assuming you go through the blinds at each level three times,

$$3 \times \$150 = \$450$$

$$3 \times \$300 = \$900$$

$$3 \times \$550 = \$1,650$$

Add up the blind costs: $450 + $900 + $1,650 = $3,000.

That's a total of only 9 rounds.

This measure of the true "…number of rounds of the table that you can survive before being blinded off, assuming you play no pots in the meantime," is crucial in evaluating your likelihood of getting "…a better hand in a better situation, with a reasonable amount of money left," and it is entirely dependent on this tournament's blind structure. For the rest of this section, I will refer to this more accurate structure-based measure as "True M." True M for this real-world tournament would indicate to the player that his survival time (9 rounds) was less than half that (20 rounds) predicted by Harrington's M.

TRUE M IN FAST POKER TOURNAMENTS

To really drill home the flaw in M—as Harrington defines it—let's look at a fast tournament structure. Let's assume the exact same $3,000 in chips, and the exact same $50/$100 blind level, but with the 20-minute blind levels we find in many small buy-in tournaments. With this blind structure, the blinds will be one level higher each time we go through them. How many rounds of play will our $3,000 in chips survive, assuming we play no pots? (Again, I'll use the Caesars WSOP Circuit levels, as above, changing only the blind length from 60 minutes to 20 minutes.)

$150 + $300 + $550 + $1,100 (4 rounds) = $1,950

The next round the blinds are $300/$600 with a $75 ante, so the cost of a ten-handed round is $1,650, and we only have $1,050 remaining. That means that with this faster tournament structure, our True M at the start of that $50/$100 blind level is actually about 4.6, a very far cry from the 20 that Harrington's M would give you, and quite far from the 9 rounds we would survive in the 60-minute structure described above.

And, in a small buy-in tournament with 15-minute blind levels—and these fast small buy-in tournaments are very common in poker rooms today—this same $3,000 chip position starting at this same blind level would indicate a True M of only 3.9.

TRUE M IN SLOW-STRUCTURED POKER TOURNAMENTS

But what if you were playing in the $10,000 main event of the WSOP, where the blind levels last 120 minutes? In this tournament, if you were entering the $50/$100 blind level with $3,000 in chips, your True M would be 12.6. Unfortunately, that's still nowhere near the 20 rounds Harrington's M gives you.

TRUE M ADJUSTS FOR TOURNAMENT STRUCTURE

Note that in each of these tournaments, 20 M means something very different as a survival indicator. True M shows that the survival equivalent of $3,000 in chips at the same blind level can range from 3.9 rounds (39 hands) to 12.6 rounds (126 hands), depending solely on the length of the blinds.

Furthermore, even within the same blind level of the same tournament, True M can have different values, depending on how deep you are into that blind level. For example, what if you have $3,000 in chips but instead of being at the very start of that $50/$100 blind level (assuming 60-minute levels), you are somewhere in the middle of it, so that although the blinds are currently $50/$100, the blinds will go up to the $100/$200 level before you go through them three more times? Does this change your True M?

It most certainly does. That True M of 9 in this tournament, as demonstrated above, only pertains to your chip position at the $50/$100 blind level if you will be going through those $50/$100 blinds *three times* before the next level. If you've already gone through those blinds at that level one or more times, then your True M will not be 9, but will range from 6.4 to 8.1, depending on how deep into the $50/$100 blind level you are.

Most important, if you are under the mistaken impression that at any point in the $50/$100 blind level in any of the tournaments described above, $3,000 in chips is sufficient to go through 20 rounds of play (200 hands), you are way off the mark. What Harrington says "M tells you" is not at all what M tells you. If you actually stopped and calculated True M, as defined above, then True M would tell you what Harrington's M purports to tell you.

If Harrington had actually realized that his M was not an accurate survival indicator, and he had stopped and calculated True M for a variety of tournaments, would he and his publisher still be advising you to employ the same starting hand standards and playing strategies at a True M of 3.9 (with 39 hands before blind-off) that you would be employing at a True M of 12.6 (with 126 hands before blind-off)? If he believes that a player with 20 M has 20 rounds of play to wait for a good hand before he is blinded off (and again, 20 rounds at a ten-player table would be 200 hands), then his assessment of your likelihood of getting "…a better hand in a better situation, *with a reasonable amount of money left*," would be quite different than if he realized that his True M was 9 (90 hands remaining till blind-off), or in a faster blind structure, as low as 3.9 (only 39 hands remaining until blind-off). Those radically different blind-off times would drastically alter the frequencies of occurrence of the premium starting hands, and the likelihood of getting those hands, what he tells us his M theory and strategy are based on.

A BLACKJACK ANALOGY

For blackjack players—and I know a lot of my readers come from the world of blackjack card counting—Harrington's M might best be compared to the "running count." If I am using a traditional balanced card counting system at a casino blackjack table, and I make my playing and betting decisions according to my running count, I will often be playing incorrectly, because the structure of the game—the number of decks in play and the number of cards that have already been dealt since the last shuffle—must be taken into account in order for me to adjust my running count to a "true" count. A +6 running count in a single-deck game means something entirely different from a +6 running count in a six-deck shoe game. And even within the same game, a +6 running count at the beginning of the deck or shoe means something different from a +6 running count toward the end of the deck or shoe.

Professional blackjack players adjust their running count to the true count to estimate their advantage accurately and make their strategy decisions accordingly. The unadjusted running count cannot do this with any accuracy. Harrington's M could be considered a kind of *Running M*, which must be adjusted to a True M in order for it to have validity as a survival gauge.

WHEN HARRINGTON'S RUNNING M IS OCCASIONALLY CORRECT

Harrington's Running M can "accidentally" become correct without a True M adjustment when a player is very short-stacked in a tournament with lengthy blind levels. For example, if a player has an M of four or five in a tournament with 2-hour blind levels, then in the early rounds of that blind level, since he could expect to go through the same blind costs four or five times, Harrington's unadjusted M would be the same as True M. This might also occur when the game is short-handed, since players will be going through the blinds more frequently. (This same thing happens in blackjack games where the running count equals the true count at specific points in the deal. For example, if a blackjack player is using a count-per-deck adjustment in a six-deck game, then when the dealer is down to the last deck in play, the running count will equal the true count.) In rare situations like these, where Running M equals True M, Harrington's "red zone" strategies may be correct—not because Harrington was correct in his application of M, but because of the tournament structure and the player's poor chip position at that point.

In tournaments with 60-minute blind levels, this type of "Running M = True M" situation could only occur at a full table when a player's M is 3 or less. And in fast tournaments with 15 or 20-minute blind levels, Harrington's M could only equal True M when a player's M = 1 or less.

Harrington's yellow and orange zone strategies, however, will always be pretty worthless, even in the slowest tournaments, because there are no tournaments with blind levels that last long enough to require no True M adjustments.

WHY HARRINGTON'S STRATEGIES CAN'T BE SAID TO ADJUST AUTOMATICALLY FOR TRUE M

Some Harrington defenders may wish to make a case that Dan Harrington made some kind of automatic adjustment for approximate True M in devising his yellow and orange zone strategies. But in *HOH II*, he clearly states that M tells you how many rounds of the table you will survive—period. In addition, in order to select which hands a player should play in these zones, based on the likelihood of better hands occurring while the player still has a reasonable chip stack, it was necessary for Harrington to specify some number of rounds in order to develop a table of the frequencies of occurrence of the starting hands. His book tells us that he assumes an M of 20 simply means 20 rounds remaining—which we know is wrong for all real-world tournaments.

But for those who wish to make a case that Harrington made some kind of a True M adjustment that he elected not to inform us about, my answer is that it's impossible that whatever adjustment he used would be even close to accurate for all tournaments and blind structures. If, for example, he assumed 20 M meant a True M of 12, and he developed his starting-hand frequency charts with this assumption, then his strategies would be fairly accurate for the slowest blind structures we find in major events. But they would still be very wrong for the faster blind structures we find in events with smaller buy-ins and in most online tournaments.

In *HOH II*, he does provide quite a few sample hands from online tournaments, with no mention whatsoever of the blind structures of these events, but 15-minute blind levels are less common online than 5-, 8-, and 12-minute blind levels. Thus, I have to believe that Harrington considers his strategies correct for tournaments of all speeds, and it is doubtful that he made any True M adjustments, even for slower tournament structures.

I suspect that Harrington has not actually played a lot of small buy-in tournaments with their typical 15- or 20-minute blind lengths. When I look up his tournament record in *Card Player's* online database, of the thirteen cashes they show for him in the past four years, eleven of them are in major events with buy-ins of $5,000 or more, mostly $10,000 WSOP and WPT events. *Card Player* doesn't track the results of tournaments with buy-ins below $300, which most of the tournaments with 15- and 20-minute levels would have. So we don't know for sure that he's not playing the Orleans $60 tournaments a few days a week. But I doubt it, as it appears that he does not even play many of the faster pro-level events with buy-ins ranging from $300 to $2,500, since he shows only two cashes in the past four years in tournaments with buy-ins below $5,000. If he is playing these smaller buy-in events regularly, his record in them is dismal.

As Harrington's treatment of M is contained entirely in *HOH II*, a book which he subtitled "The Endgame," I believe that when writing about M, he really was writing about what the subtitle indicates the book is about—final-table, short-handed play in major tournaments with typical blind lengths of 90 to 120 minutes. For this type of endgame play—which is where he does have experience—M as described by Harrington would be a far more accurate survival measure and strategy guide than it is if we attempt to apply it to ten-handed games with faster blind structures, as if it should be used from the start to the finish of any and every tournament, as his publisher has asserted online.

It's unfortunate that Harrington used online examples in his book without specifying their blind structures. I suspect he has not played a lot of online poker and may not even know that they typically have very short blind lengths. I believe he used these online examples in his book, possibly at the urging of his publisher, in order to give his book a more universal appeal. The online market is huge. Obviously, he is a very smart guy, and I don't think he ever really considered the effects of tournament structure on strategy, because he was only familiar with one structure—long, slow, and deep-stacked.

SIMPLIFYING TRUE M FOR REAL-LIFE TOURNAMENT STRATEGY

If all poker tournaments had the same blind structure, then we could just memorize chart data that would indicate True M with any chip stack at any point in any blind level. Unfortunately, there are almost as many blind structures as there are tournaments. There are ways, however, that Harrington's Running M could be adjusted to an *approximate* True M without literally figuring out the exact cost of each blind level at every point in the tournament. With 90-minute blind levels, after dividing your chip stack by the cost of a round, simply divide your Running M by two, and you'll have a reasonable approximation of your True M. With 60-minute blind levels, take about 40 percent of the Running M. With 30-minute blind levels, divide the Running M by three. And with 15- or 20-minute blind levels, divide the Running M by five. These will be far from perfect adjustments, but they will be much closer to reality than Harrington's unadjusted Running M numbers.

BUT DO TOURNAMENT PLAYERS NEED TO KNOW THEIR "TRUE M"?

Am I suggesting that poker tournament players should start estimating their True M, instead of the Running M that Harrington proposes? No, because I disagree with Harrington's emphasis on survival and basing so much of your play on your cards. I just want to make it clear that M, as defined and described in *HOH II*, is *wrong*, a bad measure of what it purports and aims to measure. It is based on an error in logic, in which a crucial factor in the formula—tournament structure—is ignored.

Although it would be possible for a player to correct Harrington's mistake by estimating his True M at any point in a tournament, I don't advise it. Admittedly, it's a pain in the ass trying to calculate True M exactly, not something most players could do quickly and easily at the tables. But that's not the reason I think True M should be ignored. The reason is related to the overarching difference between Harrington's strategies and mine. That is: It's a grave error for tournament players to focus on how long they can survive if they just sit and wait for premium cards. That's not what tournaments are about. It's a matter of perspective. When you look at your stack size, you shouldn't be thinking, "How long can I survive?" but "How much of a threat do I pose to my opponents?"

> **IT'S A GRAVE ERROR FOR TOUR-NAMENT PLAYERS TO FOCUS ON HOW LONG THEY CAN SURVIVE IF THEY JUST SIT AND WAIT FOR PREMIUM CARDS.**

The whole concept of M is geared to the player who is tight and conservative, waiting for premium hands (or premium enough at that point). Harrington's strategy, at least as expressed in his books, is overly focused on cards as the primary pot-entering factor, as opposed to entering pots based predominately (or purely) on position, chip stack, and opponents.

In *PTF1*, I suggest that players assess their chip position by considering their chip stacks as a simple multiple of the current big blind. If you have $3,000 in chips, and the big blind is 100, then you have 30 big blinds. This number, 30, tells you nothing about how many rounds you can survive if you don't enter any pots. But frankly, that doesn't matter. What matters in a tournament is that you have sufficient chips to employ a full range of skills, and—just as important—that you have sufficient chips to threaten your opponents with a raise, and an all-in raise if that is what you need for the threat to be successful to win you the pot. Your ability to threaten is directly related to the health of your chip stack in relation to the current betting level, which is most strongly influenced by the size of the blinds. In my *PTF1* strategy, tournaments are not so much about survival as they are about stealing pots. If you're going to depend on surviving until you get premium cards to get you to the final table, you're going to see very few final tables. You must outplay your opponents with the cards you are dealt, not wait and hope for cards that are superior to theirs.

I'm not suggesting that you ignore the size of the preflop pot and focus all of your attention on the size of the big blind. You should always know the total of the chips in the pot preflop, but not because you want to know how long you can survive if you sit there waiting for miracle cards. You simply need to know the size of the preflop pot so you can make your betting and playing decisions, both pre- and post-flop, based on all of the factors in the current hand. What other players, if any, have entered the pot? Is this a pot you can steal if you don't have a viable hand? Is this pot worth the risk of an attempted steal? If you have a drawing hand, do you have the odds to call, or are you giving an opponent the odds to call? Are any of your opponents pot-committed? Do you have sufficient chips to play a speculative hand for this pot? There are dozens of reasons why you need to know the size of a pot you are considering getting involved in, but M is not a factor in *any* of these decisions.

So, again, although you will always be totaling the chips in the pot in order to make betting and playing decisions, sitting there and estimating your blind-off time by dividing your chip stack by the total chips in the preflop pot is an exercise in futility. It has absolutely nothing to do with your actual chances of survival. You shouldn't even be thinking in terms of survival, but of domination.

HOH II VERSUS PTF1: A SAMPLE SITUATION

Let's say the blinds are $100/$200, and you have $4,000 in chips. Harrington would have you thinking that your M is 13 (yellow zone), and he advises: "...you have to switch to small-ball moves: get in, win the pot, but get out when you encounter resistance." (*HOH II*, p. 136) In the *PTF1* basic strategy for fast tournaments (*PTF1* p. 158), I categorize this chip stack equal to 20 big blinds as "very short," and my advice is: "...you must face the fact that you are not all that far from the exit door. But you still have enough chips to scare any player who does not have a really big chip stack and/or a really strong hand. Two things are important when you are this short on chips. One is that unless you have an all-in raising hand as defined below, do not enter any pot unless you are the first in. And second, any bet when you are this short will always be all in."

The fact is, you don't have enough chips for "small ball" when you're this short on chips in a fast tournament, and one of the most profitable moves you can make is picking on Harrington-type players who think it's time for small ball.

Harrington sees this yellow zone player as still having 13 rounds of play (130 hands—a huge overestimation) to look for a pretty decent hand to get involved with. My thinking in a fast tournament, by contrast, would be: "The blinds are now $100/$200. By the time they get around to me fifteen minutes from now, they will be $200/$400. If I don't make a move before the blinds get around to me, and I have to go through those blinds, my $4,000 will become $3,400, and the chip position I'm in right now, which is a stack equal to 20 times the big blind, will be reduced to a stack of only 8.5 times the big blind. Right now, my chip stack is moderately scary. Ten to fifteen minutes from now (in 7-8 hands), any legitimate hand will call me down."

> **WHEN YOU'RE VERY SHORT ON CHIPS YOU MUST TAKE RISKS, BECAUSE THE RISK OF TOURNAMENT DEATH IS GREATER IF YOU DON'T PLAY THAN IF YOU DO.**

So, my advice to players this short on chips in a fast tournament is to raise all in with any two cards from any late position seat in an unopened pot. My raising hands from earlier positions include all pairs higher than 6-6, and pretty much any two high cards. And my advice with these hands is to raise or reraise all in, including calling any all ins. You need a double up so badly here in a fast tournament that you simply can't wait any longer. As per *PTF1* (p. 159): "When you're this short on chips you must take risks, because the risk of tournament death is greater if you don't play than if you do."

There is also a side effect of using a loose-aggressive strategy when you have enough chips to hurt your opponents, and that is that you build an image of a player who is not to be messed with, and that is always the preferred image to have in any no-limit hold'em tournament. But while Harrington sees this player surviving for another thirteen rounds of play, the reality is that he will survive fewer than four more rounds in a fast tournament, and within two rounds he will be so short-stacked that he will be unable to scare anybody out of a pot, and even a double up will not get him anywhere near a competitive chip stack.

My advice at this chip level in slow-structured tournaments as per this book is not nearly as aggressive as the advice I provided in *PTF1* for fast-structured events, but then I provide very little advice in this book on which hands to play in slow-structured tournaments because I think hand selection is so much less important than other game factors.

THE GOOD NEWS FOR POKER TOURNAMENT PLAYERS

The good news for poker tournament players is that Harrington's books have become so popular, and his M strategy so widely accepted by players and "experts" alike, that today's no-limit hold'em tournaments are overrun with his disciples, who all play the same tight, conservative style through the early blind levels, then predictably start entering pots with more marginal hands as their M diminishes—and their tight early play almost always guarantees diminished M. And, though many of the top players know that looser, more aggressive play is what's getting them to the final tables, I doubt that tight M-based strategies will be abandoned by the masses any time soon.

In the March 28, 2007 issue of *Card Player* magazine, columnist Steve Zolotow reviewed *PTF1*, stating: "Snyder originates a complicated formula for determining the speed of a tournament, which he calls the patience factor. Dan Harrington's discussion of M and my columns on CPR cover this same material, but much more accurately. Your strategy should be based not upon the speed of the tournament as a whole, but on your current chip position in relation to current blinds. If your M (the number of rounds you can survive without playing a hand) is 20, you should base your strategy primarily on that fact. Whether the blinds will double and reduce your M to 10 in fifteen minutes or four hours should not have much influence on your strategic decisions." Zolotow's "CPR" articles were simply a couple of columns he wrote in 2006 in which he did nothing but explain Harrington's M theory, as if it were 100 percent correct. He added nothing to the theory of M, and is clearly as ignorant of the math as Harrington and Harrington's publisher. So, money-making opportunities in poker tournaments continue to abound.

[This chapter was initially published as an article in the Spring 2007 issue of *Blackjack Forum Online* in somewhat different form. I want to thank "SlackerInc" for posting a question on the poker discussion forum at my website, www.pokertournamentformula.com, in which he pointed out many of the key differences between Harrington's short-stack strategies and those in *PTF1*. He wanted to know why our pot-entering strategies were so far apart. The answer is that the strategies in PTF1 were specifically identified as strategies *for fast tournaments* of a specific speed, so my assumptions, based on a player's current chip stack, would usually be that the player is about five times more desperate than Harrington would see him (his Running M of 20 being roughly equivalent to my True M of about 4).]

GLOSSARY

ace master: A player who will play any hand in any pot from any position if one of his cards is an ace and will often stay in a pot too long hoping to hit the ace. See *PTF1* for a more detailed discussion.

aces up: To have two pair, one of which is aces.

action: The total amount bet by players; any betting by the players in a round is the "action."

add on: In tournaments, an option to purchase a specified number of chips over-and-above the starting chip allotment.

advertising: Common gamblers' slang for getting involved in a bet at a disadvantage in order to get more action later when you have an advantage.

aggressive: A style of play characterized by raising and reraising frequently.

all in: When a player has all his chips committed to the pot.

ante: A forced bet, in addition to the blinds, that must be placed by all players at the table before any cards have been dealt.

GLOSSARY

attack dynamics: Optimal stealing strategy for the minefield portion of a tournament, based on relative stack size. See Chapter Eleven.

baby full: In hold'em, a full house that is not the best possible full house because the three-of-a-kind are made with one of the lower denomination community cards.

baby pair: A small pair, generally 6-6 or lower.

backdoor: In hold'em, to make a straight or flush by drawing to it on both the turn and river. Often an accidental improvement, as when a player with top pair backdoors a flush.

bad beat: To have a strong hand beaten by an opponent's suck out.

ball-cap kid: Typically, a young, loose aggressive player who sports a ball-cap, though it could be any player who plays with this style. See *PTF1* for a more detailed discussion.

bank/ bankroll: The total amount of money a player has to gamble with.

basic strategy: The mathematically correct strategy for any gambling game.

BB: Big blind.

belly buster: An inside straight draw.

big slick: In hold'em, any A-K in the hole.

bitch slap: A raise or reraise by a player with a big chip stack designed to put a shorter stacked opponent to a decision on whether to pot-commit himself. See Chapter Eleven.

blank: A card that comes down on the turn or river that seems irrelevant to the cards on board and the hand in play.

blind: In hold'em, a forced bet that must be placed preflop instead of, or in addition to, an ante before any cards have been dealt. Usually, only two players, on a rotating basis, are required to place blind bets.

blind defender: A player who frequently calls or reraises late position players when he is in one of the blinds, and especially when in the big blind.

blind level: In tournament hold'em, the current amount of the blinds. As the tournament progresses, the level rises.

blinded off: In a tournament, to be eliminated by having one's chips steadily dwindled by the blinds and antes.

blind-off time: The amount of time it would take a starting chip stack to be blinded off if no hand was ever played, but blinds and antes were paid.

bluff: To place a bet with a weak hand in order to represent a strong hand and win a pot by causing opponents to fold.

GLOSSARY

board: In hold'em, the face-up community cards on the table.

boat: A full house, also *full boat.*

boat person: A fearless, aggressive player comfortable with high-risk play. See *PTF1* for a more detailed discussion.

bot: A computer program that plays poker, either for practice, or in real games online.

bottom pair: In hold'em, a pair made by matching the lowest card on the board with one of your hole cards.

bubble: The time period in a tournament just before the remaining players are guaranteed a prize payout.

build a pot: To increase the amount of money in a pot by betting and/or raising in such a way that other players are induced to call.

busted draw: A hand in which a player fails to make the straight or flush, for which he was remaining in the pot, by the time the river card is dealt.

bust out: In a poker tournament, to lose all of your chips.

button: In hold'em, the disk that rotates clockwise from player to player, indicating which player has the "dealer" position and bets last.

buy-in: In a tournament, the amount you pay to obtain your initial chips for playing the tournament.

cagey codger: Typically, an older experienced male player who is fairly tight and will slowplay strong hands to trap opponents. See *PTF1* for a more detailed discussion.

call: To match a bet without raising in order to keep your hand alive in a pot.

calling station: A derogatory term for a passive player who rarely raises, but often calls with any hand, whether weak or strong.

camouflage: Any bet or play intended to mislead an opponent, usually into thinking one's hand is weaker than it is.

canasta lady: A very tight player who never bluffs and will only stay in a pot with a very strong hand. See *PTF1* for a more detailed discussion.

card dead: A lengthy time period in which you are dealt no playable starting hands.

catch: In hold'em, to make a hand stronger than an opponent's because of a card or cards dealt on the flop, turn, or river.

change gears: To suddenly play more (or less) aggressively than you have been playing for the purpose of confusing opponents.

charge: To bet in order to make other players pay to stay in a pot.

check: To stay active in a pot in which no bet is required, and without betting yourself.

GLOSSARY

check-raise: To raise or reraise a player who has bet, after having checked to him before his bet.

chip leader: In tournaments, the player who currently has the most chips.

chip position: In tournaments, the size of a player's current chip stack in relation to the size of his opponents' chip stacks.

chip utility: The *usefulness* or *serviceability* of your chips. See Chapters 1, 2 and 3 for more detailed information.

chopping the prize pool: In tournaments, to divide up the prize money at the final table, before the tournament ends, by mutual agreement of the remaining players.

coin flip: An all-in hand in which one player has a pocket pair and his opponent has two overcards (or similar situations), with neither player having a great edge over the other. Also called a *race*.

cold deck: See "cooler."

competitive factor: The equivalent number of big blinds in a tournament's starting chip stack divided by 60. See Chapter Two for more detailed information.

competitive stack: A player's current chip stack divided by 60 times the current big blind, an indicator of chip utility. See Chapter One.

community cards: In hold'em, the face-up cards on the table that all players may combine with the cards in their hands to make the best possible five-card hand.

connectors: Hole cards that are consecutive in value, such as J-Q or 7-6.

continuation bet: A bet placed after the flop by the preflop raiser.

cooler: A hand in which one player is dealt a very strong hand that he cannot lay down against an opponent whose hand is even stronger.

counterfeit: In hold'em, for a card to come down on the turn or river that cripples a player's formerly strong hand, usually by pairing one of the cards on the board.

crunch time: In fast tournaments, the last opportunity players have to use skillful play before the rising blinds reduce the tournament to a matter of luck.

cutoff seat: The seat to the right of the button.

dead money: Any weak player who has little chance of winning, or money put into the pot by a player who has already folded.

defender: See "blind defender."

deep stack: A lot of chips in relation to the size of the current blind and ante costs.

GLOSSARY

deep-stack tournament: A tournament with a "utility rank" of 4, 5, or 6, where the players typically start with chips stacks equivalent to more than 120 times the size of the starting big blind. See Chapter Two.

define a hand: To bet in such a way as to reveal the strength of your hole cards to your competitors.

disguised hand: A strong hand where strength is not suspected by a competitor.

dominated hand: In hold'em, hole cards in which one card matches another player's hole card, while the other player's kicker is stronger. K-Q is dominated by A-Q.

dominant utility: To have a chip stack equal to at least 100 times the size of the current big blind *and* at least four times the size of the average stack on the table. See Chapter Two.

double belly buster: A straight draw that can be made two ways, though not on the two ends.

drawing dead: In hold'em, to draw to a hand with no chance of winning because another player already has a hand ranked higher than any hand you could make.

draw out: In hold'em, to beat a player who had a better hand prior to the cards that appeared on the flop, turn or river.

early position: The players who must bet first; generally, the first four betting positions in a ten-handed game.

emotional intelligence: At a poker table, acute awareness of and empathy for opponents' feelings and states of mind. See Chapter One.

entry fee: In a tournament, the amount a player pays to the house that does not go into the prize pool.

expected value (or EV): Common professional gamblers' term for the mathematically expected dollar return for a wager or series of wagers.

fast: Aggressive betting.

fast-structured tournament: A tournament that has short blind levels and/or few starting chips in relations to the starting blinds, and that will often play out in a short time period as players are eliminated quickly. See Chapter One and *PTF1*.

fifth street: In hold'em, the fifth community card. Also called the *river*.

final table: In a tournament, the last table of players remaining after all others have been eliminated.

flop: In hold'em, the first three community cards dealt onto the table after the first betting round.

flush: Any five suited cards in the same hand.

flush draw: A hand in which it is possible to make a flush with one or two cards needed to complete the hand.

flush master: A term for a player who will enter a pot with any two suited cards, and who will stay in the pot as long as his flush draw is still alive. See *PTF1* for a more detailed discussion.

fluctuations: The inevitable short-term winning and losing streaks caused by good and bad luck, as opposed to any actual advantage or disadvantage.

flux: Common gamblers' slang for fluctuations.

fold: To discard a hand and no longer be active in a pot.

fourth street: In hold'em, the fourth community card dealt face-up onto the table. Also called the *turn*.

free card: In hold'em, a turn or river card that any player can see without having to put more money into the pot.

free roll: Common gamblers' slang for any bet or game that costs nothing but has a potential monetary return.

full house: A hand consisting of a pair and three of a kind. Also called a *boat* or *full boat*.

full-ring game: A nine- or ten-handed game.

full utility: To have a chip stack equivalent to the size of 100 or more big blinds and no serious restrictions on play caused by aggressive players or bigger chip stacks. See Chapter Two.

gap concept: The idea that it takes a stronger hand to call a raise than to make a raise, possibly valid in some limit games, but not valid in no-limit hold'em tournaments.

gapped connectors: Hole cards that are separated in rank but still close enough in rank to be part of a straight, such as 10-7 or 8-6.

game theory: A branch of mathematics that deals with optimal strategies in conflicts between two or more opposing entities. See Chapter One.

grand theft: A bold move to steal a big pot from an opponent who has a strong hand.

green zone: From *Harrington on Hold'em II*, a chip stack that allows a player to be what Harrington considers "fully functional," equal to 20 M or better. See "M."

groupie: An amateur player who enters major tournaments simply to be close to famous players.

gutshot: An inside straight draw, or any straight draw that can only be made on one end. Also called a *one-way straight draw*, or a *belly buster*.

hanger-on: An amateur player who enters tournaments for the purpose of socializing with well-known pros and posturing as a pro himself. Often drops the names of famous players in an attempt to enhance his image.

Harringbot: A player who typically plays tight in the early portion of a tournament, taking few risks, then starts pushing in aggressively as his chip stack gets low.

heads up: A game or a pot played by two players, one against the other. Also *head-on* or *head-to-head*.

high-low hand: A hand that contains one high card and one low card, such as K-3 or Q-6; also often called a *trash hand*.

hijack seat: Two seats to the right of the button.

hit: In hold'em, for the board cards to increase the value of a player's hand. If a player has a pocket pair and a trip card comes down on the flop, the flop *hit* him.

hit the money: To arrive at that portion of a tournament where all remaining players are in the prize pool.

hold up: To have a hand that is better than an opponent's hand go on to win the pot.

hole cards: In hold'em, the players' first two cards, dealt face down.

implied odds: The mathematical relationship of the current bet you must make to the total you ultimately expect to win if you take the pot, after taking into account the probable betting action after your bet.

in the dark: Without looking at one's hole cards.

in the money: In tournaments, any finishing position that pays a portion of the prize pool.

information bet: A bet placed when you have a legitimate hand (that may be the winning hand) for the purpose of seeing an opponent's response in order to determine his strength (or lack of).

information bluff: A bet placed when you have no legitimate hand (and little chance of winning on the strength of your cards) for the purpose of stealing the pot based on a weak response from an opponent.

inside straight draw: A hand in which you have four cards to a straight, but need a card that falls between two of your cards to make the straight, or can fall on only one end of your cards. Also called a *gutshot*, a *belly-buster*, or a *one-way straight draw*.

instacall: An instant call to a bet or raise.

jam: To push all in.

keep the lead: For a player who raised on one betting round to automatically lead out with a bet on the next betting round.

GLOSSARY

kicker: In hold'em, a hole card that will be used to determine a winner if two players otherwise have identical hands.

killer: A player who typically overbets small pots and frequently pushes all in even when not short-stacked.

late position: In hold'em, the last players to bet on a round, with the button being the latest position.

laydown: A fold of a strong hand because of perceived danger.

lead out: To enter a pot with a raise as the first one in on a round.

legitimate hand: Any hand that has a reasonable chance of winning a pot based on its strength.

limit: A game in which bets are limited to a specified betting structure, as opposed to no-limit.

limit the field: To raise in order to discourage marginal hands from entering a pot and possibly drawing out on you.

limp in: In hold'em, to enter a pot on the first betting round by calling the big blind.

limper: Any player who enters a pot preflop by just calling the big blind.

load up: To grab chips as if threatening to bet or raise when the action is on another player.

long ball: A tournament strategy that consists of aggressive betting, raising and reraising, with an attempt to make the pot big and intimidate weak players. See Chapter Four.

longballer: A player who primarily employs a long-ball style.

loose: A player who plays a higher percentage of hands than normal; a table where many players consistently enter the pot; a call with a marginal hand that either could be easily beaten by many other hands given the cards on board, or one that does not have the mathematical odds of winning necessary to justify the call as a good bet.

low utility: To have a chip stack size equivalent to the cost of only 15 to 30 big blinds. A player with low utility is hampered by his short stack in the use of his poker skills. See Chapter One.

M: A player's current chip stack divided by the cost of going through one orbit of the blinds and antes, a term attributed to Paul Magriel, but popularized by Dan Harrington in *Harrington on Hold'em II*.

maniac: A very loose and aggressive player whose bets seem to have little relation to his cards or chances of winning.

marginal call: To call a bet when the odds of winning the hand are very close to the minimal odds needed to make the call profitable.

marginal utility: To have many of your poker skills restricted, usually by being short-stacked.

middle position: In hold'em, any of three seats located halfway between the first betting positions and the button.

minefield: The second phase of a tournament when the short-stacked players start pushing all in, hindering "normal" poker action. See Chapter Eleven.

min-raise: A raise of the minimum amount allowed.

miss: For the board cards to fail to increase the value of a hand.

mix up: To play the same hands in different ways at different times in order to keep competitors from figuring out your cards; to engage in action frequently is to *mix it up*.

moderate utility: A chip stack equal to the cost of 30 to 60 big blinds. A player with moderate utility can use only a subset of his poker skills. See Chapter One.

monster: Any highly-ranked hand that is unlikely to be beaten, such as a full house or a straight flush.

muck: To fold. Also, the pile of already discarded cards on the table.

multiway pot: Any pot contested by more than two players.

neuro-economics: The science of how people make choices about risk, based on the biochemistry of the brain.

NLH: No limit hold'em.

no-limit: A betting structure in which there is no upper limit to the amount a player can bet or raise.

no utility: To have a chip stack totaling less than the cost of 15 big blinds. Players with no utility have very few skill options available. See Chapter One.

nuts: A hand that cannot be beaten by any other possible hand in play.

oaf: A player with very little understanding of the game of poker. See *PTF1* for a more detailed discussion.

odds: The chances against something happening.

offsuit: Cards that are not of the same suit.

on a draw: To have a potential, but not yet made hand that could improve if the right cards came down.

on tilt: A player who plays erratically and poorly, usually as a result of a bad beat or losing streak.

one-way straight draw: A hand in which you have four cards to a straight that can only be completed by a card that falls between two of your cards or a card on one end, rather than either end. Also called a *gutshot*, a *belly buster*, or *inside straight draw*.

open-end (straight draw): Four consecutive cards to a straight, which can be made with one more card on either end. Also called a *two-way straight draw*.

orange zone: A chip stack that is not fully functional according to Dan Harrington's "M" rating system.

out: A card that will increase the value of your hand to a winner.

outchip: To have more chips than an opponent.

overbet: To bet an amount that seems very big based on the size of the pot.

overcard: In hold'em, a card in the hole that is higher than the highest card on the board, or a card on the board that is higher than a player's pocket pair.

overpair: In hold'em, a pocket pair that is higher than the highest card on the board.

overplay: To bet too aggressively with a marginal hand.

over-the-top: To raise a bet or a raise.

pace stalker: Borrowed from horse racing, a poker tournament player who attempts to keep up with the field with the intention of coming on strong later as opponents tire. See Chapter Thirteen.

pair master: A player who has difficulty laying down a pocket pair, even in the face of aggressive betting when overcards are on the board, often in hopes of making a set on the turn or river. See *PTF1* for a more detailed discussion.

passive: A non-aggressive playing style or a table with mostly checking and calling, and very little raising.

patience factor: A measure of a tournament's speed based on the number of starting chips and the blind structure. See Chapter Two.

percentage payback tournament: A tournament with a prize structure that pays multiple winners, with first place getting the highest payout and lower finishes getting lesser amounts.

petty larceny: Theft of small pots, such as stealing the blinds.

phase one: The early stack-building portion of a tournament. See Chapter Ten.

phase two: The second period of a tournament, called the "minefield," when short stacks start making desperate moves. See Chapter Eleven.

phase three: The bubble portion of a tournament, just before all players are in the money. See Chapter Twelve.

phase four: The money portion of a tournament. See Chapter Thirteen.

GLOSSARY

phase five: The final table portion of a tournament. See Chapter Fourteen.

play back: To continue to give action, particularly aggressive counteraction, to a player who is betting aggressively.

pocket: In hold'em, the hole cards, mostly used to describe a pair in the hole, such as "pocket pair" or "pocket jacks."

position: The order in which a player must act on his hand. Often used to mean "later position," as in "I had position on him."

position play or position bet: To bet in an attempt to take a pot based on having position on an opponent but no legitimate hand.

post oak bluff: Old-timers' term for a very small bet compared to the size of the pot, meant to take down a pot with minimal risk.

post-flop: The decisions and action that occur on betting rounds after the flop.

pot: The total amount bet by all players in a current hand.

pot-committed: In a poker tournament, to have approximately half or more of one's chips already in a pot, so that a player will be committed to putting the rest in if there is a bet or raise he has to meet.

pot odds: The ratio of the total amount in the pot to the amount of the current bet a player must call to stay in the hand.

power poker: An aggressive long-ball style of play.

preflop: In hold'em, the action that occurs based on the players' hole cards, and before the flop.

price: The cost of playing a hand in relation to the potential return.

price out: To raise in order to make the price of playing mathematically incorrect for any competitor on a draw. "His all-in bet priced me out of the pot."

prize pool: The total amount of all prize money to be awarded to the winners, based on the total buy-ins of all players in a tournament.

probe bet: A bet placed, usually with a less-than-premium hand, for the purpose of seeing if a competitor will relinquish the pot without a fight.

pro-level tournament: Any tournament of Rank 1 or higher, with a utility factor of 5 or higher, a patience factor of 10 or higher, and a buy-in of $300 or more. See Chapter Two.

protecting a hand: Betting with a made hand to give opponents the mathematically wrong pot odds to try to draw out.

PTF1: *Poker Tournament Formula 1*

push in: For a player to bet all of his chips. Same as "Go all in."

Q: From *Harrington on Hold'em II*, a player's current chip stack in relation to the average chip stack in the tournament.

quads: Four of a kind.

race: See "coin flip."

rag: Any low card (usually 2-8).

rainbow: In hold'em, cards of all different suits on the board after the flop.

raise: To increase the bet from the previous bet.

raising seat: The seating position two seats to the right of the button, also called the *hijack seat*.

rammin' and jammin': To play very aggressively with lots of raising.

rank: See "utility rank."

read (a player): To deduce the strength of a player's hand from his actions, betting, or physical mannerisms.

read (the board): In hold'em, to figure out the possible hands in play based on the community cards.

rebuy: In tournaments which allow this option, to purchase more chips after a tournament has begun.

red zone: A desperately short chip stack as defined in *Harrington on Hold'em II*.

reraise: To raise a prior bettor's raise.

resteal: To reraise a late position player whose raise is suspected of being a steal.

reverse chip value theory: A long-standing but erroneous theory regarding tournament "chip value" that states that the more chips you have, the less each of your chips is worth. See Chapter One.

ring game: A full-table non-tournament game, usually with nine to ten players.

risk of ruin: The statistical chance that a player will go broke based on his betting and his advantage or lack of advantage. Also called *gambler's ruin*.

river: In hold'em, the fifth and last community card to be dealt. Also known as *fifth street*.

rock: A very tight, conservative player.

royal flush: The highest-ranking hand, a straight flush to the ace.

runner-runner: In hold'em, to make a strong hand by catching needed cards on both the turn and river.

run over: To bully a player or players with very aggressive play.

satellite: A poker tournament played to win a seat in a bigger tournament.

GLOSSARY

scare card: A card that appears on the board that makes a superior hand by an opponent possible.

Seabiscuit: A sudden aggressive play, or series of plays, by a player with a solid image in order to exploit off-guard opponents. See Chapter Thirteen.

second pair: In hold'em, a hand where the second-highest card on the board is matched by a card in a player's hand.

semibluff: A bet made when your hand is not yet a strong hand, but might improve to a strong hand if the right card falls.

set: In hold'em, to make trips by holding a pocket pair and getting the third card on the board.

set a trap: To slowplay a very strong hand in order to disguise its strength and win more from your opponents.

shift gears: Same as "change gears."

shoot back: To reraise.

shot: Any bet you can make that will cause an opponent to fold and win you the pot whether or not you have the strongest hand.

short-handed: In hold'em, a game in which there are fewer than seven players at a table.

short stack: A small amount of chips to play with.

**short-stack
tournament:** Any tournament with a utility rank of 1, 2, or 3, in which players typically start out with chip stacks equivalent to the cost of 120 big blinds or less. See Chapter Two.

showdown: The revelation of the hands to determine the winner of the pot after all betting is completed.

**show'n'
teller:** A player who often shows his hand unnecessarily when he folds and talks incessantly about his own hands and others, usually to show off his understanding of the game by using poker jargon. See *PTF1* for a more detailed discussion.

sit-and-go: A popular type of online tournament, now often found in some live poker rooms, that has no scheduled time, but begins as soon as the required number of seats are filled with players.

slowplay: To deliberately refrain from playing aggressively when you have a very big hand, usually to keep other players in the pot in order to draw more money out of them.

**slow-
structured
tournament:** Any live tournament in which the blind levels are 40 minutes or longer, or an online tournament in which players average 20 hands or more per blind level. See Chapter Two.

small ball: A playing style that consists of playing a wide range of starting hands, while keeping the pots small. The goal is to hit unsuspected strong hands to win big pots, or to steal pots that seem to be available for a modest bet. See Chapter Four.

smallballer: A player who primarily employs the small-ball style of play.

speculative hand (or spec hand): Small pairs, medium connected cards, suited cards, and weaker combinations that are unlikely to have much value on their own, but would have high implied odds if the board cards turn them into a strong and unexpected hand.

split pot: A pot that is divided between two or more players who have identical hands.

standard deviation: A mathematical term that quantifies the normal amount of fluctuation in results due to luck. See Appendix A.

standard raise: In no-limit tournaments, a bet of 3 to 5 times the size of the big blind preflop. A raise of about half the size of the current pot post-flop.

starting competitive factor: See "competitive factor."

starting hand: A player's hole cards.

steal: To take a pot by betting when you have a weak hand.

straight: A premium hand that consists of five consecutive cards with no gaps.

straight flush: One of the highest ranking hands. It consists of five consecutive cards, all of the same suit.

suck out: The same as *draw out*. To beat a player who has a better hand by making a superior hand with cards that come on the board.

suited: Two cards that are the same suit.

super-satellite: A multitable satellite that awards multiple seats to a bigger tournament.

superstar: A poker pro (or sometimes an author who is not a pro) who is well-known to the public, usually through television appearances. See Chapter Six.

surrender: To fold.

survival-oriented strategies: A strategy of seeing few flops, and only with premium starting cards, in order to preserve chips and give the player a greater chance of being dealt strong starting cards with which to play strongly.

survivalist: A player who employs survival-oriented strategies.

table image: The style a player projects through his actions and demeanor, such as aggressive, timid, conservative, and crazy.

take a shot: To bet at the pot, usually hoping to win it with no callers or raises.

take a stand: To remain in a pot in the face of danger posed by either scare cards on the board or an opponent with a superior chip position.

take down: To win the pot.

tell: A player's subconscious action or mannerism that reveals something about his hand to an opponent.

tight: A player who plays relatively few hands, also said of a table where there is little action because of the presence of many such players.

tilt: See "on tilt."

top pair: In hold'em, to have a card in the hole that matches the top card on the board.

top set: For the highest card on the board to match a player's pocket pair giving that player the highest three of a kind possible

trash hand: Any starting hand that most players would throw away before the flop, such as K-3, J-5 and 5-2, because of the unlikelihood of those cards improving to become a strong hand.

trap: Same as *set a trap*.

trapping hand: A starting hand such as a small pair or suited connectors that improves to a set or better after the flop, that can be used to trap unsuspecting opponents into putting a lot of chips into the pot.

trips: Three of a kind.

true M: The actual number of rounds of play a player would have left, based on his chip stack and the blind structure, as opposed to M as described in *Harrington on Hold'em II*. See Appendix C.

turn: In hold'em, the fourth community card dealt on the board. Also known as *fourth street*.

two live cards: Any two starting cards that do not match an opponent's starting cards. See Chapter Four.

two-way straight draw: To have four cards to a straight that can be made with one of two cards. Also called an *open-end straight draw*.

under the gun: The first player to act on his hand preflop.

under-chipped: To have few chips relative to the size of the blinds and/or bets in a game.

unraised pot: A preflop pot in which any active players simply called the big blind (limped in) without raising.

utility: See "chip utility."

utility factor: A mathematical gauge for measuring a tournament's value for skillful players based on its blind structure. See Chapter Two.

utility odds: The amount of chips a player would have if he calls a bet and wins a pot compared to the number he would have if he folds instead of calling. See Chapter Three.

utility rank: A system of categorizing tournaments based on their utility factors. See Chapter Two.

value bet: A modest bet placed on the river by a player who believes he has the best hand and that his opponent has a hand strong enough to call one more small bet.

variance: A math term that denotes the amount of fluctuation in results that is normal for a game.

walk: When all players at the table fold preflop, giving the blinds (and antes, if any) to the big blind.

wimp: A weak player who checks, calls and folds much more often than he bets, raises or reraises. See *PTF1* for a more detailed discussion.

win rate: The amount of money won divided by the amount of money bet. A way of measuring return on investment.

WMPP: World's Most Patient Player. See Chapter Two.

WPT: World Poker Tour.

WSOP: World Series of Poker.

yellow zone: A chip stack that is somewhat less than "fully functional" as defined in *Harrington on Hold'em II*.

INDEX

INDEX

INDEX

FREE!
Poker & Gaming Magazines

www.cardozabooks.com

3 GREAT REASONS TO VISIT NOW!

1. FREE GAMING MAGAZINES

Go online now and read all about the exciting world of poker, gambling, and online gaming. Our magazines are packed with tips, expert strategies, tournament schedules and results, gossip, news, contests, polls, exclusive discounts on hotels, travel, and more to our readers, prepublication book discounts, free-money bonuses for online sites, and words of wisdom from the world's top experts and authorities. Also, you can sign up for Avery Cardoza's free email newsletters.

2. MORE THAN 200 BOOKS TO MAKE YOU A WINNER

We are the world's largest publisher of gaming and gambling books and represent a who's who of the greatest players and writers on poker, gambling, chess, back-gammon, and other games. With more than 10 million books sold, we know what our customers want. Trust us.

3. THIS ONE IS A SURPRISE

Visit us now to get the goods!

So what are you waiting for?

CARDOZA PUBLISHING ONLINE

GREAT CARDOZA POKER BOOKS
ADD THESE TO YOUR LIBRARY - ORDER NOW!

DANIEL NEGREANU'S POWER HOLD'EM STRATEGY by Daniel Negreanu. This power-packed book on beating no-limit hold'em is one of the three most influential poker books ever written. Negreanu headlines a collection of young great players—Todd Brunson, David Williams. Erick Lindgren, Evelyn Ng and Paul Wasicka—who share their insider professional moves and winning secrets. You'll learn about short-handed and heads-up play, high-limit cash games, a powerful beginner's strategy to neutralize professional players, and how to mix up your play and bluff and win big pots. The centerpiece, however, is Negreanu's powerful and revolutionary small ball strategy. You'll learn how to play hold'em with cards you never would have played before—and with fantastic results. The preflop, flop, turn and river will never look the same again. A must-have! 520 pages, $34.95.

POKER WIZARDS by Warwick Dunnett. In the tradition of Super System, an exclusive collection of champions and superstars have been brought together to share their strategies, insights, and tactics for winning big money at poker, specifically no-limit hold'em tournaments. This is priceless advice from players who individually have each made millions of dollars in tournaments, and collectively, have won more than 20 WSOP bracelets, two WSOP main events, 100 major tournaments and $50 million in tournament winnings! Featuring Daniel Negreanu, Dan Harrington, Marcel Luske, Kathy Liebert, Mike Sexton, Mel Judah, Marc Salem, T.J. Cloutier and Chris "Jesus" Ferguson. This must-read book is a goldmine for serious players, aspiring pros, and future champions! 352 pgs, $19.95.

HOW TO BEAT LOW-LIMIT POKER by Shane Smith and Tom McEvoy. If you're a low-limit player frustrated by poor results or books written by high-stakes players for big buy-in games, this is exactly the book you need! You'll learn how to win big money at the little games—$1/$2, $2/$4, $4/$8, $5/$10—typically found in casinos, cardrooms and played in home poker games. After one reading, you'll lose less, win more and play with increased confidence. You'll learn the top 10 tips and winning strategies specifically designed for limit hold'em, no-limit hold'em, Omaha high-low and low-limit poker tournaments. Great practical advice for new players. 184 pages, $9.95.

OMAHA HIGH-LOW: How to Win at the Lower Limits by Shane Smith. Practical advice specifically targeted for the popular low-limit games you play every day in casinos and online will have you making money, and show you how to avoid losing situations and cards that can cost you a bundle—the dreaded second-nut draws, trap hands, and two-way second-best action. Smith's proven strategies are spiced with plenty of wit and wisdom. You'll learn the basics of play against the typical opponents you'll face in low-limit games—the no-fold'em players and the rocks—and get winning tactics, illustrated hands, and tournament tips guaranteed to improve your game. 144 pages, $12.95.

TOURNAMENT TIPS FROM THE POKER PROS by Shane Smith. Essential advice from poker theorists, authors, and tournament winners on the best strategies for winning the big prizes at low-limit rebuy tournaments. Learn proven strategies for each of the four stages of play—opening, middle, late and final—how to avoid 26 potential traps, advice on rebuys, aggressive play, clock-watching, inside moves, top 20 tips for winning tournaments, more. Advice from Brunson, McEvoy, Cloutier, Caro, Malmuth, others. 160 pages, $14.95.

NO-LIMIT TEXAS HOLD'EM: The New Player's Guide to Winning Poker's Biggest Game by Brad Daugherty & Tom McEvoy. For experienced limit players who want to play no-limit or rookies who has never played before, two world champions show readers how to evaluate the strength of a hand, determine the amount to bet, understand opponents' play, plus how to bluff and when to do it. Seventy-four game scenarios, unique betting charts for tournament play, and sections on essential principles and strategies show you how to get to the winner's circle. Special section on beating online tournaments. 288 pages, $24.95.

GREAT CARDOZA POKER BOOKS
ADD THESE TO YOUR LIBRARY - ORDER NOW!

POKER TOURNAMENT FORMULA 2: Advanced Strategies for Big Money Tournaments *by Arnold Snyder*. Probably the greatest tournament poker book ever written, and the most controversial in the last decade, Snyder's revolutionary work debunks commonly (and falsely) held beliefs. Snyder reveals the power of chip utility—the real secret behind winning tournaments—and covers utility ranks, tournament structures, small- and long-ball strategies, patience factors, the impact of structures, crushing the Harringbots and other player types, tournament phases, and much more. Includes big sections on Tools, Strategies, and Tournament Phases. A must buy! 496 pages, $24.95.

HOW TO WIN AT OMAHA HIGH-LOW POKER *by Mike Cappelletti*. Clearly written strategies and powerful advice shows the essential winning strategies for beating Omaha high-low poker! This money-making guide includes more than sixty hard-hitting sections on Omaha. Players learn the rules of play, best starting hands, strategies for the flop, turn, and river, how to read the board for both high and low, dangerous draws, and how to beat low-limit tournaments. Includes odds charts, glossary and low-limit tips. 304 pgs, $19.95.

WINNER'S GUIDE TO TEXAS HOLD'EM POKER *by Ken Warren*. New edition shows how to play every hand from every position with every type of flop. Learn the 14 categories of starting hands, the 10 most common hold'em tells, how to evaluate a game for profit, the value of deception, the art of bluffing, eight secrets to winning, starting hand categories, position, and more! Includes detailed analysis of the top 40 hands and the most complete chapter on hold'em odds in print. Over 500,000 copies sold! 224 pages, $14.95.

KEN WARREN TEACHES TEXAS HOLD'EM *by Ken Warren*. This is a step-by-step comprehensive manual for making money at hold'em poker. 42 powerful chapters teach you one lesson at a time. Great practical advice and concepts with examples from actual games and how to apply them to your own play. Lessons include: Starting Cards, Playing Position, Raising, Check-raising, Tells, Game/Seat Selection, Dominated Hands, Odds, and much more. This book is already a huge fan favorite and best-seller! 416 pages, $26.95.

WINNER'S GUIDE TO OMAHA POKER *by Ken Warren*. Concise and easy-to-understand, Warren shows beginning and intermediate Omaha players how to win from the first time they play. You'll learn the rules, betting and blind structure, why you should play Omaha, the advantages of Omaha over Texas hold'em, glossary, reading the board, basic strategies, Omaha high, Omaha hi-low split 8/better, how to play draws and made hands, evaluation of starting hands, counting outs, computing pot odds, the unique characteristics of split-pot games, the best and worst Omaha hands, how to play before the flop, how to play on the flop, how to play on the turn and river, and much more. 224 pages, $19.95

CHAMPIONSHIP TOURNAMENT POKER *by Tom McEvoy*. Enthusiastically endorsed by more than five world champions, this is a *must* for every player's library. McEvoy lets you in on the secrets he has used to win millions of dollars in tournaments and the insights he has learned competing against the best players in the world. Packed solid with winning strategies for 11 games with extensive discussions of 7-card stud, limit hold'em, pot and no-limit hold'em, Omaha high-low, re-buy, half-half tournaments, satellites, and includes strategies for each stage of tournaments. 416 pages, $29.95.

HOW TO WIN NO-LIMIT HOLD'EM TOURNAMENTS *by McEvoy & Don Vines*. Learn the basic concepts of tournament strategy and how to win big by playing small buy-in events, graduate to medium and big buy-in tournaments, adjust for short fields, huge fields, slow and fast-action events. Plus, how to win online tournaments. You'll also learn how to manage a tournament bankroll and get tips on table demeanor for televised tournaments. See actual hands played by finalists at WSOP and WPT championship tables with card pictures, analysis and useful lessons from the play. 376 pages, $29.95.

Order now at 1-800-577-WINS or go online to: www.cardozabooks.com

GREAT CARDOZA POKER BOOKS
ADD THESE TO YOUR LIBRARY - ORDER NOW!

CRASH COURSE IN BEATING TEXAS HOLD'EM *by Avery Cardoza*. Perfect for beginning and somewhat experienced players who want to jump right in on the action and play cash games, local tournaments, online poker, and the big televised tournaments where millions of dollars can be made. Both limit and no-limit hold'em games are covered along with the essential strategies needed to play profitably on the preflop, flop, turn, and river. The good news is that you don't need to memorize hands or be burdened by math to be a winner—just play by the no-nonsense basic principles outlined here. 208 pages, $14.95

INTERNET HOLD'EM POKER *by Avery Cardoza*. Learn how to get started in the exciting world of online poker. The book concentrates on Internet no-limit hold'em, but also covers limit and pot-limit hold'em, five- and seven-card stud, and Omaha. You'll learn everything from how to play and bet safely online to playing multiple tables, using early action buttons, and finding easy opponents. Cardoza gives you the largest collection of online-specific strategies in print—more than 6,500 words dedicated to 25 unique strategies! You'll also learn how to get sign-up bonuses worth hundreds of dollars! 176 pages, $9.95

HOW TO PLAY WINNING POKER *by Avery Cardoza*. New and completely updated, this classic has sold more than 250,000 copies. Includes major new coverage on playing and winning tournaments, online poker, limit and no-limit hold'em, Omaha games, seven-card stud, and draw poker (including triple draw). Includes 21 essential winning concepts of poker, 15 concepts of bluffing, how to use psychology and body language to get an extra edge, plus information on playing online poker. 256 pages, $14.95.

POKER TALK: Learn How to Talk Poker Like a Pro *by Avery Cardoza*. This fascinating and fabulous collection of colorful poker words, phrases, and poker-speak features more than 2,000 definitions. No longer is it enough to know how to walk the walk in poker, you need to know how to talk the talk! Learn what it means to go all in on a rainbow flop with pocket rockets and get it cracked by cowboys, put a bad beat on a calling station, and go over the top of a producer fishing with a gutshot to win a big dime. You'll soon have those railbirds wondering what *you* are talking about. 304 pages, $9.95.

OMAHA HIGH-LOW: Play to Win with the Odds *by Bill Boston*. Selecting the right hands to play is the most important decision to make in Omaha. This is the *only* book that shows you the chances that every one of the 5,278 Omaha high-low hands has of winning the high end of the pot, the low end of it, and how often it is expected to scoop all the chips. You get all the vital tools needed to make critical preflop decisions based on the results of more than 500 million computerized hand simulations. You'll learn the 100 most profitable starting cards, trap hands to avoid, 49 worst hands, 30 ace-less hands you can play for profit, and the three bandit cards you must know to avoid losing hands. 248 pages, $19.95.

KEN WARREN TEACHES 7-CARD STUD *by Ken Warren*. You'll learn how to play and win at the main variations of seven-card stud (high-low split and razz—seven-card stud where the lowest hand wins), plus over 45 seven-card stud home poker variations! This step-by-step manual is perfect for beginning, low-limit, and somewhat experienced players who want to change their results from losses to wins, or from small wins to bigger wins. Lessons include starting cards, playing position, which hands to play to the end, raising and check-raising strategies, how to evaluate your hand as you receive every new card, and figure out what hands your opponents likely have. 352 pages, $14.95.

Order now at 1-800-577-WINS or go online to: www.cardozabooks.com

GREAT CARDOZA POKER BOOKS
ADD THESE TO YOUR LIBRARY - ORDER NOW!

HOLD'EM WISDOM FOR ALL PLAYERS *By Daniel Negreanu.* Superstar poker player Daniel Negreanu provides 50 easy-to-read and right-to-the-point hold'em strategy nuggets that will immediately make you a better player at cash games and tournaments. His wit and wisdom makes for great reading; even better, it makes for killer winning advice. Conversational, straightforward, and educational, this book covers topics as diverse as the top 10 rookie mistakes to bullying bullies and exploiting your table image. 176 pages, $14.95.

MILLION DOLLAR HOLD'EM: Winning Big in Limit Cash Games *by Johnny Chan and Mark Karowe.* Learn how to win money consistently at limit hold'em, poker's most popular cash game, from one of poker's living legends. You'll get a rare opportunity to get into the mind of the man who has won ten World Series of Poker titles—tied for the most ever with Doyle Brunson—as Johnny picks out illustrative hands and shows how he thinks his way through the betting and the bluffing. No book so thoroughly details the thought process of how a hand is played, the alternative ways it could have been played, and the best way to win session after session. *Essential* reading for cash players. 400 pages, $29.95.

THE POKER TOURNAMENT FORMULA *by Arnold Snyder.* Start making money now in fast no-limit hold'em tournaments with these radical and never-before-published concepts and secrets for beating tournaments. You'll learn why cards don't matter as much as the dynamics of a tournament—your position, the size of your chip stack, who your opponents are, and above all, the structure. Poker tournaments offer one of the richest opportunities to come along in decades. Every so often, a book comes along that changes the way players attack a game and provides them with a big advantage over opponents. Gambling legend Arnold Snyder has written such a book. 368 pages, $19.95.

HOW TO BEAT SIT-AND-GO POKER TOURNAMENTS by Neil Timothy. There is a lot of dead money up for grabs in the lower limit sit-and-gos and Neil Timothy shows you how to go and get it. The author, a professional player, shows you how to reach the last six places of lower limit sit-and-go tournaments four out of five times and then how to get in the money 25-35 percent of the time using his powerful, proven strategies. This book can turn a losing sit-and-go player into a winner, and a winner into a bigger winner. Also effective for the early and middle stages of one-table satellites.176 pages, $14.95.

HOW TO BEAT INTERNET CASINOS AND POKER ROOMS *by Arnold Snyder.* Learn how to play and win money online against the Internet casinos. Snyder shows you how to choose safe sites to play. He goes over every step of the process, from choosing sites and opening an account to how to take your winnings home! Snyder covers the differences between "brick and mortar" and Internet gaming rooms and how to handle common situations and predicaments. A major chapter covers Internet poker and basic strategies to beat hold'em and other games online. 272 pages, $14.95..

I'M ALL IN: High Stakes, Big Business, and the Birth of the World Poker *Tour by Lyle Berman with Marvin Karlins.* Lyle Berman recounts how he revolutionized and revived the game of poker and transformed America's culture in the process. Get the inside story of the man who created the World Poker Tour, plus the exciting world of high-stakes gambling where a million dollars can be won or lost in a single game. Lyle reveals the 13 secrets of being a successful businessman, how poker players self-destruct, the 7 essential principles of winning at poker. Foreword by Donald Trump. Hardback, photos. 232 pages, $24.95.

7-CARD STUD: The Complete Course in Winning at Medium & Lower Limits *by Roy West.* Learn the latest strategies for winning at $1-$4 spread-limit up to $10/$20 fixed-limit games. Covers starting hands, 3rd-7th street strategy, overcards, selective aggressiveness, reading hands, pro secrets, psychology, and more in an informal 42 lesson format. Includes bonus chapter on 7-stud tournament strategy by Tom McEvoy. 224 pages, $19.95.

Order now at 1-800-577-WINS or go online to: www.cardozabooks.com

DOYLE BRUNSON'S EXCITING BOOKS
ADD THESE TO YOUR COLLECTION - ORDER NOW!

SUPER SYSTEM by Doyle Brunson. This classic book is considered by the pros to be the best book ever written on poker! Jam-packed with advanced strategies, theories, tactics and money-making techniques, no serious poker player can afford to be without this hard-hitting information. Includes fifty pages of the most precise poker statistics ever published. Features chapters written by poker's biggest superstars, such as Dave Sklansky, Mike Caro, Chip Reese, Joey Hawthorne, Bobby Baldwin, and Doyle. Essential strategies, advanced play, and no-nonsense winning advice on making money at 7-card stud (razz, high-low split, cards speak, and declare), draw poker, lowball, and hold'em (limit and no-limit).This is a must-read for any serious poker player. 628 pages, $29.95.

SUPER SYSTEM 2 by Doyle Brunson. The most anticipated poker book ever, SS2 expands upon the original with more games and professional secrets from the best in the world. Superstar contributors include Daniel Negreanu, winner of multiple WSOP gold bracelets and 2004 Poker Player of the Year; Lyle Berman, 3-time WSOP gold bracelet winner, founder of the World Poker Tour, and super-high stakes cash player; Bobby Baldwin, 1978 World Champion; Johnny Chan, 2-time World Champion and 10-time WSOP bracelet winner; Mike Caro, poker's greatest researcher, theorist, and instructor; Jennifer Harman, the world's top female player and one of ten best overall; Todd Brunson, winner of more than 20 tournaments; and Crandell Addington, no-limit hold'em legend. 672 pgs, $34.95.

CARO'S GUIDE TO DOYLE BRUNSON'S SUPER SYSTEM by Mike Caro. Working with World Champion Doyle Brunson, the legendary Mike Caro has created a fresh look to the "Bible" of all poker books, adding new and personal insights that help you understand the original work. Caro breaks 36 concepts into either "Analysis, Commentary, Concept, Mission, Play-By-Play, Psychology, Statistics, Story, or Strategy. Lots of illustrations and winning concepts give even more value to this great work. 86 pages, 8 1/2 x 11, $19.95.

ACCORDING TO DOYLE by Doyle Brunson. Learn what it takes to be a great poker player by climbing inside the mind of poker's most famous champion. Fascinating anecdotes and adventures from Doyle's early career playing poker in roadhouses are interspersed with lessons from the champion who has made more money at poker than anyone else in history. Learn what makes a great player tick, how he approaches the game, and receive candid, powerful advice from the legend himself. 208 pages, $14.95.

MY 50 MOST MEMORABLE HANDS by Doyle Brunson. This instant classic relives the most incredible hands by the greatest poker player of all time. Great players, legends, and poker's most momentous events march in and out of fifty years of unforgettable hands. Sit side-by-side with Doyle as he replays the excitement and life-changing moments of the most thrilling and crucial hands in the history of poker: from his early games as a rounder in the rough-and-tumble "Wild West" years—where a man was more likely to get shot as he was to get a straight flush—to the nail-biting excitement of his two world championship titles. Relive million dollar hands and the high stakes tension of sidestepping police, hijackers and murderers. A thrilling collection of stories and sage poker advice. 168 pages, $14.95.

ONLINE POKER by Doyle Brunson. Ten compelling chapters show you how to get started, explain the safety features which lets you play worry-free, and lets you in on the strategies that Doyle himself uses to beat players in cyberspace. Poker is poker, as Doyle explains, but there are also strategies that only apply to the online version, where the players are weaker!—and Doyle reveals them all in this book.192 pages, illustrations, $14.95.

BOBBY BALDWIN'S WINNING POKER SECRETS by Mike Caro with Bobby Baldwin. The fascinating account of 1978 World Champion Bobby Baldwin's early career playing poker against other legends is packed with valuable insights. Covers the common mistakes average players make at seven poker variations and the dynamic winning concepts needed for success. Endorsed by superstars Doyle Brunson and Amarillo Slim. 208 pages, $14.95.

Order now at 1-800-577-WINS or go online to: www.cardozabooks.com

MIKE CARO'S EXCITING WORK
POWERFUL BOOKS YOU <u>MUST</u> HAVE

CARO'S MOST PROFITABLE HOLD'EM ADVICE *by Mike Caro.* When Mike Caro writes a book on winning, all poker players take notice. And they should: The "Mad Genius of Poker" has influenced just about every professional player and world champion alive. You'll journey far beyond the traditional tactical tools offered in most poker books and for the first time, have access to the entire missing arsenal of strategies left out of everything you've ever seen or experienced. Caro's first major work in two decades is packed with hundreds of powerful ideas, concepts, and strategies, many of which will be new to you—they have never been made available to the general public. This book represents Caro's lifelong research into beating the game of hold em. 408 pages, $24.95

MASTERING HOLD'EM AND OMAHA *by Mike Caro and Mike Cappelletti.* Learn the professional secrets to mastering the two most popular games of big-money poker: hold'em and Omaha. This is a thinking player's book, packed with ideas, with the focus is on making you a winning player. You'll learn everything from the strategies for play on the preflop, flop, turn and river, to image control and taking advantage of players stuck in losing patterns. You'll also learn how to create consistent winning patterns, use perception to gain an edge, avoid common errors, go after and win default pots, recognize and use the various types of raises, play marginal hands for profit, the importance of being loved or feared, and Cappelletti's unique point count system for Omaha. 328 pages, $19.95.

CARO'S BOOK OF POKER TELLS *by Mike Caro.* One of the ten greatest books written on poker, this must-have book should be in every player's library. If you're serious about winning, you'll realize that most of the profit comes from being able to read your opponents. Caro reveals the the secrets of interpreting *tells*—physical reactions that reveal information about a player's cards—such as shrugs, sighs, shaky hands, eye contact, and many more. Learn when opponents are bluffing, when they aren't and why—based solely on their mannerisms. Over 170 photos of players in action and play-by-play examples show the actual tells. These powerful ideas will give you the decisive edge. 320 pages, $24.95.

CARO'S SECRETS OF WINNING POKER *by Mike Caro.* New 2008 edition features more hold'em strategeis. Learn the essential strategies, concepts, and plays that comprise the very foundation of winning poker play. Learn to win more from weak players, equalize stronger players, bluff a bluffer, win big pots, where to sit against weak players, and the six factors of strategic table image. Includes selected tips on hold 'em, 7 stud, draw, lowball, tournaments, more. 160 pages, $12.95.

CARO'S PROFESSIONAL POKER REPORTS

Each of these three powerful insider poker reports is centered around a daily mission, with the goal of adding one weapon per day to your arsenal. Theoretical concepts and practical situations are mixed together for fast in-depth learning. For serious players.

11 DAYS TO 7-STUD SUCCESS. Bluffing, playing and defending pairs, different strategies for the different streets, analyzing situations—lots of information within. One advantage is gained each day. A quick and powerful method to 7-stud winnings. Essential. Signed, numbered. $19.95.

12 DAYS TO HOLD'EM SUCCESS. Positional thinking, playing and defending against mistakes, small pairs, flop situations, playing the river, are just some sample lessons. Guaranteed to make you a better player. Very popular. Signed, numbered. $19.95.

PROFESSIONAL 7-STUD REPORT. When to call, pass, and raise, playing starting hands, aggressive play, 4th and 5th street concepts, lots more. Tells how to read an opponent's starting hand, plus sophisticated advanced strategies. Important revision for serious players. Signed, numbered. $19.95.

Order now at 1-800-577-WINS or go online to: www.cardozabooks.com

THE CHAMPIONSHIP SERIES
POWERFUL INFORMATION YOU <u>MUST</u> HAVE

CHAMPIONSHIP NO-LIMIT & POT-LIMIT HOLD'EM *by T. J. Cloutier & Tom McEvoy.* The bible for winning pot-limit and no-limit hold'em tournaments gives you all the answers to your most important questions: How do you get inside your opponents' heads and learn how to beat them at their own game? How can you tell how much to bet, raise, and reraise in no-limit hold'em? When can you bluff? How do you set up your opponents in pot-limit hold'em so that you can win a monster pot? What are the best strategies for winning no-limit and pot-limit tournaments, satellites, and supersatellites? Rock-solid and inspired advice you can bank on from two of the most recognizable figures in poker. 304 pages, $29.95.

CHAMPIONSHIP HOLD'EM *by T. J. Cloutier & Tom McEvoy.* Hard-hitting hold'em the way it's played *today* in both limit cash games and tournaments. Get killer advice on how to win more money in rammin'-jammin' games, kill-pot, jackpot, shorthanded, and full table cash games. You'll learn the thinking process for preflop, flop, turn, and river play with specific suggestions for what to do when good or bad things happen. Includes play-by-play analyses, advice on how to maximize profits against rocks in tight games, weaklings in loose games, experts in solid games, plus tournament strategies for small buy-in, big buy-in, rebuy, add-on, satellite and big-field major tournaments. Wow! 392 pages, $29.95.

CHAMPIONSHIP OMAHA (Omaha High-Low, Pot-limit Omaha, Limit High Omaha) *by Tom McEvoy & T.J. Cloutier.* Clearly-written strategies and powerful advice from Cloutier and McEvoy who have won four World Series of Poker Omaha titles. You'll learn how to beat low-limit and high-stakes games, play against loose and tight opponents, and the differing strategies for rebuy and freezeout tournaments. Learn the best starting hands, when slowplaying a big hand is dangerous, what danglers are (and why winners don't play them), why you sometimes fold the nuts on the flop and would be correct in doing so, and overall, how you can win a lot of money at Omaha! 296 pages, illustrations, $29.95.

CHAMPIONSHIP HOLD'EM TOURNAMENT HANDS *by T. J. Cloutier & Tom McEvoy.* An absolute must for hold'em tournament players, two legends show you how to become a winning tournament player at both limit and no-limit hold'em games. Get inside the authors' heads as they think their way through the correct strategy at 57 limit and no-limit starting hands. Cloutier & McEvoy show you how to use skill and intuition to play strategic hands for maximum profit in real tournament scenarios and how 45 key hands were played by champions in turnaround situations at the WSOP. Gain tremendous insights into how tournament poker is played at the highest levels. 368 pages, $29.95.

CHAMPIONSHIP HOLD'EM SATELLITE STRATEGY *by World Champions Brad Dougherty & Tom McEvoy.* Every year satellite players win their way into the $10,000 WSOP buy-in and emerge as millionaires or champions. You can too! Learn the specific, proven strategies for winning almost any satellite from two world champions. Covers the ten ways to win a seat at the WSOP, how to win limit hold'em and no-limit hold'em satellites, one-table satellites, online satellites, and the final table of super satellites. Includes a special chapter on no-limit hold'em satellites! 320 pages, $29.95.

HOW TO WIN THE CHAMPIONSHIP: Hold'em Strategies for the Final Table, *by T.J. Cloutier.* If you're hungry to win a championship, this is the book that will pave the way! T.J. Cloutier, the greatest tournament poker player ever—he has won 60 major tournament titles and appeared at 39 final tables at the WSOP, both more than any other player in the history of poker—shows how to get to the final table where the big money is made and then how to win it all. You'll learn how to build up enough chips to make it through the early and middle rounds and then how to employ T.J.'s own strategies to outmaneuver opponents at the final table and win championships. You'll learn how to adjust your play depending upon stack sizes, antes/blinds, table position, opponents styles, chip counts, and the specific strategies for six-handed, three handed, and heads-up play. 288 pages, $29.95.

Order now at 1-800-577-WINS or go online to: www.cardozabooks.com

POWERFUL WINNING POKER SIMULATIONS
A MUST FOR SERIOUS PLAYERS WITH A COMPUTER!
IBM compatible CD ROM Win 95, 98, 2000, NT, ME, XP

These incredible full color poker simulations are the best method to improve your game. Computer opponents play like real players. All games let you set the limits and rake and have fully programmable players, plus stat tracking, and Hand Analyzer for starting hands. Mlke Caro, the world's foremost poker theoretician says, "Amazing... a steal for under $500... get it, it's great." Includes free phone support. "Smart Advisor" gives expert advice for every play!

1. TURBO TEXAS HOLD'EM FOR WINDOWS - $59.95. Choose which players, and how many (2-10) you want to play, create loose/tight games, and control check-raising, bluffing, position, sensitivity to pot odds, and more! Also, instant replay, pop-up odds, Professional Advisor keeps track of play statistics. Free bonus: Hold'em Hand Analyzer analyzes all 169 pocket hands in detail and their win rates under any conditions you set. Caro says this "hold'em software is the most powerful ever created." Great product!

2. TURBO SEVEN-CARD STUD FOR WINDOWS - $59.95. Create any conditions of play; choose number of players (2-8), bet amounts, fixed or spread limit, bring-in method, tight/loose conditions, position, reaction to board, number of dead cards, and stack deck to create special conditions. Features instant replay. Terrific stat reporting includes analysis of starting cards, 3-D bar charts, and graphs. Play interactively and run high speed simulation to test strategies. Hand Analyzer analyzes starting hands in detail. Wow!

3. TURBO OMAHA HIGH-LOW SPLIT FOR WINDOWS - $59.95. Specify any playing conditions; betting limits, number of raises, blind structures, button position, aggressiveness/ passiveness of opponents, number of players (2-10), types of hands dealt, blinds, position, board reaction, and specify flop, turn, and river cards! Choose opponents and use provided point count or create your own. Statistical reporting, instant replay, pop-up odds high speed simulation to test strategies, amazing Hand Analyzer, and much more!

4. TURBO OMAHA HIGH FOR WINDOWS - $59.95. Same features as above, but tailored for Omaha High only. Caro says program is "an electrifying research tool...it can clearly be worth thousands of dollars to any serious player." A must for Omaha High players.

5. TURBO 7 STUD 8 OR BETTER - $59.95. Brand new with all the features you expect from the Wilson Turbo products: the latest artificial intelligence, instant advice and exact odds, play versus 2-7 opponents, enhanced data charts that can be exported or printed, the ability to fold out of turn and immediately go to the next hand, ability to peek at opponents hand, optional warning mode that warns you if a play disagrees with the advisor, and automatic mode that runs up to 50 tests unattended. Tough computer players vary their styles for a great game.

---

6. TOURNAMENT TEXAS HOLD'EM - $39.95
Set-up for tournament practice and play, this realistic simulation pits you against celebrity look-alikes. Tons of options let you control tournament size with 10 to 300 entrants, select limits, ante, rake, blind structures, freezeouts, number of rebuys and competition level of opponents. Pop-up status report shows how you're doing vs. the competition. Save tournaments in progress to play again later. Additional feature allows quick folds on finished hands.

Order now at 1-800-577-WINS or go online to: www.cardozabooks.com